The Economics and Business of Sustainability

Given the emergence of sustainability as the defining issue of our time, it is essential for university graduates, and especially business and economics students, to have a fundamental grasp of the key issues in this emerging multidisciplinary field of study.

Nemetz provides a comprehensive, detailed overview of the interlinked economic and ecological concepts central to this new discipline. Accompanying the introduction of the underlying theory is a broad array of real-world supporting data from Asia, Europe and North America. This volume also features a chapter on the threat of emerging pandemics and their significance for the achievement of a truly sustainable world.

This book accentuates the value and importance of a strong sustainability approach in an age of climate change emergency. It is an ideal companion for instructors and students of sustainability in business, economics and related disciplines such as geography and political science.

Peter N. Nemetz is Professor of Strategy and Business Economics at the University of British Colombia, Canada.

The Economics and Business of Sustainability

Peter N. Nemetz

Routledge
Taylor & Francis Group

LONDON AND NEW YORK

First published 2022
by Routledge
2 Park Square, Milton Park, Abingdon, Oxon OX14 4RN

and by Routledge
605 Third Avenue, New York, NY 10158

Routledge is an imprint of the Taylor & Francis Group, an informa business

© 2022 Peter N. Nemetz

British Library Cataloguing-in-Publication Data
A catalogue record for this book is available from the British Library

Library of Congress Cataloging-in-Publication Data
Names: Nemetz, Peter N., 1944- author.
Title: The economics and business of sustainability / Peter N. Nemetz.
Description: Milton Park, Abingdon, Oxon ; New York, NY : Routledge, 2021. |
    Includes bibliographical references and index.
Subjects: LCSH: Sustainable development. | Business--Environmental aspects. |
    Climatic changes—Economic aspects.
Classification: LCC HC79.E5 N446 2021 | DDC 338.9/27—dc23
LC record available at https://lccn.loc.gov/2021013614

ISBN: 978-0-367-77311-3 (hbk)
ISBN: 978-0-367-77309-0 (pbk)
ISBN: 978-1-003-17073-0 (ebk)

DOI: 10.4324/9781003170730

Typeset in Bembo
by Apex CoVantage, LLC

To my dearest wife, Roma, and daughter, Fiona, the grandest stars in my universe – may they continue to burn bright for many years to come.

Contents

Figures

Tables

Other books by the author

Editor, *Energy Policy: The Global Challenge*, Butterworth & Co. (Canada) Ltd., for the Institute for Research on Public Policy, Montreal, 1979.

Editor, *Resource Policy: International Perspectives*, Institute for Research on Public Policy, Montreal, 1980.

Editor, *Energy Crisis – Policy Response*, Institute for Research on Public Policy, Montreal, 1981.

Editor (with Marilyn Hankey), *Economic Incentives for Energy Conservation*, Wiley-Interscience, New York, 1984.

Editor, *The Pacific Rim: Investment, Development and Trade*, U.B.C. Press, 1987.

Editor, *The Pacific Rim: Investment, Development and Trade*, 2nd rev. ed., U.B.C. Press, 1990.

Editor, *Emerging Issues in Forest Policy*, U.B.C. Press, 1992.

Editor, *The Vancouver Institute: An Experiment in Public Education*, JBA Press, 1998.

Editor, *Bringing Business on Board: Sustainable Development and the B-School Curriculum*, JBA Press, 2002, co-sponsored by the National Round Table for the Environment and the Economy and distributed by UBC Press.

Editor, *Sustainable Resource Management: Reality or Illusion?*, Edward Elgar, 2007.

Business and the Sustainability Challenge, Routledge, 2013.

Co-editor (with Philippe Tortell and Margot Young), *Reflections of Canada: Illuminating our Opportunities and Challenges at 150+ years*, Peter Wall Institute for Advanced Studies, 2017.

Corporate Strategy and Sustainability, Routledge, 2022, forthcoming.

Unsustainable World: Are We Losing the Battle to Save the Planet?, Routledge, 2022, forthcoming.

Front cover picture acknowledgement
Glacier front, Kongsfjorden, Svalbard, 79°N. Photograph by Dr. Fiona S. Danks

Preface

The rationale for undertaking this work arose after many years of teaching courses in environmental policy, energy economics and, more recently, sustainability and business. The subject matter of sustainable development is, by definition, multidisciplinary, and this presents numerous challenges to amassing its diverse subject matter within the covers of one book. It is a tribute to the power of the modern concept of sustainability that so many books are now available on this subject. However, instructors tasked with distilling this material within a classroom setting, whether for junior- and senior-level undergraduates or master's students in business, economics, geography, public policy and government, must grapple with the lack of any relatively comprehensive treatment of the subject.

I suspect that most instructors in the area of sustainability and business, like myself, have been forced to cobble together a broad range of snippets from articles and books rather than being able to rely, to some degree, on a single work as a core source of material. This book is an attempt to fill this gap. As explained in more detail in the introduction, this textbook focuses primarily on the interrelated areas of science, policy, economics and ecology. A companion volume addresses the issue of corporate strategy and sustainability.

Despite these disclaimers, the production of this work has been a labor of love, driven by hundreds of hours of lively classroom interaction with students with inquiring and open minds from the United States, Canada and a broad range of countries in Latin America, Europe and Asia. It is because of them that I undertook this task, which, in retrospect, was much more work than I ever realized. In addition to the many students who inspired me to continue teaching in this field for almost four decades, I owe a deep debt of gratitude to numerous individuals who have contributed, in one way or another, to this book. To name but a few: the late Bert Allsopp, the late Ray Anderson, Sergey Avramenko, Ken Baker, Dyhia Belhabib, David Brand, Bill Cafferata, Linda Coady, Duncan Dow, Buddy Hay, Ian Gill, Edward Gregr, Bettina von Hagen, Richard D. Hansen, Chris Milly, John Lampman, Jane Pan, Cassie Phillips, Rob Prins, Juan Reyero, Andrew Simms, Michael Vitt and Donovan Woolard. I also owe thanks to my academic colleagues, Werner Antweiler, Kai Chan, John Grace, Charlie Krebs, David Shindler, Rashid Sumaila, Peter Timmer, and Andy Yan. Finally, I wish to single out several former students in particular who have been of immense help in this undertaking: Jana Hanova, Simon Bager, Patrick Dore, Cristina Infante, Jane Lister, Judy Feng and Rebecca Gu. It goes without saying that all of these individuals must be absolved of any responsibility for any oversights or errors I may have committed.

Finally, I owe my deepest gratitude to two people in particular: my daughter, Dr. Fiona Danks, who brought her scientific expertise to the task of proofreading chapters for errors in both science and grammar, and especially my dearly beloved wife, Roma, who stoically endured the many evenings when I barricaded myself in our home office until all hours, feverishly engaged in yet another revision of this textbook.

Peter N. Nemetz
Vancouver, BC
May 2021

1   Book outline, rationale and introduction

Why study sustainability in a business school? This is a legitimate question for an undergraduate or master's level student who has chosen his/her specific discipline within business and is finishing all course requirements in anticipation of graduation and impending employment. The principal answer to this question and the message of this book is four-fold: (1) there is a significant probability that within the next decade or two at most, the national and international business environment will be radically different from today; (2) this may be, in no small part, because of the enormous ecological challenges facing the globe and the feedback effects they have on our economic systems; (3) by necessity, issues of sustainability will be central to the *strategic* decision-making of mid-sized and major corporations; and (4) any middle-level or senior manager unfamiliar with the issues, both theoretical and empirical, will be placing themselves and their firms at a serious competitive disadvantage. The most recent addition to these modern global transformations is the impact of the potential re-emergence of pandemics on the path to sustainable future ecological, economic and social structures (a topic addressed in Chapter 11).

It can be argued that the goal of achieving sustainable development is probably the greatest challenge humankind has ever faced. It will require a concerted and coordinated effort among consumers, business and government. If sustainable development is indeed to be achieved, it can also be argued that the sine qua non is the education of the emerging business elite in the fundamental principles of sustainability, for only with the active engagement of the business community is there any realistic hope that our economic, social and ecological systems can achieve sustainability.

This presents a major challenge within the confines of a business school, as traditional business education has adopted the reductionist approach pioneered by the sciences. This model has withstood the test of time, producing highly educated young graduates who are focused on the theory and empirical data of their chosen discipline. The study of sustainability, within business as in other subject areas, represents a fundamental divergence from this traditional model. This new educational model requires multidisciplinary integration across a wide range of disciplines in the areas of business, ecology, economics, geography, political science, psychology and social issues. Aside from the occasional capstone course at the end of a business degree, there are few, if any, precedents for this holistic approach.

The mission of business schools is to lead in the area of business education, developing new theory and exploring the significance of a vast array of empirical data. It is also their mission, however, to identify and respond to emerging trends in their environment. One need only read the national press, business magazines and corporate reports to see the

DOI: 10.4324/9781003170730-1

emergence of a dramatic change in the environment of business. Issues of sustainability have been the focus of cover pages from such high-profile journals as *Business Week*, the *Economist, Time* and *Vanity Fair*.

This phenomenon has been mirrored in the proliferation of corporate reports devoted to sustainability and/or corporate social responsibility. For example, the Governance & Accountability Institute (G&A 2020a, 2020b) reported that in 2019, 65% of the Russell 1000 Index companies and 90% of the S&P 500 Index companies published sustainability reports.

What has focused all these companies on an issue that received very little corporate attention just two decades ago? Consider the following headlines from corporate, governmental and academic reports:

"Human Society Under Urgent Threat from Loss of Earth's Natural Life," *Guardian*, May 6, 2019.

"Bank of England Chief Mark Carney Issues Climate Change Warning," BBC, December 30, 2019.

"JP Morgan Economists Warn Climate Crisis Is Threat to Human Race," *Guardian*, February 21, 2020.

"Why Blackrock's Larry Fink Warns Climate Change Is on the Edge of Reshaping Finance," MarketWatch, January 14, 2020.

"Flooding from Sea Level Rise Could Cost Our Planet $14.2 Trillion, Study Says," CNN, July 30, 2020.

"Federal Report Warns of Financial Havoc from Climate Change," *New York Times*, September 8, 2020.

"Fifth of Countries at Risk of Ecosystem Collapse, Analysis Finds. Trillions of Dollars of GDP Depend on Biodiversity, According to Swiss RE Report," *Guardian*, October 12, 2020.

"UN Warns That World Risks Becoming 'Uninhabitable Hell' for Millions Unless Leaders Take Climate Action," CNN, October 13, 2020.

"Merkel: Tackling Climate Change a Matter of 'Survival,'" Politico, November 10, 2020.

While much of the discussion of sustainability issues within the popular press has focused on negative aspects, many of these sustainability challenges represent extraordinary opportunities for business. This double-sided interpretation is not new to history. The ancient Chinese phrase for "crisis" is composed of two characters: the first represents "danger," but the second represents "opportunity." The modern re-interpretation of this historical characterization was enunciated by Michael Porter of Harvard University in a *Scientific American* essay in April 1991 where he stated that "the conflict between environmental protection and economic competitiveness is a false dichotomy" (Porter 1991, p. 168). This thesis has been further developed by Porter in several seminal articles from the *Harvard Business Review* and the *Journal of Economic Perspectives* (Porter and van der Linde 1995a, 1995b; Porter and Kramer 2006, 2011). The key message of these articles is simple: there has been a false dichotomy between expenditures on pollution control and corporate profitability. The gist of the authors' argument is that corporate strategy – the highest level of decision-making within a corporation – which recognizes, addresses and incorporates issues of sustainability can yield significant and "sustainable" competitive advantage.

Several high-profile investors, including Warren Buffett, have recognized the business opportunities associated with addressing climate change (Inside Climate News February 29, 2016). In particular, Buffet has focused on wind energy (Bloomberg Green February 22, 2020), a major component of renewable energy – a market which is expected to reach $2,152.9 billion by 2025 (MarketWatch March 25, 2021). A major economic initiative has been underway for several years to finance this transformation in the form of green finance, an industry which reached over $31 trillion in 2019 (Bloomberg June 6, 2019). Among the major players are HSBC, which has earmarked an investment of $1 trillion to achieve net zero emissions by 2050 (Reuters October 9, 2020).

The holistic approach to sustainability advanced by this book is based on three interrelated components. First and foremost is corporate strategy. But the formation and execution of such strategy cannot be understood without knowledge and appreciation of the economic and political environment in which this strategy must be crafted. Hence, the second major component is government policy – incorporated in legislation and regulations, as well as economic and political theory, which help shape much of this immediate corporate environment. Finally is the scientific framework, largely in the form of ecological theory, which – at least in principle – provides the intellectual rationale for a significant portion of government policy relating to sustainability issues.

This volume presents a detailed description of the economic and ecological issues which must inform decision-making within the corporate and governmental sectors; a companion volume (Nemetz, *Corporate Strategy and Sustainability*, Routledge, 2022) outlines how businesses can incorporate sustainability considerations into their highest levels of corporate strategy.

The context

Few concepts have had such a major impact on public discourse over the past few decades as sustainability. In this period, a vast array of initiatives have been taken by governments, business, non-governmental organizations and individuals to advance the cause of sustainability. While there are numerous examples of relatively successful policies and practices, the achievement of sustainability at the level that matters most – the global scale – has been an unmitigated failure. Recent evidence in support of this discouraging conclusion has been provided by several major international scientific reports. The most recent reports from the Intergovernmental Panel on Climate Change (IPCC) paint a bleaker picture than their previous report of 2014, with greater impacts and a foreshortened deadline in which to act in order to forestall potentially catastrophic results. These comprehensive studies by the IPCC, representing the consensus views of thousands of scientists, have concluded that greenhouse gas emissions (esp. carbon dioxide and methane) continue to increase, the temperature of the atmosphere and oceans continues to rise, land- and sea-based ice continues to melt, sea levels and ocean acidification continue to rise and climate extremes have and will continue to worsen (see NAS March 2016; NOAA 2019; Nisbet et al. 2019; BAMS 2018, 2019; WMO 2019; IPCC 2018; IPCC 2019). In their annual surveys of several dozen anthropogenic global risks, the World Economic Forum (2019, 2020) identifies climate change with all its manifestations as the most likely risk with the greatest impact.

In May 2019, it was reported that carbon dioxide levels in the atmosphere had reached levels higher than those recorded in the past 800,000 to 2 million years (Smithsonian. com May 15, 2019; *Washington Post* May 11, 2019). Symptomatic of this phenomenon was the extraordinary temperature of 84 degrees Fahrenheit (29 Celsius) recorded near the entrance to the Arctic Ocean in northwest Russia, approximately 30–40 degrees higher than average (Smithsonian.com May 15, 2019; *Washington Post* May 11, 2019). One year later, the Arctic Circle saw its highest ever recorded temperature with the Siberian town of Verkhoyansk reaching 38 degrees Celsius on June 20, 2020 (BBC June 22, 2020). It is accepted fact that the Arctic is experiencing the effects of global warming at a much faster rate than the rest of the world (AMAP-SWIPA 2017; Jeong et al. 2018; Struzik 2015; Washington Post May 14, 2019; Fischetti 2019; Francis 2020; Hu et al. 2020; Lai et al. 2020; Landrum and Holland 2020; Garbe et al. 2020; King et al. 2020; Previdi et al. 2020). This provides the equivalent of a crystal ball for scientists to see what lies in store for the rest of the world in the years to come, as there are significant climatological linkages between the Arctic and mid-latitudes (Francis and Vavrus 2012; UNEP 2019). The United Nations Environment Programme report (2019) concluded that a sharp rise in Arctic temperatures in the order of 3–5 degrees Celsius is now inevitable. In 2018, the world experienced the breaking of all-time global heat records (*Washington Post* July 5, 2018). These provide clear signals of the direction and magnitude of the changes the globe is undergoing, with profound implications for the future. Similar dramatic changes are occurring in Greenland and Antarctica with the threat of rapid loss of ice cover and subsequent sea-level rise (Lai et al. 2020; Garbe et al. 2020; King et al. 2020).

All these climate-related changes are marked by positive feedback loops, lags, potential abrupt shifts (so-called tipping points) and irreversibilities that pose a direct threat to humanity if left uncontrolled (US CCSP 2008, 2009a, 2009b; NAS 2013, 2019, 2020; Barnosky et al. 2012; Steffen et al. 2018). A similar bleak outlook is reflected in the work of the Intergovernmental Science-Policy Platform on Biodiversity and Ecosystem Services (IPBES 2019), which states that "Nature's Dangerous Decline [is] 'Unprecedented'; Species Extinction Rates [are] 'accelerating.'"

The IPCC has concluded that future global temperature changes must not exceed 1.5 degrees Celsius to limit potentially devastating impacts to our ecological and economic systems. Figure 1.1 depicts the expected consequences of a range of global temperature increases.

While the sustainability challenge is multifaceted, encompassing economic and social as well as ecological variables, it is climate change that has assumed preeminence, with its potentially massive direct and indirect effects on the fabric of our economic and social systems. The threat to global sustainability appears to rest on three variables: (1) rising population; (2) increasing industrialization and wealth with a concomitant rise in demand for food and other natural resources; and (3) technological innovations that may have environmentally detrimental effects. Total pollution can increase from any one of these factors. If the goal is to decrease humanity's environmental impact on the planet, it is clearly insufficient to tackle only one or two of these factors; an increase in the residual may offset any beneficial changes in the others.

In light of the depth of intellectual resources devoted to addressing the problem of climate change, the question remains as to why global change not only continues unabated but also appears to be accelerating, pushing the limits of planetary boundaries (Steffen et al. 2015, see also WMO 2019). The two principal agents capable of addressing this issue are the corporate and governmental sectors with the help of civil society, but, to date, the record has been mixed at best. At least part of the problem has been the existence of powerful and pervasive myths that have had a broad influence on public opinion, corporate

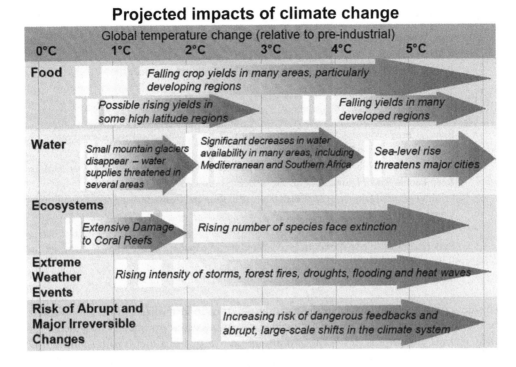

Figure 1.1 IPCC-predicted effects of temperature increases

strategy and government policy. These include: the myth that countries can grow their way out of pollution; the myth that international trade and globalization have an unambiguously positive effect on sustainability; the myth that humankind's technological ingenuity will overcome any barriers to sustainability; and the myth that humankind can adapt to continuing climate change (Nemetz 2015).

What is sustainable development?

It is useful to begin a discussion of sustainable development with a *thought experiment* from a seminal work by William McDonough and Michael Braungart in the *Atlantic Monthly* (1998) entitled, "The Next Industrial Revolution":

> If someone were to present the Industrial Revolution as a retroactive design assignment, it might sound like this:
>   Design a system of production that
>
> • Puts Billions Of Pounds Of Toxic Material Into The Air, Water, And Soil Every Year
> • Measures Prosperity By Activity, Not Legacy
> • Requires Thousands Of Complex Regulations To Keep People And Natural Systems From Being Poisoned Too Quickly

- Produces Materials So Dangerous That They Will Require Constant Vigilance From Future Generations
- Results In Gigantic Amounts Of Waste
- Puts Valuable Materials In Holes All Over The Planet, Where They Can Never Be Retrieved, And
- Erodes The Diversity Of Biological Species And Cultural Practices.

Eco-Efficiency Instead:

- Releases *Fewer* Pounds Of Toxic Material Into The Air, Water, And Soil Every Year
- Measures Prosperity By *Less* Activity
- *Meets* Or *Exceeds* The Stipulations Of Thousands Of Complex Regulations That Aim To Keep People And Natural Systems From Being Poisoned Too Quickly
- Produces *Fewer* Dangerous Materials That Will Require Constant Vigilance From Future Generations
- Results In *Smaller* Amounts Of Waste
- Puts *Fewer* Valuable Materials In Holes All Over The Planet, Where They Can Never Be Retrieved
- Standardizes and homogenizes biological species and cultural practices

This quotation cogently describes the path the Western industrialized world has followed for the last two centuries. It has clearly yielded enormous economic and social benefits for many nations, and yet it is clearly the authors' intent to argue that such a path is unsustainable. This view is reflected in the challenging piece by the well-known Harvard biologist E. O. Wilson entitled, "Is Humanity Suicidal?" (*New York Times Magazine* June 20, 1993).

The challenge of sustainability is to find another path for business and government which will continue to generate wealth but with considerably less environmental impact. Two other brief quotations help set the stage for the definition of sustainable development.

1 "Only 7% of physical U.S. throughput winds up as product, and only 1.4% is still product after six months."

(Friend 1996)

2 "Business has ignored its major product lines: pollution and waste. Why would anyone set out to produce something which it cannot sell, for which it has no conceivable use, and for which it might be potentially liable?"

(Smith 2007, p. 306)

The phrase "sustainable development" emerged from the report of the World Commission on Environment and Development (also known as the *Brundtland Report* after its chairperson, Prime Minister Gro Harlem Brundtland of Norway). The report was published as *Our Common Future* in 1987 by Oxford University Press. The definition is beguilingly simple: "development that meets the need of the present without compromising the ability of future generations to meet their own needs." As originally conceived, sustainable development has three components: (1) the economy, (2) society and (3) the environment. All must achieve sustainability for the general goal to be realized.

The Brundtland Commission took a fairly optimistic view of the possibilities for *decoupling* economic activity and environmental impact, thereby permitting increased economic development in the third world. To some, this is overly optimistic and the concept "sustainable development" is an oxymoron. One of the major conceptual problems raised by the theory of sustainable development is how to define it in a manner which can be operationalized. There are numerous studies of sustainable development, many with their own more precise definition than the Brundtland Commission. Several common conceptual threads run throughout these studies: (1) a direct or indirect articulation of the concept of *natural capital* – where maintenance of a constant natural capital stock (including the renewable resource base and the environment) yields an indefinite stream of output or "income"; (2) a focus on social stability, empowerment and equity with particular emphasis on reducing poverty and maintaining an adequate quality of life for all global inhabitants alive and to be born (i.e. both intra- and intergenerational equity); (3) a critical distinction between qualitative and quantitative changes in the utilization of our technology and natural resource base (i.e. development versus growth) – for example, technological advances which may permit us to raise our standard of living without increasing the throughput of material and energy resources – sometimes defined as *dematerialization*; and (4) the *precautionary principle* – which states that society cannot wait for definitive scientific proof of a potential threat to the global ecosystem before acting if that threat is both large and credible. The underlying theory is based on scientific principles, largely associated with the pioneering work of ecologists such as C. S. Holling (Holling 2005; Allen and Holling 2008; Gunderson and Holling 2001), that suggest that by the time one recognizes or begins to feel the tangible effects of certain types of ecological threats, it may be too late to act to prevent or reverse serious negative effects.

One central concept of sustainability is the proposition that our generation must leave the next generation a stock of capital no less than we have now. Implicit in this proposition is that we must, to the best of our ability, live off the "interest" on this capital stock and not draw it down. If part of this capital is drawn down, it must be replaced by substitute capital. The ability to achieve this goal hinges on which of two major definitions of sustainable development is adopted: *weak* sustainability or *strong* sustainability. Under the *Weak Sustainability Constant Capital Rule*, our society may pass on less environment to future generations so long as this loss is offset by increasing the stock of roads and machinery or other man-made (physical) capital. In contrast, under the *Strong Sustainability Constant Capital Rule*, perfect substitution among different forms of capital is not a valid assumption. Some elements of the natural capital stock cannot be substituted for (except on a very limited basis) by man-made capital. Many of the functions and services of ecosystems are essential to human survival; they are life support services (such as biogeochemical cycling) and cannot be replaced. To implement a policy of sustainable development, it is necessary to have more accurate measures of the various types of capital (natural, human and physical). Without these measures, society cannot make the right decisions.

While much public attention has been focused on global warming, the broad challenge of sustainable development includes other major ecological threats to the continued viability of global economic systems. Significant local, regional and global pressures on the earth's renewable resource base are occurring in fisheries, forestry, biodiversity, agriculture, water supply and human health, and many of these are directly linked to climate change.

Thinking about sustainability and systems analysis

As stated, the principal goal of this textbook is to introduce business students to the broad range of sustainability issues they will encounter in their careers. The concepts and examples presented in this volume are intimately linked under the general rubric of *integration* – a key characteristic of sustainability. In approaching the broad range of material covered in this volume, students are encouraged to adopt a *systems-theory* approach to their analysis. This approach can be applied within or among the disparate disciplines of geography, business, economics, policy analysis, strategic management and ecology. The critical question to address in any analysis of a policy, strategy or event is, "What are its effects on other system components, and how has it, in turn, been affected by other policies, strategies or events?" Many of the tools and theories described in this volume specifically address these questions, including, among others, revenge theory (or the law of unintended consequences), the ecological footprint, net energy analysis, trophic cascades, non-linear dynamics and feedback, tipping points, and a range of economic, ecological and cross-disciplinary modeling techniques. Even the basic economic concept of externalities represents a manifestation of systems thinking as it embodies the potentially system-wide effects of an economic transaction between two parties where these effects are invisible to the market. The adoption of a systems-theory perspective frequently highlights and clarifies the complex interrelationships among disparate disciplinary spheres such as ecology and economics. Appendix 1.1 to this chapter provides a simple example of this concept, and Appendix 1.2 discusses some similarities between economic and ecological systems.

After reading this textbook, students should, at a minimum, be comfortable in addressing the following set of fundamental issues in sustainable development.

1   Be able to define sustainable development as originally enunciated and be familiar with key components such as natural capital, intergenerational equity, development versus growth and dematerialization, the precautionary principle, weak vs. strong sustainability.

2   Be familiar with the debate over the meaning of standard economic measures of well-being (such as GDP/capita) and some of the proposed alternatives.

3   Be familiar with the basics of environmental economics (esp. the principles of public goods and externalities and common property resources vs. open access resources) as well as some of the basic methods of measuring environmental benefits and the debate over appropriate social discount rates.

4   Be conversant with major policy tools such as pollution taxes, marketable permits and offsets.

5   Have a working knowledge of some fundamental ecological issues such non-linear dynamics, positive feedback loops, thresholds and tipping points.

6   Be familiar with some of the basic principles of ecological economics (especially how ecological principles are integrated into this new discipline and the measurement problems associated with ecological services).

7   Be familiar with some of the metrics and data sources associated with sustainable development such as ecological and carbon footprints, the US Toxic Release Inventory (TRI), Canada's National Pollutant Release Inventory (NPRI) and greenhouse gas databases.

8   Have a basic knowledge of some major market responses to climate change such as the US market for SO_2 and the EU Emissions Trading System for carbon dioxide.

Appendix 1.1
A simple example of systems theory

The forest sector has made, and continues to make, a significant contribution to economic activity in the US Pacific Northwest, Southeast, Northeast and several provinces of Canada. The traditional view of this sector focused on the economic value from the exploitation of dimensional timber and fiber for pulp and paper. The resulting economic decision-making framework focused on the rate of harvest, subject to a constraint based on maintaining a sustainable yield of forest products for the indefinite future. This historical view has been supplanted by a more extensive and nuanced view of the broad contributions from forests, including not only marketable non-timber values but also the complex interlinkages with both ecological systems and other disparate economic and social activities. Figure 1.2 illustrates some of the more important of these linkages and focuses specifically on the effects of loss of forest cover. Such loss can be due to excessive harvesting with inadequate replacement or natural or anthropogenic phenomena such as forest fires, disease and insect predation. What is apparent from this systems graphic is that the effects of the loss of forest cover are multifaceted and have an ultimately significant negative impact across a broad spectrum of economic values and business activity. The nature of these complex linkages is, in many cases, just now being thoroughly researched. What is missing in this diagram – and a subject discussed in Chapter 8 – are the multiple feedback loops and irreversibilities in this system which can make system restoration and recovery exceedingly difficult.

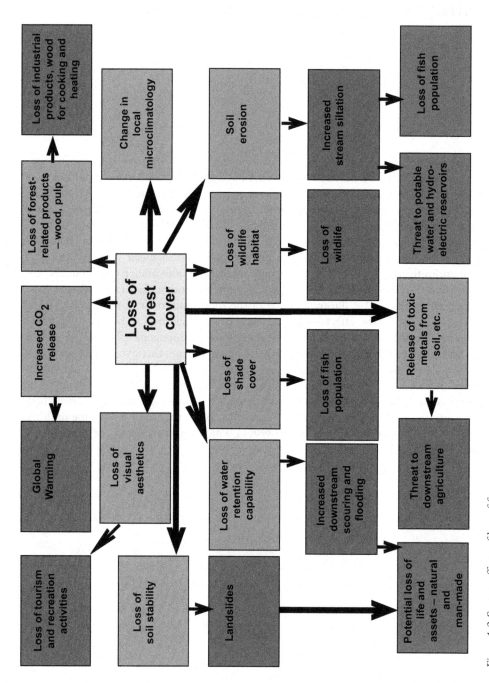

Figure 1.2 System effects of loss of forest cover

Appendix 1.2
Business and ecosystems as complex adaptive systems

One of the fundamental contributions of the discipline of environmental economics (see Chapter 5) was the realization that economic systems – and business, in particular – have profound, measurable and monetizable impacts on the environment. With the emergence of ecological economics (see Chapter 9) as a companion discipline, the circle of influence was completed with the identification of ecological systems as providing the underpinnings of economic activity. In fact, both economic and ecological systems have profound similarities and much to learn from each other. Both are manifestations of what have been described as complex adaptive systems. Levin (1998, p. 432) defines such systems by three essential components: "sustained diversity and individuality of components; localized interactions among those components; and an autonomous process that selects from among those components, based on the results of local interactions, a subset for replication or enhancement." Walker and Salt (2006, pp. 34–35) focus on a critical characteristic of such systems, namely their emergent behavior; i.e. a characteristic that forecloses the opportunity to predict system behavior solely from the observation of the "individual mechanics of its component parts or any pair of interactions. . . . Changes in one component can sometimes result in complete reconfigurations of the system; the system changes to a different stable state (or regime)."

C. S. Holling, one of the fathers of modern ecological theory, has developed a powerful paradigm for understanding the underlying behavior of a vast array of disparate systems which are, in essence, all complex and adaptive. Holling and Gunderson (2002, pp. 3–34) identify four critical phases in the evolution of such systems: (1) exploitation or rapid growth (called the r phase); (2) conservation (called the k phase); (3) release (called the omega phase); and (4) reorganization (called the alpha phase). The significance of each phase is best illustrated by reference to Table 1.1, which draws upon the work of Walker and Salt (2006, pp. 75–78) to demonstrate the applicability to both ecological and business models. It is interesting to note that the underlying theoretical foundation of the omega phase is essentially similar to the creative destruction process in economic systems articulated by Joseph Schumpeter in his classic 1950 work, *Capitalism, Socialism and Democracy*. In light of such strong similarities between economic and ecological systems, it should come as no surprise that conceptual models used in one area may be transferable in complete or modified form to the other. This two-way exchange has been illustrated in several studies which have attempted to apply financial models to the management of natural resources. By way of example, Edwards et al. (2004) and Sanchirico et al. (2006) use portfolio theory, an approach which uses diversification to balance and reduce risk, to recommend a shift from single- to multiple-species optimization in fisheries management. Several authors have also recommended the application of portfolio theory to address forest restoration (Crowe and Parker 2008), agroecosystems (Acutt 1988) and the monumental loss of global biodiversity (Hockstra 2012; Figge 2004; Doremus 2003).

On the other side of the ledger, Kambhu et al. (2007a, 2007b), Soramaki et al. (2006), May et al. (2008) and Haldane and May (2011) illustrate how critical ecological and epidemiological principles can aid the understanding of financial markets, thereby leading to improved methods of controlling contagion and large and undesirable effects of systemic risk such as those witnessed in the financial crisis of 2007–2008. Despite the promising emergence of cross-system learning proffered by the underlying similarity of economic and ecological systems, the analyst and policymaker must also be cognizant of system differences which may attenuate the power of such conceptual transferences. The most obvious difference is that in contrast to ecosystems, economic systems are composed of human agents who create as well as respond to system rules (Ehrenfeld 2003, p. 3; Kambhu et al. 2007a, 2007b). Nevertheless, this new avenue of intellectual inquiry has opened up many new possibilities for understanding and influencing the behavior of superficially distinct, complex adaptive systems.

Table 1.1 Business and ecosystems as complex adaptive systems

	Phase	*Characterization*	*Ecological model*	*Business model*
r phase	Exploitation or rapid growth	System components weakly interconnected, and the internal state is weakly regulated	Weeds, alder, dock and pigweed on newly exposed sites or cleared lands	Innovators, entrepreneurs, start-ups
k phase	Conservation	Increasing efficiency and interconnectedness at the cost of resilience; rigidity increases and redundancy and flexibility decrease	More biomass bound up in unavailable forms stored in tree heartwood and dead organic matter	Greater specialization, greater efficiencies, economies of scale
Omega phase	Release	A sudden regime shift from even a small stimulus if system resilience is low (i.e. a tipping point phenomenon)	Fires, droughts, pests and disease	Emergence of new technology or market shock
Alpha phase	Reorganization	A chaotic state with no stable equilibrium; this state evolves back toward a new r phase	New species, growth from suppressed vegetation, germination of buried seeds	Emergence of new groups in organizations, with new inventions, creative ideas and people

References

Acutt, Melinda (1988) "Biodiversity: A portfolio analysis model for efficient conservation decisions," Department of Economics, Lancaster University, UK.

Allen, Craig R. and C.S. Holling (2008) *Discontinuities in Ecosystems and Other Complex Systems*, New York: Columbia University Press.

Arctic Monitoring and Assessment Programme (AMAP-SWIPA) (2017) *Snow, Water, Ice and Permafrost in the Arctic*, Oslo.

Barnosky, Anthony D. et al. (2012) "Approaching a state shift in Earths' biosphere," *Nature*, June 7.

BBC (2020) "Arctic Circle sees 'highest-ever' recorded temperatures," June 22.

Bloomberg (2019) "Green financing is now $31 trillion and growing," June 6.

Bloomberg Green (2020) "Buffett touts wind energy following climate-change criticism," February 22.

Brundtland Commission (1987) *Our Common Future*, New York: Oxford University Press.

Bulletin of the American Meteorological Society (BAMS) (2018) "Explaining extreme events of 2017 from a climate perspective," Special Supplement, 99(12), December.

Bulletin of the American Meteorological Society (BAMS) (2019) "State of the climate in 2018," Special Supplement, 100(9), September.

Crowe, Kevin A. and William H. Parker (2008) "Using portfolio theory to guide reforestation and restoration under climate change scenarios," *Climate Change*, 89, pp. 355–370.

Doremus, Holly (2003) "A policy portfolio approach to biodiversity protection on private lands," *Environmental Science & Policy*, 6, pp. 217–232.

Edwards, Steven F. et al. (2004) "Portfolio management of wild fish stocks," *Ecological Economics*, 49, pp. 317–329.

Ehrenfeld, John (2003) "Putting a spotlight on metaphors and analogies in industrial ecology," *Journal of Industrial Ecology*, 7(1), pp. 1–4.

Figge, Frank (2004) "Bio-folio: Applying portfolio theory to biodiversity," *Biodiversity and Conservation*, 13, pp. 827–849.

Fischetti, Mark (2019) "A new reality: Climate change is dramatically altering life at the top of the world," *Scientific American*, Summer, Special edition.

Francis, Jennifer A. (2020) "Meltdown," *Scientific American*, Summer, Special edition.

Francis, Jennifer A. and Stephen J. Vavrus (2012) "Evidence linking Arctic amplification to extreme weather in mid-latitudes," *Geophysical Research Letters*, March 17.

Friend, Gil (1996) "A cyclical materials economy: What goes around comes around . . . or does it?," *New Bottom Line*, 5(6), March 12.

Garbe, Julius et al. (2020) "The hysteresis of the Antarctic ice sheet," *Nature*, September 23.

Governance & Accountability Institute, Inc. (G&A) (2020a) *Flash Report 1000: Trends on the Sustainability Reporting Practices of the Russell 1000 Index Companies*.

Governance & Accountability Institute, Inc. (G&A) (2020b) *Flash Report S&P 500: Trends on the Sustainability Reporting Practice of S&P 500 Index Companies*.

Gunderson, Lance H. and C.S. Holling (2001) *Panarchy: Understanding Transformations in Hunan and Natural Systems*, Washington: Island Press.

Haldane, Andrew G. and Robert M. May (2011) "Systemic risk in banking ecosystems," *Nature*, January 20.

Hockstra, Jonathan (2012) "Improving biodiversity conservation through modern portfolio theory," *PNAS*, April 24.

Holling, C.S. (2005) *Adaptive Environmental Assessment and Management*, Caldwell, NJ: Blackburn Press.

Holling, C.S. and Lance H. Gunderson (2002) "Resilience and adaptive cycles," in Lance H. Gunderson and C.S. Holling (eds.) *Panarchy: Understanding Transformations in Human and Natural Systems*, Washington: Island Press, pp. 25–62.

Hu, Siyu et al. (2020) "Marine heatwaves in the Arctic region: Variations in different ice covers," *Geophysical Research Letters*, August 6.

Inside Climate News (2016) "Warren Buffett delivers cold-blooded view of global warming to share-holders," February 29.

Intergovernmental Science-Policy Platform on Biodiversity and Ecosystem Services (IPBES) (2019) *The Global Assessment Report on Biodiversity and Ecosystem Services.*

IPCC (2018) *Global Warming of 1.5 C.* IPCC special report.

IPCC (2019) "Polar regions," Chapter 3 in *IPCC Special Report on the Ocean and Cryosphere in a Changing Climate.*

Jeong, Su-Jong et al. (2018) "Accelerating rates of Arctic carbon cycling revealed by long-term atmosphere CO2 measurements," *Science Advances,* July 11.

Kambhu, John et al. (2007a) *New Directions for Understanding Systemic Risk,* Washington, DC: National Research Council.

Kambhu, John et al. (2007b) "Systemic risk in ecology and engineering," Part 3, *Federal Reserve Bank of New York Policy Review,* November.

King, Michalea D. et al. (2020) "Dynamic ice loss from the Greenland Ice sheet driven by sustained glacier retreat," *Communications Earth & Environment,* August 13, pp. 1–6.

Lai, Ching-Yao et al. (2020) "Vulnerability of Antarctica's ice shelves to meltwater-driven fracture," *Nature,* August 27.

Landrum, Laura and Marika M. Holland (2020) "Extremes become routine in an emerging new Arctic," *Nature Climate Change,* September 14, pp. 1–7.

Levin, Simon A. (1998) "Ecosystems and the biosphere as complex adaptive systems," *Ecosystems,* 1, pp. 431–436.

MarketWatch (2020) "Renewable energy market: Global industry analysis, size, share, growth, trends and forecast, 2018–2025," August 28.

MarketWatch (2021) "Renewable energy market size research report growth forecast 2025," March 25.

May, Robert M. et al. (2008) "Ecology for bankers," *Nature,* 451, February 21, pp. 893–895.

McDonough, William and Michael Braungart (1998) "The next industrial revolution," *The Atlantic Monthly,* October, pp. 82–92.

NAS (2013) *Abrupt Impacts of Climate Change: Anticipating Surprises,* Washington, DC: National Academies Press.

NAS (2016) *Attribution of Extreme Weather Events in the Context of Climate Change,* Washington, DC: National Academies Press.

NAS (2019) *Climate Change and Ecosystems,* Washington, DC: National Academies Press.

NAS (2020) *Climate Change: Evidence and Causes: Update 2020,* Washington, DC: National Academies Press.

Nemetz, Peter N. (2015) "Reconstructing the sustainability narrative: Separating myth from reality," Chapter 2 in Helen Kopnina and Eleanor Shoreman-Ouimet (eds.) *Sustainability: Key Issues,* London: Routledge.

Nemetz, Peter N. (2022) *Corporate Strategy and Sustainability,* London: Routledge.

Nisbet, E.G. et al. (2019) "Very strong atmospheric methane growth in the 4 years 204–2017: Implications for the Paris agreement," *Global Biogeochemical Cycles,* March 18.

NOAA (2019) *Executive Summary in Arctic Report Card.*

Porter, Michael E. (1991) "America's green strategy," *Scientific American,* April, p. 168.

Porter, Michael E. and Mark R. Kramer (2006) "Strategy & society: The link between competitive advantage and corporate social responsibility," *Harvard Business Review,* December, pp. 78–92.

Porter, Michael E. and Mark R. Kramer (2011) "Creating shared value," *Harvard Business Review,* January–February, pp. 62–77.

Porter, Michael E. and Claas van der Linde (1995a) "Green and competitive: Ending the stalemate," *Harvard Business Review,* September/October, pp. 120–134.

Porter, Michael E. and Claas van der Linde (1995b) "Toward a new conception of the environment-competitiveness relationship," *Journal of Economic Perspectives,* 9(4), pp. 97–118.

Previdi, Michael et al. (2020) "Arctic amplification: A rapid response to radiative forcing," *Geophysical Research Letters,* August 25.

Reuters (2020) "HSBC targets net zero emissions by 2050, earmarks $1 trln green financing," October 9.

Sanchirico, James N. et al. (2006) "An approach to ecosystem-based fishery management," RFF discussion paper DP-6-40, September.

Smith, William G.B. (2007) "Accounting for the environment: Can industrial ecology pay double dividends for business?," in Peter N. Nemetz (ed.) *Sustainable Resource Management: Reality or Illusion?*, Cheltenham: Edward Elgar, pp. 304–341.

Smithsonian.com (2019) "Carbon dioxide levels reach highest point in human history," May 15.

Soramaki, Kimmo et al. (2006) "The typology of interbank payment flows," *Federal Reserve Bank of New York Staff Report 243*, March.

Steffen, Will et al. (2015) "Planetary boundaries: Guiding human development on a changing planet," *Science*, February 13.

Steffen, Will et al. (2018) "Trajectories of the Earth system in the anthropocene," *PNAS*, August 14.

Struzik, Ed (2015) "Defending the 'right to be cold'," *The Tyee*, February 2.

UNEP (2019) *Global Linkages: A Graphic Look at the Changing Arctic*.

US Climate Change Science Program (CCSP) (2008) *Abrupt Climate Change*, December.

US Climate Change Science Program (CCSP) (2009a) *Thresholds of Climate Change in Ecosystems*.

US Climate Change Science Program (CCSP) (2009b) *The Effects of Climate Change on Agriculture, Land Resources, Water Resources, and Biodiversity in the United States*.

Walker, Brian and David Salt (2006) *Resilience Thinking*, Washington: Island Press.

Washington Post (2018) "Red-hot planet: All-time heat records have been set all over the world during the past week," July 5.

Washington Post (2019) "It was 84 degrees near the Arctic Ocean this weekend as carbon dioxide hit its highest level in human history," May 14.

Wilson, E.O. (1993) "Is humanity suicidal?," *New York Times Magazine*, June 20.

WMO (2019) *Provisional Statement on the State of the Global Climate in 2019*.

World Economic Forum (2019) *The Global Risks Report 2019*, 14th edition.

World Economic Forum (2020) *The Global Risks Report 2020*, 15th edition.

2 A brief historical overview of economic development and the environment

Pre- and post-agricultural revolution

We begin with an allegorical tale. On Easter Sunday, 1722, Dutch explorers landed on a remote island in the south Pacific Ocean. (See Figure 2.1.) This land, appropriately named Easter Island, revealed a remarkable and disconcerting sight to the explorers. Standing astride the shoreline were hundreds of massive stone figurines – as tall as 65 feet in height and weighing up to 270 tons (Diamond 2005; Ponting 2007). Clearly the result of a relatively advanced civilization, these statues stood in marked contrast to the decay and desolation which surrounded them. The island's inhabitants were reduced to living in caves or reed huts and verged on the brink of extinction from starvation.

Recent research has been able to reconstruct the rise and fall of Easter Island's civilization. First peopled in the 5th century by Polynesians, the island had witnessed the flowering of a society with elaborate religious rituals. Central to the practice of this religion was the quarrying and carting of massive stones from the center of the island to the coastline where they were erected. Absent wheels and other means of conveyance, it appears the locals adopted a method of transport used by the ancient Egyptians when building the great pyramids. Logs were used to roll the stones to the coast. The earliest inhabitants also relied on the once flourishing forest cover to provide fuel for cooking, heat for their homes and canoes for offshore fishing.

The explorers found no such forest – the island had been virtually stripped of all trees, and the inhabitants had lost their capacity to build homes, fish offshore and provide food from once fertile soil eroded from loss of forest cover. The inhabitants were trapped on their island, no longer able to reverse the decline of their civilization by escaping back to other distant islands in Polynesia.

While this chronology has become the subject of some debate (Hunt and Lipo 2006, 2011; Diamond 2007), there is, nevertheless, a profound allegorical significance to the apparent plight of the Easter Islanders which resonates to this day. Despite the fact that the islanders could presumably observe the exhaustion of the forest resource which was essential for their survival, they were unable to devise a social-economic-political system that allowed them to find the right balance with their fragile environment. One suggested explanation for this suicidal behavior was the increasingly fierce competition for the remaining dwindling resources among rival groups on the island. This bears a disturbing resemblance to modern-day national and international behavior toward dwindling marine resources such as the Atlantic cod and other fish species. The dismal history of Easter Island provides a striking example of the dependence of human societies on their ecosystem and the consequences of irreversibly damaging that environment. Like Easter Island, the earth has only limited resources to support human society and all its demands.

DOI: 10.4324/9781003170730-2

Figure 2.1 Easter Island
Source: David Wright

Like the islanders, the human population of planet earth has no currently practical means of escape. The economist Kenneth Boulding (1966) coined the phrase "Spaceship Earth" in an attempt to capture the essence of this dilemma faced by mankind.

To place this dilemma in a modern context, consider the challenge facing NASA in their goal to send humans to the planet Mars. For just a one-way trip (Krauss 2009), the space agency would have to provide enough food, water and oxygen for a small crew of astronauts as well as find a way to dispose of waste from their activities. It is obviously impractical (read impossible) to load this material into one spaceship for the journey. To solve this problem, NASA would have to replicate within the spaceship a minor version of the earth, creating the commodities needed for existence and recycling the waste products. To all intents and purposes, this is called an *ecosystem*. Some years ago, NASA conducted a minor experiment as a proof of concept. Illustrated in Figure 2.2 is the result of NASA's first experiment: a small glass container, or "biosphere," which holds a plant and a small shrimp (www.eco-sphere.com). This is basically a closed system like the earth – with the similar exception of the inflow of external energy in the form of sunlight. The process within the container replicates, on a greatly simplified scale, the fundamental principles of a natural ecosystem. The shrimp feeds on the plant, and its detritus acts as a food source for the plant. The system is theoretically self-sustaining.

ECOSPHERE

Hold a world in the palm of your hand. Developed by NASA, the EcoSphere is a complete bio-regenerative ecological system sealed in handblown glass. Fascinating to view, it demonstrates the delicate balance of a closed ecosystem (like our Earth) and contains the same elements: earth, water, air, and life—algae, shrimp, and microbes that provide each other with nutrients. All it needs to sustain itself is indirect sunlight. Limited warranty. *No PO box or international deliveries available. Business address for delivery preferred. Allow 3 weeks. No gift box.*

5¼" Pod • 42045...$98.00
5¼" Sphere • 47072...$185.00
4" Sphere • 42044...$85.00

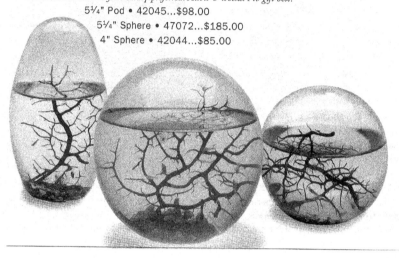

Figure 2.2 Ecosphere

With a proof of concept in hand, the next obvious requirement was to scale up the experiment to reflect more accurately the circumstances and requirements of spaceship travel. In 1991, Biosphere 2 was born in Oracle, Arizona (Sherman 1993; Schellnhuber 2001). Four women, four men, and 3,800 other species of animal and plants were placed within a massive sealed building (see www.biospheres.com/images/bio2diagram3.jpg) in an attempt to create a model for space stations on the moon or Mars. Contained within the structure were miniature representations of many of the earth's ecosystems, including a rainforest, a coral reef, mangrove wetlands, grasslands and a desert (www.b2science.org/who/fact). The results of the experiment, if successful, could also meet the requirements of a nine-month space flight. The experiment failed within one year as it was revealed that fresh air was secretly pumped in to compensate for a potentially deadly imbalance occurring between oxygen and carbon dioxide which threatened the collapse of all species within Biosphere 2.

The sobering conclusions from this experiment were aptly summarized by Cohen and Tilman (1996, pp. 1150–1151):

At present there is no demonstrated alternative to maintaining the viability of Earth. No one yet knows how to engineer systems that provide humans with the life-supporting services that natural ecosystems produce for free. Dismembering major biomes into small pieces, a consequence of widespread human activities, must be regarded with caution. Despite its mysteries and hazards, Earth remains the only known home that can sustain life.

At this point, it is legitimate to pose the question: why worry? Modern humankind has achieved the greatest degree of wealth in history, and it has proven technical skills which have successfully overcome every serious threat to civilization so far. It is here that one must look outside the fields of technology, politics and economics and consider the lessons of ecological history. As Chapter 9 explores, the global economy is imbedded in a larger system – called the earth's ecosystem – which provides the necessary resources for survival. This system is basically "closed" (or finite) and will ultimately constrain the level of human activity. Nature has worked out an elaborate system of checks and balances to maintain some form of equilibrium. A good example of this concept is provided by the relationship between predators and prey, as illustrated in the classic representation of Figure 2.3 (Krebs, see also Huffaker 1958; Forsyth and Caley 2006). Predators (lynx) increase in numbers as their food supply (snowshoe hares) increases, then decrease in number as the prey population is depleted. Prey then increase in the face of the reduced number of predators, and this almost sinusoidal cycle repeats itself indefinitely. When, for some reason or another, natural controls are removed on one species, it may experience exponential growth until it finally reaches a binding constraint such as limited food supply. The result is frequently sudden population collapse, as illustrated in Figure 2.4 (derived from Scheffer 1951).

What does this have to do with humanity? Figure 2.5 provides the US Census Bureau's (2021) best estimates of global population over the last 5,000 years. One may posit the rhetorical question: does this look like a state of equilibrium? To understand the significance of this population trend, one must turn to another ecological term known as *carrying capacity*, defined as the number of organisms of a particular species (whether human, animal or plant) that a geographic area can support without irreversibly reducing its capacity to support them in the future at the desired level of living. Carrying capacity is a function

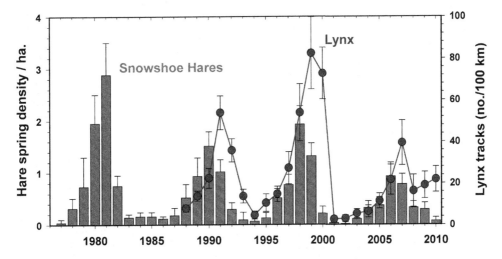

Figure 2.3 Typical predator-prey interaction

Source: Reproduced with the permission of Professor Charles Krebs.

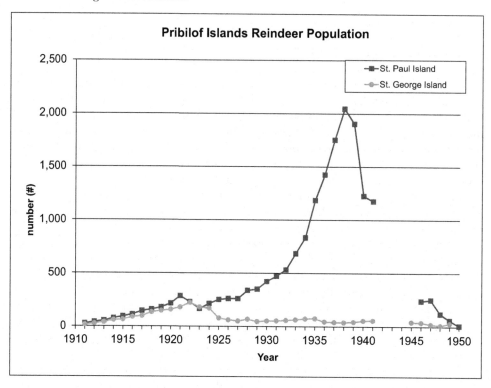

Figure 2.4 Typical population collapse

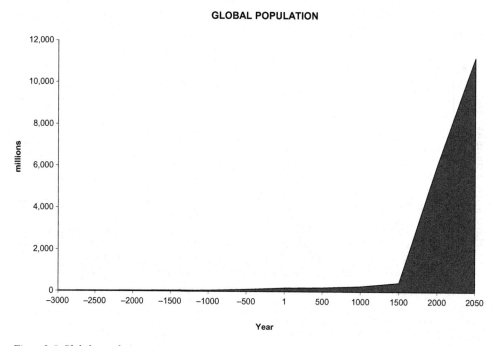

Figure 2.5 Global population estimates

Table 2.1 Estimates of global carrying capacity

Conditions	Carrying capacity (billion people)
Using present agro technologies, vegetarian diet only and equal food distribution	5.5
If humans derive 15% of calories from animal products, as do many in South America	3.7
If humans gained 25% of their calories from animal protein, as is the case with most people in North America	2.8
Current population	6.1

of many interacting factors including food, energy supplies and ecosystem services such as the provision of fresh water and recycling of nutrients. Carrying capacity is ultimately determined by the component that has the lowest capacity. The relevant question is: when will we reach the global carrying capacity? Table 2.1 answers this question on the basis of the best ecological data available today. With a current population of 6.1 billion, it appears that the earth has already passed the point of global carrying capacity (Brown University Global Hunger Program n.d.; see also Heilig 1993 and Cohen 1995). Does this mean the Brundtland Commission's goal of raising the living standard of the vast majority of global inhabitants is unattainable? In Chapter 3, the question is posed whether it is possible to delink economic growth and environmental despoliation.

The exponential growth of human population in the last 500 years is a central, but not only, factor that must be considered. Gerard Piel, former publisher of *Scientific American*, wrote a prescient book entitled *The Acceleration of History* which discussed the ethical obligations of a citizenry in the face of rapidly advancing science and technology (Piel 1972). A cogent illustration of this modern phenomenon of unprecedented exponential change is provided in historical graphs from Steffen et al. (2005). (See Figure 2.6.) The two most important time series are human population growth (Figure 2.5) and global GDP (Figure 2.7 from De Long 1998). In contrast to the historical growth of human population represented in Figure 2.5, the scale of the graph of GDP growth is logarithmic, signifying the extraordinary achievement of human ingenuity in creating wealth through the application of technology to the earth's resources.

In 1798, the Reverend Thomas Malthus published the first edition of his *An Essay on the Principle of Population*. This work, more than any other, may have contributed to the characterization of the field of economics as "the dismal science." Malthus hypothesized that humankind would remain in a perpetual state of near starvation as the arithmetic increase in food production would be outpaced by an exponential increase in human population. Few works in traditional economics have been so vilified, as generations of economists have declared that Malthus was "wrong" and that increasing production of per capita global food supplies through continued breakthroughs in global food production technology has proved this beyond a reasonable doubt.

The United Nations has projected that global population will increase from 7.7 billion in 2019 to 10.9 billion in 2100 (UN 2019). If the earth's nations are to feed this growing number of citizens, major new technological breakthroughs will be required to raise the yield of current food crops. What are the prospects for these continued advances in technology and its application to food production? One of the great technological advances in agriculture occurred in the period 1950 to 1984 and is referred to as the "green

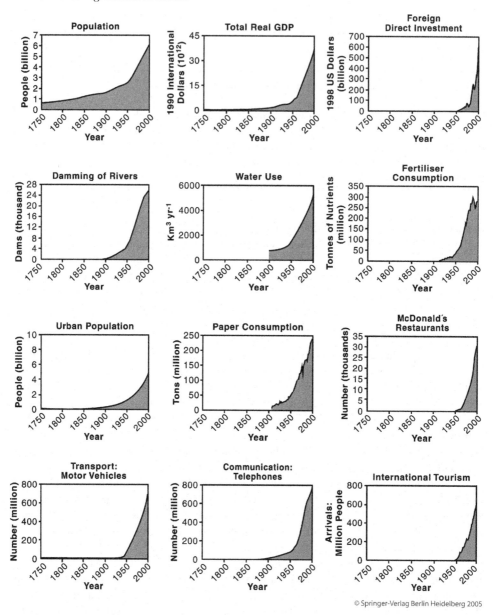

Figure 2.6 Some exponential growth examples

Source: Steffan et al. 2005, reproduced with permission of the publisher

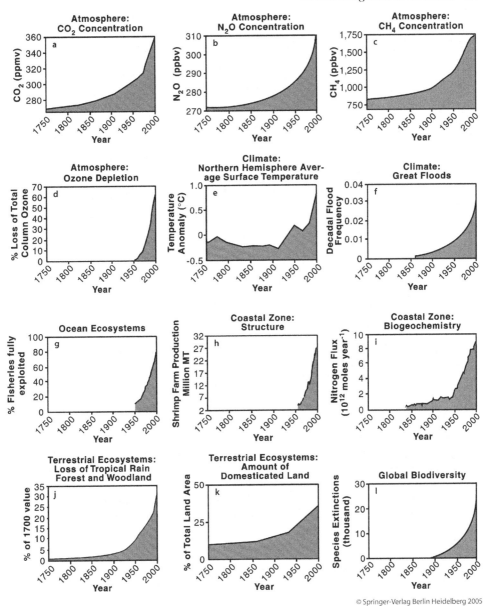

Figure 2.6 (Continued)

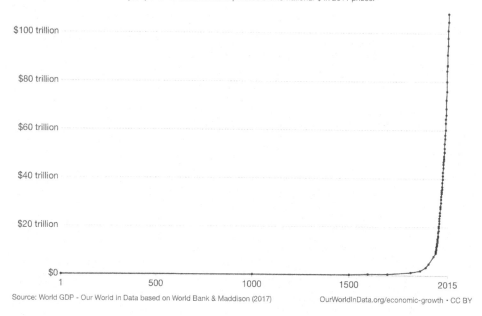

World GDP over the last two millennia
Total output of the world economy; adjusted for inflation and expressed in international-$ in 2011 prices.

Source: World GDP - Our World in Data based on World Bank & Maddison (2017)   OurWorldInData.org/economic-growth · CC BY

Figure 2.7 Estimated gross world product

revolution." This was a concerted effort on the part of the Western industrialized nations to stimulate staple food production in India and other third world countries through an agricultural system which relied on five critical factors: hybrid seeds which are high yield, fast growing and disease resistant; heavy use of fertilizer (e.g. India increased its consumption of fertilizer from 69,800 tons in 1950–1951 to 27.228 million tons in 2018–2019; Fertiliser Association of India – faidelhi.org); increased use of pesticides; mechanization and high-energy-intensity agriculture such as tractors, combines and irrigation pumps; and increased reliance on monoculture (UNEP 2011, p. 40).

As with all technological advances, there are both benefits and costs. The benefits were clear: between 1950 and 1984, there was a 2.6-fold increase in world grain output. This represented an average increase of almost 3% per year and rising per capita production by more than one third. In contrast, world population growth during 1980–1985 was only 1.75% per year. The costs, however, have been substantial and include land degradation, ground water contamination, social dislocation due to land aggregation and the displacement of small landowners and significant economic and ecological costs associated with the production and use of fertilizers, pesticides and commercial energy products. Since 1961 to 2017, there has been a steady increase in cereal production and an accompanying commensurate increase in average grain production per capita at the global level (World Bank World Development Indicators -WDI 2019). However, the declining trend in the proportion of undernourished people in the world over the period 2005–2015 has reversed and is back to the levels of 2010–2011 (see Figure 2.8 from FAO 2019). Principal explanatory factors include conflicts, misdirection, spoilage and extreme weather events, most particularly what the Food and Agriculture Organization (FAO) characterizes as the "dramatic, longer term impact on food security . . . associated with exposure to drought" (FAO 2019, p. 7).

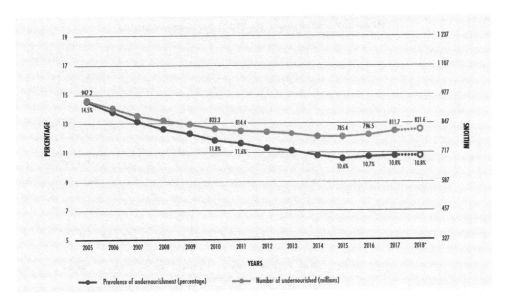

Figure 2.8 Percentage of undernourished population in the developing world

Notes: * Values for 2018 are projections as illustrated by dotted lines and empty circles. The entire series was carefully revised to reflect new information made available since the publication of the last edition of the report; it replaces all series published previously. See Box 2.

Source: FAO.

Initial conclusion

There are several fundamental forces driving the current pressure on the environment: (1) rising population; (2) increasing industrialization and wealth with a concomitant rise in demand for food and other natural resources; and (3) technological innovations which may have environmentally detrimental effects. The interrelationship among these factors can be captured in the following basic equation:

$$P \times M/P \times E/M = \text{total pollution}$$

where P = population, M = material consumption and E = environmental impact.

The message from this simple relationship is that total pollution can increase from any one of three factors: population growth, increased per capita consumption and the increased pollution intensity of products. If the goal is to decrease the environmental burden of the planet, it is clearly insufficient to tackle only one or two of these factors; an increase in the residual may offset any positive effects in the others. What does the empirical evidence tell us?

Despite popular opinion to the contrary, it is often the nature of scientific evidence that it is open to divergent interpretations. An optimist would take consolation in the fact that the annual rate of population increase falls as per capita income rises. The underlying dynamic process is referred to as the *demographic transition* and includes a pattern of changes in birth rates, death rates and resulting population growth rates that accompany

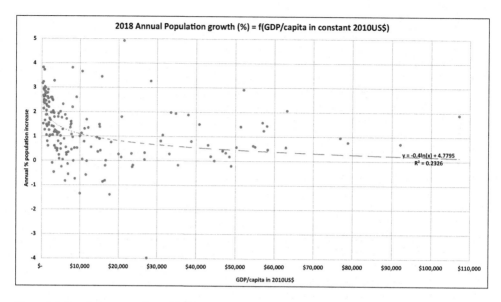

Figure 2.9 Population growth vs. GDP/capita in 2000

economic development. Net population growth is a function of the phase of economic development. Historically, three such phases have been documented: (1) a pre-industrial phase, characterized by both high birth and death rates, producing low or stable population growth; (2) an industrial phase, marked by high birth rates and major reduction in death rates due to the increased application of public health measures, leading, in turn, to explosive growth; and (3) a mature or post-industrial phase characterized by both low birth and death rates, producing a return to low or stable population growth rates.

These transitions are based on historical time-series analysis but can also be observed in cross-sectional examination of global nations today which span a broad range of per capita income. The data provided in Figure 2.9 compare the annual growth rates in national population with GDP per capita. It can be hypothesized on the basis of these data that past a certain point in per capita income, population growth rate stabilizes at a low level, in some cases below the level of population replacement. Even more important is the relatively low level of per capita income (at approximately $10,000) at which this stabilization appears to occur. This suggests that it is not necessary to raise the standard of living of the world's poorest countries to the level of the wealthiest in order to solve the problems associated with rapid population increase.

Another way of observing the significantly different national population growth paths is to examine *population pyramids*, which show the percentage of the population, by gender, in each major age category. Figure 2.10 provides sample international population pyramid data for six countries (US Census Bureau 2021). The two wealthiest countries in this sample, the United States and Canada, have an approximately even age distribution, suggesting a relatively stable population. In contrast, the four developing nations, China, India, Egypt and Pakistan, have a much greater proportion of their population in their child-bearing years, suggesting a potential for a significant continuing increase in population. By raising the standard of living of these countries, it is hoped that they will replicate the historical pattern of the developed world as illustrated in Figure 2.11, which shows

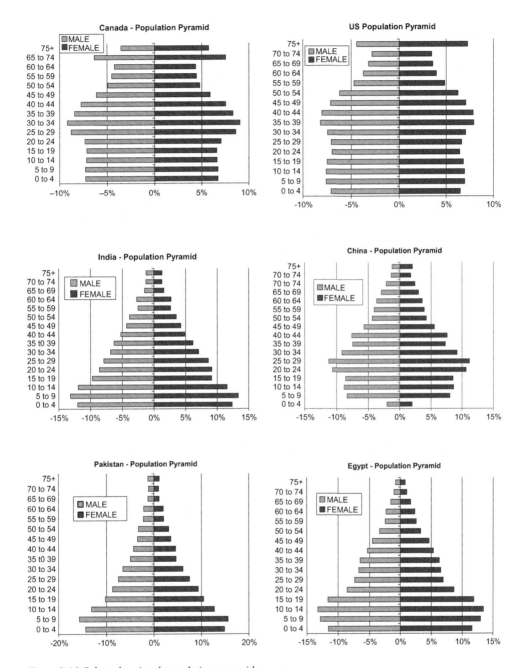

Figure 2.10 Selected national population pyramids

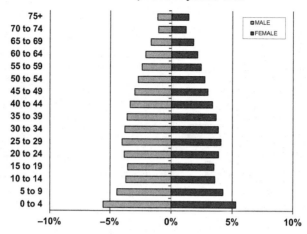

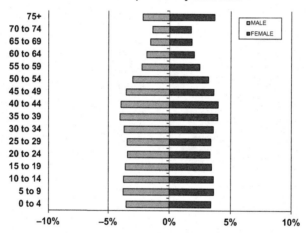

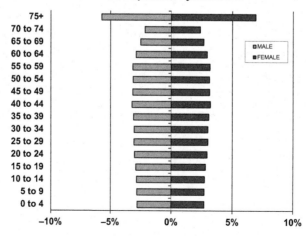

Figure 2.11 US national population pyramids

the past and projected shift in the US population pyramid as national wealth increases. Nevertheless, the increasing proportion of middle-aged and elderly persons accompanying industrial development tends to generate its own particular challenges, as there is a decrease in the percentage of working people in the total population, putting additional stress on national pension funds.

In sum, the optimist's position is that increased wealth brings reduced population growth and, therefore, by simply raising the standard of living of the rest of the world, the problem of population growth will take care of itself. There are several positive sides to this argument: it seems altruistic and ethical; it may avoid the problem of forced population control, such as China's controversial program to reduce births and the concomitant perverse incentives created by this policy; it will avoid the contentious perception that the industrialized world is forcing population control on the third world for self-serving reasons; and it may finesse the delicate religious issue of birth control and abortion.

In marked contrast, the pessimist's interpretation of these same data is based on three arguments: first, the process of raising global standards of living will take a long time; second, the drain on essential natural resources (in such areas as fisheries and agriculture) may be enormous; and, finally and perhaps most importantly, the environment poses a binding constraint in the form of the adequacy of fresh clean water; the assimilative capacity of air, water and soil; and the burden on the ecosystem from the increased utilization of energy.

Summary overview of human historical impact on the environment

Throughout the broad sweep of human history, global inhabitants have progressed through four major historical phases: (1) pre-agricultural, (2) agricultural to pre-industrial, (3) industrial and (4) post-industrial. The last of these phases is restricted to only a subset of modern nations, as the majority of the global population remains in an earlier stage. Figure 2.12 links the exponential increase in population over the last 12,000 years to major technological transitions. Each of the four principal phases can be associated with specific forms of economic organization, human impacts on the natural environment and the nature of the risks faced by humankind.

1   **The pre-agricultural period**, characterized by hunting, gathering and herding, lasted for about 2 million years and was marked by localized ecological disturbance from controlled burning, overhunting and some resulting extinction of species. The human population remained in relative balance with resource availability by frequent changes of location, and some measure of population control was achieved through infanticide. One study (Doughty et al. 2010) has suggested that even at this early stage of human development, humankind exerted a subtle influence on global climate. It is posited that ancient hunters helped warm the Arctic and subarctic regions by intensive hunting of wooly mammoths. By largely eliminating this herbivorous species whose diet consisted largely of leaves, humankind created an ecosystem response which led to the proliferation of dwarf birch trees, changing the reflective surface of the region (i.e. its *albedo*) and increasing its heat absorption. This systemic response led to a subtle increase in global warming. This is but one example of the importance of systems analysis not only in the study of ecology but also in the interrelationship of economic and ecological systems. (See Chapter 8 on systems theory.)

2   **The agricultural revolution** occurred about 10,000 years ago and represents the most important transition in human history. In the space of a few thousand years,

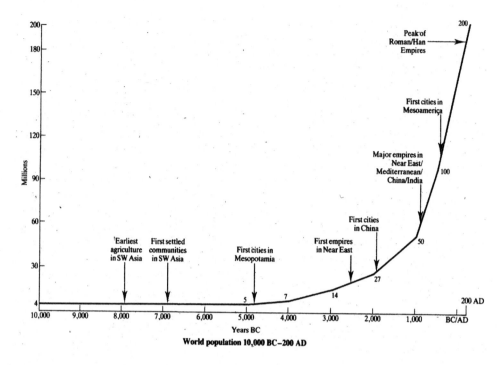

Figure 2.12 Landmarks in global economic development

a radically different way of life emerged based on a major alteration to natural ecosystems in order to produce crops and provide pasture for animals. This intensive system of food production was developed separately in at least three areas of the world: Mesoamerica, Southwest Asia and China.

Agriculture allowed the emergence of a large hierarchical social structure supported by, but not engaged directly in, agricultural production, including administration, religion, culture, military forces and early industrial activity. According to Ponting (1991), the first true cities started to emerge by about 5000 BC:

> Human history in the 8000 years or so since the emergence of settled agricultural societies has been about the acquisition and distribution of the surplus food production and the uses to which it has been put. The size of the food surplus available to a particular society has determined the number and extent of other functions . . . the link may have been more obvious in earlier, simpler societies, but it is still present in contemporary societies.
>
> (p. 54)

Settled agricultural societies provide the first examples of intensive human alteration of the environment and their major destructive impact. They also provide examples of societies that so damaged the environment as to bring about their own collapse – an event characterized by Jared Diamond (2005) as "Ecocide." At least two major factors associated with agricultural activity had a historically devastating environmental impact: deforestation and irrigation.

Deforestation through forest clearing for agriculture, fuel and building materials leads to soil erosion, declining crop yields and eventual inability to grow enough food. Much of the Mediterranean area, now distinguished by bare rock and deserts, was once covered in forests. In his insightful book on the forest history of the Mediterranean literal, J. V. Thirgood (1981, p. 3) observed:

> No other part of the world so strikingly drives home the story of man's failure to maintain his environment. . . . Once the focal point of western civilization, the Balkans, Anatolia, the Levant and North Africa is now economically depressed. Southern Italy, where the Hellenes settled Graecia Magna nearly three thousand years ago (974– 443 B.C.) and developed a centre of Grecian culture – where Herodotus, the historian, lived, where Pythagoras advanced the science of Geometry, and where Aeschylus wrote his plays – was a land of forests. It was here in the scorched heart of Sicily at Piazza Armerina, that a mosaic extending over a quarter of an acre was discovered – the floor of a fourth century Roman villa, depicting woodland hunting and wildlife scenes at a site now surrounded by a landscape of barren grey hills.

Ponting (1991) describes a similar situation in North Africa, which

> contains a whole series of impressive Roman remains . . . from what were once some of the most flourishing and highly productive provinces of the Roman Empire. But they now lie surrounded by vast deserts, a memorial to widespread environmental degradation brought about by human actions.

One of the most famous and controversial cases of environmental collapse leading to the demise of a society comes from the Maya, who developed – in what are now parts of Mexico, Guatemala, Belize and Honduras – one of the most extraordinary societies of its type found anywhere in the world. The old empire existed during the period AD 300– 900. Population was estimated to have peaked in AD 800 at between 2.7 and 3.4 million. The civilization collapsed within a few decades due to declining food production due to the compound effects of deforestation and drought (Hodell et al. 1995, 2001; Diamond 2005; Fagan 2008; Ponting 2007; Global Heritage Fund 2011; Evans 2018).

Irrigation, the process which facilitates the transformation of arid regions to highly productive agricultural areas, is a double-edged sword and has been labeled the second major destructive force of the agricultural era. Its benefits are multifold. In addition to allowing crop production in areas where none could occur before, it permits increased crop yield, allows multiple cropping in a year and broadens the array of crops which can be cultivated. In contrast, however, its costs are significant, as it can deplete the soil of nutrients and raise the water table, increasing water logging and producing progressive salinization of the soil which can lead to the gradual decline of crop production through lower yields and elimination of salt-intolerant crops such as wheat. The only way this process can be prevented is by very carefully using irrigation, avoiding overwatering and leaving the ground fallow at periodic intervals. Unfortunately, in many parts of the world, these procedures, especially fallowing, are luxuries, as every bit of arable land is required to feed their populations. There are numerous civilizations in human history which are suspected of collapsing due to soil salinization. Among the most prominent of these are

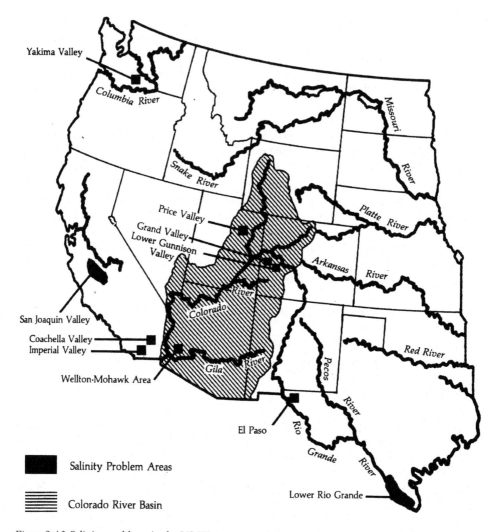

Figure 2.13 Salinity problems in the US West

Source: El-Ashry et al. 1985, p. 49, reproduced with permission of the publisher.

the agricultural societies of ancient Mesopotamia and the Indus Valley, now parts of the Middle East and South Asia (Turner et al. 1990, Ponting 2007).

While salinization and other major effects of vast irrigation projects have received relatively little public attention, it is still a critical issue wherever intensive irrigation-based agriculture is practiced in both the developing and developed worlds. It has been estimated that between 21% and 24% of global arable land is damaged by salt (UNEP 2006; Lenntech 2011). For a cogent example, one need look no further than the US with the drawdown of the Colorado River and the extensive depletion of the Ogallala Aquifer, which have provided vast quantities of water for agriculture and urban development in the Southwest. (See Woods et al. 2000; Welle and Mauter 2017; Philpott 2020; Figure 2.13 from El-Ashry et al. 1985). Figure 2.14 provides a dramatic example of the effect of

Colorado River Discharge Near US-Mexico Border

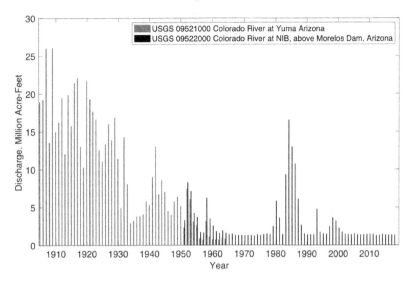

Figure 2.14 Colorado River flows

Source: Reproduced with permission of the author.

excess demand on Colorado River water over the past century (Milly 2020). Both these phenomena represent unsustainable practices which must be resolved if current agriculture and urbanization is to continue in the western states.

On a positive note, while the San Joaquin Valley in California has lost thousands of acres from cultivation due to irrigation-induced salinization, solar farms have emerged as a welcome supplement to farm income threatened by the threat of increasing water scarcity (*Sacramento Bee* September 27, 2019). This offers the promise of using this land in a sustainable manner while contributing to US energy self-sufficiency. All critical stakeholders, including farmers and environmentalists, agreed to use this land for the creation of a 13,000-acre solar energy facility. This novel approach has been termed "the vanguard of a new approach to locating renewable energy projects," overcoming traditional objections to the use of land for non-agricultural purposes (*New York Times* August 10, 2010).

While both deforestation and irrigation have had devastating impacts on many ancient civilizations, deforestation has been the recent focus of global concern in both tropical and temperate forests – all the way from Brazil, Central America and Southeast Asia to Africa (ASEAN Post 2017; FAO 2020; Escobar 2020; Khelifa 2020). This is a critical issue today, with immense implications not only directly for global agriculture but also indirectly for global warming and all its concomitant effects.

References

ASEAN Post (2017) "Deforestation: A modern-day plague in Southeast Asia," September 23.

Boulding, Kenneth (1966) "The economics of the coming spaceship Earth," http://dieoff.org/page160. htm; reprinted as Ch. 5 in Herman E. Daly (ed.) 1973 *Toward a Steady-State Economy*, New York: W.H. Freeman & Co., pp. 121–132.

Brown University (n.d.) "World Global Hunger Program," http://www.brown.edu/Departments/World_Hunger_Program/

Cohen, Joel E. (1995) *How Many People Can the Earth Support?*, New York: W.W. Norton & Co.

Cohen, Joel E. and David Tilman (1996) "Biosphere 2 and biodiversity: The lessons so far," *Science*, 274, November 15, pp. 1150–1151.

De Long, J. Bradford (1998) "Estimates of World GDP, one million B.C.: Present," http://econ161.berkeley.edu.

Diamond, Jared (2005) *Collapse: How Societies Choose to Fail or Succeed*, New York: Viking.

Diamond, Jared (2007) "Easter Island revisited," *Science*, 317, September 21, pp. 1692–1694.

Doughty, Christopher et al. (2010) "Biophysical feedbacks between the Pleistocene megafauna extinction and climate: The first human-induced global warming?," *Geophysical Research Letters*, 37, L15703, 5 pages.

El-Ashry, Mohamed et al. (1985) "Salinity pollution from irrigated agriculture," *Journal of Soil and Water Conservation*, 40(1), January–February, pp. 48–52.

Escobar, Herton (2020) "Deforestation in the Brazilian Amazon is still rising sharply," *Science*, 369(6504), August 7, p. 613.

Evans, Nicholas P. et al. (2018) "Quantification of drought during the collapse of the classic Maya civilization," *Science*, August 3.

Fagan, Brian (2008) *The Great Warming: Climate Change and the Rise and Fall of Civilizations*. New York: Bloomsbury Press.

Food and Agriculture Organization (FAO) (2019) *The State of Food Security and Nutrition in the World*, Rome: United Nations.

Food and Agriculture Organization (FAO) (2020) *The State of the World's Forests*, Rome: United Nations.

Forsyth, David M. and Peter Caley (2006) "Testing the irruptive paradigm of large-herbivore dynamics," *Ecology*, 87(2), pp. 297–303.

Global Heritage Fund (2011) "Mighty Maya cities succumbed to environmental crisis," September 1.

Heilig, Gerhard K. (1993) *How Many People can be Fed on Earth?* IIASA WP 93-40, August.

Hodell, David A. et al. (1995) "Possible role of climate in the collapse of classic Maya civilization," *Nature*, 375, June 1, pp. 391–394.

Hodell, David A. et al. (2001) "Solar forcing of drought frequency in the Maya Lowlands," *Science*, 202, May 18, pp. 1367–1370.

Huffaker, C.B. (1958) "Experimental studies on predation: Dispersion factors and predator-prey oscillations," *Hilgardia*, 27, pp. 343–383.

Hunt, Terry L. and Carl P. Lipo (2006) "Late colonization of Easter Island," *Science*, 311, March 17, pp. 1603–1606.

Hunt, Terry L. and Carl P. Lipo (2011) *The Statues That Walked: Unraveling the Mystery of Easter Island*, New York: Free Press.

Khelifa, Rassim (2020) "North African forests falling to charcoal," *Science*, Letter, August 28.

Krauss, Lawrence M. (2009) "A one-way ticket to Mars," *New York Times*, August 31, OPED.

Krebs, Charles (2018) Department of Zoology, University of British Columbia, Personal communication.

Lenntech, B.V. (2011) Rotterdamseweg, The Netherlands. www.lenntech.com/applications/irrigation/salinity/salanity-hazard-irrigation.htm.

Malthus, Thomas (1798) *An Essay on the Principle of Population*, reprinted 2002, Boston: IndyPublish.com.

Milly, Chris (United States Geological Survey) (2020) Personal communication, May 30.

New York Times (2010) "Recycling land for green energy ideas," August 10.

Philpott, Tom (2020) *Perilous Bounty: The Looming Collapse of American Farming and How We Can Prevent It*, London: Bloomsbury Publishing.

Piel, Gerard (1972) *The Acceleration of History*, New York: Alfred A. Knopf.

Ponting, Clive (1991) *A Green History of the World*, Harmondsworth, Middlesex: Penguin Books.

Ponting, Clive (2007) *A New Green History of the World*, London: Vintage Books.

Sacramento Bee (2019) "'Farming the sun:' as water goes scarce, can solar farms prop up the Valley?" September 27.

Scheffer, Victor B. (1951) "The rose and fall of a Reindeer Herd," *Science*, 73(6), December, pp. 356–362.

Schellnhuber, H.-J. (2001) "Earth system analysis and management," Chapter two in Eckart Ehlers and Thomas Krafft (eds.) *Understanding the Earth System: Compartments, Processes and Interactions*, Berlin: Springer, pp. 17–56.

Sherman, Francine Shonfeld (1993) "Biosphere 2: Hard science of soft sell?," in *Encyclopaedia Britannica Yearbook*, Chicago: Encyclopaedia Britannica, p. 166.

Steffen, W. et al. (2005) *Global Change and the Earth System*, Berlin: Springer.

Thirgood, J.V. (1981) *Man and the Mediterranean Forest: A History of Resource Depletion*, London: Academic Press.

Turner, B.L. et al. (1990) *The Earth as Transformed by Human Action: Global and Regional Changes in the Biosphere over the Past 300 Years*, Cambridge: Cambridge University Press.

UN Environment Programme (UNEP) (2006) *Global Environment Outlook 3 (GEO3)*.

UN Environment Programme (UNEP) (2011) *Towards a Green Economy: Pathways to Sustainable Development and Poverty Eradication*.

United Nations (2019) *World Population Prospects*, June.

US Census Bureau (2021). website. http:www.census.gov/.

Welle, Paul D. and Meagan S. Mauter (2017) "High-resolution model for estimating the economic and policy implications of agricultural soil salinization in California," *Environmental Research Letters*, 12, p. 94010.

Woods, J.J. et al. (2000) *Water Level Decline in the Ogallala Aquifer*, United States Geological Service, Kansas City.

World Bank (2019) "World development indicators."

Wright, David. Photo credit for Easter Island.

www.eco-sphere.com [website of Ecosphere Associates, Inc., Tucson, AZ].

3 A brief historical overview of economic development and the environment

The Industrial Revolution and sequel

The second most significant change in recent human history was the Industrial Revolution of the late 1700s and early 1800s. This dramatic change in technology, economics and the organization of business and society occurred in England during the period 1760–1840. Termed the "Workshop of the World" (Chambers 1961), the island nation established the framework on which our modern industrial economy rests. This revolution was characterized by a shift from an agrarian to an industrial society, and the locus of production shifted from the home and workshop to the factory. The principal features of this radical transformation included several major changes in the technological and non-industrial spheres:

> (1) the use of new basic materials, chiefly iron and steel, (2) the use of new energy sources, including both fuels and motive power, such as coal, the steam engine, electricity, petroleum, and the internal-combustion engine, (3) the invention of new machines, such as the spinning jenny and the power loom that permitted increased production with a smaller expenditure of human energy, (4) a new organization of work known as the factory system, which entailed increased division of labour and specialization of function, (5) important developments in transportation and communication, including the steam locomotive, steamship, automobile, airplane, telegraph, and radio, and (6) the increasing application of science to industry. These technological changes made possible a tremendously increased use of natural resources and the mass production of manufactured goods.
>
> (*Encyclopaedia Britannica* 1993, Vol. 6, p. 305)

New developments in non-industrial spheres included:

> (1) agricultural improvements that made possible the provision of food for a larger non-agricultural population, (2) economic changes that resulted in a wider distribution of wealth, the decline of land as a source of wealth in the face of rising industrial production, and increased international trade, (3) political changes reflecting the shift in economic power . . . , (4) sweeping social changes, including the growth of cities, the development of working-class movements . . . , and (5) cultural transformations of a broad order. The worker acquired new and distinctive skills, and his relation to his task shifted; instead of being a craftsman working with hand tools, he became a machine operator, subject to factory discipline.
>
> (*Encyclopaedia Britannica* 1993, Vol. 6, p. 305)

DOI: 10.4324/9781003170730-3

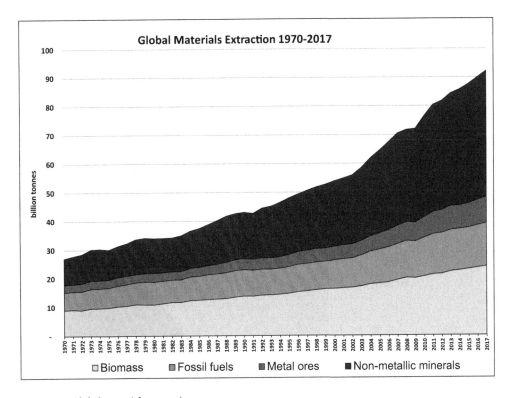

Figure 3.1 Global materials extraction

Source: www.ggdc.net/maddison; European Commission 2018.

From the perspective of environmental sustainability, there were at least four profound and interrelated changes ushered in by the Industrial Revolution: a rapid increase in the flow of materials; a massive increase in the use of energy, particularly fossil fuels; the consequent release of large quantities of anthropogenic greenhouse gases such as carbon dioxide; and the generation and release of a broad range of industrial-based air and water pollutants. Figure 3.1 displays global materials extraction measured from 1900 to 2017. Figures 3.2a and 3.2b show the dramatic increase in energy consumption in the United Kingdom (Warde 2007; Mitchell and Deane 1962; Mitchell and Jones 1971; Maddison 2006a, 2006b; Mitchell 2007a) and the United States (Mitchell 2007b, 2013; Maddison 2006b; US Department of Commerce 1975) over the past several centuries. Both these figures also display the changing mix of fuel types as fossil fossils established a dominant role in both economies. Projections of existing trends (Hatfield-Dodds et al. 2017; European Commission 2018) suggest that global energy use could increase by 69%, and material resource extraction may increase by as much as 119% by 2050, with the biggest increase in non-metallic minerals. Krausmann et al. (2017, p. 1880) observe:

> Human-made material stocks accumulating in buildings, infrastructure, and machinery play a crucial but underappreciated role in shaping the use of material and energy resources. Building, maintaining, and in particular operating in-use stocks of materials

require raw materials and energy. Material stocks create long-term path-dependencies because of their longevity. . . . About half of all materials extracted globally by humans each year are used to build up or renew in-use stocks of materials. . . . Despite efforts to improve recycling rates, continuous stock growth precludes closing material loops; recycling still only contributes 12% of inflows to stocks. Stocks are likely to continue to grow, driven by large infrastructure and building requirements in emerging economies.

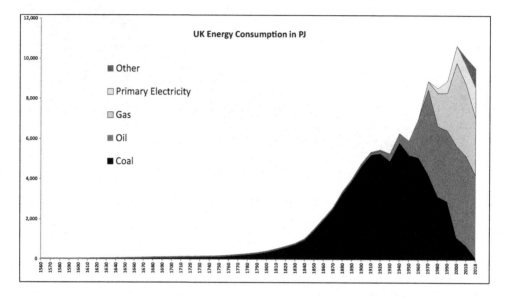

Figure 3.2a UK historical energy consumption

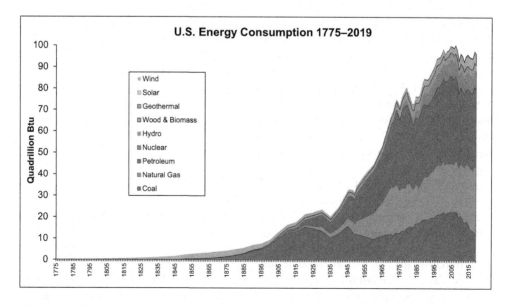

Figure 3.2b US energy consumption

In a remarkable research article in *Nature*, Elhacham et al. (2019) compare how the overall material output of human activities compares to the overall natural biomass. They conclude:

> Earth is exactly at the crossover point; in the year 2020 (± 6), the anthropogenic mass, which has recently doubled roughly every 20 years, will surpass all global living biomass. On average, for each person on the globe, anthropogenic mass equal to more than his or her bodyweight is produced every week.
>
> (p. 1)

Figures 3.3 and 3.4 illustrate the historic rise in greenhouse gases in the UK and US, most notably carbon dioxide, as a consequence of energy consumption (data from ORNL).

The results of the Industrial Revolution were dramatic, allowing a commensurate increase in wealth and standard of living among the industrializing nations of the world. The fundamental challenge now faced by the global community is how to share this development with the vast majority of world citizens who reside within the third world without engendering the same deleterious environmental consequences. This challenge can be posited as follows: is it possible to delink economic growth and environmental despoliation, or, more simply, is there more than one path to economic development? It is now generally accepted that raising the standard of living of the third world to any significant proportion of that experienced by the developed nations would involve massive increases in energy and material flows that would threaten the very foundation of the global ecological system which supports human life and economic activity.

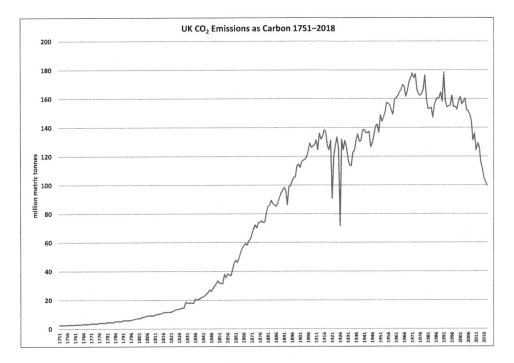

Figure 3.3 UK CO$_2$ emissions

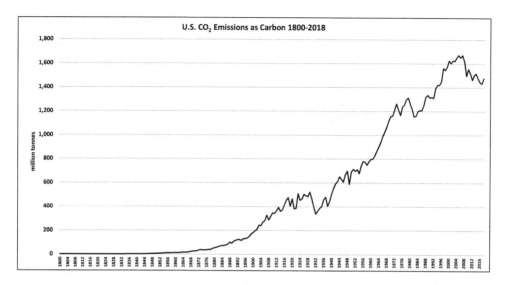

Figure 3.4 US CO_2 emissions

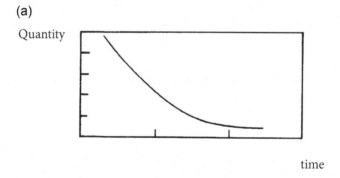

Figure 3.5a Traditional environmental Kuznets curves (I)

There is a commonly held view that economies can grow their way out of pollution in a manner analogous to the demographic transition. This conventional wisdom is epitomized by the famous *environmental Kuznets curve*, named after the late Simon Kuznets of Harvard University's Economics Department. There are two principal variants of this function. The first class of curves, as illustrated in Figure 3.5a, represents monotonically *decreasing* environmental problems associated with increasing standards of living, such as the percentage of population without safe water or adequate sanitation. The second class of curves (see Figure 3.5b) are *concave* functions for such pollutants as airborne particulates and sulfur dioxide. In this case, it is posited that as economies move from primary to secondary and tertiary industry, they can both afford greater pollution control and switch to more environmentally benign production processes.

(b)

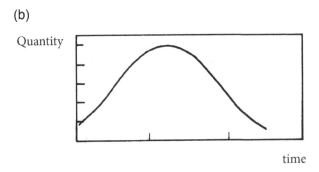

Figure 3.5b Traditional environmental Kuznets curves (II)

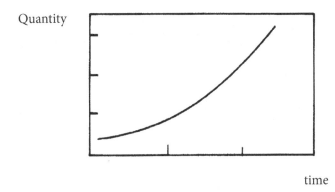

Figure 3.6 Revised environmental Kuznets curve

While these two types of transformations appear to be supported by historical evidence, they portray a seriously incomplete and misleading picture of the environmental consequences of industrialization. Figure 3.6 typifies what is missing. The monotonically *increasing* functions portrayed in this figure represent the increasing levels of pollutants which rise in tandem with increasing national income: solid waste, radioactive waste and persistent organic pollutants (POPs), etc. Unlike traditional pollutants associated with the early stages of industrialization, many of these new hazards transcend local or regional effects and pose global-level threats to the environment. These include POPs such as aldrin, chlordane, dieldrin, dioxins (PCDDs), DDT, endrin, furans (i.e. polychlorinated dibenzofurans), heptachlor, hexachlorobenzene, mirex, polychlorinated biphenyls (PCBs) and toxaphene. These substances have three critical properties which render them especially problematic: they persist in the environment, bioaccumulate (see Chapter 8) in the food web and are subject to long-range transport (UNEP 2007; NRC 2009; Breivik et al. 2002a, 2002b, 2007). While many POPs are pesticides, others have been used extensively as solvents and ingredients in both industrial processes and pharmaceutical production.

POPs have multiple diffusion pathways in the environment and can be deposited far from their point of manufacture or use (EMEP 2005; Wania and Mackay 1993; Ottesen et al. 2010). Several studies of the blood, tissues and maternal milk of Arctic mammals, including humans, have found pollutant levels many times those of populations in the temperate regions (Indian Affairs and Northern Affairs Canada 2003; Schindler 2007). One research study conducted in the Arctic found a growing gender imbalance among human births, with females far outnumbering males. In one Greenland village, no males were born in the period under study (Schindler 2007; LOE 2007). In an attempt to understand the potential causal relationships in this phenomenon, one study (UNEP 2004) found a convex relationship between total PCB concentrations in maternal serum and the male/female sex ratio at birth (see Figure 3.7). There is recent emerging evidence that many of the POPs deposited in the Arctic over the past half century are now being re-volatized by climate change (Ma et al. 2011).

One research paper (Mackenzie 2005) cited several scientific studies suggesting that changes in human birth sex ratios are not confined to the Arctic regions. One of the principal explanations advanced for this phenomenon is the class of environmental and occupational chemicals called *endocrine disruptors* (EDs), which can interfere with human hormonal systems. (See also James 1995; Sakamoto et al. 2001.) An exhaustive study on the state of knowledge with respect to EDs was published in May 2012 by the European Environment Agency (EEA 2012). The research suggested that these globally pervasive chemicals can affect multiple human body systems and processes such as reproduction, thyroid, immune, digestive, cardiovascular and metabolic systems as well as neurodevelopmental processes. The report posited a causal relationship between the growth of the global chemical industry and the increasing rates of endocrine diseases and disorders, citing by way of example the decreasing quality of semen among many European males,

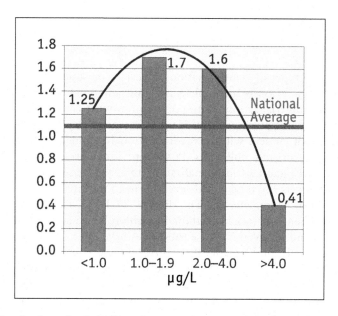

Figure 3.7 Ratio of male to female births as function of PCB concentration in maternal serum in the Arctic

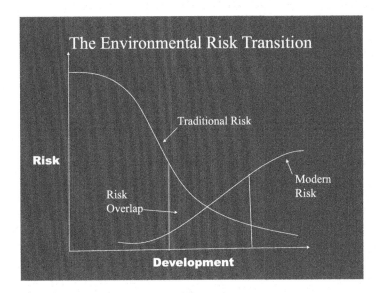

Figure 3.8 The risk transition

Source: Smith 2009, reproduced with permission of the author.

where fertility in approximately 40% of males is impaired. A range of similar reproductive-related effects have also been observed in several wildlife species considered to be valuable sentinels of human health. The extent of these "early warning signals" has led the EEA to suggest a precautionary approach (see Chapter 10) to the introduction and use of this broad range of chemicals. In fact, the ubiquitous presence of modern chemicals in the environment has been graphically summarized by Williams (2012) in her summary of scientific research on contaminants in human milk:

> When we nurse our babies, we feed them not only the fats and sugars that fire their immune systems, cellular metabolisms, and cerebral synapses. We also feed them, in albeit miniscule amounts, paint thinners, dry-cleaning fluids, wood preservatives, toilet deodorizers, cosmetic additives, gasoline by-products, rocket fuel, termite poisons, fungicides, and flame-retardants.
>
> (pp. 197–198)

Unfortunately, the third world does not escape the impact of chemicals generated in large quantities in the developed nations. Professor Kirk Smith of the University of California at Berkeley developed the concept of the *environmental risk transition*, which describes how third world countries experience the deleterious impacts of both traditional and modern pollutants. As Figure 3.8 illustrates, many developing nations in the process of industrialization are caught within a zone of risk overlap between traditional and modern risks (Smith and Ezzati 2005; Smith 2009; see also Messerli et al. 2001). A tripartite classification of countries in different stages of development illustrates the major types of morbidity and mortality risks faced by each category.

Undeveloped countries: Traditional causes of death are largely from contaminated water, poor sewage disposal, infectious diseases, parasites and underdeveloped systems of public health.

Industrializing countries: These nations experience a mix of both traditional and modern risk factors with the additional impact of chemical contaminants from uncontrolled industrial processes leading to lung diseases, poisonings, etc.

Developed countries: Modern causes of death include heart disease, stroke and cancer largely associated with longevity, lifestyle (including diet) and exotic contaminants.

The full environmental risk transition (Smith 2009) is presented in Figure 3.9, which shows the shifting environmental burdens from local to global, from immediate to delayed, and from risks principally to human health to risks to global life support systems. In sum, the environmental Kuznets curve is both oversimplified and misleading. While the original curves purport to show some hypothetical aggregation of pollution, in fact there are a series of curves – each relating to the temporal significance of a particular class of pollutants. If these curves could be aggregated using some common metric, they would portray the overall pollutant level of an economy at any given level of development. The more conceptually correct way of treating these disparate curves would be to include them on one graph in a stacked manner and then take the envelope of these curves to represent the overall burden on the economy and its ecosystem. This final curve would resemble that proposed by Smith in his conceptual model of risk transition where traditional sources of pollution are reduced but new forms of environmental risks emerge, thus leading to a U-shaped function where risk begins to rise again quite rapidly with the nature of the modern industrial system.

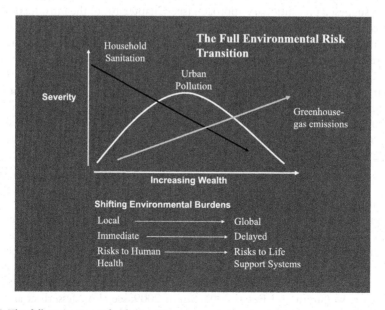

Figure 3.9 The full environmental risk transition

Source: Smith 2009, reproduced with permission of the author.

Ironically, it is sometimes the case that modern pollutants generated in the developed world and transported globally by natural processes may have a greater impact on the developing world because of its increased vulnerability due to poverty, malnutrition and lack of protective institutions and infrastructure (IPCC 2001; Yohe et al. 2006; Fussel 2009; Maplecroft 2011).

The special case of greenhouse gases

As illustrated in Figures 3.3 and 3.4, the advent of climate change through the release of greenhouse gases has been inexorably linked to the use of fossil fuels in the process of industrialization. Over the course of this history, a select group of now developed countries have been responsible for the lion's share of these emissions. Wei et al. (2016) have estimated that from 1850 to 2005, developed countries contributed between 53%–61% and developing countries 39%–47% to the critical elements of climate change: increase in global air temperature, upper oceanic warming, sea ice reduction in the Northern Hemisphere and permafrost degradation.

Yet the balance has changed, as a multipart categorization of global nations based on United Nations Development Programme (UNDP)'s Human Development Index (UNDP 2020) suggests that, following 2011, emissions of CO_2 from the less developed world had exceeded those of the developed world. (See Figure 3.10). The choice of

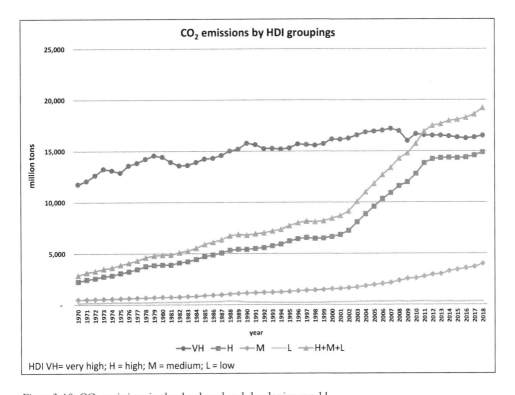

Figure 3.10 CO_2 emissions in the developed and developing world

categorization of nations can make a difference, as a dichotomous analysis of developed and developing nations by Jiang et al. (2019) suggests that the crossover occurred as early as 2004. Whichever categorization one chooses, the paths are expected to continue on their current trajectories for the immediate future driven in no small part by the rapidly growing economies of China and India (IEA 2020). Figure 3.11 shows changes in the

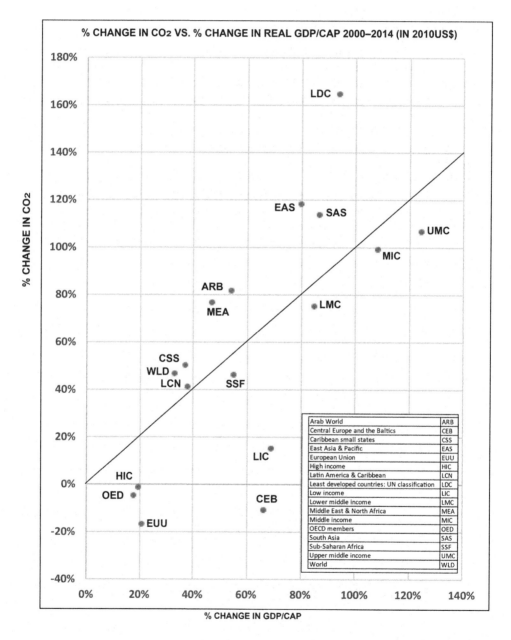

Figure 3.11 Change in GHG and GDP by HDI groupings

growth of greenhouse gases (GHG) and GDP by Human Development Index (HDI) groupings.

Figures 3.12a and 3.12b compare the recent emissions of three developed nations (Germany, France and Japan) with two fast-growing, less developed countries (China and India.) As indicated prior, there is a clear dichotomy, with the developed nations experiencing a decrease in total carbon dioxide emissions and the two major developing nations experiencing a continued increase. This distinction raises a critical question about the effect of economic growth on total GHG emissions. Is the curve similar to the concave version depicted in Figure 3.5a or the near exponential version of Figure 3.6? This is an important distinction as it determines whether greenhouse gases will eventually peak and fall after a certain level of development is reached; i.e. is there *decoupling* or *delinkage* between economic growth and GHG production? It is worth postulating about the reason for the decrease in GHG emissions among developed nations. Several explanations come immediately to mind: (1) increased efficiency of the capital stock in the use of energy; (2) the one-time transition to lower carbon fuels through the replacement of coal by natural gas in the electric power sector; (3) the increased use of the largely non-carbon-emitting energy source of nuclear power; (4) the gradual shift to renewable energy sources such as solar, wind, hydro, biomass and other more exotic forms such as geothermal and tidal power; and (5) a shift to a service economy, typical of post-industrial economies.

This last possible explanation requires further examination. In an insightful quote from his 1985 book *The Zero-Sum Solution*, Professor Lester Thurow, former dean of MIT's

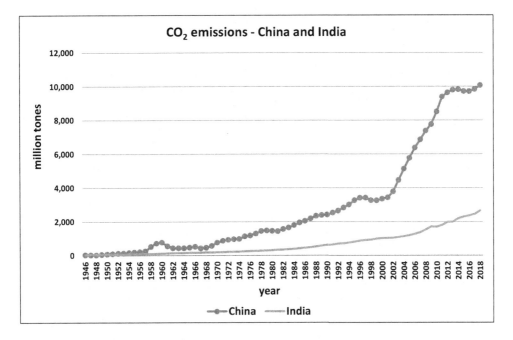

Figure 3.12a CO$_2$ emissions – China and India

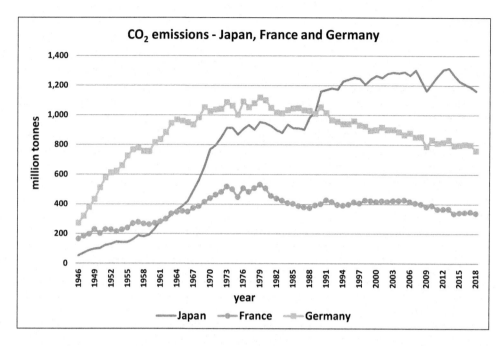

Figure 3.12b CO₂ emissions – Japan, France and Germany

Sloan School of Management, concluded that the service economy cannot be divorced from the production of goods:

> The first industrial revolution saw a shift from agriculture to industry; the second industrial revolution represents a shift from industry to services. . . . [In the US] between 1977 and 1982 . . . 37 percent of all those new service workers went into health care. Whatever you believe about the desirability of more health care, Americans are not going to generate a high standard of living giving each other heart transplants. . . . Another 33 percent of all those new service workers went into business or legal services. . . . Suing each other is good clean fun and generates a lot of jobs, but it is not productive.
>
> (Thurow 1986, pp. 56–58)

The clear implication of this observation is that countries transitioning to a service-based economy must still rely on a base of manufacturing whether this manufacturing occurs *within or without* their geographic boundaries. This phenomenon helps explain the concurrent reduction in manufacturing in developed countries and the increase in manufacturing in countries such as China of exports destined for the developed world. Developed countries may see a fall in their production of greenhouse gases

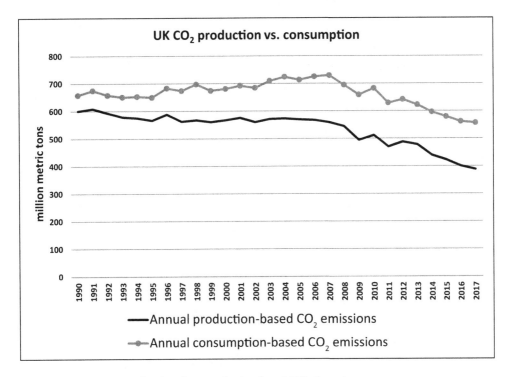

Figure 3.13 UK consumption-based vs. production-based CO_2 footprint

associated with deindustrialization but are importing *embodied* carbon in goods produced overseas. The net result is that data on national GHG production may give an
erroneous picture of a country's contribution to total global GHG production. The
most common way of resolving this dilemma is the construction of a *consumption-based*,
as opposed to a *production-based*, accounting of national greenhouse gas contributions
to global climate change where the GHG intensity of imports is added to domestic
GHG production minus GHG embodied in national exports. Figures 3.13 and 3.14
illustrate this calculation for both the United Kingdom and the United States. As
expected, consumption-based CO_2 exceeds production-based CO_2 for both countries
(data derived from OWID). During the period of 1990–2007, the United Kingdom
was extolling its decrease in total CO_2 production while, in fact, their total CO_2
footprint was increasing. This fact was first brought to light in a 2007 report by the
UK-based New Economics Foundation Report entitled *Chinadependence*. The online
publication from Oxford University entitled *Our World in Data*, available on their
website (ourworldindata.org), has since conducted similar calculations for most of the
world's countries. Most of the OECD countries follow the British and American pattern, with their CO_2 consumption footprint higher than their production footprint as

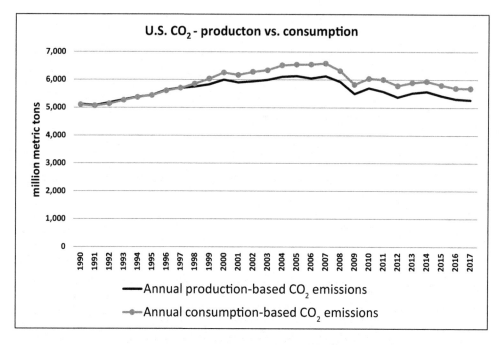

Figure 3.14 US consumption-based vs. production-based CO_2 footprint

well as falling absolute levels of CO_2 within the last decade. As one might expect, however, given its dominant role in global production and exports, the comparable curves for China are reversed, as illustrated in Figure 3.15: production-based CO_2 continues to exceed consumption-based CO_2 and at an increasing rate.

The choice of measure of national GHG footprint is an essential prerequisite to implementing targeted policies to achieve the most efficient, effective and equitable reduction of total global emissions. Parenthetically, it should be noted that production- and consumption-based accounting of GHG emissions are only two of four possible accounting systems. Davis et al. (2011) outline the nature of a possible *extraction-based* system, while Marques et al. (2012) and Lenzen and Murray (2010) have described an *income-based* system. The distinction between them is described by Steininger et al. (2016):

> First, irrespective of where they emerge in the supply chain, emissions could be attributed to the country that extracts the fossil fuels that allow for these emissions (extraction-based principle). Second, one could acknowledge that factors other than fossil fuels, such as labour and capital, also benefit from a polluting production process by earning income (wages, interest, rents). Thus, all emissions discharged along the supply chain could be attributed to specific agents (and countries) according to the value they add in production, and thus according to

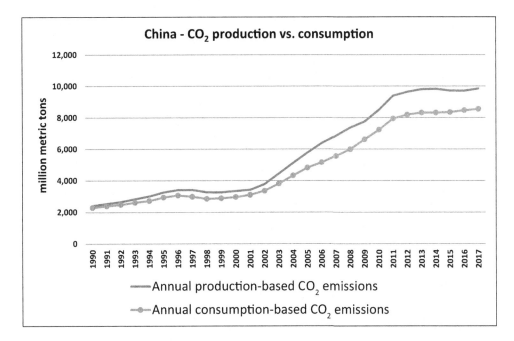

Figure 3.15 China consumption-based vs. production-based CO_2 footprint

the income they earn (income-based principle, also known as 'enabled' emissions or downstream responsibility).

(p. 35)

The allocation of responsibility for greenhouse gas–induced climate change will vary depending on which of the counting methods is chosen. Steininger et al. recommend multiple carbon accounting to overcome the possible inadequacies of any one system. Given the relative conceptual simplicity of the production- and consumption-based approaches, these will probably remain the most commonly used in decision-making.

Given the complexity of the data and intercountry variability, a focus on GHG production and consumption in any one country is a necessary but not sufficient indicator of the direction of future global climate change. It is necessary to focus on total global production of goods and services, their energy requirements and greenhouse gas emissions. Figure 3.16 depicts total global GHG emissions and Figure 3.17 a time series of the GHG intensity of gross world product (World Bank World Development Indicators, WDI and Our World In Data, OWID) while Figure 3.18 presents a graph of the GHG intensity of global energy use (World Bank 2020). Figures 3.17 and 3.18 are suggestive of increasing efficiency over time. However, from the perspective of total global impact, Figure 3.16 is clearly the most important and does not provide reassurance that

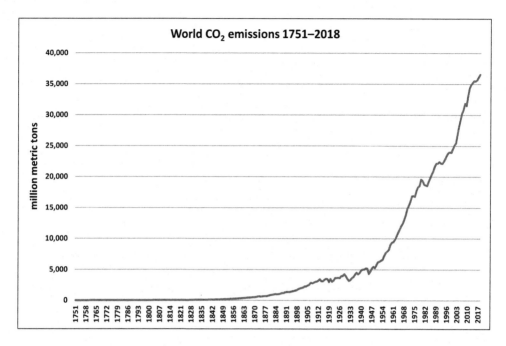

Figure 3.16 Total global GHG emissions

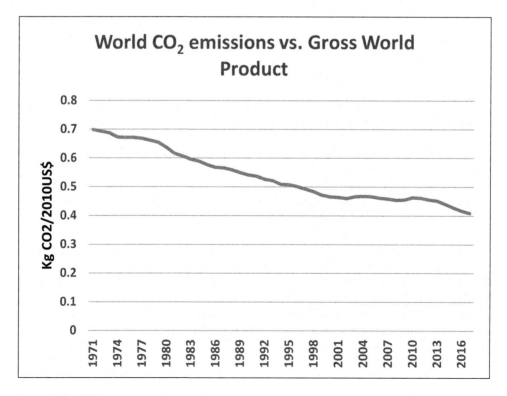

Figure 3.17 GHG intensity of gross world product

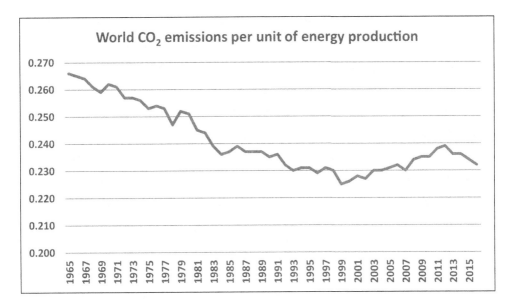

Figure 3.18 GHG intensity of global energy use

humankind has achieved any degree of control over this trend at this point. The next section of this chapter and the final chapter in this book examine various scenarios for the road forward.

Paths to economic development

These findings raise a central and critical question of whether it is possible to identify alternative paths of development for the developing world which could successfully raise their standard of living without drastic global ecological consequences; i.e. is it possible to decouple material, energy and GHG production and consequent climate change from economic growth? There are two variants of decoupling: *relative decoupling*, where the annual increase in CO_2 production trails that of GDP growth, and *absolute decoupling*, where CO_2 production falls while economic growth continues.

A partial answer to whether decoupling exists first requires deconstructing the components of industrialization. There were three essential commodities which launched England on its path to industrialization during the Industrial Revolution: textiles, coal and iron and steel. There is a distinctive temporal pattern of production and consumption for all these commodities, as illustrated in Figure 3.19. There is an initial production increase, often accompanied by commensurate exports of related intermediate and finished goods, as the economy first moves through the stages of industrialization, and then a decrease during the post-industrial period, which is characterized more by tertiary industry and a service economy. In general, this pattern tends to be repeated for other industrializing economies with some country-specific exceptions. Comparable data for the United States are presented in Figure 3.20 (US Department of Commerce 1975, various years; BP 2020,

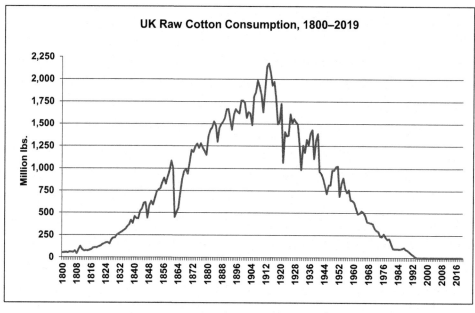

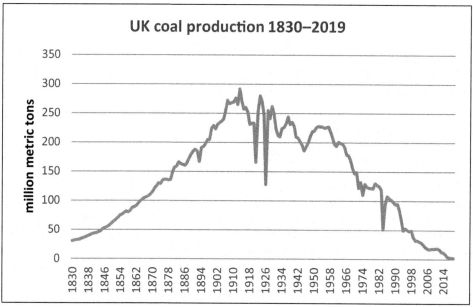

Figure 3.19 UK historical data on cotton, steel and coal

Source: Maddison, Indexbox, B.R. Mitchell, BP, World Steel Institute.

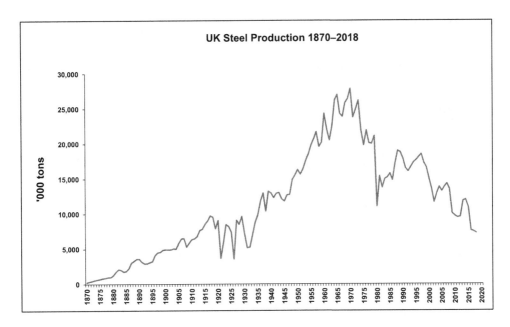

Figure 3.19 (Continued)

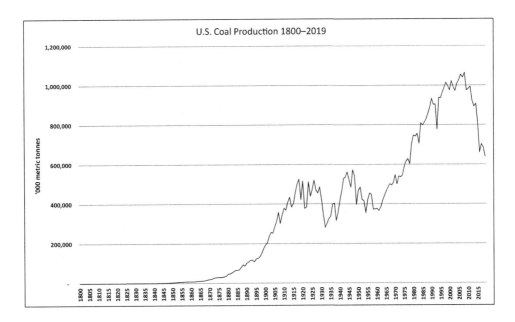

Figure 3.20 US historical data on cotton, steel and coal

Source: B.R. Mitchell.

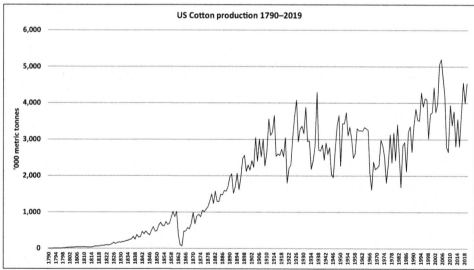

Figure 3.20 (Continued)

Mitchell 2007a; USDA 2021; AISI 2021; WSO 2021). The early stages of industrialization in both countries present a similar pattern, but there are distinct differences between these two countries across two of these major commodities.

While the UK has seen most of it coal production disappear and its use in electricity production largely backed out by natural gas, nuclear power and renewables, the United States is still a major producer and user of coal. While most of its production remains in country, representing 19% of electric power generation in 2020 (US EIA 2021), the US is the fourth largest exporter of coal in the world, devoting about 13% of its domestic production to export. Despite these facts, the status of the coal industry in the US is in a state of flux as demand for this fuel has dropped due to its relative cost and environmental impact. As a result, numerous coal companies have filed for bankruptcy.

Another distinction between the two countries is that US cotton production remains high as its highly subsidized industry has fed the global market for this commodity, and the US is among the top four nations in the global export market for cotton.

In the case of steel, both countries reached peak levels of production in the early to mid-1970s but still maintain a significant level of domestic production supplemented by imports from lower cost foreign suppliers.

One of the first rigorous academic research efforts to examine the structure of development was produced by Professor Wassily Leontief of Harvard University, a Nobel laureate in Economics. In a seminal paper in the journal *Scientific American* in 1963, Leontief applied the input-output theory he had created (see Appendix 3.1 to this chapter) to make a disaggregated comparison of the economic structure of several developed countries. His research demonstrated a "great similarity of structure" among these countries. Given the environmental consequences of historical economic growth among the developed nations, a global path to sustainability would seem to mandate a different and more benign path to industrialization for the developing world. Is there any evidence to suggest that such a path exists and has been followed? Data on steel, textiles and coal from the two most prominent countries of the developing world, China and India, appear to bear a close resemblance to the path followed by the UK and United States (see Figure 3.21). Among global producers of steel and cotton yarn as well as global consumers of coal, China and India rank first and second in the world.

If an alternative path to economic development cannot be found, raising the living standards of the third world will have potentially catastrophic impacts on the global ecosystem. Leontief (1963, p. 159) concluded: "The fact is that the choice of alternative technologies hardly exists. The process of development consists essentially in the installation and building of an approximation of the system embodied in advanced economies." Given recent patterns of economic development, there seems to be little reason to believe this conclusion has changed significantly in the past five decades. Despite the 20th-century emergence of what has been termed the Second Industrial Revolution – marked by the production of new natural and synthetic resources such as aluminum, new alloys and plastics – the environmental pattern associated with continuing production of coal, iron and steel appears to be repeating. Table 3.1 summarizes the major pollutants from iron, steel, coal and textile production.

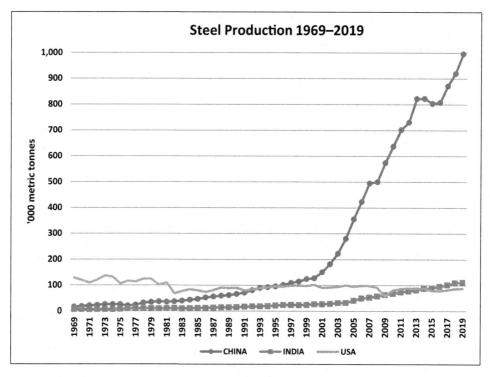

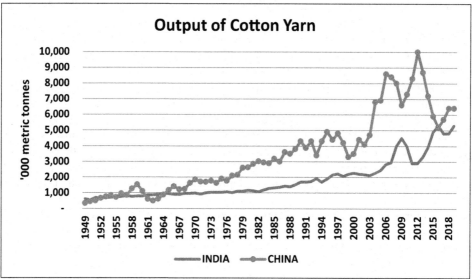

Figure 3.21 China and India production of steel, textiles and coal

Source: World Steel Institute, BP, B.R. Mitchell, P. Nemetz, Sergey Avramenko, China Statistical Yearbooks.

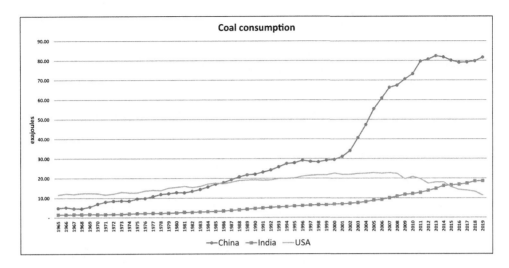

Figure 3.21 (Continued)

Table 3.1 Major pollutants from iron, steel, coal and textile production

	Iron mining	Iron/steel mills	Coal mining	Coal burning	Textiles
Air pollutants					
CO$_2$		X	X	X	
Fluorides (F)		X			
Mercury (Hg)				X	
Nitrogen oxides (NOx)		X		X	
Particulate matter (PM)		X			
Sulfur oxides (SOx)		X		X	
Water pollutants					
Halogenated organic compounds (AOX)					X
Arsenic (As)	X				
Biochemical oxygen demand (BOD)					X
Cadmium (Cd)	X	X			
Chromium (Cr)	X	X			X
Cobalt (Co)					X
Chemical oxygen demand (COD)	X	X			X
Coliform bacteria					X
Copper (Cu)	X				X
Cyanide	X	X			
Iron (Fe)	X		X		
Lead (Pb)	X	X			

(Continued)

Table 3.1 (Continued)

	Iron mining	Iron/steel mills	Coal mining	Coal burning	Textiles
Mercury (Hg)	X	X			
Nickel (Ni)	X				X
Oil and grease	X	X	X		X
Pesticides					X
pH	X	X	X	X	X
Phenol		X			X
Sulfide					X
Temperature		X			X
Total suspended solids (TSS)	X	X	X		X
Zinc (Zn)	X	X			X

The challenge of decoupling economic activity and environmental degradation such as climate change remains contentious and has received considerable attention in the last decade (Smith et al. 2010; UNEP 2011; Rawlings 2020). In a survey of 179 scientific articles, Vaden et al. (2020a, p. 243) conclude:

> The evidence does not suggest that decoupling towards ecological sustainability is happening at a global (or even regional) scale. The literature finds evidence of impact decoupling, especially between GHG emissions (such as COX and SOX emissions) in wealthy countries for certain periods of time, but not of economy-wide resource decoupling, least of all on the international and global scale. Quite the opposite: there is evidence of increased material intensity and re-coupling.

These findings are supported by Hickel and Kallis (2019, p. 1) and Vaden et al. (2020b, p. 1), who conclude, respectively, that "there is no empirical evidence that absolute decoupling from resource use can be achieved on a global scale against a background of continued economic growth" and "compared to 2017, 'successful' decoupling has to result in 2.6 times more GDP out of every ton of material use, including in-use material stocks. There are no realistic scenarios for such an increase in resource productivity." Wiedmann et al. (2015, p. 2671) conducted a study of 186 countries and concluded:

> Achievements in decoupling in advanced economies are smaller than reported or even nonexistent. . . . As wealth grows, countries tend to reduce their domestic portion of materials extraction through international trade, whereas the overall mass of material consumption generally increases.

The next chapter explores what it means to raise gross domestic product – the most common measure of national well-being – and what might be a realistic and desirable target for the third world. Whether this pattern can be broken as the world continues on the path to further economic growth depends on the achievement of the aforementioned *decoupling* of materials, energy and GHG from growth as well as the possible existence of alternatives to growth itself. (See Chapter 9.)

Case study: The Asia–Pacific

Much of the extraordinary expansion in the global economy during the post–World War II era can be attributed to the engine of economic growth in the Asia-Pacific region. What patterns of growth can one observe here, and what implications do these patterns have for the global environment? One model which has been developed to explain the dynamic growth of this region is the *flying geese metaphor* of development. (See Figure 3.22.)

This postwar phenomenon was facilitated by a conscious change in government policy from protectionist import substitution to open-market, export promotion in the Asia-Pacific. During this transition, the production of labor-intensive and low-technology

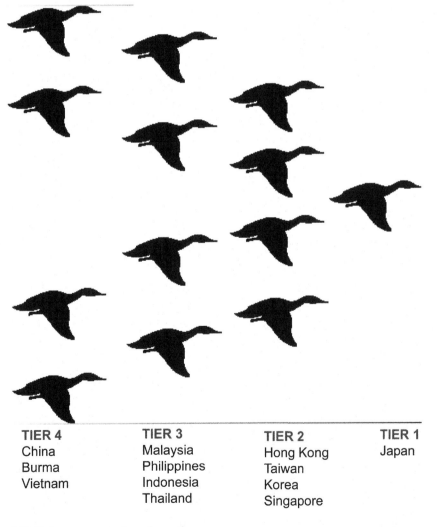

TIER 4	TIER 3	TIER 2	TIER 1
China	Malaysia	Hong Kong	Japan
Burma	Philippines	Taiwan	
Vietnam	Indonesia	Korea	
	Thailand	Singapore	

Figure 3.22 Flying geese metaphor of growth

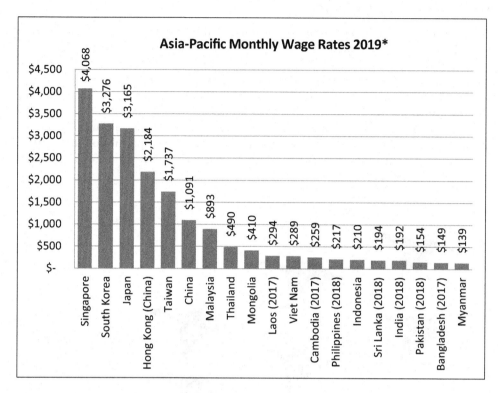

Figure 3.23 Wage rates in the Asia-Pacific
Source: ILO.

goods is passed from one country to the next as new, more sophisticated technologies/ goods are produced in response to changing comparative advantage. This change is based, to a significant degree, on the rising price of labor and the availability of other critical inputs such as an educated and trained labor force. Historically, Tier 1 was composed of only one country, Japan, which was the first to engage in massive industrialization in the postwar era. Tier 2 was composed of the Four Asian Tigers (Hong Kong, Korea, Taiwan and Singapore), Tier 3 by four countries in Southeast Asia (Malaysia, the Philippines, Indonesia and Thailand) and Tier 4 by China, Myanmar and Vietnam but more recently joined by Bangladesh. With sustained double-digit growth, China has moved past most of its Asian neighbors and has recently surpassed the United States as the world's largest economy based on purchasing power parity. While China remains the world's largest producer of steel, user of coal and exporter of textiles, the flying geese metaphor explains how high rising wage rates in China have forced the movement of certain types of textile production out of China to lower-wage countries such as Bangladesh and smaller countries in Southeast Asia such as Vietnam and Cambodia (*Business Week* March 27, 2006; *New York Times* August 16, 2010, August 14, 2011; BBC September 15, 2011). Figure 3.23 shows comparative wage rates for the Asia-Pacific region for 2019.

A companion model, entitled the *S curve*, describes how countries pass through four stages of structural transformation as they travel along an economic growth curve: Stage 1: primary production; Stage 2a: labor-intensive manufacturing typically involving light manufactures like textiles, apparel and household equipment – in Stage 2a countries, comparative advantage lies in a large, cheap labor supply; Stage 2b: heavy industry; Stage 3: high-tech manufacturing (e.g. electronic chips, consumer electronics, technically sophisticated machinery and equipment); and Stage 4: a post-industrial service economy where comparative advantage is no longer in manufacturing but rather in domestic and international services, including communication, finance, transportation and entertainment – this stage usually requires sophisticated technology such as IT, etc. The McKinsey Global Institute (Tonby et al. 2020) has produced an extensive report examining the different stages of technological development among four categories of Asian states – what they call Advanced Asia, China, Merging Asia and Frontier Asia and India. The hypothesis of this study is that it may be possible for Asia to boost economic growth through technological leapfrogging in at least four areas: (1) accelerated digitization; (2) mobile application processors, advanced displays and next-generation electric vehicle batteries; (3) boosting business technology services at the global level; and (4) renewable energy sources. The achievement of these goals will be dependent on "speed, collaboration and resilience" (p. 90).

The result of the dynamic change in comparative advantage is illustrated by the extraordinary rise in Asia-Pacific national GDP in the postwar period. Unfortunately, the environmental impact of this growth is reflected in rapidly rising levels of carbon dioxide. Figure 3.24 plots the ratio of real GDP in 2018 to 1984 values against

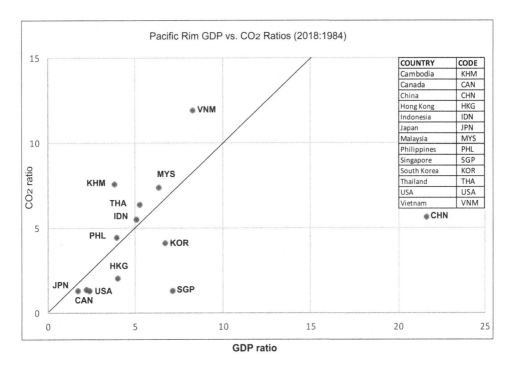

Figure 3.24 Asia-Pacific GDP and CO_2 growth

the comparable ratio of CO_2 emissions (for Cambodia, the comparative values are 2018:1993). Those countries which lie above the diagonal line have CO_2 emissions rising faster than real GDP, while those lying below the line have achieved what is term *relative decoupling*. Laos is an outlier and has been omitted from the graph as its CO_2 ratio is 105.6 and its GDP ratio only 8.33 over the 1984–2018 time period. Laotian emissions of CO_2 underwent a dramatic increase following 2014 and ended up at 19.32 million tons in 2018. The recent and projected increase is due principally to the Laotian government's policy to become a major supplier of electricity to its neighbors in Southeast Asia. While most of this will be produced by hydropower, a program of coal-fired power plant installations, along with coal's use in industry, account for much of the increase in GHGs (Our World In Data, Global Energy Monitor n.d., ERIA and Lao Energy and Mines 2018).

Appendix 3.1
A short primer on input-output analysis

Developed by Wassily Leontief in the 1930s, input-output analysis, sometimes referred to as "inter-industry analysis," is a comprehensive and systematic methodology for representing an economic system, be it local, regional or national (see Leontief 1966). While the theory has been extant for some time, it was not until the advent of modern computers that the complex computations required to carry out the analysis became possible. Today, these models are used throughout the globe by both free and centralized planned economies (GTAP n.d.; OECD n.d.). Input-output (or I-O) is a model of the flows of goods and services among sectors of the economy. It is represented as a system of simultaneous linear equations which capture the direct and indirect economic interrelationships among all the sectors of the economy, no matter how detailed the degree of disaggregation. A principal use of input-output methodology is to determine the impact on any and all sectors of an economy resulting from an increase or decrease in demand for a final product. For example, what is the economic effect of increasing final (i.e. consumer) demand in the US for automobiles?

Input-output can also be used to track the implications of sectoral increases on economy-wide emissions of conventional air, water and soil pollutants, as well as toxic chemicals and greenhouse gases. This requires linkages with environmental databases in the US such as the Toxic Release Inventory (TRI), the US EPA greenhouse gas inventory databases and the US EPA air pollution emission inventory. The methodology of measuring system-wide environmental effects involves the use of pollution coefficients in input-output tables. This permits the tracking of pollution changes throughout the economy as any one product or sector experiences increased or decreased demand as a result of market forces or government intervention (Lave et al. 1995).

There are three analytical tables associated with traditional input-output analysis: the dollar-flow table, the coefficient table and the inverse coefficient table. Each is briefly described in turn.

The *dollar-flow table* tracks the sales of goods and services among sectors of an economy. Table 3.2 illustrates a highly simplified representation with an economy divided into three sectors (agriculture and two manufacturing sectors). In the original Leontief square formulation of the input-output table, these sectors are arrayed on both the x-axis and y-axis. Row industries sell to column industries, and column industries buy from row industries. It is important to note that some sectors sell to themselves. This square matrix, which forms the core of the I-O analysis, is converted into a series of simultaneous linear equations in the next two tables which can be solved algebraically. Note also that there are additional columns and additional rows flanking the square matrix. Their number will

Table 3.2 Sample input-output matrix

	Agricultural sector	Manufacturing sector #1	Manufacturing sector #2	Final demand	Total outputs
Agricultural sector	$20	$60	$40	$80	$200
Manufacturing sector #1	$80	$60	$80	$80	$300
Manufacturing sector #2	$40	$60	$120	$180	$400
Household (labor)	$60	$120	$160	$140	
Total inputs	$200	$300	$400		$900

depend on the complexity of the model but always include household labor, total inputs, final demand, total output, imports and exports.

In practice, most extant I-O models, be they regional or national, have subdivided the economy into many more categories. Table 3.3 presents a somewhat high level of disaggregation for the US economy with 81 sectors, although the number may be as large as thousands. The principal challenge in assembling this table is the time and effort required to gather the data for the whole economy. As a consequence, I-O tables frequently incorporate data which may be several years old. There are several limitations to the basic I-O model: first, it represents a snapshot of the economy at one period in time; second, the square matrix implies that each industry produces one product and that each product is produced by only one industry. This problem has been addressed by the development of rectangular matrices (Statistics Canada 2010; Duchin and Levine 2012).

The *coefficient table* is derived from the dollar-flow table and contains the data in a modified form which permits more intensive analysis. Each cell is the ratio of the input from a row industry to the total output of the industry in whose vertical column the cell appears. The algebraic representation is shown here (Charnes et al. 1972):

Table 3.3 Industries in 81-sector US input-output matrix

Final non-metal	**Basic non-metal**
1 Footwear and other leather products	40 Stone and clay products
2 Misc. furniture and fixtures	41 Stone and clay mining and quarrying
3 Household furniture	42 Printing and publishing
4 Tobacco manufactures	43 Glass and glass products
5 Apparel	44 Paperboard containers and boxes
6 Misc. fabricated textile products	45 Paper and allied products, except containers
7 Drugs, cleaning and toilet preparations	46 Wooden containers
8 Food and kindred products	47 Lumber and wood products, except containers
Final metal	48 Forestry and fishery products
9 Special industry machinery and equipment	49 Misc. textile goods and floor coverings
10 Ordnance and accessories	66 State and local government enterprises
28 Electric lighting and wiring equipment	67 Hotels, personal and repair services, except automobile
29 Electric industrial equipment and apparatus	68 Automobile repair and services

Table 3.3 (Continued)

30 Electronic components and accessories

Basic metal

31 Heating, plumbing and structural metal products

32 Machine shop products

33 Metal containers

34 Stampings, screw machine products and bolts

35 Other fabricated metal products

36 Primary nonferrous metal manufacturing

37 Non-ferrous metal ores mining

56 Agricultural, forestry and fishery services

57 Plastics and synthetic materials

58 Chemicals and selected chemical products

59 Chemical and fertilizer, mineral mining

Energy

60 Petroleum refining and related industries

61 Electricity, gas and water

62 Coal mining

63 Crude petroleum and natural gas

Services

64 Federal government enterprises

65 Transportation and warehousing

11 Aircraft and parts

12 Misc. transportation equipment

13 Radio, television and communication equipment

14 Materials handling machinery and equipment

15 Misc. manufacturing

16 Optical, ophthalmic and photographic equipment

17 Service industry machines

18 Household appliances

19 Scientific and controlling instruments

20 Office, computing and accounting machines

21 Farm machinery and equipment

38 Primary iron and steel manufacturing

39 Iron and ferroalloy ores mining

69 Radio and television broadcasting

70 Amusements

71 Medical and educational services, non-profit organizations

72 Wholesale and retail trade

73 Finance and insurance

74 Communications, except radio and television broadcasting

75 Business services

76 Real estate and rental

22 Engines and turbines

23 Construction, mining and oil field machinery

24 Misc. electrical machinery, equipment and supplies

25 Metalworking machinery and equipment

26 Motor vehicles and equipment

27 General industrial machinery and equipment

50 Rubber and misc. plastics products

51 Broad and narrow fabrics, yarn and thread mills

52 Paints and allied products

53 Leather tanning and industrial leather products

54 Livestock and livestock products

55 Misc. agricultural products

77 Maintenance and repair construction

Misc.

78 Research and development

79 Office supplies

80 Business travel, entertainment and gifts

81 Scrap, used and second-hand goods

Each cell in the matrix is derived as follows:

$$X_{ij} = a_{ij} X_j$$

where:

X_{ij} = the amount of goods and services provided by industry in row i to industry in column j

a_{ij} = a constant which relates the activity level of industry j to its requirements from industry i; i.e. each unit increase in the total activity of industry j will occasion an input of a_{ij} units from industry i

X_j = total amount of activity of industry j

Each row in the matrix:

$$\Sigma X_{ij}/y_i = X_i$$

where:

y_i = amount of goods and services flowing from (row) industry i to final demand (rather than to other industries as intermediate inputs)

X_i = total amount of output (or activity) of (row) industry i

Example

Row #1

$$X_{11} + X_{12} + X_{13} + \ldots + y_1 = X_1$$

or by substitution $(X_{ij} = a_{ij} X_j)$ =

$$a_{11} X_1 + a_{12} X_2 + a_{13} X_3 + \ldots + Y_1 = X_1$$

Sample three-sector table:

$$X_{11} + X_{12} + X_{13} + y_1 = X_1$$
$$X_{21} + X_{22} + X_{23} + y_2 = X_2$$
$$X_{31} + X_{32} + X_{33} + y_3 = X_3$$

or

$$a_{11} X_1 + a_{12} X_2 + a_{13} X_3 + y_1 = X_1$$
$$a_{21} X_1 + a_{22} X_2 + a_{23} X_3 + y_2 = X_2$$
$$a_{31} X_1 + a_{32} X_2 + a_{33} X_3 + y_3 = X_3$$

Charnes et al. (1972, p. 89) provide a highly simplified numeric example which divides national output into three commodities: corn, cloth and shoes.

The third table, the *inverse-coefficient table*, is perhaps the most important, as it allows the tracking of changes in one industry's output throughout the entire economy. In this table, the coefficient in each cell gives, per dollar of delivery to final demand made by the

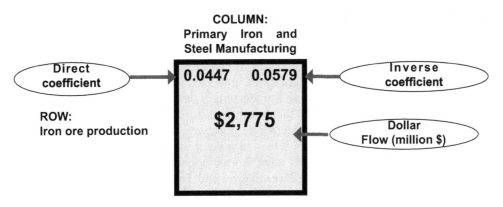

Figure 3.25 Sample cell from US input–output matrix: iron ore and primary iron and steel manufacturing.

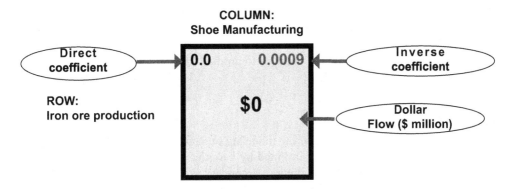

Figure 3.26 Sample cell from US input–output matrix: iron ore and shoe manufacturing.

sector at the column head, as well as the total input *directly and indirectly* required from the industry listed at the left of each row. An illustration of these entries is provided in Figures 3.25 and 3.26.

Brief numerical example

For convenience of display, the three sub-tables are sometimes combined in one graph in large input–output tables. In Figure 3.25, for example, the sample cell represents the sale of iron ore as an input to the primary iron and steel manufacturing sector in 1980 (*Scientific American* 1981). The dollar flow is $2,775 million; the direct coefficient is 0.0447 (i.e. $2,775 million iron ore input divided by $62,031 million, which is the gross domestic output of primary iron and steel manufacturing); and the inverse coefficient is 0.0579, which is derived by matrix inversion. In contrast to the *direct coefficient*, which represents the increment in iron ore production required as a direct input for one additional unit output of iron and steel, the *inverse coefficient* captures not only the additional direct iron ore input but also any indirectly induced requirements for iron ore as a consequence of any other sector products required for one additional unit of iron and steel output.

The critical information imparted by the indirect coefficient is illustrated by a second example (Figure 3.26). In this case, the cell captures the relationship between iron ore production and shoe manufacturing. There are no direct sales of iron ore to the shoe manufacturing industry. This does not mean, however, that there are not indirect effects on iron ore demand from the increased production of shoes. For example, the cell representing the dollar sales of iron ore to the shoe manufacturing industry will be zero, as well as the comparable cell in the coefficient table. However, there will be a positive value for the inverse coefficient since iron ore is used to make steel, and steel is ultimately used in shoe manufacturing (e.g. steel lasts or other shoe components, etc.).

This type of analytical tool can be exceedingly useful. For example, input-output analysis can be used to answer important questions such as: (1) how will an industry be affected by increased or reduced demand for any product? (e.g. how will iron ore sales be affected by changes in the demand for shoes?); (2) what is the complete environmental life-cycle impact of selected products? (e.g. what will be the total environmental impact across the economy of an increase in the demand for shoes?); or, at a more conceptual level, (3) are there alternative paths to economic development, or will developing nations have to go through the same pollution-intensive process of development experienced by the developed nations? From a business and sustainability perspective, question (3) is of particular relevance, and the application of I-O analysis to product life-cycle analysis is described in a companion volume (Nemetz 2022).

Modern input-output analysis

While an important breakthrough in the modeling of national economies, the traditional square industry-by-industry matrix invented by Leontief had some significant deficiencies, not least of which was the handling of secondary products (i.e. products that were produced by an industry in addition to its principal output). A major conceptual advance was achieved in the 1970s in the United States with the adoption of a new System of National Accounts (SNA) developed under the auspices of the United Nations. This led to a major reconceptualization and restructuring of input-output analysis and the presentation of its component data. As described by the US Bureau of Economic Analysis (2009, p. 1–2), the core of the I-O accounts consists of two major tables – a "make" table and a "use" table:

> The *make table* shows the production of commodities by industries. The rows present the industries, and the columns display the commodities that the industries produce. Looking across a row, all the commodities produced by that industry are identified, and the sum of the entries is that industry's output. Looking down a column, all the industries producing that commodity are identified, and the sum of the entries is the output of that commodity.
>
> The *use table* shows the uses of commodities by intermediate and final users. In contrast to the make table, the rows in the use table present the commodities or products, and the columns display the industries and final users that utilize them. The sum of the entries in a row is the output of that commodity. The columns show the products consumed by each industry and the three components of "value added" – compensation of employees, taxes on production and imports less subsidies, and gross

operating surplus. Value added is the difference between an industry's output and the cost of its intermediate inputs, and total value added is equal to GDP. The sum of the entries in a column is that industry's output.

Several additional subsidiary tables have been created to assist in studying the ultimate national-level effects of sectoral changes. In fact, variations of these models have been used to study economic activity at a regional level as well.

References

American Iron & Steel Institute (AISI) (2021) www.steel.org.

BBC (2011) "China 'losing edge' as low-cost manufacturer, says KPMG," September 15.

BP (2020) *Statistical Review of World Energy* (69th ed.), British Petroleum Corporation.

Breivik, K., A. Sweetman, J.M. Pacyna and K.C. Jones (2002a) "Towards a global historical emission inventory for selected PCB congeners: A mass balance approach 1: Global production and consumption," *The Science of the Total Environment*, 290, pp. 181–198.

Breivik, K., A. Sweetman, J.M. Pacyna and K.C. Jones (2002b) "Towards a global historical emission inventory for selected PCB congeners: A mass balance approach 2: Emissions," *The Science of the Total Environment*, 290, pp. 199–224.

Breivik, K., A. Sweetman, J.M. Pacyna and K.C. Jones (2007) "Towards a global historical emission inventory for selected PCB congeners: A mass balance approach 3: An update," *The Science of the Total Environment*, 377, pp. 296–307.

Business Week (2006) "How rising wages are changing the game in China," March 27.

Chambers, Johnathan D. (1961) *Workshop of the World: British Economic History from 1820 to 1880*, Oxford: Oxford University Press.

Charnes, A. et al. (1972) "Economic social and enterprise accounting and mathematical models," *The Accounting Review*, January, pp. 85–108.

Davis, Steven J. et al. (2011) "The supply chain of CO2 emissions," *PNAS*, November 8.

Duchin, Faye and Stephen H. Levine (2012) "The rectangular sector-by-technology model: Not very economy produces every product and some products may rely on several technologies simultaneously," Journal of Economic Structures, April 17.

Economic Research Institute for ASEAN and East Asia (ERIA) and Lao Ministry of Energy and Mines (2018) "Lao PDR Energy outlook 2020," Research Project Report No. 19.

Elhacham, Emily et al. (2019) "Global human-made mass exceeds all living biomass," *Nature*, 588, December 9, pp. 442–444.

Encyclopaedia Britannica (1993) "Industrial revolution," 6, pp. 304–305.

European Commission (2018) *Raw Materials Scoreboard, European Innovation Partnership on Raw Materials*.

European Environment Agency (EEA) (2012) *The Impacts of Endocrine Disruptors on Wildlife, People and Their Environments*, The Weybridge+15 (1996–2011) Report.

European Monitoring and Evaluation Programme (EMEP) (2005) "Regional multicompartment model MSCE-POP," Convention on Long-Range Transboundary Air Pollution, Technical Report 5/2005.

Fussel, Hans-Martin (2009) *Development and Climate Change Background Note: Review of Quantitative Analysis of Indices of Climate Change Exposure, Adaptive Capacity, Sensitivity and Impacts*, World Bank.

Global Energy Monitor (n.d.) "Laos and coal."

Global Trade Analysis Project (GTAP) "Purdue university," website. www.gtap.agecon.purdue.edu.

Hatfield-Dodds, Steve et al. (2017) "Assessing global resource use and greenhouse emissions to 2050, with ambitious resource efficiency and climate mitigation policies," *Journal of Cleaner Production*, 144, 25(4), pp. 403–414.

Hickel, Jason and Girogos Kallis (2019) "Is green growth possible?," *New Political Economy*, Routledge, pp. 1–18.

Indian Affairs and Northern Affairs Canada (2003) *Human Health*, Ottawa.

Intergovernmental Panel on Climate Change (IPCC) (2001) *Impacts, Adaptation and Vulnerability: Technical Summary*, Switzerland.

International Energy Agency (IEA) (2020) *World Energy Scenarios 2020*.

James, William H. (1995) "Evidence that Mammalian sex ratios at birth are partially controlled by parental hormone levels at the times of conception," *Journal of Theoretical Biology*, 180, pp. 271–286.

Jiang, Jingjing et al. (2019) "Applied energy: Research on the peak of CO2 emissions in the developing world: Current progress and future prospects," February.

Krausmann, Fridolin et al. (2017) "Global socioeconomic material stocks rise 23-fold over the 20th century and require half of annual resource use," *PNAS*, February 21.

Lave, Lester B. et al. (1995) "Using input-output analysis to estimate economy-wide discharges," *Environmental Science & Technology*, 29(9), pp. 420A–426A.

Lenzen, Manfred and Joy Murray (2010) "Conceptualizing environmental responsibility," *Ecological Economics*, October 20.

Leontief, Wassily (1963) "The structure of development," *Scientific American*, 20, pp. 148–166.

Leontief, Wassily (1966) *Input-Output Economics*, New York: Oxford University Press.

Living on Earth (LOE), podcast September 21, 2007. www.loe.org.

Ma, Jianmin et al. (2011) "Revolatilization of persistent organic pollutants in the Arctic induced by climate change," *Nature Climate Change*, July 24, pp. 255–260.

Mackenzie, Constanza A. (2005) "Declining sex ratio in a first nation community," *Environmental Health Perspectives*, 113(1), October, pp. 1295–1298.

Maddison, Angus (2006a) *The World Economy: Volume 1 a Millennial Perspective*, Development Centre Studies OECD, Paris.

Maddison, Angus (2006b) *The World Economy: Volume 2 Historical Statistics*, Development Centre Studies OECD, Paris.

Maddison, Angus updated information available at: www.ggdc.net/maddison/ [website of Groningen Growth and Development Centre, University of Groningen, The Netherlands].

Maplecroft (2011) "World's fastest growing populations increasingly vulnerable to the impacts of climate change: 4th global atlas reports," http://mplecroft.com/about/news/ccvi_2012.html.

Marques, Alexandra et al. (2012) "Income-based environmental responsibility," *Ecological Economics*, October 23.

Messerli, B. et al. (2001) "From nature-dominated to human-dominated environmental changes," in Chapter 13 in Eckart Ehlers and Thomas Krafft (eds.) *Understanding the Earth System: Compartments, Processes and Interactions*, Berlin: Springer, pp. 195–208.

Mitchell, B.R. (2007a) *International Historical Statistics: The Americas 1750–2005*, Houndmills, Basingstoke, Hampshire: Palgrave Macmillan.

Mitchell, B.R. (2007b) *International Historical Statistics: Europe 1750–2005*, Houndmills, Basingstoke, Hampshire: Palgrave Macmillan.

Mitchell, B.R. (2013) *International Historical Statistics: Europe 1750–2010*, Houndmills, Basingstoke, Hampshire: Palgrave Macmillan.

Mitchell, B.R. and Phyllis Deane (1962) *Abstract of British Historical Statistics*, Cambridge: Cambridge University Press.

Mitchell, B.R. and H.G. Jones (1971) *Second Abstract of British Historical Statistics*, Cambridge: Cambridge University Press.

National Research Council (NRC) (2009) *Global Sources of Local Pollution: An Assessment of Long-Range Transport of Key Air Pollutants to and from the United States*, Washington, DC.

Nemetz, Peter N. (2022) *Corporate Strategy and Sustainability*, London: Routledge.

New Economics Foundation and the Open University (2007) *Chinadependence: The Second UK Interdependence Report*, London.

New York Times (2010) "China's labor tests its muscle," August 16.

New York Times (2011) "Cheap robots vs. cheap labor," August 14.

Oak Ridge National Laboratory (ORNL) "Greenhouse Gas," website. http://cdiac.ornl.gov/.

Organization for Economic Cooperation and Development (OECD) (n.d.) *The OECD Input-Output Database*. www.oecd.org/dataoecd/48/43/2673344.pdf.

Ottesen, Rolf Tore et al. (2010) "Norges Geologiske Undersokelse (NGU)," *Geochemical Atlas of Norway Part 2 Geochemical Atlas of Spitsbergen*, Trondheim.

Oxford University, *Our World in Data* (OWID). Ourworldindata.org.

Rawlings, Luke (2020) "The myth of decoupling and green economic growth," Atlas Institute for International Affairs, August 16.

Sakamoto, Mineshi et al. (2001) "Declining Minamata male birth ratio associated with increased male fetal death die to heavy methylmercury pollution," *Environmental Research*, Section A 87, pp. 92–98.

Schindler, David (2007) "A life with pesticides," Lecture to The Vancouver Institute, November 3.

Scientific American (1981) "Input-output chart of the United States economy in 1980," [poster].

Smith, Kirk (2009) "Combustion, climate, health, and the environmental risk transition," September 10–11.

Smith, Kirk and Majid Ezzati (2005) "How environmental health risk change with development: The epidemiologic and environmental risk transitions revisited," *Annual Review of Environment and Resources*, pp. 291–333.

Smith, Michael H. et al. (2010) *Cents and Sustainability: Securing Our Common Future by Decoupling Economic Growth from Environmental Pressures*, London: Earthscan.

Statistics Canada (2010) *The Input-Output Structure of the Canadian Economy 2006–2007*, Ottawa.

Steininger, Karl W. et al. (2016) "Multiple carbon accounting to support just and effective climate policies," *Nature Climate Change*, November 23, pp. 35–41.

Thurow, Lester (1986) *The Zero-sum Solution*, Colorado: Touchstone.

Tonby, Oliver et al. (2020) *The Future of Asia: How Asia can Boost Growth through Technological Leapfrogging*, McKinsey Global Institute, New York.

UK Central Statistical Office (various years) *Annual Abstract of Statistics*, London.

United Nations Development Programme (UNDP) (2020) *Human Development Report*.

United Nations Environment Programme (UNEP) (2007) *Global Environment Outlook GEO4*.

United Nations Environment Programme (UNEP) (2011) *Decoupling Natural Resource Use and Environmental Impacts from Economic Growth*.

United Nations Environment Programme (UNEP) Global Environment Facility (GEF) (2004) *Persistent Toxic Substances, Food Security and Indigenous Peoples of the Russian North*.

US Bureau of Economic Analysis (BEA) (2009) *Concepts and Methods of the U.S. Input-Output Accounts*, Washington, DC.

US Department of Agriculture (USDA) (2021) *Cotton Sector at a Glance*, Washington, DC.

US Department of Commerce (1975) *Historical Statistics of the United States*, Washington, DC.

US Department of Commerce (various years) *Statistical Abstracts of the United States*, Washington, DC.

US Energy Information Administration (2021) *Monthly Energy Review*, April, Washington, DC.

Vaden, T. et al. (2020a) "Decoupling for ecological sustainability: A categorisation and review of research literature," *Environmental Science and Policy*, 112, pp. 236–244.

Vaden, T. et al. (2020b) "Raising the bar: On eth type, size and timeline of a successful, decoupling," *Environmental Politics*, June 24.

Wania, Frank and Donald Mackay (1993) "Global fractionation and cold condensation of low volatility organochlorine compounds in polar regions," *Ambio*, 22(1), February, pp. 10–18.

Warde, Paul (2007) *Energy Consumption in England and Wales 1560–2000*, Italy: Cosiglio Nazionale delle Recherche.

Wei, Ting et al. (2016) "Developed and developing world contributions to climate system change based on carbon dioxide, methane and nitrous oxide emissions," *Advances in Atmospheric Sciences*, 33, May, pp. 632–643.

Wiedmann, Thomas O. et al. (2015) "The material footprint of nations," *PNAS*, May 19.

Williams, Florence (2012) *Breasts: A Natural and Unnatural History*, New York: W.W. Norton & Co.

World Bank (2020) "CO2 intensity (kg per kg of il equivalent energy use)," Data.

World Steel Organization (WSO) (2021) www.worldsteel.org.

Yohe, Gary et al. (2006) "Global distributions of vulnerability to climate change," *The Integrated Assessment Journal*, 6(3), pp. 35–44.

4 What are we trying to achieve?

Measuring wealth and well-being

Ever since the invention of national accounts (i.e. methods of measuring the total economic activity of a country) in the 1930s, the prevailing worldview has been that the well-being of a society could be measured by looking at the economy and calculating the gross domestic product (or, more specifically, the gross domestic product per capita). This fundamental concept has come under increasing scrutiny in the last few decades. Perhaps the most articulate critique was spoken by the late senator Robert Kennedy, who stated in a speech delivered on March 18, 1968, at the University of Kansas:

> Our Gross National Product, now, is over $800 billion dollars a year, but that Gross National Product – if we judge the United States of America by that – that Gross National Product counts air pollution and cigarette advertising, and ambulances to clear our highways of carnage. It counts special locks for our doors and the jails for the people who break them. It counts the destruction of the redwood and the loss of our natural wonder in chaotic sprawl. It counts napalm and counts nuclear warheads and armored cars for the police to fight the riots in our cities. It counts Whitman's rifle and Speck's knife, and the television programs which glorify violence in order to sell toys to our children. Yet the gross national product does not allow for the health of our children, the quality of their education or the joy of their play. It does not include the beauty of our poetry or the strength of our marriages, the intelligence of our public debate or the integrity of our public officials. It measures neither our wit nor our courage, neither our wisdom nor our learning, neither our compassion nor our devotion to our country, it measures everything in short, except that which makes life worthwhile. And it can tell us everything about America except why we are proud that we are Americans.
>
> (Kennedy 1968)

There are several ways of addressing the issues raised by Robert Kennedy: (1) developing measures of happiness and social well-being, (2) creating alternative metrics to GDP and measures of wealth, (3) exploring the role of the distribution of income, and (4) creating goals, motivating action and measuring progress. Each is discussed in turn in the following.

Measuring happiness and social well-being

Sustainability requires its simultaneous achievement in all three areas of economy, ecology and society, yet what we actually measure with national income data is focused solely on

DOI: 10.4324/9781003170730-4

the economic. Clearly, there are a significant number of factors which matter to people and are not captured in GDP data. One of these factors surely must be satisfaction or happiness. This has been a difficult variable to measure because of its intangible nature, its cultural characteristics and its potentially changing components. Fortunately, several outstanding research advances in the last few years have offered a glimpse of temporal trends in happiness in such countries as the United States as well as permitting cross-national and cross-cultural comparisons (Ingelhart 2004; Graham 2009; Diener et al. 2010; Helliwell et al. 2020). Research from the National Opinion Research Center at the University of Chicago (Smith 2011; Smith et al. 2015) has shown that Americans seem to be no happier than they were almost 50 years ago despite increased median income (Helliwell et al. 2020). (See Figure 4.1a.) In fact, Figure 4.1b suggests there may be a modest inverse but statistically insignificant relationship between the two variables in the United States. (t stat −0.597, p = 0.558; F 0.356, p = 0.5575). Research conducted by Twenge et al. (2015, p. 136) covering the period 1972–2014 suggests that trends in happiness may vary by age groupings:

> Recent adolescents are happier and more satisfied with their lives than adolescents in past decades and generations; however, adults over age 30 are less happy than their predecessors. While adults over age 30 were once happier than young adults aged 18–29, the two groups did not differ in happiness by the early 2010s, and the positive correlation between age and happiness found in past eras disappeared by the early 2010s. Similarly, the happiness advantage of mature adults over adolescents has dwindled. Mixed-effects models show that these effects were primarily due to time period rather than generation/cohort. While previous studies of adults found few time period effects in happiness, we find that the time trend differs based on age, with opposite trends for young people versus mature adults.

A study entitled *The Economics of Happiness* by Mark Anielski (2007) examined several dozen factors which were deemed to be desirable to the average person and then looked at the progress in achieving these goals over the past five decades. As is apparent in

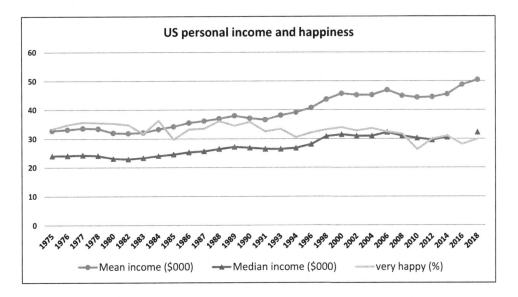

Figure 4.1a US income and happiness time trends

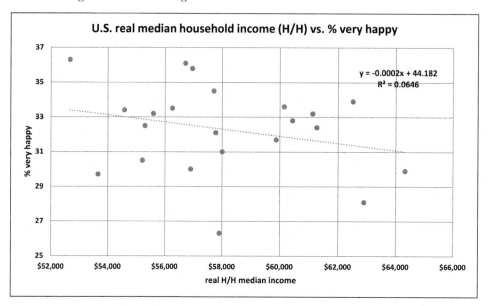

Figure 4.1b US median household income vs. happiness

Table 4.1, quantitative measures of these variables were worse than they were in 1950 in most cases. Comparing data from another study (Ingelhart 2004) on happiness in several dozen countries with GDP per capita yields a broad range of values. (See Figure 4.2.) Of particular note is the somewhat counterintuitive nature of the data. While most poor countries have low levels of happiness, several others have unusually high levels – higher than many modern industrialized economies. Many of the countries lying above the trend line are from Latin America, while many below are former members of the communist bloc (Ingelhart 2010). In general, the data suggest that past a certain level of income, there is little improvement in levels of happiness. This is an important finding that we will see elsewhere in analysis of sustainability since it suggests that one need only raise per capita income levels to between $10,000 and $20,000 per year to achieve a significant degree of happiness – a value considerably lower than the per capita income of much of the industrialized world. A common explanation for the declining marginal increment in happiness is that "more income improves happiness only until basic needs are met. Beyond the point where there is enough income so that people are no longer hungry and absolute poverty has been eliminated, income does not matter for happiness" (Di Tella and MacCulloch 2010, p. 218).

Richard Layard, in his book *Happiness: Lessons From a New Science* (2006), identified seven meta-variables which he felt affect happiness: family relationships, financial situation, work, community and friends, health, personal freedom and personal values. The critical importance of many of these factors has been independently verified in numerous other studies.

More recent international efforts to recast the debate over the components of well-being have been produced by the UNDP and the OECD. The first study by UNDP published in 2010 represented an attempt by the international body to look beyond the conventional measures of welfare, as typified by GDP/capita, and generate alternative measures of well-being across countries and over time. The first such effort in 1990 was

Table 4.1 State of progress indicators

What we want more of	Progress indicator	Better	Worse	No change
Happiness	Self-rated happiness		X	
Longer lives	Life expectancy	X		
Overall societal well-being	Index for social health		X	
Healthy youth	Youth suicide rate		X	
Prosperous economy	GDP	X		
Healthy markets	Stock market values	X		
More money	Personal income	X		
	Real wages		X	
Genuine progress	Genuine progress indicator (GPI)		X	
More material possessions	Consumption expenditures	X		
More leisure time and time with friends and family	Leisure time		X	
Strong and healthy relationships	Divorce rate		X	
Healthy farmland	Productive farmland		X	
More time to give to others	Volunteer time	X		
Reduced dependence on fossil fuels	Fossil fuel use vs. renewables		X	
Debt	US total outstanding debt		X	
Violence	Violent crime rate		X	
Inequality of income and wealth	Gini coefficient		X	
Poverty	Poverty rates			X
Work	Hours of work		X	
Work-related commuting time	Commuting time		X	
Underemployment	Underemployment rate		X	
Automobile crashes, deaths and injuries	Auto crashes		X	
Long-term environmental damage	Cost of environmental damage		X	
Loss of wetlands	Area of wetlands		X	
Loss of old-growth forests	Area of old-growth forest		X	
Air pollution	Air quality indexes	X		
Reliance on foreign borrowing and debt	Foreign debt outstanding		X	

a Human Development Index which measured life expectancy at birth, the adult literacy rate, mean years of schooling and educational attainment. Realizing that the HDI represented only part of the broader picture of well-being, the UNDP produced a family of additional indexes (see Table 4.2). Figure 4.3 outlines the derivation of the environmental and socioeconomic sustainability indexes (UNDP 2019).

It is important to remember that much of the data reported by the UN and relied upon in the construction of these indexes is based upon surveys conducted by individual countries. As such, the degree of accuracy may be difficult to ascertain. In matters of national pride, such as adult literacy rates, there might be a tendency to err on the upside in the reporting process. Even in most of the developed nations – where literacy rates

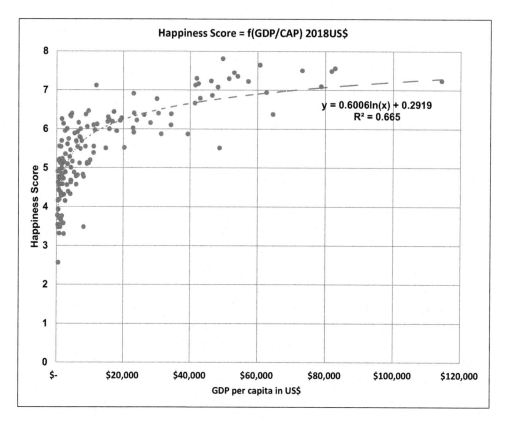

Figure 4.2 International income and happiness

Table 4.2 UNDP family of indexes of well-being

UNDP indexes and dashboards
Human Development Index
Inequality-adjusted Human Development Index
Gender Development Index
Gender Inequality Index
Multidimensional Poverty Index
Quality of Human Development
Life-course gender gap
Women's empowerment
Environmental Sustainability
Socioeconomic Sustainability

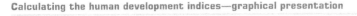

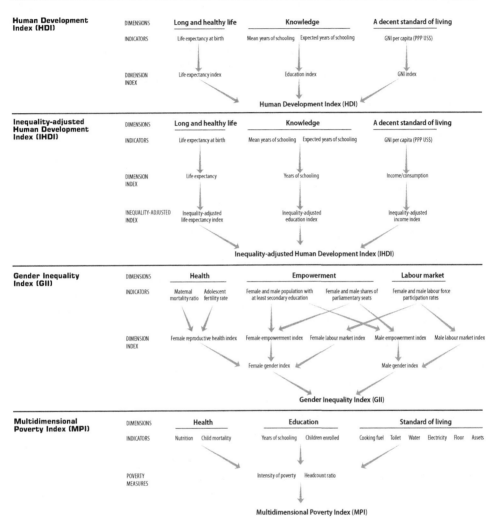

Figure 4.3 Derivation of UN HDI indexes

are considered to be 99% – there is a reason to be circumspect. For example, in both the United States and Canada, where in-depth analysis has been conducted of disaggregated levels of literacy and numeracy (e.g. proficient, intermediate, basic and below basic), the results fall far short of 100% (US DoE NCES 2005; Statistics Canada 2003). The UNDP discontinued the use of this variable in its index construction in 2009 and replaced it with mean years of schooling. The underlying lesson from these reports is that the construction of any index – whether it concerns matters social, economic or ecological – must be based on meaningful and verifiable data.

A second major study, by the OECD (2011a), compared 34 countries across 21 indicators under the general rubrics of "material conditions" and "quality of life" (see Appendix 4.2). Only six of these variables were conventional measures of economic welfare.

The top seven countries (in descending order) were Australia, Canada, Sweden, New Zealand, Norway, Denmark and the United States. It is important to note that the OECD index is distinct from the other indexes in that is interactive and allows the reader to vary the importance of the components, thereby creating potentially different ranking results. After identifying and measuring these types of variables, the challenge remains as to how such information is to be used. A remarkable effort to use these data to complement GDP figures has taken place in the mountain kingdom of Bhutan (*New York Times* October 4, 2005). In 2008, the country adopted a quantitative Gross National Happiness (GNH) Index to measure the progress of the government in promoting the emotional well-being of its citizenry. The GNH Index has nine major categories, each composed of several sub-components: psychological well-being, ecology, health, education, culture, living standards, time use, community vitality and good governance (Centre for Bhutan Studies & GNH 2015). (See Table 4.3.) Table 4.4 displays the subcomponents for the psychological component questions and how they are measured. (See also Ura et al. 2012.)

Table 4.3 Bhutan's Gross National Happiness Index

GNH Index variables

Psychological wellbeing

1 General mental health
2 Frequency of prayer recitation
3 Frequency of meditation
4 Taking account of karma in daily life
5 Frequency of feeling of selfishness
6 Frequency of feeling of jealousy
7 Frequency of feeling of calmness
8 Frequency of feeling of compassion
9 Frequency of feeling of generosity
10 Frequency of feeling of frustration
11 Occurrence of suicidal thought

Ecology

1 Pollution of rivers
2 Soil erosion
3 Method of waste disposal
4 Names and species of plants and animals
5 Tree plantations around your farm or house

Health

1 Self reported health status
2 Long term disability
3 # of healthy days in the past 30 days
4 Body Mass Index
5 Knowledge of transmission of HIV/AIDS virus

6 Duration for a child to be breast fed only
7 Walking distance to health care centre

Education

1 Level of education
2 Literacy rate
3 Ability to understand lozey
4 Historical literacy (Knowledge on local legend and folk stories)

Culture

1 Speaking first language
2 Frequency of playing traditional games
3 Zorig chusum skills
4 Teaching children importance of discipline
5 Teaching children importance of impartiality
6 Knowledge of mask and other dances performed in tshechus
7 Importance of reciprocity as a life principle
8 Attitude towards killing
9 Attitude towards stealing

Living standards

1 Household income
2 Income sufficiency to meet everyday needs
3 Food insecurity
4 House ownership

Measuring wealth and well-being 81

Table 4.3 (Continued)

GNH Index variables

5	Room ratio	8	There is a lot of understanding in your family
6	Purchase of second hand clothes	9	Your family is a real source of comfort to you
7	Difficulty in contributing to the community festivals	10	No. of relatives living in the same community
8	Postponement of urgent repairs and maintenance of house	11	Victim of crime
		12	Feelings of safety from human harm
		13	Sense of enmity in the community

Time use

14 No. of days volunteered

1 Total working hours

15 Amount of donation in cash value

2 Sleep hours

16 Availability of social support

Community vitality

Good governance

1 Sense of trust in neighbours

1 Performance of central govt in reducing income gap

2 Neighbours helping each other in the community

2 Performance of central govt in fighting corruption

3 Labour exchange with community members

3 Right to freedom of speech and opinion

4 Socialising with friends

4 Freedom from discrimination

5 Members of your family really care about each other

5 Trust in central ministries

6 Trust in dzongkhag administration

6 You wish you were not part of your family

7 Trust in media

7 Members of your family argue too much

Table 4.4 Bhutan's Gross National Happiness Index – psychological components

#	Indicators	Indexes	Question	Range	Threshold (deprived if variable is below threshold)
1	General mental health	Mental Health Index	General Health Questionnaire	**1(Worst)–37(Best)** **Categories:** **22–37 (Normal mental wellbeing)** **17–21 (Some distress)** **1–16 (Severe distress)**	**22 (Normal mental wellbeing)**
2	Frequency of prayer recitation	Spirituality Index	Do you say/ recite prayers?	**1(Worst)–3(Best)** **Categories:** **1 (Never)** **2 (Occasionally)** **3 (Daily)**	**3 (Daily)**
3	Frequency of meditation	Spirituality Index	Do you practise meditation?	**1(Worst)–3(Best)** **Categories:** **1 (Never)** **2 (Occasionally)** **3 (Daily)**	**2 (Occasionally)**

(Continued)

Table 4.4 (Continued)

#	Indicators	Indexes	Question	Range	Threshold (deprived if variable is below threshold)
4	Taking account of karma in daily life	Spirituality Index	Do You consider karma in the course of your daily life?	1(Worst)–3(Best) **Categories:** **1 (Never)** **2 (Occasionally)** **3 (Daily)**	**3 (Daily)**
5	Frequency of feeling of selfishness	Emotional Balance Index	How often do you experience selfishness?	1(Worst)–3(Best) **Categories:** **1 (Often)** **2 (Sometimes)** **3 (Never)**	**3 (Never)**
6	Frequency of feeling of jealousy	Emotional Balance Index	How often do you experience jealousy?	1(Worst)–3(Best) **Categories:** **1 (Often)** **2 (Sometimes)** **3 (Never)**	**3 (Never)**
7	Frequency of feeling of calmness	Emotional Balance Index	How often do you experience calmness?	1(Worst)–3(Best) **Categories:** **1 (Never)** **2 (Sometimes)** **3 (Often)**	**3 (Often)**
8	Frequency of feeling of compassion	Emotional Balance Index	How often do you experience compassion?	1(Worst)–3(Best) **Categories:** **1 (Never)** **2 (Sometimes)** **3 (Often)**	**3 (Often)**
9	Frequency of feeling of generosity	Emotional Balance Index	How often do you experience generosity?	1(Worst)–3(Best) **Categories:** **1 (Never)** **2 (Sometimes)** **3 (Often)**	**3 (Often)**
10	Frequency of feeling of frustration	Emotional Balance Index	How often do you experience frustration?	1(Worst)–3(Best) **Categories:** **1 (Often)** **2 (Sometimes)** **3 (Never)**	**3 (Never)**
11	Occurrence of suicidal thought	Emotional Balance Index	Have you ever seriously thought of committing suicide?	1(Worst)–2 (Best) **Categories:** **1 (Yes)** **2 (No)**	**2 (No)**

Perhaps the most ambitious to track cross-national and temporal trends in happiness and subjective well-being has been the comprehensive series of studies conducted by Helliwell et al. from 2012 to 2020. Of 153 countries surveyed, Finland was deemed the happiest and Afghanistan the least happy. The critical criteria used by Helliwell et al. and other major studies in determining well-being are listed in Table 4.5. Table 4.6 lists the top ten countries in each of these alternative measurement systems. In general, the rank correlation between GDP/capita and the other three global measures is weak: Human Poverty Index (HPI) (–0.128), Human Development Index (HDI) (0.467) and World Happiness Report (WHR) (0.228).

Table 4.5 Principal criteria used in alternative indexes

Determinants/components of alternative measures of well-being

Variables	GDP/ cap	HPI	UN HDI	Global Hunger Index (GHI)	Better Life Index (BLI)	OECD	World Happiness Report (WHR)	Gross National Happiness (GNH)	Genuine Progress Indicator (GPI)
GDP/capita	X			X			X	See	See
Personal income			X		X	X		Table 4.4 in text	Table 4.7 in text
Civic engagement					X	X			
Dystopia				X					
Ecological footprint		X							
Education			X		X	X			
Environment					X	X			
Well-being and safety		X			X	X			
Freedom to make life choices				X			X		
Generosity				X			X		
Health				X	X	X			
Housing					X	X			
Jobs						X			
Life expectancy		X	X		X		X		
Perceptions of corruption				X			X		
Social support					X	X	X		
Work-life balance					X	X			
Trust in government							X		
Life satisfaction						X			

Table 4.6 Top ten countries in each index

Top dozen countries in each index				
Global data				OECD
GDP/cap	HPI	HDI	WHR	BLI – life-satisfaction component
Luxembourg (1)	Costa Rica (59)	Norway (4)	Finland (15)	Norway (4)
Macao (2)	Mexico (69)	Switzerland (3)	Denmark (10)	Australia (11)
Switzerland (3)	Colombia (88)	Ireland (5)	Switzerland (3)	Iceland (6)
Norway (4)	Vanuatu (130)	Germany (17)	Iceland (6)	Canada (19)
Ireland (5)	Vietnam (133)	Hong Kong (16)	Norway (4)	Denmark (10)
Iceland (6)	Panama (55)	Australia (11)	Netherlands (13)	Switzerland (3)
Qatar (7)	Nicaragua (142)	Iceland (6)	Sweden (12)	Netherlands (13)
Singapore (8)	Bangladesh (148)	Sweden (12)	New Zealand (23)	Sweden (12)
US (9)	Thailand (82)	Singapore (8)	Austria (14)	Finland (15)
Denmark (10)	Ecuador (90)	Netherlands (13)	Luxembourg (1)	US (9)
Australia (11)	Jamaica (99)	Denmark (10)	Canada (19)	Luxembourg (1)
Sweden (12)	Norway (4)	Finland (15)	Australia (11)	New Zealand (23)

Generating alternative metrics

Several pioneering attempts have been made in the West to create independent measures of national income and wealth which can be compared to conventional GDP measurements. Figure 4.4 captures the essence of the problem with current economic measures of well-being. Produced by a non-governmental organization (NGO) called Redefining Progress (n.d.), the figure's accompanying explanatory text reads:

> According to the most popular index of prosperity – the Gross Domestic Product – this family should be celebrating. Their "persona GDP" goes higher every time they have to spend more money, no matter the reason why. Big jump in health insurance premiums? Splendid. Expensive divorce settlements? Even better. Is this any way to measure the real economic progress of a family . . . or a society? We don't think so. That's why we created the Genuine Progress Indicator or GPI. More than 400 leading economists, including several Nobel Prize winners, have called for measures like GPI that offer a more meaningful view of the economic realities most Americans face in their day-to-day lives. Using GDP as a starting point, GPI adds benefits (like the economic value of housework) and deducts costs (like crime and pollution) that GDP ignores. The results are frankly troubling. Both GDP and GPI consistently grew from 1950 – the first GPI calculation – until the late 1970s. But for the last 20 years GPI has tumbled, even as total GDP continues to soar. Maybe that's why for too many American families, the "booming" economy doesn't translate into a better quality of life. So the next time politicians and pundits start cheering about the rising GDP, tell them you're still waiting for a measure of genuine progress.

Figure 4.4 The downside of GDP growth

A comparison of US GDP and GPI per capita for the half century following 1950 is presented in Figures 4.5 and 4.6. The calculations behind these figures are reported in Table 4.7 (Talberth et al. 2006). More recent research has expanded the theoretical and methodological foundations of this indicator and applied it to numerous political entities (Kubiszewski et al. 2013; Talberth and Weisdorf 2017; Fox and Erickson 2018, 2020). Kubiszewski et al. compare GDP/capita and GPI/capita for 17 nations over the period 1950–2003. With the exception of Japan and Poland, all other countries studied reproduce the results of the US studies – GPI/capita lagging behind GDP/capita. Fox and Erickson extend the analysis to the subnational level, using a ranking methodology to compare trends in GPI with more a standard measure of economic performance for all 50 US states. Not unexpectedly, they found significant divergence of GPI per capita among the 50 states, with 7 having a negative GPI, "suggesting that total costs of annual consumption in those states outweigh the benefits" (Fox and Erickson 2018, pp. 30–31). They conclude their analysis by reviewing some of the theoretical issues with the GPI methodology:

> At the center of the theoretical debate over GPI has been the weak sustainability critique, a recognition that depletion of natural or social capital remains a viable economic development strategy due to the substitution of expanding income and consumption to produce rising per capita GPI.
>
> (p. 34)

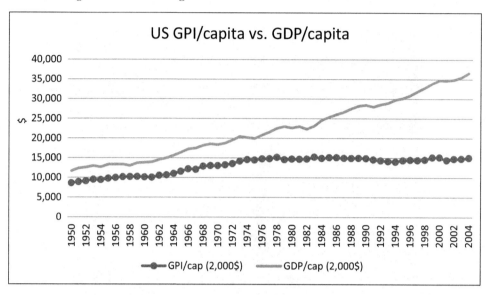

Figure 4.5 US GPI/capita vs. GDP/capita

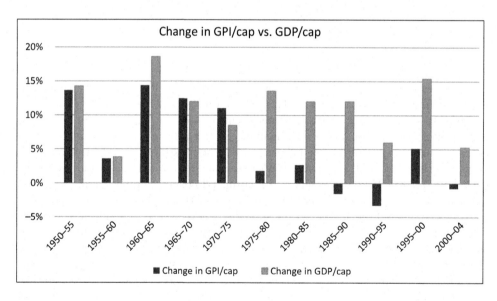

Figure 4.6 Changes in US GPI/capita vs. GDP/capita

Table 4.7 US genuine progress indicator (2004)

	Billion $
Personal consumption	*7,589*
Income distribution	120
Personal consumption adjusted for income inequality	6,318
Adjustments	
Value of housework and parenting	2,542
Value of higher education	828
Services of consumer durables	744
Services of highways and streets	112
Value of volunteer work	131
Net capital investment	389
Cost of household pollution abatement	−21
Cost of noise pollution	−18
Cost of crime	−34
Cost of air pollution	−40
Cost of water pollution	−120
Loss of old-growth forests and damage from logging roads	−51
Cost of underemployment	−177
Cost of automobile accidents	−175
Loss of farmland	−264
Net foreign borrowing	−254
Loss of leisure time	−402
Cost of ozone depletion	−479
Loss of wetlands	−53
Cost of commuting	−523
Cost of consumer durables	−1,090
CO_2 emissions damages	−1,183
Depletion of non-renewable energy resources	−1,761
Net genuine progress	*4,419*

Another conceptually similar index was constructed by a prominent economist, Herman Daly, former senior economist for the World Bank, and John B. Cobb, Jr., professor of theology and philosophy at the Claremont Graduate School in California. The results of their measure, called an Index of Sustainable Economic Welfare (ISEW), was compared over four decades with per capita GDP in Figure 4.7, and the underlying economic calculations are displayed in Table 4.8 (Daly and Cobb 1994, 2002).

Both the GPI and ISEW address the social component in sustainable development.

Finally, it is necessary to specifically add a focus on natural resource depletion and degradation (i.e. natural capital) to address the ecological component of sustainability.

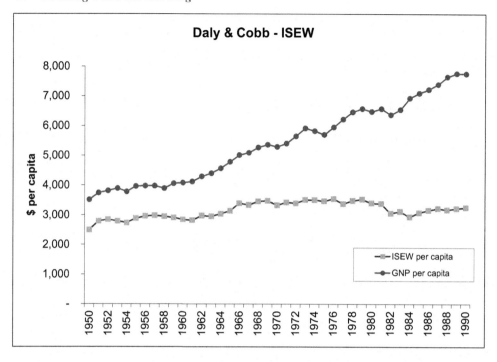

Figure 4.7 US Index of Sustainable Economic Welfare

Consider the following quote by Robert Repetto (1989, p. 2), a researcher with the World Resources Institute: "A country could exhaust its mineral resources, cut down its forests, erode its soils, pollute its aquifers, and hunt its wildlife and fisheries to extinction, but measured income would not be affected as these assets disappeared." What analytical methodologies can be used to address this problem?

In his pioneering study, Repetto used Indonesia, with a major natural-resource-based economy, as a case study to demonstrate a novel methodology to adjust the country's national accounts to incorporate estimates of the depletion of natural capital. Repetto looked specifically at petroleum, forest and soil depletion to make adjustments to Indonesia's GDP. The analytical methodology entailed several distinct steps. For example, for petroleum, annual estimates were made of opening and closing physical stocks in barrels of oil considered as economically recoverable reserves. An estimate was then made of economic rent per barrel by subtracting the production costs from the Free on Board (FOB) export price. Finally, the physical estimates and rent data were combined in a monetary account to determine the economic value of the opening and closing stocks. The calculation was the following:

Closing stock (m bbl) × rent/bbl = closing stock ($m) + net change in physical stock × rent/bbl = net change in monetary accounts ($m)

Table 4.8 US Index of Sustainable Economic Welfare

Billion $	1990
Personal consumption	*1,266*
Distributional inequality	109
Weighted personal consumption	1,164
Adjustments	
Services: Household labor	520
Services: Consumer durables	225
Services: Highways and streets	18
Improvement in health and education public expenditures	45
Expenditures on consumer durables	−235
Defensive private expenditures health and education	−63
Cost of commuting	−35
Cost of personal pollution control	−5
Cost of auto accidents	−32
Costs of water pollution	−15
Costs of air pollution	−19
Costs of noise pollution	−5
Loss of wetlands	−21
Loss of farmland	−37
Depletion of non-renewable resources	−313
Long-term environmental damage	−285
Cost of ozone depletion	−85
Net capital growth	29
Change in net international position	−34
Index of Sustainable Economic Welfare (ISEW)	*818*

Table 4.9 reproduces the results of these calculations for petroleum over the period 1980–1984. As is evident from these data, the value of the physical stock declined over this period in study. A similar methodology is used for the calculation in the changes in the value of forests as a component of Indonesia's natural capital.

Repetto uses a somewhat different methodology for estimating the change in the value of the nation's soils. Again, a multistep calculation is used: first, an annual cost of erosion is based on annual productivity losses from soil erosion, and then these costs are capitalized using a discount rate of 10%. The issue of the appropriate discount rate to use in evaluating natural capital is somewhat contentious, and this issue is discussed further in Chapter 6.

Finally, Repetto uses these data to calculate net domestic product and net domestic investment – representing adjustments to conventional measures of GDP and GDI after adjusting for the value of resource depletion. The results are displayed in Figures 4.8 and 4.9. The conclusions from this landmark study are noteworthy as this methodology

Table 4.9 Indonesian petroleum accounts

Physical accounts (million barrels)	1980	1981	1982	1983	1984
Opening stock	11,742	11,306	10,943	10,631	10,181
Additions					
Discoveries	141	223	172	71	67
Upward revisions	0	0	0	0	0
Depletions	577	586	484	521	517
Net change	−436	−363	−312	−450	−450
Closing stock	11,306	10,943	10,631	10,181	9,731
Unit values (US$/barrel)					
FOB export price	28.11	35.83	35.74	34.75	31.94
Production costs	3.80	5.50	8.59	9.15	7.64
Rent/barrel	24.31	30.33	27.15	25.60	24.30
Monetary accounts (million US$)					
Opening stock	141,138.80	274,848.86	331,901.19	288,631.65	260,633.60
Additions					
Discoveries	3,427.71	6,763.59	4,669.80	1,817.60	1,628.10
Upward revisions	$0.00	$0.00	$0.00	$0.00	$0.00
Depletions	14,026.87	17,773.38	13,140.60	13,337.60	12,563.10
Net change	−10,599.16	−11,009.79	−8,470.80	−11,520.00	−10,935.00
Revaluation	144,309.20	68,062.10	−34,798.70	−16,478.10	−13,235.30
Closing stock	274,848.86	331,901.19	288,631.65	260,633.60	236,463.30

Source: Reproduced with permission of the publisher.

can be used to assess the impact of any nation's depletion of its natural capital on its real wealth. To quote Repetto (1989, p. 4):

> For resource-based economies, evaluations of economic performance and estimates of macroeconomic relationships are seriously distorted by failure to account for natural resource depreciation. . . . Over the past 20 years [1970–1989], Indonesia drew heavily on its considerable natural resource endowment to finance development expenditures.

In fact, the overstatement of income and its growth may actually be considerably more than these estimates indicate because the analysis is restricted to only petroleum, timber and soils on the principal island of Java. Excluded from this analysis are non-renewables such as natural gas, coal, copper, tin and nickel and renewable resources such as non-timber forest products and fisheries. Repetto concludes: "Should gross investment be less than resource depletion, then, on balance, the country is drawing down, rather than building up, its asset base, and using its natural resource endowment to finance current consumption" (p. 5). If any corporation were to deplete its capital and claim it as income, the management would probably be fired. This is a clear example of how the adoption of

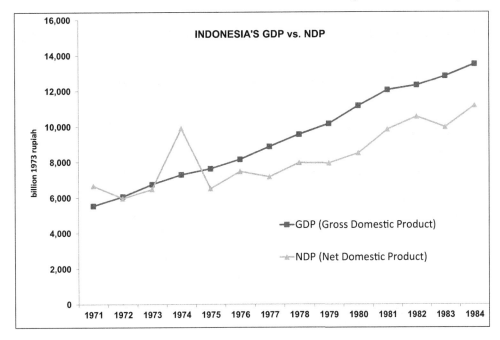

Figure 4.8 Indonesian Gross Domestic Product (GDP) vs. Net Domestic Product (NDP)

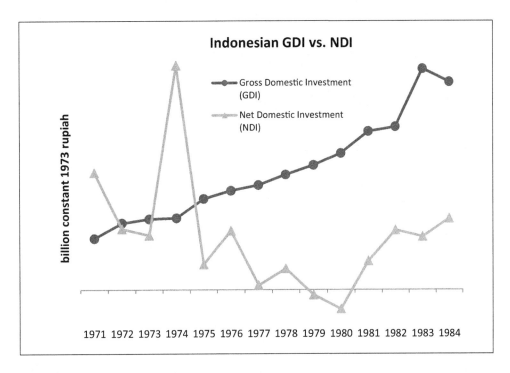

Figure 4.9 Changes in annual Indonesian GDP and NDP

certain corporate accounting principles could improve the interpretation of government economic data immeasurably.

This major conceptual advance from an NGO in the private sector was paralleled by work conducted by the World Bank. World Bank has produced several methodologies in order to create a more comprehensive measure of the wealth of nations. It began with the recognition that the traditional definition of physical or "produced" capital must be complemented by at least two other types of capital: (1) natural capital, as described prior, which includes not only land, fossil fuel deposits and other mineral wealth but also such critical natural resources as clean water, and (2) human capital, as embodied in skills, health and social organization. Table 4.10 presents some example data from the World Bank's original attempt in 1990 to redefine wealth and apply it to a comparison of national economies (Serageldin 1995, Annex 1, pp. 1–4). What are the implications of these revised measures of national wealth? Robert Solow, Nobel laureate in economics, has stated that "what we normally measure as capital is a small part of what it takes to sustain human welfare" (*New York Times* September 19, 1995). Economic development policies have focused on what is easily measured – namely physical capital – to the exclusion of such critical components of national well-being as education, health, social organization and the environment.

The data in Table 4.10 show that natural-resource-rich countries such as Australia and Canada come out on top on a per capita basis – especially in light of the fact that their resources are shared by a relatively small population base. Countries such as Switzerland

Table 4.10 World Bank's original estimates of total national wealth 1990

Country	Wealth per person ($)	Composition of wealth		Produced or manufactured (%)	Human and social (education, skills, etc.) (%)
		Natural			
		land (crops, etc.) (%)	other (subsoil minerals and water) (%)		
Australia	835,000	64	8	7	21
Canada	704,000	64	5	9	22
Japan	565,000	1	0	18	81
US	421,000	22	3	16	59
Germany	399,000	3	1	17	79
Singapore	306,000	0	0	15	85
Saudi Arabia	184,000	26	28	18	28
Russia	98,000	34	36	15	15
Mexico	74,000	11	5	11	73
China	6,600	3	5	15	77
India	4,300	2	9	25	64
Vietnam	2,600	2	9	15	74
Ethiopia	1,400	12	27	21	40
World	**86,000**	**15**	**5**	**16**	**64**

and Japan have radically different resource mixes but also ranked near the top because of their investment in human capital. It has been posited that countries that derive most of their wealth from human and social capital are better positioned to create a sustainable economic advantage in the post-industrial era and information age, where a high premium is placed on human creativity, education and technical skills.

The World Bank undertook a major revision and expansion of this analysis in 2000 and 2006 and then again in 2011. An example of their comparative international data is displayed in Table 4.11. In this case, the categories have been renamed as produced capital, natural capital and intangible capital. *Produced capital* represents the sum of machinery and structures and development on urban land. *Natural capital* includes energy and mineral resources, timber and non-timber forest resources, crop and pasture land and protected areas. The category of *intangible capital* is calculated as a residual, representing the difference between total wealth and the sum of produced and natural capital. It includes human capital, institutional infrastructure and social capital. (Total wealth is defined as the net present value of sustainable consumption. See Appendix 4.1 for the World Bank's calculation of total wealth.)

While interesting in and by themselves, these "stock" estimates are considered less important than efforts to estimate national sustainability by incorporating depletion of natural capital. To address this specific issue, the World Bank created a new metric, first called genuine savings measure (GSM) but subsequently labeled *adjusted net savings (ANS)* (World Bank 2011). In conventional national income accounts, net savings rate is calculated by deducting depreciation of physical capital from gross savings:

$$NS = (GDS - Dp) / GDP$$

where:

NS = net savings

GDS = gross domestic savings

Dp = depreciation of physical capital

GDP = gross domestic product

The World Bank's adjusted net savings rate is calculated as follows:

$$GENSAV = (GDS - Dp + EDU - Rni - CO_2 \text{ Damage})/GDP$$

where:

GENSAV = genuine domestic savings rate

GDS = gross domestic savings

Dp = depreciation of physical capital

EDU = current expenditure on education

Rni = rent from depletion of i-th natural capital resource (energy, mineral and forest depletion are included)

CO2 Damage = estimated at US$20 per ton of carbon times number of tons of carbon emitted

GDP = gross domestic product at market prices

Table 4.11 Recent World Bank estimates of total national wealth (US$)

Rank	Country	Subsoil assets	Timber	Non-timber forest resources	Protected areas	Crop land	Pasture land	Natural capital	Produced capital + urban land	Net foreign assets	Intangible capital	Total wealth per capita
1	Luxembourg	0	255	85	1,413	718	3,621	6,092	213,425	99,449	598,563	917,530
2	Iceland	0	0	103	8,382	81	3,797	12,363	137,470	-45,995	799,123	902,960
3	Norway	99,706	669	1,417	4,788	505	3,078	110,162	183,078	36,436	532,121	861,797
4	Denmark	8,536	217	587	2,463	2,808	5,005	19,616	130,827	1,288	591,224	742,954
5	Switzerland	0	299	155	3,521	845	4,590	9,411	165,561	55,211	506,613	736,795
6	US	3,478	831	462	3,625	2,598	2,827	13,822	100,075	-6,947	627,246	734,195
17	Canada	12,644	3,980	4,302	11,293	2,603	2,103	36,924	89,811	-2,977	414,938	538,697
44	Mexico	3,525	1	149	316	1,360	1,290	6,641	21,320	-3,085	106,508	131,385
101	China	804	231	45	107	2,501	325	4,013	6,017	284	8,921	19,234
149	Ethiopia	2	8	48	261	522	281	1,123	324	97	2,089	3,439
150	Liberia		2,012	198	16	955	20	3,201	217	-1,709	1,659	3,368
151	Congo Dem. Rep.	77	443	546	19	500	14	1,599	200	-183	678	2,294
152	Burundi	2	1,054	3	13	1,541	84	2,697	166	-145	-527	2,191

Table 4.12 Adjusted net savings of selected petrostates (as % of Gross National Income)

Country	Adjusted net savings	
	2011	*2015–2017*
Algeria	21.4	21.2
Iran	20.0	n/a
Norway	16.2	16.9
Kuwait	9.7	14.6
Mexico	9.0	7.5
Argentina	7.7	5.4
Canada	7.6	6.5
Venezuela	6.5	7.2
Brazil	5.2	6.1
Kazakhstan	2.5	5.8
Colombia	1.5	2.8
Russia	1.5	8
Ecuador	0.4	11.4
Azerbaijan	−0.1	9.5
Saudi Arabia	−1.8	13.4
Indonesia	−2.4	12
Angola	−42.6	−16.3
Chad	−49.9	n/a

Table 4.12 shows the results of these calculations for a selected number of petrostates. These countries have widely different genuine savings rates, with some experiencing significant negative values. There is a longstanding debate over the special role of petroleum in economic development and sustainability, frequently referred to as the *resource curse* or *Dutch disease* (see Maass 2009; Margonelli 2007). One recent report (Carbon Tracker 2021) has estimated the significant financial difficulties facing some of the poorer petrostates in the face of potential falling demand for fossil fuels. Over 400 million people live in 19 of the most vulnerable countries, and the most vulnerable face potential revenue shortfalls of over 40%.

At least one major critique of the original genuine savings measure was voiced by Pillarisetti in the journal *Ecological Economics* (2005). According to this author, the metric has both positive and negative features. On the plus side, GSM highlights the need for investment in physical and social capital and subtracts natural resource depletion and environmental damage from conventional measures such as GDP. On the negative side, however, its conceptual problems include the omission of some major pollutants such as sulfur dioxide and nitrogen dioxide. Its foundational assumption is based on the principle of weak sustainability, which assumes that the loss of natural capital can be replaced by increased expenditures on other forms of capital (see Chapter 1). Because of the components and structure of the GSM, an apparently misleading impression may be given that many advanced countries are sustainable despite contrary evidence from other major measures such as the *ecological footprint* (see Chapter 8). This critique remains valid for the revised adjusted net savings rates.

A special commission was formed in 2009 by French president Nicholas Sarkozy and co-chaired by two Nobel laureates in economics, Stiglitz et al. (2009). Their report, titled *Report by the Commission on the Measurement of Economic Performance and Social Progress*, is one of the most comprehensive analytical examinations of the issues to date. To quote the authors (pp. 7–8, 12, 17–18):

> The Commission's aim has been to identify the limits of GDP as an indicator of economic performance and social progress, including the problems with its measurement; to consider what additional information might be required for the production of more relevant indicators of social progress; to assess the feasibility of alternative measurement tools, and to discuss how to present the statistical information in an appropriate way. . . . In effect, statistical indicators are important for designing and assessing policies aiming at advancing the progress of society, as well as for assessing and influencing the functioning of economic markets. . . . Choices between promoting GDP and protecting the environment may be false choices, once environmental degradation is appropriately included in our measurement of economic performance. So too, we often draw inferences about what are good policies by looking at what policies have promoted economic growth; but if our metrics of performance are flawed, so too may be the inferences that we draw. . . . It has long been clear that GDP is an inadequate metric to gauge well-being over time particularly in its economic, environmental, and social dimensions, some aspects of which are often referred to as *sustainability*. . . . The time is ripe for our measurement system to *shift emphasis from measuring economic production to measuring people's well-being. . . . There is a need for a clear indicator of our proximity to dangerous levels of environmental damage (such as associated with climate change or the depletion of fishing stocks.)*

One additional piece of evidence which suggests that GDP/capita is an inadequate if not misleading indicator of well-being was provided in a controversial book by Charles Kenny (2011) of the World Bank. In this work, Kenny stated that many nations in the third world are considerably better off than indicated by their per capita income when one considers the decrease in rates of infant mortality, increased school attendance and general improvement in health, including increases in life expectancy. According to Kenny (2011, p. 10–11): "the biggest success of development has not been making people richer, but, rather, has been making the things that really matter – things like health and education – cheaper and more widely available."

The impact of income distribution

Table 4.13 illustrates how GDP per capita can lead to a seriously skewed interpretation of the relative well-being of alternative countries. In this table, two pairs of countries with relatively similar per capita gross domestic product have been chosen. It should be apparent from a cursory examination of this table that there are profound differences between the two sets of countries despite their superficial similarity based on an average

Table 4.13 Pairwise comparisons of countries

	Namibia	*Ukraine*	*S. Africa*	*Albania*
GDP/capita ($)	9,683	7,994	11,756	12,300
Gini index	59.1	25	63	29
Bottom 40% share	8.6	24.5	7.2	22.1
Top 10% share	47.3	21.2	50.5	22.2
Top 1% share	n/a	n/a	19.2	6.4
Human Development Index	0.645	0.75	0.705	0.791
Rank	129	88	111	69
Life expectancy at birth	63.4	72	63.9	78.5
Expected years of schooling	12.6	15.1	13.7	15.2
Mean years of schooling	6.9	11.3	10.2	10.1
Happy Planet Index	21.6	26.4	15.9	36.8
Rank	103	70	128	13
World Happiness Index	4.571	4.561	4.814	4.883
Rank	122	123	109	105
Gender Development Index	n/a	0.995	0.984	0.971
Gender Inequality Index	n/a	0.284	0.422	0.234
Rank	n/a	60	97	51

economic value (UNDP 2019). One of the most important distinctions is related to the level of income inequality. There are two common methods for measuring this variable: the Gini coefficient and comparative shares of income between the highest and lowest decile or centile. The World Bank (n.d., p. 1) defines and illustrates the Gini concept as follows:

> It is based on the Lorenz curve, a cumulative frequency curve that compares the distribution of a specific variable (for example, income) with the uniform distribution that represents equality. To construct the Gini coefficient, graph the cumulative percentage of households (from poor to rich) on the horizontal axis and the cumulative percentage of income (or expenditure) on the vertical axis. The Gini captures the area between this curve and a completely equal distribution. If there is no difference between these two, the Gini coefficient becomes 0, equivalent to perfect equality, while if they are very far apart, the Gini coefficient becomes 1, which corresponds to complete inequality.

The Lorenz curve for Brazil in 2018 is displayed in Figure 4.10 and the Gini index for 2017 is 53.3 (World Bank 2020). Figure 4.11 maps GDP/capita versus the Gini coefficient for 75 countries for which data were available in 2015. It is noteworthy that countries with remarkably different GDP/capita can have similar Gini indexes, but what is even more remarkable is the number of countries with similar GDP/capita and widely divergent Gini indexes.

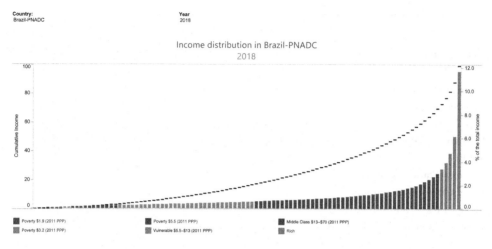

Figure 4.10 Lorenz curve for Brazil 2018

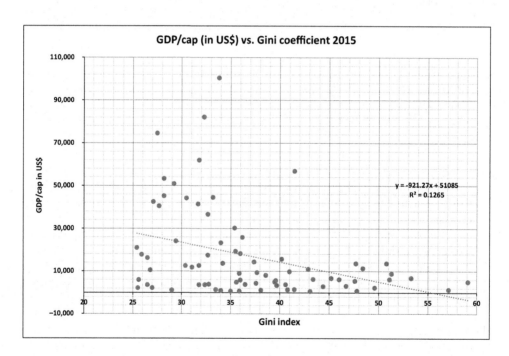

Figure 4.11 GDP per capita vs. Gini index in 2015

Alternatively, as started prior, a quicker assessment of income or wealth inequality may be generated by a simple comparison of upper and lower deciles, percentiles or any other similar division. For example, the US Federal Reserve Bank of St. Louis (2019) reported that income inequality in the US has risen from 1989 to 2016, with the share of the top 1% of income earners rising from 42% to 50% and the share of the bottom 50% of income earners falling from 15% to 13%. The bank also concluded that wealth is even more inequitably distributed: the top 10% of Americans increased their share of total wealth from 67% in 1989 to 77% in 2016. This change has been accompanied by a largely non-ameliorated white-black wealth gap. Similar gaps have continued to exist for whites/Hispanics, educational attainment and older versus younger families. Other findings are even more striking. *Forbes* (October 8, 2020) reports that the top 1% of US households hold 15 times more wealth than the bottom 50% combined, and an earlier study from the National Bureau of Economic Research (Saez and Zucman 2014) concluded:

> Wealth concentration has followed a U-shaped evolution over the last 100 years: It was high in the beginning of the twentieth century, fell from 1929 to 1978, and has continuously increased since then. The rise of wealth inequality is almost entirely due to the rise of the top 0.1% wealth share, from 7% in 1979 to 22% in 2012 – a level almost as high as in 1929. The bottom 90% wealth share first increased up to the mid-1980s and then steadily declined. The increase in wealth concentration is due to the surge of top incomes combined with an increase in saving rate inequality. Top wealth-holders are younger today than in the 1960s and earn a higher fraction of total labor income in the economy.

Time-series analysis conducted by the Resolution Foundation (2020) in the United Kingdom found that the while the share of wealth held by the richest 1% and 10% of UK citizens fell during the early and mid-20th century, these shares have stabilized or slightly increased since 1985. The authors observe that this trend has been largely replicated across many countries, according to the monumental study of inequality authored by Thomas Piketty (2014) entitled *Capital in the Twenty-First Century*.

The fundamental question is why this all matters. The clearest and most articulate answer to this question has been provided by Professor Joseph Stiglitz, who has devoted much of his academic career to the study of the extent and impact of income inequality. Stiglitz (2013) concluded:

> Much of America's concentration of wealth at the top was the result of rent seek-ing. . . . . We are paying a high price for our inequality – an economic system that is less stable and less efficient, with less growth, and a democracy that has been put into peril.

(p. xv)

He also observed:

> These disturbing trends in income and wealth inequality were outdone by even more
> disturbing evidence about inequalities in health. . . . Today, women in the United
> States, on average, have the lowest life expectancy of women in any of the advanced
> countries. Educational attainment, which is often tied in with income and race, is
> a large and growing predictor of life span. . . . Decreases in income and decline in
> standards of living are often accompanied by a multitude of social manifestation –
> malnutrition, drug abuse, and deterioration in family life, all of which take a toll on
> health and life expectancy. Indeed these declines in life expectancy are often consid-
> ered more telling than income numbers themselves.
>
> (p. xiii)

An interesting historical footnote to the subject of income inequality comes from the
1914 decision of Henry Ford, one of America's most prominent industrialists, to double
the wages of his workers compared to the average wage for automakers. He voiced the
following justification for his action (Ford 1926):

> The owner, the employees, and the buying public are all one and the same, and unless
> an industry can so manage itself as to keep wages high and prices low it destroys itself,
> for otherwise it limits the number of its customers. One's own employees ought to
> be one's own best customers. . . . We increased the buying power of our own people,
> and they increased the buying power of other people, and so on and on. . . . It is this
> thought of enlarging buying power by paying high wages and selling at low prices
> that is behind the prosperity of this country.

Ford was articulating the concept generally accepted in the economics profession that one
cannot have a healthy economy without sufficient purchasing power in the working and
middle classes. And yet, in recent times, a not insignificant proportion of the population
has experienced just the opposite: trapped in a vicious circle of low-paying work and
unable to purchase anything but "cheap goods" from companies unable to pay decent
wages. In her book *Cheap: The High Cost of Discount Culture*, Shell (2009, p. 161) states:
"As Woolworth himself pronounced in 1892, cheap goods cannot be had without 'cheap
help'. America is now awash in cheap help who distribute the cheap goods." In the same
vein, Barbara Ehrenreich (2011), in her *book Nickle and Dimed: On (Not) Getting By in
America*, presents a graphic portrayal of the lives of those Americans on the lowest rung of
the socioeconomic ladder earning "poverty-level wages." In his landmark book, *Bowling
Alone*, Robert Putnam (2000, updated to 2020), a Harvard social scientist, described the
loss of many institutions, such as churches, clubs and bowling leagues, that had traditionally provided the social glue that helped hold communities together. Several causes were
identified, but foremost among these has been the increasing financial pressures on a significant proportion of the population.

Compounding the financial and social burdens on the poorest members of society are
the findings that pollution, in general – and climate change, in particular – have the greatest impact on this group, which also has the least ability to mitigate these impacts (Carson

et al. 1997; Hajat et al. 2015; Islam and Winkel 2017; Muller et al. 2018; US Fourth National Climate Assessment 2018). In their innovative research, Muller et al. (2018) adjust the distribution of income data in the United States for both 2011 and 2014 by deducting damages due to exposure to air pollution from reported market income. Their findings suggest that the distribution of income is worse when air pollution is taken into consideration (p. 1):

> The Gini coefficient for this measure of adjusted income is 0.682 in 2011, as compared to 0.482 for market income. By 2014, we estimate that the Gini for adjusted income fell to 0.646, while the market income Gini did not appreciably change. The inclusion of air pollution damage acts like a regressive tax: with air pollution, the bottom 20% of households lose roughly 10% of the share of income, while the top 20% of households gain 10%.

To this point, the discussion has largely focused on the extent and significance of domestic-level inequality in developed nations such as the United States and United Kingdom. Of even greater potential import is the level of income and wealth inequality across nations, particularly the contrast between the developed world and developing nations. The extent of poverty in the developing world has varied by study and time. For the year 2008, the World Bank (2012) estimated that 2.5 billion people earned less than $2 per day and 1.3 billion less than $1.25 (see also Collins et al. 2009; Collier 2007). More recent estimates from the United Nations (UNDP 2019) estimate that some 600 million people currently live below the $1.90 poverty line, and this number increases to 1.3 billion when measured by the UN's Multidimensional Poverty Index. Yet, as the UNDP reports, significant progress has been made in the past few decades in addressing some of this inequality, recognizing that simple measures of per capita GDP fail to capture the true nature and extent of these disparities.

The UNDP report presents five key messages: (1) while many people are stepping above minimum floors of achievement in human development, widespread disparities remain; (2) a new generation of severe inequalities in human development is emerging, even if many of the unresolved inequalities of the 20th century are declining; (3) inequalities in human development can accumulate through life, frequently heightened by deep political imbalances; (4) assessing inequalities in human development demands a revolution in metrics; and (5) redressing inequalities in human development in the 21st century is possible – if we act now, before imbalances in economic power translate into entrenched political dominance.

The report stresses the existence of "two seismic shifts that will shape the 21st century: climate change and technological transformations" (p. 6). In order to address the challenges of technological change, the report concludes that "having a set of basic capabilities – those associated with the absence of extreme deprivations – is not enough. Enhanced capabilities are becoming crucial for people to own the 'narrative of their lives'" (p. 6). Despite the fact that inequalities in basic capabilities are slowly narrowing, inequalities in enhanced capabilities are widening (typified by life expectancy at age 70, population with a tertiary education and the extent of fixed broadband subscriptions).

The potential impact of climate change is equally momentous. According to the UNDP (2019, p. 17):

> Climate change will hurt human development in many ways beyond crop failures and natural disasters. Between 2030 and 2050 climate change is expected to cause an additional 250,000 deaths a year from malnutrition, malaria, diarrhoea and heat stress. Hundreds of millions more people could be exposed to deadly heat by 2050, and the geographic range for disease vectors – such as mosquitoes that transmit malaria or dengue – will likely shift and expand. The overall impact on people will depend on their exposure and their vulnerability. Both factors are intertwined with inequality in a vicious circle. Climate change will hit the tropics harder first, and many developing countries are tropical. Yet developing countries and poor communities have less capacity than their richer counterparts to adapt to climate change and severe weather events. So the effects of climate change deepen existing social and economic fault lines. There are also effects in the other direction, with evidence that some forms of inequality may make action on climate harder.

Other studies have produced similar results, describing "extreme carbon inequality" among nations (Oxfam 2015) and concluding that global warming has increased global inequality (Diffenbaugh and Burke 2019).

This raises a fundamental question: to what extent should the developed world divert resources required for domestic climate change preparedness to the much greater pool of population in the developing world. There are clearly humanitarian reasons for doing so. All of humanity faces the threat of global climate change. Yet there are also many more mainstream arguments why extending, and indeed augmenting, aid to the developing world is in the self-interest of the industrial nations. The third world has traditionally been a supplier of raw materials and offered a market for goods produced by the first world. Unfortunately, this relationship has historically been profoundly asymmetrical, with subsidies and tariff and non-tariff barriers imposed by the industrialized world significantly diminishing the capabilities of many nations of the developing world to full capitalize on their natural comparative advantage.

There is at least one more rationale for the increased level of assistance to developing nations in light of recent events. The emergence of the latest pandemic to afflict humanity in the form of COVID-19 has highlighted what Laurie Garrett (1994, 2000) has referred to as the global petri dish capable of incubating and transmitting new, or even preexisting, pathogens at a global scale. As Chapter 11 discusses, this phenomenon has been intensified by increased population pressure and density, as well as certain agricultural practices and the conversion and destruction of natural habitat, which have placed humanity in closer contact with domesticated and wild animals as well as other disease reservoirs in the natural environment.

Setting goals, motivating action and measuring progress

In 2015, the United Nations developed the Sustainable Development Goals (SDG), a list of 17 goals to guide nations' assessment of their progress toward sustainability (UN 2020a). (See Figure 4.12.) Each year, the international agency produces a detailed progress report

Figure 4.12 UN Sustainable Development Goals

on each goal. The latest report, issued in 2020, paints a mixed picture. The accompanying press release (UN 2020b) quotes UN Secretary-General Antonio Guterres:

> Global efforts to date have been insufficient to deliver the change we need, jeopardizing the Agenda's promise to current and future generations. Now, due to COVID-19, an unprecedented health, economic and social crisis is threatening lives and livelihoods, making the achievement of Goals even more challenging.
>
> (p. 1)

To quote the summary:

> The 2020 Report notes that progress had been made in some areas, such as improving maternal and child health, expanding access to electricity and increasing women's representation in government. Yet even these advances were offset elsewhere by growing food insecurity, deterioration of the natural environment, and persistent and pervasive inequalities. Now, in only a short period of time, the COVID-19 pandemic has unleashed an unprecedented crisis, causing further disruption to SDG progress, with the world's poorest and most vulnerable affected the most.
>
> (p. 1)

Table 4.14 summarizes the status of the 17 goals in the immediate pre-COVID period.

In their latest biannual *World Happiness Report*, Helliwell et al. (2020) attempt to map the 17 UN Sustainable Development Goals to their determinants of subjective well-being (see Figure 4.13). They are then able to compare the relative importance of SDG groups in explaining the variance of perceived well-being within regions. (See Figure 4.14). Not

Table 4.14 Summary of progress toward the UN SDGs

State of the UN SDGs pre-COVID

#	Goal	Before COVID-19
1	End poverty in all its forms everywhere	The world was off track to end poverty by 2030 (projection: 6%)
2	End hunger, achieve food security and improved nutrition and promote sustainable agriculture	Population affected by moderate or severe food insecurity has risen from 22.4% in 2014 to 25.9% in 2019
3	Ensure healthy lives and promote well-being for all at all ages	Progress in many health areas continued but needs acceleration
4	Ensure inclusive and equitable quality education and promote lifelong opportunities for all	Over 200 million children will still be out of school in 2030
5	Achieve gender equality and empower all women and girls	Despite improvements, full gender equality remains unreached
6	Ensure availability and sustainable management of water and sanitation for all	2.2 billion people lack safely managed drinking water, and 4.2 billion people lack safely managed sanitation
7	Ensure access to affordable, reliable, sustainable and modern energy for all	789 million people lack electricity, and 1 in 4 not electrified in some developing countries
8	Promote sustained, inclusive and sustainable economic growth, full and productive employment and decent work for all	Global GDP per capita growth has slowed from 2.0% in 2010–2018 to 1.5% in 2019
9	Build resilient infrastructure, promote inclusive and sustainable industrialization and foster innovation	Manufacturing growth was declining due to tariffs and trade tensions
10	Reduce inequality within and among countries	Income inequality was falling in some countries (the Gini index fell in 38 out of 84 countries in the period 2010–2017)
11	Make cities and human settlements inclusive, safe, resilient and sustainable	The share of urban population living in slums rose to 24% in 2018
12	Ensure sustainable consumption and production patterns	The global material footprint was 73.2 billion metric tons in 2010 and rose to 85.9 billion metric tons in 2017
13	Take urgent action to combat climate change and its impacts	The global community shies away from commitments to reverse the climate crisis (global temperatures are projected to rise by up to 3.2 degrees Celsius by 2100)
14	Conserve and sustainably use the oceans, sea and marine resources for sustainable development	A 100%–150% rise in ocean acidity is projected by 2100, affecting half of all marine life
15	Protect, restore and promote sustainable use of terrestrial ecosystems, sustainably manage forests, combat desertification, halt and reverse land degradation and halt biodiversity loss	Over 31,000 species are threatened with extinction, which is 27% of over 116,000 assessed species in the International Union for Conservation of Nature (IUCN) Red List
16	Promote peaceful and inclusive societies for sustainable development, provide access to justice for all and build effective, accountable and inclusive institutions at all levels	Every day 100 civilians are killed in armed conflicts
17	Strengthen the means of implementation and revitalize the global partnership for sustainable development	Net official development assistance totaled $147.4 billion in 2019, almost unchanged from 2018, but aid to Africa rose by 1.3% from 208 and aid to the less developed countries rose by 2.6% from 2018

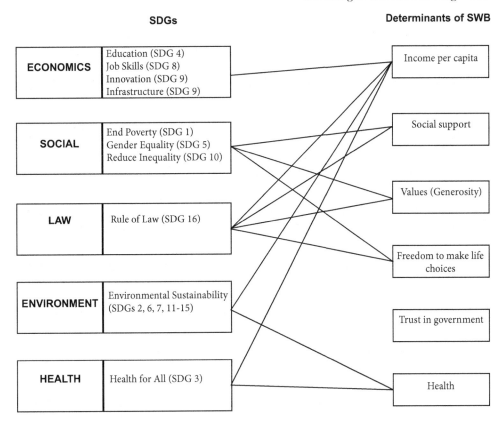

Figure 4.13 Mapping SDGs to determinants of subjective well-being

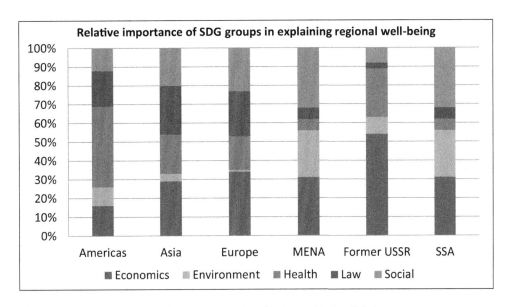

Figure 4.14 Relative important of SDG groups in explaining regional well-being

surprisingly, some of these findings correspond with our intuition about the importance of various factors in such disparate groups as the Americas, Asia, Europe, the former Soviet Union countries, the Middle East and North Africa (MENA) and sub-Saharan Africa (SSA).

Conclusion

In sum, it is clear that the sustainability challenges we face today – economic, social and ecological – are the result of the long period of global economic growth, and continuation of this trend poses even greater challenges. As such, it is essential to understand the evolution of modern economic theory designed to address these issues. The next three chapters describe the origins, development and principal components of the subfield of environmental economics, and the following three chapters outline the basic principles of ecology and the relatively new discipline of ecological economics.

Appendix 4.1
The World Bank's calculation of total wealth (World Bank 2011, pp. 142–143, reproduced with permission)

Total wealth

Total wealth can be calculated as $Wt = \int_t^\infty C(s) \times e^{-r(s-t)} ds$; where Wt is the total value of wealth, or capital, in year t; $C(s)$ is consumption in year s; and r is the social rate of return to investment. The social rate of return from investment is equal to:

$$r = \rho + \eta \frac{C}{C}$$

where ρ is the pure rate of time preference, η is the elasticity of utility with respect to consumption. Under the assumption that $\eta = 1$, and that consumption grows at a constant rate, then total wealth can be expressed as:

$$(A.1) \quad Wt = \int_t^\infty C(t) \times e^{-r(s-t)} ds$$

The current value of total wealth at time t is a function of the consumption at time t and the pure rate of time preference.

Expression (A.1) implicitly assumes that consumption is on a sustainable path, that is, the level of saving is enough to offset the depletion of natural resources. The calculation of total wealth requires that two issues be considered in computing the initial level of consumption:

- *The volatility of consumption.* To solve this problem we used the five-year centered average of consumption for each of the three years: 1995, 2000 and 2005.
- *Negative rates of adjusted net saving.* When depletion-adjusted saving is negative, countries are consuming natural resources, jeopardizing the prospects for future consumption. A measure of sustainable consumption needs to be derived in this instance.

Hence, the following adjustments were made:

- Wealth calculation for 2005, for example, considered consumption series for 2003–07.
- For the years in which saving adjusted for depletion of produced and natural capital was negative, this measure of depletion-adjusted saving was subtracted from consumption to obtain *sustainable* consumption, that is, the consumption level that would have left the capital stock intact.

- The corrected consumption series were then expressed in constant 2005 U.S. dollars. Deflators are country-specific: they are obtained by dividing gross domestic product (GDP) in current dollars by GDP in constant dollars. This rule was also applied to natural capital and net foreign assets.
- The average of constant-dollars consumption between 2003 and 2007, for example, was used as the initial level of consumption for wealth calculation of 2005.

For computation purposes, we assumed the pure rate of time preference to be 1.5 percent, and we limited the time horizon to 25 years. This time horizon roughly corresponds to a generation. We adopted the 25-year truncation throughout the calculation of wealth, in particular, of natural capital.

Appendix 4.2
Well-being indicator variables used by the OECD (2011b)

A MATERIAL CONDITIONS

   1   Income and Wealth

      a   Household net adjusted disposable income per person
      b   Household financial net wealth per person

   2   Jobs and Earnings

      a   Employment rate
      b   Long-term unemployment rate

   3   Housing

      a   Number of rooms per person
      b   Dwelling with basic facilities

B QUALITY OF LIFE

   1   Health Status

      a   Life-expectancy at birth
      b   Self-reported health status

   2   Work and Life

      a   Employees working very long hours
      b   Time devoted to leisure and personal care
      c   Employment rate of women with children 6–14 years

   3   Education and Skills

      a   Educational attainment
      b   Students' cognitive skills

   4   Social Connections

      a   Contacts with others
      b   Social network support

   5   Civic Engagement and Governance

      a   Voter turn-out
      b   Consultation on rule-making

References

Anielski, Mark (2007) *The Economics of Happiness: Building Genuine Wealth*, Gabriola Island: New Society Publishers.

Carbon Tracker (2021) *Beyond Petrostates: The Burning Need to Cut Oil Dependence in the Energy Transition*, February.

Carson, Richard T. et al. (1997) "The relationship between air pollution emissions and income: US data," *Environment and Development Economics*, 2, pp. 433–450.

Centre for Bhutan Studies & GNH (2015) 2015 GNH Survey Report.

Collier, Paul (2007) *The Bottom Billion. Why the Poorest Countries Are Failing and What Can be Done About It*, Oxford: Oxford University Press.

Collins, Daryl et al. (2009) *Portfolios of the Poor. How the World's Poor Live No $2 a Day*, Princeton: Princeton University Press.

Daly, Herman and John Cobb (1994) *For the Common Good*, Boston: Beacon Press.

Daly, Herman and John Cobb (2002) "For the common good," in Peter N. Nemetz (ed.) *Bringing Business on Board: Sustainable Development and the B-School Curriculum*, Vancouver: JBA Press, pp. 65–86.

Diener, Ed, John F. Helliwell and Daniel Kahneman (eds.) (2010) *International Differences in Well-Being*, Oxford: Oxford University Press.

Diffenbaugh, Noah S. and Marshall Burke (2019) "Global warming has increased global economic inequality," *PNAS*, May 14.

Di Tella, Rafael and Robert MacCulloch (2010) "Happiness adaptation to income beyond 'basic needs'," in Ed Diener, John F. Helliwell and Daniel Kahneman (eds.) *International Differences in Well-Being*, Oxford: Oxford University Press, pp. 217–246.

Ehrenreich, Barbara (2011) *Nickle and Dimed: On (Not) Getting by in America*, New York: Henry Holt and Company.

Forbes (2020) "Top 1% of U.S. households hold 15 times more wealth than bottom 50% combined," October 8.

Ford, Henry (1926) *Today and Tomorrow: Timeless Wisdom for a Modern Digital Age*, Vintage, reprinted in 2018 by Generosity Press, Washington State.

Fox, Mari-Jane V. and Jon D. Erickson (2018) "Genuine economic progress in the United States: A fifty state study and comparative assessment," *Ecological Economics*, 147, pp. 29–35.

Fox, Mari-Jane V. and Jon D. Erickson (2020) "Design and meaning of the genuine economic progress indicator: A statistical analysis of the U.S. fifty-state model," *Ecological Economics*, J167, p. 106441.

Garrett, Laurie (1994) *The Coming Plague: Newly Emerging Diseases in a World Out of Balance*, New York: Farrar, Straus and Giroux.

Garrett, Laurie (2000) *Betrayal of Trust: The Collapse of Global Public Health*, New York: Hyperion.

Graham, Carol (2009) *Happiness Around the World: The Paradox of Happy Peasants and Miserable Millionaires*, Oxford: Oxford University Press.

Hajat, Anjum et al. (2015) "Socioeconomic disparities and air pollution exposure: A global review," *Current Environmental Health Reports*, 2, December, pp. 440–450.

Helliwell, John F., Richard Layard and Jeffrey Sachs (2012–2020) *World Happiness Report*. The Earth Institute, Columbia University, CIFAR, Centre for Economic Performance, New York.

Ingelhart, Ronald F. (2004) *Human Beliefs and Values*, Mexico: Siglo Veintiuno Editores.

Ingelhart, Ronald F. (2010) "Faith and freedom: Traditional and modern ways to happiness," in Ed Diener, John F. Helliwell and Daniel Kahneman (eds.) *International Differences in Well-Being*, Oxford: Oxford University Press, pp. 351–397.

Islam, Nazrul and John Winkel (2017) "Climate change and social inequality," UN Working Paper 152, October.

Kennedy, Robert F. (1968) "Remarks at the university of Kansas," University of Kansas Library, March 18.

Kenny, Charles (2011) *Getting Better: Why Global Development Is Succeeding: And How We Can Improve the World Even More*, New York: Basic Books.

Kubiszewski, Ida et al. (2013) "Beyond GDP: Measuring and achieving global genuine progress," *Ecological Economics*, 93, pp. 57–68.

Layard, Richard (2006) *Happiness: Lessons from a New Science*, New York: Penguin.

Maass, Peter (2009) *Crude World: The Violent Twilight of Oil*, New York: Alfred A. Knopf.

Margonelli, Lisa (2007) *Oil on the Brian, Adventures from the Pump to the Pipeline*, New York: Doubleday.

Muller, Nicholas Z. et al. (2018) "The distribution of income is worse than you think: including pollution impacts into measures of income inequality," *PLOS One*, March 21, pp. 1–15.

New York Times (1995) "The wealth of nations: A 'greener' approach turns list upside down," September 19.

New York Times (2005) "A new measure of well-being from a happy little Kingdom," October 4.

Organization for Economic Co-operation and Development (OECD) (2011b) *How's Life? Measuring Well-Being*, Paris: OECD, October.

Organization for Economic Co-operation and Development (OECD) (2011a) *Compendium of OECD Well-Being Indicators*, Paris: OECD, May.

Oxfam (2015) "Extreme carbon inequality," December 2.

Piketty, Thomas (2014) *Capital in the Twenty-First Century*, Cambridge, MA: Bellknap Press of Harvard University Press.

Pillarisetti, J. Ram (2005) "The World Bank's 'genuine savings' measure and sustainability," *Ecological Economics*, 55, pp. 599–609.

Putnam, Robert D. (2000 and 2020) *Bowling Alone: The Collapse and Revival of American Community*, New York: Simon & Schuster.

Redefining Progress (n.d.) newspaper advertisement, Oakland, CA.

Repetto, Robert (1989) *Wasting Assets: Natural Resources in the National Income Accounts*, Washington, DC: World Resources Institute.

Resolution Foundation (2020) "The UK's wealth distribution and characteristics of high-wealth households," December.

Saez, Emmanuel and Gabriel Zucman (2014) "Wealth inequality in the United States since 1913: Evidence from capitalized income tax data," NBER Working Paper 20625, October.

Serageldin, Ismail (1995) *Sustainability and Wealth of Nations: First Steps in an Ongoing Journey*, World Bank, Third Annual World Bank Conference on Environmentally Sustainable Development, September 30, Washington, DC.

Shell, Ellen (2009) *Cheap: The High Cost of Discount Culture*, New York: Penguin Press.

Smith, Tom W. (2011) "Trends in well-being, 1972–2010," National Opinion Research Center, University of Chicago, March.

Smith, Tom W. et al. (2015) *Trends in Psychological Well-Being, 1972–2014*, General Social Survey Final Report, NORC, University of Chicago.

Statistics Canada (2003) *Building on Our Competencies: Canadian Results of the International Adult Literacy and Skills Survey*, Ottawa.

Stiglitz, Joseph E. (2013) *The Price of Inequality, How Today's Divided Society Endangers Our Future*, New York: W.W. Norton.

Stiglitz, Joseph E., Amaryta Sen and Jean-Paul Fitoussi (2009) *Report by the Commission on the Measurement of Economic Performance and Social Progress.* Published as *Mis-Measuring Our Lives: Why GDP Doesn't Add Up*, 2010, The New Press, New York.

Talberth, John and Michael Weisdorf (2017) "Genuine Progress Indicator 2.0: Pilot accounts for the US, Maryland, and city of Baltimore 2012–2014," *Ecological Economics*, 142, pp. 1–11.

Talberth, John et al. (2006) *The Genuine Progress Indicator 2006: A Tool for Sustainable Development*, Oakland: Redefining Progress.

Twenge, Jean M. et al. (2015) "More happiness for young people and less for mature adults: Time period differences in subjective well-being in the United States, 1972–2014," *Social Psychological and Personality Science*, 7(2), pp. 131–141.

UN (2020a) *The Sustainable Development Goals Report 2020.*

UN (2020b) "Sustainable Development Goals," *Press Release.*

United Nations Development Programme (UNDP) (2019) *Human Development Report.*

Ura, Karma, Sbna Alkire and Tshoki Zangmo (2012) "Case study" Bhutan: Gross national happiness and the GNH Index," in John F. Helliwell et al. (eds.) *World Happiness Report*, New York: The Earth Institute, Columbia University, CIFAR, Centre for Economic Performance.

US (2018) *Fourth National Climate Assessment.*

US Department of Education (DoE) National Center for Education Statistics (NCES) National Assessment of Adult Literacy (NAAL) (2005) "A first look at the literacy of America's adults in the 21st century."

US Federal Reserve Bank of St. Louis (2019) "What wealth inequality in America looks like: Key facts & figures," Open Vault Blog.

World Bank (2006) *Where Is the Wealth of Nations?* Washington, DC: World Bank.

World Bank (2011) *The Changing Wealth of Nations*, Washington, DC: World Bank.

World Bank (2012) "World Bank sees progress against extreme poverty but flags vulnerabilities," *Press Release*, February 29.

World Bank (2020) LAC equity lab: Income inequality: Income distribution.

5 An overview of environmental economics

The subdiscipline of environmental economics emerged in the 1960s in the wake of the publication of Rachel Carson's *Silent Spring* and the increased awareness of environmental issues among the general public, media and government. Much of conventional economic thinking concerning environmental degradation focuses on the general concept of "market failure," as expressed in several interrelated issues: externalities, public goods, property rights and issues of common property and open access resources. Although some of these concepts had been in currency for some time (for example, the English economist Arthur Pigou (1920) discussed the concept of externalities, although he did not cast his analysis in terms of environmental degradation), they became central pillars of the new discipline. Despite the new focus on the environment, the subdiscipline was the intellectual child of neo-classical economics and, as such, relied on many of the theoretical constructs of this traditional economic analysis.

Externalities are usually defined as unintentional side-effects of production and consumption that affect a third party either positively or negatively. The key point is that these effects are not reflected in the price of the good – i.e. they do not enter into market transactions. Good examples of positive externalities include clean air and water and beautiful private gardens; by contrast, negative externalities include polluted air and water and poorly maintained private residential yards, etc. Because of the existence of externalities, the marginal private cost (MPC) of an activity does not equal its marginal social cost (MSC). MPC is the cost born by the producer; MSC is the cost borne by society. When MPC does not equal MSC, goods or activities with negative externalities are underpriced (since the MPC is artificially lower than the MSC) and overproduced, and goods or activities with positive externalities are overpriced and underproduced. The distinction between private and social cost is illustrated in Figure 5.1. Individuals and corporations respond to private costs as they are the direct, visible costs which affect their personal or business decisions. Social cost, in contrast, includes *all costs* associated with the production of a good or service (including externalities) and, as such, is of relevance to government policy, which must address the total costs faced by society. In fact, externalities should be of concern to corporations and individual citizens, as well, since their decisions generate much of the costs. To personalize the concept, one need only ask the question: why should I pay (or incur an additional cost) because someone else has produced or purchased a product or service which may be of little or no interest to me? The fact that these additional costs often indirectly impact such things as personal health, peace of mind and longevity serves to underscore the importance of externalities.

DOI: 10.4324/9781003170730-5

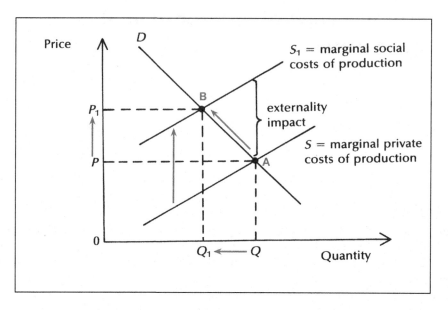

Figure 5.1 Social cost vs. private cost

The majority of environmental goods fall into a category in which market values are not available. These goods – termed *public goods* – generally have two key characteristics: *non-exclusion*, meaning that one person could not prevent (i.e. "exclude") another from consuming the resource, and *joint consumption,* meaning that when a good is consumed by one person, it does not diminish the amount consumed by another person. For example, in theory, one person's consumption of clean air does not diminish any other person's consumption. With non-exclusion and joint consumption, it is never in the interest of a private, profit-maximizing enterprise to produce such a good because the enterprise could not reap the economic rewards of doing so. Consumers would "free ride." Parenthetically, it could be argued that some environmental goods are only quasi-public goods in the sense that consumption by one individual or corporation (of clean river water, for example) may indeed diminish the amount available for others.

Finally, common property resources are those owned by no one and hence overconsumed. The classic elaboration of this theory was provided by Garret Hardin (1968) in a seminal article entitled "The Tragedy of the Commons," which appeared in the prestigious journal *Science*. In this article, Hardin based his assessment on the classic problem faced by English farmers who had unlimited access to the commons to graze their cattle. When farmers took advantage of this opportunity, the inevitable result was overgrazing, which impoverished them all. It was Hardin's conclusion that this problem could be solved by the creation of property rights to the commons and the assignment of these rights to a single individual who would have an economic incentive to maintain restricted access, thereby guaranteeing indefinite productivity. This model has been used to explain the continuing overexploitation of global fisheries resources. Since the date of its original exposition, however, this theory has been subject to increased scrutiny and criticism.

It is important to note that there are at least two major conceptual problems with Hardin's original formulation. First, Hardin was essentially referring to *open access resources* as opposed to *commons*. The inability to control access to a resource may or may not be characteristic of any one common property resource. In many parts of the third world, communities have had, or currently have, common property resources which have elaborate institutional mechanisms for preventing excess use and degradation. Examples include former social networks called "water temples" for the coordination of water use in rice fields in Bali, alpine pastures in Switzerland, irrigated rice fields in northern Philippines (*Zanjera*), historical commons-based irrigation systems in Spain (*Huerta*), some local areas in Africa and Southeast Asia and some local fisheries in the South Pacific (Dietz et al. 2003 supplementary material). Unfortunately, many of these functioning commons have been destroyed because of several factors, including increasing population pressure, increasing commercialization of resources resulting from globalization of markets and the increasing intrusion of remote central government into local forms of government and their traditional means of resource control (even in those circumstances where the intentions are good).

The late Nobel laureate Elinor Ostrom and colleagues outlined the criteria for successful management of commons (Ostrom et al. 2002; Dietz et al. 2003):

> (i) the resources and use of the resources by humans can be monitored, and the information can be verified and understood at relatively low cost; (ii) rates of change in resources, resource-user populations, technology, and economic and social conditions are moderate; (iii) communities maintain frequent face-to-face communication and dense social networks – sometimes called social capital – that increase the potential for trust, allow people to express and see emotional reactions to distrust, and lower the cost of monitoring behavior and inducing rule compliance; (iv) outsiders can be excluded at relatively low cost from using the resource (new entrants add to the harvesting pressure and typically lack understanding of the rules); and (v) users support effective monitoring and rule enforcement.
>
> (Dietz et al. 2003, p. 8)

The authors, however, recognize that there are few locations in the world that meet all these conditions. Nevertheless, when a constellation of these factors is present, commons management generally can act to control and preserve resources.

The second main critique of Hardin is that single ownership of the resource base is no guarantee that the resources will avoid being degraded or exhausted. For example, if the owner's personal discount rate is higher than the rate of renewal of the resource, it is economically rational (and profit maximizing) for the owner to deplete the resource, take these earnings and invest them elsewhere (Clark 1973, 1990; Clark and Munro 1978, 1979). Examples abound of entrepreneurs engaging in "high-grading," where they skim off the best of the resource (or deplete most of it) and then abandon the business, taking their profits. This particularly was the case in the early history of commercial forestry. This is the reason for the very strict forestry requirements on how much can be harvested and how much must be replanted each year in North American and most European jurisdictions.

As governments began to respond to perceived environmental threats in the late 1960s, the most common regulatory approach adopted was what has been referred to as "command and control" (CAC). Under this approach, regulatory agencies frequently instruct a company (specifically a production operation such as a mill, smelter, mine, etc.) not to exceed a specific level of pollutant output for each source of air and water pollution, such as a stack or other in-plant source of emissions. There are several broad sources of economic inefficiency in this approach: first, CAC requires the regulator to spend resources to acquire information about control technology and levels of pollution that corporations already possess; second, industrial operations vary in the ease (i.e. cost) with which they can abate pollution, and imposing one standard on all is economically inefficient; third, the polluter has no incentive to do better than the standard; and fourth, if the regulations are based on rates of product or effluent output, there is no precise control over total emissions. For example, industrial plants could increase the level of production and concomitant pollution discharges while remaining within the law by meeting standards based on amount of pollutant per unit of output. This is clearly not in keeping with the intent of the original legislation and accompanying regulations which sought to control the environmental impact of industrial operations.

There is one additional problem associated with command-and-control regulation with its concomitant structure of legal sanctions, usually fines. In some circumstances, firms may view the regulations as licenses to pollute, with the monetary fine representing the de facto cost of the license. This "cost of doing business" interpretation can be particularly problematic when the amount of the fine is considerably less than the cost of pollutant reduction or avoidance. The problem is compounded by the fact that the probability of being caught is invariably less than 1.0 in any given period, thereby encouraging some firms to adopt a strategy of non-compliance because of the significantly lower expected value of the ultimate financial penalty.

One early solution to the problem of the inefficiency of CAC was the adoption of *performance standards* for some large industrial complexes. Under this approach, often called a bubble regulation (see Figure 5.2), the government may set a limit on the total amount of a particular air pollutant emanating from the complex and let the company achieve that target with the least-cost mix of alternative measures within the complex itself. It is important to note that air emissions can come from point sources (such as stacks), area sources (such as ponds) or fugitive sources (such as pipe leaks and loose fittings). Pollution abatement options may include process changes, changes in the mix of inputs, improvements in "end-of-pipe" control or any combination thereof.

This approach has been somewhat controversial. For example, the United States Environmental Protection Agency (US EPA) sued the Texas air pollution authority in 2010 to discontinue the practice (*New York Times* June 11, 2010); however, the concept remains sound. For example, the current use of a cap-and-trade system for the control of sulfur dioxide emissions in the US (see Appendix 5.1) can be considered a meta-bubble approach with two modifications: (1) the bubble is large enough to encompass a geographic region or the entire country, and (2) the method of achieving the desired performance standard is through the use of marketed permits since *interfirm* coordination is required as opposed to *intrafirm* optimization in the original one-plant bubble.

One of the first major shifts from command and control toward economic incentives for environmental control was undertaken by the OECD in 1972 under the general rubric of the *polluter pays principle* (PPP). The basic tenet of this policy was that the price of the good or service produced should fully reflect its total social cost of production, including the cost of all the resources used. In other words, this principle attempts to make polluters "internalize" their externalities so they and their consumers are ultimately guided by the social cost rather than the private cost of production. There are several important aspects

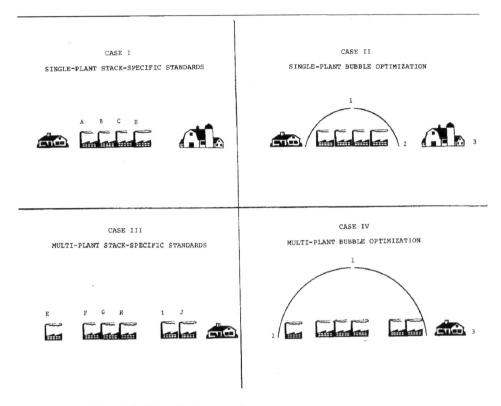

Figure 5.2 Bubble model of air pollution control

of this principle. First, as in all economic decisions, the rational (and efficient) producer is expected to equate marginal costs and marginal revenues (MC = MR), which can also be more generally stated as MC = MB (marginal costs equal marginal benefits). In this case, the scope is widened to consider marginal social costs and benefits rather than marginal private costs and benefits. The rule therefore becomes MSC = MSB.

Second, because of the nature of the marginal cost and benefit curves, it will rarely be socially optimal to reduce pollution by 100% (i.e. to have zero levels of pollution). And, third, the name of the concept is somewhat misleading, as the cost of pollution does not fall exclusively on the producer; instead, the distribution of additional cost will be split between the producer and the consumer depending on the slope of the demand curve faced by the producer. This principle is illustrated in Figure 5.3, which describes the allocation of the tax burden. Two examples illustrate this varying distributional impact. Figure 5.4a represents the case of gasoline, while Figure 5.4b portrays the case for laundry detergent. The underlying variable which determines the ultimate distribution of de facto tax liability is the elasticity of demand for the product itself. [fn 1] Gasoline consumption is considered to be relatively insensitive to price changes in the short term since most motorists have few options they can pursue short of investing in a new, more fuel-efficient automobile. Interestingly enough, recent experience in the US with respect to motorists' response to rising gas prices has suggested there may be more flexibility than previously measured. US motorists have been able to reduce their leisure driving, increase their use of

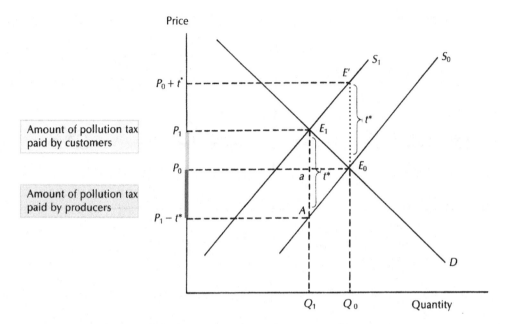

Figure 5.3 Who pays for a pollution tax?

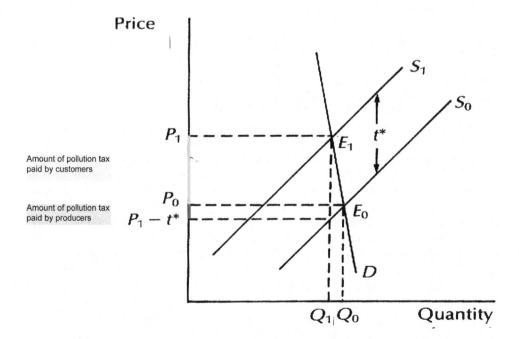

Figure 5.4a Inelastic demand for gasoline

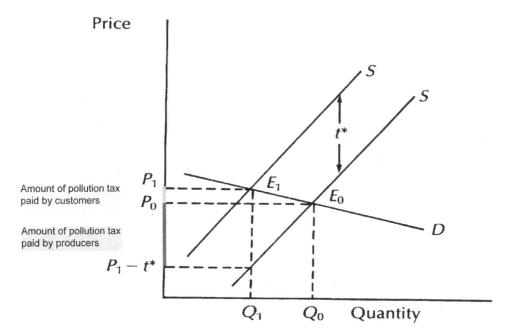

Figure 5.4b Elastic demand for detergent

carpooling and switch, where possible, to alternative modes of transport, including buses and other forms of mass transit (*New York Times* May 17, 2011). However, the general principle remains the same: there are some commodities for which there are few substitutes in the short term, and, as a consequence, the seller has a better ability to pass along the ultimate incidence of the tax increase. In contrast, in the case of laundry detergent, two factors limit the ability of the manufacturer to pass along the tax: the existence of alternative detergent brands which may vary in their pollution impact and other non-detergent alternatives such as soap.

There are a myriad of economic incentives for pollution control already in place in Europe, and a United Nations Environment Programme report (2007) provided a comprehensive summary. Tables 5.1 and 5.2 are drawn from this report and provide a classification of environmental policy instruments as well as examples of their use in practice. (See also OECD 2010b.) With so many options available, a critical issue is determining selection criteria for the choice of appropriate policy instruments. When one moves from the world of economic theory to the world of practical use, it is necessary to consider an array of criteria in choosing economic instruments for pollution control. In the "real world," governments consider not only economic efficiency but also important variables such as information requirements, administrative feasibility and costs, distributional equity (such as the effect on different income groups or regions), dependability, adaptability, dynamic incentives for continuous improvement, political acceptability and predictability.

Economic incentives in the area of environmental control are generally of four types: effluent charges, marketable permits, miscellaneous charges (such as user charges, product

Table 5.1 Classification of environmental policy instruments

Command-and-control regulations	Direct provision by governments	Engaging the public and private sectors	Using markets	Creating markets
Standards	Environmental infrastructure	Public participation	Remove perverse subsidies	Property rights
Bans	Eco-industrial zones or parks	Decentralization	Environmental taxes and charges	Tradeable permits and rights
Permits and quotas	National parks, protected areas and recreation facilities	Information disclosure	User charges	Offset programs
Zoning	Ecosystem rehabilitation	Eco-labeling	Deposit-refund systems	Green procurement
Liability		Voluntary agreements	Targeted subsidies	Environmental investment funds
Legal redress		Public-private partnerships	Self-monitoring (such as ISO 14000)	Seed funds and incentives
Flexible regulations				Payment for ecosystem services

charges and administrative charges) and subsidies. From an economic perspective, the two most important are emissions fees or taxes (called effluent charges when applied to liquid waste) and marketable emission permits (generally, but not exclusively, used in the context of air pollution). Jaccard (2005) summarizes some of the trade-offs among the major policies, and Table 5.3 expands upon this analysis by scoring the alternatives by criteria on a three-part scale. Emission fees, marketable permits and information dissemination with voluntary response are discussed in the following.

Emission fees

Derived conceptually from the work of Pigou, such fees or taxes are usually of the form: $x per pound or ton of the target pollutant. At least four principle advantages of this instrument have been expressed in the academic literature:

1   By forcing the polluter to internalize his/her externalities, this system will drive the level of pollution to its social optimum.
2   Many advocates of this tax instrument claim that since these taxes would be administered via the government's existing tax framework, there is a lower risk of evasion compared to fixed emissions standards, which are policed via irregular on-site inspections.
3   Pollution taxes always provide an incentive for further reductions in emissions, as reducing the amount of emissions means a reduction in the amount of taxes.
4   Because of #3, firms have an added incentive to devote funds to research and development for new pollution abatement technology.

Table 5.2 Economic instruments and applications

	Property rights	Market creation	Fiscal instruments	Charge systems	Financial instruments	Liability systems	Bonds and deposits
Forests	Communal rights	Concession building	Taxes and royalties		Reforestation incentives	Natural resource liability	Reforestation bonds; forest management bonds
Water resources	Water rights	Water shares	Capital gains tax	Water pricing; water protection charge			
Oceans and seas		Fishing rights; individual quotas; licensing					Oil spill bonds
Minerals	Mineral rights		Taxes and royalties				Local reclamation bonds
Wildlife		Access fees				Natural resource liability	
Biodiversity	Patents; prospecting rights	Tradeable development rights		Charges for scientific tourism		Natural resource liability	
Water pollution		Tradeable effluent permits	Effluent charges	Water treatment fees	Low-interest loans		
Land and soils	Land rights; use rights		Property taxes; land use taxes		Soil conservation incentives (such as loans)		Local reclamation bonds
Air pollution		Tradeable emission permits	Emission charges	Technology subsidies; low-interest loans			
Hazardous waste				Collection charges			Deposit-refund systems
Solid waste			Property taxes	Technology subsidies; low-interest loans			

(Continued)

Table 5.2 (Continued)

	Property rights	Market creation	Fiscal instruments	Charge systems	Financial instruments	Liability systems	Bonds and deposits
Toxic chemicals			Differential taxation			Legal liability; liability insurance	Deposit refund
Climate	Tradeable emission entitlements; tradeable forest protection obligations	Tradeable CO$_2$ permits; tradeable chlorofluorocarbon (CFC) quotas; CFC quota auction; carbon offsets	Carbon taxes; British Thermal Units tax		CFC replacement incentives; forest compacts		
Human settlements	Land rights	Access fees; tradeable development quotas; tradeable development rights	Property taxes; land use taxes	Betterment charges; development charges; land use charges; road tolls; import fees			Development completion bonds

Table 5.3 Some trade-offs among policy instruments for pollution control

	Command and control	Effluent charges or taxes	Marketable permits	Information and voluntary response	Subsidies
Effectiveness	Good	Medium	Medium-good (depending on design)	Poor	Medium
Efficiency	Poor	Good	Good	Poor	Poor
Administrative feasibility	Good	Good	Medium-good	Good	Medium
Political acceptability	Medium	Poor	Medium	Good	Medium-good [b]
Information requirements	Medium	Medium	Good	Good	Poor
Distributional equity (esp. regressivity)	n/a	Potentially poor [a]	Potentially poor [a]	n/a	n/a
Dependability	Good	Medium	Medium-good [b]	Poor	Poor
Adaptability	Good, in theory	Good	Good	Good	Poor
Predictability (of results)	Good	Medium	Medium-good [b]	Poor	Poor
Dynamic incentives for continuous improvements	Poor	Good	Good	Medium	Poor

Notes:
[a] depending on the nature of the price change in final goods
[b] depending on design

Despite the potential efficiency gains inherent in this type of regulatory instrument, there are certain problems and complexities in its real-world implementation. First, the assertion that the risk of evasion would be lower (and that monitoring costs would also be lower) with emission fees is false. The government must continue to monitor at the same (or greater) frequency as before in order to determine the quantity of pollutant to be taxed.

Second, it is extremely difficult to set the optimal level of tax because of the uncertainty surrounding the actual damage costs associated with any particular pollutant. Therefore, the government requires data on the following: (1) the firm's output of goods, (2) the pollution this output produces, (3) any long-term accumulation of pollution, (4) human exposure to this pollution, (5) the damage response function of this exposure, and (6) the monetary evaluation of the cost of pollution damage. Third, price changes in the product as a result of pollution charges will probably be regressive – i.e. with a bigger relative impact on people with a lower income. Fourth, a pollution tax is less likely to be effective where demand for the final product is inelastic (i.e. unresponsive) to price changes and/ or there are few suitable substitutes available. (See Figures 5.4a and 5.4b.) And, fifth, countries which unilaterally impose such taxes may face a competitive disadvantage in international trade, losing out to "pollution havens." However, evidence suggests that this last point may be less of a problem than first anticipated (Mani and Wheeler 1997). Despite these complexities, emission fees or taxes remain a powerful and widely used weapon in the armory of governments seeking to find an efficient method of pollution abatement.

Marketable permits

The second major economic incentive is marketable pollution permits, of which an important variant is called *cap and trade*. The basic principle is enticingly simple: an acceptable level of pollution is determined for a geographic region, permits are then issued for the level of emissions (i.e. up to the allowable level according to some procedure deemed equitable) and the holders of such permits (as potential sellers) and other polluters (as potential buyers) are encouraged to form a market and trade these permits.

The emergence of this policy tool can be credited to the theoretical work of Ronald Coase and John Dales. Coase's work (1960) was the first to articulate the critical role that property rights could play in environmental and resource-based issues. The Coase theorem states that the problem of pollution externalities could be directly addressed through the simple allocation of property rights to *either* the generator or the victim of pollution. Regardless of the allocation of these rights, either one of the parties would have an incentive to seek an agreement between the two that would invariably lead to an efficient economic solution. For example, in the case of a pulp mill upstream of a fishing ground, if the mill had the rights to pollute, a fisherman who suffered the effects of this pollution would have the incentive to pay the polluter to reduce this pollution to the point where the marginal cost to the fisherman equaled his/her marginal benefit from pollution reduction. Conversely, if the fisherman had the right to clean water, the pulp mill would have the incentive to pay the fisherman to accept the pollution. In practice, however, there are several real-world barriers to the achievement of this result. To quote Coase himself:

> The assumption [is] that there were no costs involved in carrying out market transactions. This is, of course, a very unrealistic assumption. In order to carry out a market transaction it is necessary to discover who it is that one wishes to deal with, to inform people that one wishes to deal and on what terms, to conduct negotiations leading up to a bargain, to draw up the contract, to undertake the inspection needed to make sure that the terms of the contract are being observed, and so on. These operations are often extremely costly, sufficiently costly at any rate to prevent many transactions that would be carried out in a world in which the pricing system worked without cost.
>
> (1960, p. 15)

In other words, the achievement of this economically efficient result could be stymied by a range of transaction costs associate with the number of individuals involved, their relative bargaining strength, asymmetric information, etc. Despite the barriers to the application of this theorem, Coase's seminal contribution relating to property rights and resources, where such resources include clean air and clean water, established a conceptual framework which underpins much of modern environmental economics. It led to the concept of transferable property-like rights which could be extended to the area of environmental control, and Dales (1968) advanced this theory by suggesting it could be operationalized by creating a market for such rights in the form of pollutant permits.

The underlying economic rationale for marketable permits is based on the premise that there is an incentive to *sell* permits if a firm's marginal abatement costs are below the ruling price for permits, *and* there is an incentive to *buy* permits if a firm's marginal abatement

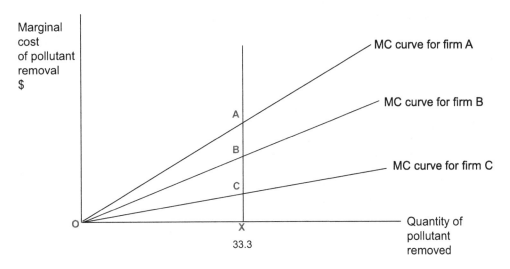

Figure 5.5 Traditional command-and-control regulation

costs are above the price of the permits. As a result of this market trading, the control of pollution will tend to be concentrated among those polluters who find it cheapest to control pollution, and permit holding will tend to be concentrated among those who find it expensive to control pollution. Therefore, system wide, society will have achieved the most efficient, least cost solution for any desired target level of pollution. Figures 5.5 and 5.6 schematically portray the economic benefits of this type of approach. (Note that the marginal cost curves for pollution removal in this diagram are assumed to be linear for simplicity. In reality, the nature of pollution control technology and economics usually implies non-linearity, with MC (marginal cost) rising exponentially as the percentage of pollutant removal approaches 100%.) In this simplified example, the social goal is to remove 100 tons of pollutant from an economy assumed to be composed of three equally sized industrial plants, each with different marginal costs of pollutant removal. These differences may stem from differences in currently installed pollution control capacity, different product mix or different technology. The traditional approach of command and control is represented in Figure 5.5 – a universal standard requiring each firm to remove an equal amount of pollution. The total cost is the summation of the integrals under the three marginal cost curves, here equal to the areas of the triangles AXO + BXO + CXO. Note the radically different marginal pollutant removal costs across the three firms.

In contrast, Figure 5.6 portrays the alternate approach using an economic instrument. All firms face the same effluent price (P) per unit of pollutant. They reduce their pollutant output up to the point where their marginal cost of pollutant removal equals the market-based effluent price. Why is this so? If their marginal cost were higher than the price, they would rather pay the price at the margin, whereas if the marginal cost were lower than the price, they would sooner reduce the amount of pollutant at the margin. Note that $Aq + Bq + Cq = 100$ tons and that $Aq < Bq < Cq$ (in other words, the firm with the lowest marginal cost of pollutant removal removes the most pollutant and vice versa). It can be shown by simple geometric or algebraic methods that the economic

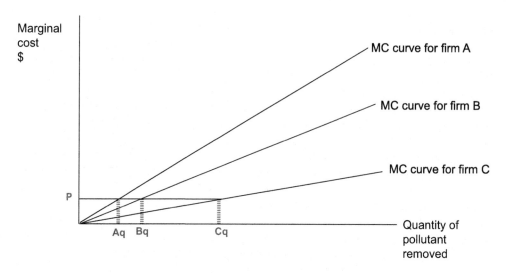

Figure 5.6 Pollution control with an economic instrument

incentive approach achieves the same total level of reduction at significantly lower total cost simply because the incentive approach encourages economically efficient decisions by each firm and, consequently, across the entire economy. Appendix 5.1 presents a case study of perhaps the most successful application of marketable permits – the US system of sulfur dioxide trading.

It is important to remember that a marketable pollutant system is not universally applicable and relies on certain characteristics for successful operation. First, there must be a large enough number of industrial plants to act as traders in order to establish a smoothly functioning market for permits. Equally important, however, are certain critical characteristics of the pollutant to be traded that can make or break a market. In his exhaustive study of the theory and practice of emissions trading, Tietenberg (2006) distinguishes among three categories of pollutants: (1) uniformly mixed assimilative pollutants, (2) non-uniformly mixed assimilative pollutants and (3) uniformly mixed accumulative pollutants.

Uniformly mixed assimilative pollutants

This class of pollutants includes greenhouse- and ozone-destroying chemicals. Because they act globally, it does not matter where they are emitted. This spatial equivalence or independence means that the simple conceptual model described prior for the efficient allocation of responsibility for abatement is appropriate where the marginal costs of control are equalized across all emitters.

Non-uniformly mixed assimilative pollutants

The simple theoretical model of market-based trading becomes considerably more complex when the environmental impact of pollutant is spatially dependent. Tietenberg identifies common pollutants such total suspended particulates (TSP), sulfur dioxide (SO_2)

and nitrogen oxides (NOx) as typical of this category. The spatial dependence may derive from two potentially interdependent characteristics: spatial clustering of emitters and spatial "hot spots" where high levels of pollutant may accumulate because of local meteorological or topographical features as well as characteristics of the pollutant which lead to rapid deposition. According to Tietenberg:

> For this class of pollutants, it is not the marginal costs of emissions reduction that are equalized across sources in a cost-effective allocation (as was the case for uniformly mixed assimilative pollutants); it is the marginal costs of concentration reduction at each receptor location that are equalized.
>
> (2006, p. 34)

This clearly creates a much more complex policy and market challenge, as each receptor represents its own market in which each pollutant emitter must participate.

Uniformly mixed accumulative pollutants

This classification is typified by pollutants which accumulate in the environment but where the location of discharge is not important. It is unclear how many pollutants actually satisfy this criterion, as location is critical for many of the chemicals which are accumulative, such as lead, cadmium, mercury and other heavy metals. In these cases, the present value of control costs and benefits must be incorporated into the analysis (see Tietenberg, pp. 38–40 for more details).

Real-world complexities

A number of significant empirical complexities are relevant to the design of marketable pollution permits in the presence of these diverse characteristics of pollutants and the environment into which they are emitted. First, as Tietenberg observes, despite the fact that SO_2 clearly falls into category #2, the complexity of the theoretically required policy instrument essentially reduces its applicability. As such, the US EPA has adopted approach #1, which seems to implicitly assume that SO_2 is a uniformly mixed assimilative pollutant. The regulatory agency addresses the issue of potential local hot spots through a process called "regulatory tiering" where SO_2 emissions must conform to two distinctive regulatory regimes: (1) a national cap and trade and (2) a set limit on local emissions based on ambient pollutant levels in order to prevent the occurrence of hot spots.

Second, some pollutants have both local and regional or international effects. A large percentage of sulfur dioxide emissions occur in the Ohio River valley where there are a large number of coal-fired power plants. A significant amount of this pollutant is subject to long-range transport and has been historically responsible for the acidification of soil and waterbodies in New England, upstate New York and Eastern Canada (*New York Times* October 22, 1990). Fortunately, the adoption of a cap-and-trade policy across all major emitters of sulfur dioxide in the US has had a decisive salutary impact on acidified lakes and forests in the Northeast. (See Appendix 5.1.) A similar phenomenon of local and long-range transport has been more recently identified with respect to mercury, where significant quantities of this heavy metal found in the high European Arctic have been traced to emissions in North America (Chaulk et al. 2011; Steen et al. 2010).

Third, Tietenberg's categorization misses a fourth class of pollutants which is relevant to the design and application of market-based trading regimes. This category is exemplified by pollutants (such as particulates) which are neither homogeneous nor uniformly mixed. Total suspended particulates can vary in at least two important respects: (1) size – which affects the spatial dimension of deposition and the potential for deep inhalation of smaller particles (i.e. designated particulate matter 2.5 micrometers or less in size) into the lungs, where their effects are much more deleterious; and (2) their toxicity – which varies by their source. For example, the toxicity of particulates will vary markedly if they are produced by road dust, metal smelters, chemical plants, electric power plants, coal-related or petroleum operations, motor vehicles, etc. By way of example, the US EPA lists 40 types of health effects from a broad range of pollutants listed under 9 different rubrics: crustal/soil, salt, secondary sulfate/long-range transport, traffic, oil combustion, coal combustion, other metals, woodsmoke/vegetative burning and miscellaneous unnamed factors (US EPA 2008, pp. 2-21 to 2-23). Under these circumstances, a significant problem may emerge if all these disparate types of particulates are subject to a cap-and-trade regime which assumes homogeneity in order to facilitate trading. Despite this drawback, several jurisdictions have experimented with a market for particulates expressed as total suspended particulates (Atkinson and Lewis 1974; Montero et al. 2002).

Finally, some innovative hybrid systems have emerged in several areas. One notable example is the Regional Clean Air Incentives Market (RECLAIM) program in the South Coast Air Quality Management District around Los Angeles, which established a cap-and-trade system for over 300 industrial emitters of SO_2 and NOx. One of the principal innovations adopted was the creation of two zones (one coastal and one inland) in order to avoid the creation of hot spots by onshore winds which blow pollution inland from the coast. Within the coastal zone, trades are only permitted internally; by contrast, in the inland zone, trades may occur within and across zones (RECLAIM 2007).

Table 5.4 compares these critical attributes for several pollutants: sulfur dioxide, carbon dioxide, particulates and mercury, the last of which has been proposed as a possible candidate for a marketable permit. While the market for sulfur dioxide has worked very well, and so would carbon dioxide, it should be apparent that neither particulates nor mercury satisfy the criteria required for successful operation of a market-based control system. Particulates are a poor candidate because of their heterogeneity. In contrast, while recent research has demonstrated that a significant proportion of mercury can be vaporized and transported as far as the polar regions (Chaulk et al. 2011; Steen et al. 2010), a sizeable

Table 5.4 Critical attributes of selected air pollutants

	SO_2	CO_2	PM	Hg
Large number of traders	Yes	Yes	Yes	Yes
Homogeneity	Yes	Yes	No	Yes
Non-toxic	Relatively	Yes	Yes/No	No
Favorable meteorological and topographical conditions	Site dependent	n/a	Site dependent	Site dependent
Capacity to be vaporized and/or dispersed	Yes	Yes	Yes	Partially
Ease of measurement	Yes	Yes	Yes	Yes

remainder of this extremely toxic element may remain near the initial point of emission, creating a local hot spot. A situation could develop where an industrial plant with high costs of mercury abatement could chose to purchase permits and continue emitting large quantities of this pollutant, thus exposing the local population to serious health effects.

The success of the US cap–and–trade system for control of acid rain precursors, such as sulfur dioxide, has intensified interest in the application of economic incentive systems for the control of greenhouse gases, particularly carbon dioxide. Appendix 5.2 reviews the theory and practice of the application of both marketable permits and carbon taxes to this critical greenhouse gas.

In addition to emission fees and marketable permits, one other related policy instrument has emerged as a successor to traditional forms of regulation: the mandatory dissemination of pollution emission information to the general public. While differing from fees and permits in the absence of market prices, this approach has been termed by Konar and Cohen (1997) a system of "market-based incentives." (See Appendix 5.3.)

In sum, the development of environmental economics has had a profound impact on government regulation of the environment, as economic instruments have frequently been used to complement or back out traditional regulatory systems of command and control. This does not mean, however, that CAC has no place in the modern armory of government policy. It still has a valid use in special cases where action is required immediately and/or where the pollutant is exceedingly toxic. In these cases, it is inappropriate to rely on the corporate sector to take time to weigh the relative costs and benefits of voluntarily controlling emissions or releases.

Environmental economics has provided a very important conceptual foundation and policy toolbox for addressing many of the environmental problems faced in recent decades. However, because this area is basically unidisciplinary in nature, it cannot address the broader, multidisciplinary challenges that face us today. To address these issues, a new cross-disciplinary area, known as ecological economics, has emerged in the last two decades, and it is described in Chapter 9.

Appendix 5.1
Sulfur dioxide trading in the US

With current global concern over greenhouse gas emissions and consequent global warming, significant discussion has been undertaken by policymakers, economists and market participants with respect to adopting a cap-and-trade system for carbon dioxide emissions in the United States. In fact, such a system already exists in Europe, along with a variety of carbon taxes (Barde and Braathen 2007; EEA 2011). It is critical to note that US proposals for a CO_2 trading system have been inspired by a similar model for sulfur dioxide control which has been operating successfully in the US for several decades.

Amendments to the US Clean Air Act in 1990, undertaken during the first Bush administration (Conniff 2009), sought to lower levels of acid rain by reducing SO_2 emissions by 10 million tons from 1980 levels. The first phase of SO_2 emissions reductions was achieved in 1995, with a second phase of reduction accomplished by the year 2000. In phase 1, individual emissions limits were assigned to the 263 most SO_2-intensive emission-generating units at 110 electric utility plants operated by 61 electric utilities, located largely at coal-fired power plants east of the Mississippi River. Called "cap and trade," the SO_2 allowance trading program has achieved an extraordinary degree of success. This represents a significant benefit to public health because of the reduction in airborne fine particulate matter, much of which is due to sulfates. Monetized benefits from the entire Acid Rain Program (both SO_2 and NOx) were estimated at $122 billion annually. There is a stark contrast between the benefits of the emissions reductions and the much lower cost of compliance. When the Acid Rain Program was being considered by Congress in 1989 and 1990, the estimated cost of the program ranged from $4 billion to over $7 billion per year. But four years after its enactment, an audit of the program by the non-partisan US Government Accountability Office concluded that the cost of full implementation was likely to be closer to $2 billion per year. More recent estimates have placed the cost of compliance closer to $1 billion per year. Figure 5.7 shows early estimates of the divergence between actual emissions and those expected without the program. Within 15 years, there had been a major decrease in wet sulfate deposition in large areas of the US Northeast, with a concomitant decrease in acidified lakes and rivers (Mclean 2007). Figure 5.8 shows the remarkable decreases achieved over the period 1990 to 2019 (US EPA 2020d).

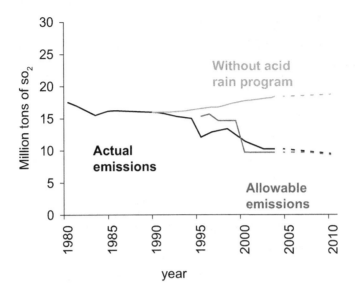

Figure 5.7 US sulfur dioxide trading system results

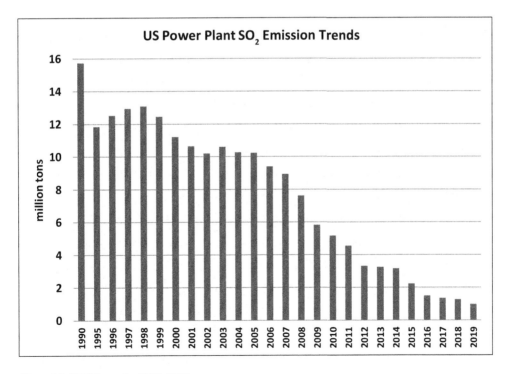

Figure 5.8 US SO$_2$ results 1990–2019

Appendix 5.2
Greenhouse gases and economic incentives

Most, if not all, economists, agree that the use of economic incentives would be the most powerful and efficient method of reducing the emissions of carbon dioxide. Table 5.5 contrasts the key elements of carbon taxes and cap-and-trade systems (Sierra Club of Canada 2008 and this author). There are trade-offs between the two, and, as such, their application must be considered in light of economic and geopolitical circumstances. A summary overview of each system in practice is presented in Table 5.5.

Table 5.5 Cap and trade vs. carbon taxes

	Carbon tax	*Cap and trade*
What is it?	Government charges polluters a set price for each ton of greenhouse gases they emit.	Government sets a legal limit on how much greenhouse gas polluters are allowed to emit (the cap). If some polluters greatly reduce their emissions and so have excess pollution permits, they can sell these to other polluters (the trade).
How does it work?	Can be applied throughout the entire economy. For industries the tax is applied based on measured emissions. For individuals the tax is applied based on carbon content of fuel purchased. Based on simple economic theory: individuals and companies will reduce their emissions-intensive behavior in order to avoid paying the tax. Can exempt certain areas of the economy from paying the tax.	Can only be applied to large industrial emissions sources (account for only 50% of Canada's GHGs). Phases of implementation: First, the government determines what the cap on emissions from industry should be. Second, the government then creates quantity of emissions permits that correspond to the cap. Third, the government then allocates these permits to industry, either free-of-charge or by auction. Fourth, companies are then able to trade permits among themselves. Each industry must ensure that it holds a sufficient number of permits for the emissions it releases. Companies that reduce their emissions can sell their additional permits on the market, while those that fail to reduce emissions must buy permits. Fifth, the government then ratchets the cap down each year, so long-term emissions reduction targets are met.

(Continued)

Table 5.5 (Continued)

	Carbon tax	Cap and trade
Price of carbon	The government directly sets the price on carbon. Price on carbon must be at least $30/ton by 2008–2010, $50/ton by 2015 and $75/ton by 2020 in order to sufficiently reduce emissions.	The government does not directly set the price on carbon (government sets cap and lets market determine price); however, government can ensure price remains high by keeping cap low and allocating permits by auction. Government should allocate all the permits by auction as soon as possible. Doing otherwise is counter to the polluter pays principle.
Certainty of emissions reductions	Provides less certainty as to level of emissions that will be reduced (government sets price and lets market determine cap); however, carbon tax will also inevitably cap emissions as long as government is willing to adjust tax until desired reduction occurs (government must outline by how much more the tax will increase if it looks as though the current price schedule will not achieve the desired targets).	Provides more certainty as to level of emissions that will be reduced; however, this is only for emissions from industry and will only be achieved if: (1) there is no price cap (or safety valve) where industry can buy permit from government for guaranteed price and (2) there are harsh penalties for those who do not comply with the system.
Economic incentives	Provides clearer economic signals. Government must lay out schedule of intended future levels of carbon tax, so that industry/investors will plan multi-billion-dollar, multi-decade investments accordingly; new, long-term infrastructure will be designed with the lowest emissions level possible as investors make decisions based on future price.	Provides less clear economic signals, as price of carbon is relatively unpredictable and will vary according to market conditions. Creates bias toward short-term solutions: if unsure that price of carbon will be much higher in future, then industry will be discouraged from making long-term investments into new green technology and infrastructure.
Administrative ease and cost	Less administratively costly and complex. Easier and faster for governments to implement. Governments have more experience with tax systems and can rely on existing structures for taxing fuels. Far more transparent and straightforward.	More costly and complex – requires negotiation between government and industry and setting up permit trading market. More potential for corruption and manipulation Will take two to three years to set up if it is designed properly.
Carbon offsets		Give industry more flexibility in how it meets cap. May give wrong type of incentive to industry, which may simply purchase cheap offsets instead of making long-term investments in new green technology. Must be accompanied with strict regulations to ensure that offset projects (1) result in a permanent and additional emissions reduction and (2) do not harm local peoples in developing countries.

Cap and trade

As described in Appendix 5.1, the United States has achieved significant reductions in sulfur dioxide emissions at minimal costs using marketable permits under a cap-and-trade policy. Europe has gone one step further and used cap and trade to address global warming by applying it to emissions of carbon dioxide. In 2005, the European Union established a carbon-trading scheme called the EU ETS (Emission Trading System) (European Commission 2009). Since its inception, some 12,000 large industrial plants in the EU have been able to buy and sell permits to release carbon dioxide into the atmosphere. There were initial problems with the EU ETS: (1) there was a free allocation of allowances driven by a desire to accommodate countries concerned about the competitiveness of their domestic industries; (2) too many allowances were handed out also due to political considerations resulting in too low a price for allowances; (3) the combination of the above two factors led to price volatility, which, in turn, created corporate uncertainly with respect to capital investments; and (4) some important sectors, such as transportation, were omitted initially.

Many of these initial difficulties have been resolved, and the program is achieving most of its goals. To quote from a recent report on the state of the EU ETS (Marcu et al. 2020, p. 1):

> In 2019 the EU ETS performance provided stakeholders reassurance that the EU ETS was now "fit for purpose" and on the right track to deliver on its main stated objectives: meeting environmental targets, deliver economic efficient decarbonization and provide good price discovery. EUA [European Unit Allowance] prices had stabilized at a level that provided a signal for decarbonization in certain areas. On the environmental side, preliminary 2019 data show that emissions from stationary sources decreased sharply, by 8.9%. This was the largest drop seen since 2009. This decrease can be attributed to a large amount of fuel switching due to a higher carbon price combined with historically low gas prices; a continuation of renewable penetration in the EU power mix; good conditions for renewables; and 2019 being a relatively 'warm' year. One important indicator of success in decarbonization, carbon intensity, showed mixed results. Data seems to indicate that the carbon intensity of sectors like glass, metals, refining, and paper & pulp are slowly decreasing, contrary to others for which the trend over Phase 3 remains largely flat. An economically efficient decarbonization should be driven by EU ETS prices. In 2019, EUAs prices were constantly above the medium-efficiency coal-to-gas switching price, and for part of the year the EUA price was even higher than the high-efficiency coal-to-gas switching price. The ERCST Market Sentiment Survey also showed an increase in confidence that the EU ETS is providing a stable and predictable framework for an investment signal.

The 2020 COVID-19 pandemic has injected significant uncertainty into the EU ETS, which cannot be resolved until the pandemic is controlled. However, at least two other important issues are in the process of resolution. First, in order to broaden the coverage of the ETS, air transport was incorporated in 2012. However, due to pushback from countries outside the EU which had flights into and out of the EU, the EU decided "to defer to ICAO which set up its own program, CORSIA. Therefore, since 2014, the scope of EU ETS has been limited to flights within the EEA" (Marcu et al. 2020, p. 14). An extension of the EU ETS is being considered to add maritime and road transport as well as buildings. However, the report by Marcu et al. (2020, p. 36) cautions that "if internal shipping is to be included in the EU ETS, it risks creating a new international diplomatic row similar to the one we saw for international aviation."

The second critical issue concerned the allocation of allowances. To quote from an EU document entitled "Free Allocation. Climate Action" (accessed December 2020):

> Auctioning is the default method for allocating emission allowances to companies participating in the EU emissions trading system (EU ETS). However, in sectors other than power generation, the transition to auctioning has been taking place progressively. Some allowances have continued to be allocated for free until 2020 and beyond. The continuation of free allocation allows the EU to pursue ambitious emissions reduction targets while shielding internationally competing industry from carbon leakage (EU accessed December 2020). This type of leakage refers to the situation that may occur if, for reasons of costs related to climate policies, businesses were to transfer production to other countries with laxer emission constraints. This could lead to an increase in their total emissions. The risk of carbon leakage may be higher in certain energy-intensive industries. To safeguard the competitiveness of industries covered by the EU ETS, the production from sectors and sub-sectors deemed to be exposed to a significant risk of carbon leakage receives a higher share of free allowances compared to the other industrial installations. This policy will continue in phase 4 (2021–2030), but based on more stringent criteria and improved data.
>
> Over the current trading period (2013–2020), 57% of the total amount of allowances will be auctioned, while the remaining allowances are available for free allocation. At the beginning of the current trading period in 2013, manufacturing industry received 80% of its allowances for free. This proportion will decrease gradually each year to 30% in 2020. Power generators since 2013 in principle do not receive any free allowances, but have to buy them. However, some free allowances have been available to modernize the power sector in some Member States. Airlines continue to receive the large majority of their allowances for free in the period 2013–2020.

The revenue from auctions is recycled back to member states to spend on climate and energy purposes.

Carbon taxes

Explicit carbon taxation has been in existence in Europe since 1990, when Finland first introduced this type of tax. There are now 17 European countries with similar initiatives. The price per metric ton of carbon ranges from a low of 1 Euro in Ukraine and Poland to over 100 Euros in Sweden (Tax Foundation October 2020). Table 5.6 from the Tax Foundation lists the 17 countries with their tax rate per ton of carbon dioxide equivalent (CO_2e) on April 1, 2020, the share of each country's GHG emission covered and the year of implementation.

Sweden is often considered as the archetypal example of the success of a carbon tax. To quote the key findings of a report by the Tax Foundation (September 2020, p. 1):

> Implemented in 1991, Sweden's carbon tax was one of the first in the world, second only to Finland's carbon tax, which was implemented a year earlier. . . . Sweden levies

Table 5.6 European countries with carbon taxes

	Tax rate (US$)	Share of emissions covered (%)	Year of implementation
Finland	68.00	36	1990
Poland	0.10	4	1990
Norway	53.00	62	1991
Sweden	119.00	40	1991
Denmark	26.00	40	1992
Slovenia	19.00	24	1996
Estonia	2.00	3	2000
Latvia	10.00	15	2004
Liechtenstein	99.00	26	2008
Switzerland	99.00	33	2008
Iceland	30.00	29	2010
Ireland	28.00	49	2010
Ukraine	0.40	71	2011
United Kingdom	22.00	23	2013
France	49.00	35	2014
Spain	16.00	3	2014
Portugal	26.00	29	2015

the highest carbon tax rate in the world, at SEK 1,190 (US $126) per metric ton of CO_2. The tax is primarily levied on fossil fuels used for heating purposes and motor fuels. . . . Since the carbon tax was implemented 30 years ago, Sweden's carbon emissions have been declining, while there has been steady economic growth. Sweden's carbon tax revenues are significant but have been decreasing slightly over the last decade.

Due to numerous exemptions, Sweden's carbon tax covers only about 40 percent of all greenhouse gases emitted nationally. While some of the exempted industries are subject to the EU ETS (the European Union Emission Trading Scheme, which generally levies a lower carbon price), others are not subject to any type of carbon pricing. Levying a single carbon tax on all sectors would eliminate these distortions and potentially further reduce emissions.

The carbon tax is one of several environmental levies in Sweden; other levies include the energy tax, aviation tax, and vehicle tax. Sweden also participates in the EU ETS.

There is some uncertainty about an appropriate level of carbon taxes required to retard or halt the process of global warming. The International Monetary Fund (2019) suggests that a price of US$75 per ton of carbon would be necessary by 2030 to hold global temperature increases to less than 2 degrees Celsius. Another report, commissioned by a Canadian think tank, Canada's Ecofiscal Commission (2019), has concluded that that country's carbon price would have to rise to CDN$210 per tonne by 2030 in order to meet its Paris commitments if the carbon tax is the principal mechanism to achieve this goal. A more recent report has suggested a price of US$600 by 2100 (Nuccitelli 2020). In theory, the carbon tax should equal the social cost of carbon – i.e. the marginal cost of the impacts from the release of carbon (in the form of carbon dioxide, of which carbon represents 27%). However, the determination of the true social cost of carbon is a complex task, and estimates range widely: Ricke et al. (2018) have estimated the 66% confidence interval of the price to range between US$177–$805 per ton of CO_2 with a median value of US$417 per ton of CO_2 while a meta-analysis conducted by Wang et al. (2019) finds an extraordinary range of US$50–$8,752/ton of carbon (equivalent to US$13.36–$2,386.91 per ton of CO_2) with a mean value of US$200.50/ton of carbon. Since the effects of greenhouse gases released into the atmosphere can last for many years, the task of cost estimation is further complicated by the choice of discount rate. Clearly, prices at the high end of these ranges would imply dramatic changes in industrial structure that would require a package of complementary government policies designed to buffer the economic system from major disruption. However, Brown and Ahmadi (2019) have concluded that carbon taxes can have a net positive impact on employment.

It is instructive to consider the impact of economic policies such as carbon taxes and marketable permits on the economies of Europe, bearing in mind that there are numerous factors which can influence total GHG emissions in any one country, as enumerated in Chapter 3. Figure 5.9 and Table 5.7 depict the percentage changes in GHG vs. real GDP for selected European countries over the period 1990–2018. There are three categories of countries depending on the relationship between these two variables: (1) GHG increases faster than GDP, (2) GHG increases at a slower pace than GDP and (3) GHGs falls while GDP grows. The apparent absolute delinkage achieved by nations in the third group must be viewed with some circumspection in light of the complexities of interpretation outlined in Chapter 3.

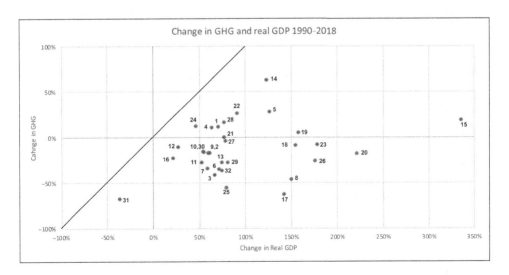

Figure 5.9 European changes in GHG and GDP 1990–2018

Table 5.7 Country codes for Figure 5.9

European country codes for Figure 5.9

1	Austria	17	Latvia (1994ff)
2	Belgium	18	Lithuania (1995)
3	Bulgaria	19	Luxembourg
4	Croatia (1995)	20	Malta
5	Cyprus	21	Netherlands
6	Czech Republic	22	Norway
7	Denmark	23	Poland
8	Estonia (1995ff)	24	Portugal
9	Finland	25	Romania
10	France	26	Slovakia (1992)
11	Germany	27	Slovenia
12	Greece	28	Spain
13	Hungary (1991)	29	Sweden
14	Iceland	30	Switzerland
15	Ireland	31	Ukraine
16	Italy	32	United Kingdom

The special case of British Columbia

In 2008, the Canadian province of British Columbia (BC) was the first political jurisdiction in North America to institute a broad-based carbon tax. This tax applies to the purchase and use of fossil fuels and covers approximately 70% of BC's GHG emissions. The rate started at $10 per ton of carbon-equivalent emissions in 2008 and rose incrementally until it reached its current level of $40. The province realized that this new tax was regressive and instituted several measures designed to offset its potentially negative effect on citizens. Each adult and child initially received a $100 rebate called a Climate Action Dividend; this was subsequently transformed into a Climate Action Tax Credit on July 1, 2019, of $154.50 per adult and $45.50 per child. Perhaps the most important change was the adoption of a policy of revenue neutrality where expected revenues from the carbon tax would be offset by reductions in personal, corporate and small business tax rates. The government has recently decided to earmark any revenue above $30/ton to provide incentives for cleaner operations among the province's major industrial emitters. This represents a partial retreat from the concept of revenue neutrality (Harrison 2019). As Harrison states:

> It will be interesting to see whether British Columbians embrace that strategy, of which industry is the immediate beneficiary, or come to resent that they are not receiving the tax credits enjoyed by Canadians in provinces subject to the federal tax.
>
> (p. 4)

The Canadian government established a coordinated nation-wide carbon price of $20 per ton in 2019 and in December of 2020 announced its intention of increasing this tax every year from $50 per ton in 2022 to $170 per ton by 2030 (*Vancouver Sun* December 12, 2020). It is currently experiencing some pushback from several of its provinces which have a heavy reliance on fossil fuel production.

BC has achieved a remarkable record of decreased GHG emissions and continued economic growth. This clearly demonstrates that the imposition of a carbon tax need not have a deleterious effect on the economy.

Other economic instruments: Offsets

There may be cases where it is not practical for an individual or corporation to directly reduce their carbon footprint. There are at least two separate cases: (1) where an activity causes an increase in GHG emissions, such as taking an air flight or building or expanding a factory, or (2) where an activity damages or destroys a carbon sink, such as removing trees or filling in wetlands for construction. In these circumstances, the individual or corporation may choose to buy offsets where a third party acts as an intermediary and invests these monies in reducing carbon emissions somewhere else on the planet. These activities may include: (1) improving the control or process technology of a company in another industry and/or country, (2) funding green power projects or (3) planting trees in a developing country.

There are a number of conceptual and logistical issues raised by offsets. First, it may be difficult to generate an accurate estimate of how much carbon is produced by engaging in a particular activity or how much carbon will be removed by any one project, especially if it is unconventional. Second, a carbon reduction project may look good on paper, but it is necessary to determine that it satisfies the condition of *additivity* – i.e. it will have an incremental effect over what would have occurred anyway. Third, it is important to ensure that the effect will be permanent and not transitory and, fourth, that the activity will not lead to displacement, where that activity simply moves to another location rather than replaces the activity that generates more net carbon. In the case of tree planting, it is essential to ascertain that the trees survive and thrive after planting and are not harvested and that compensatory woodcutting for heating and cooking does not occur in another locale. But, fifth, perhaps the most serious issue is that in the pursuit of carbon neutrality, offsets allow the individual or corporation to continue with business as usual. This is inconsistent with any serious attempt to tackle global warming and has been described as the equivalent of the medieval sale of indulgences as a means of atoning for one's sins. (See also UNEP 2020.)

Perhaps the most notorious abuse of offsets occurred in the last decade under the auspices of the UN's Clean Development Mechanism. This policy allowed countries, such as the UK, to buy offsets from developing nations such as China on the understanding that these transfers would fund the destruction of such chemicals as HFC-23, a greenhouse gas 20,000 more powerful than carbon dioxide. HFC-23 was a byproduct of the production of the refrigerant HCFC-22. Unfortunately, this well-intentioned initiative led to a perverse outcome where several companies manufactured HCFC-22 for the sole purpose of producing HFC-23 and then destroying it to gain compensation (*The Guardian* October 26, 2010).

The questionable philosophical rationale for offsets was satirized by a now defunct website called Cheat Neutral, which offered a way to compensate for a spouse cheating on his/her partner. (See Figure 5.10.)

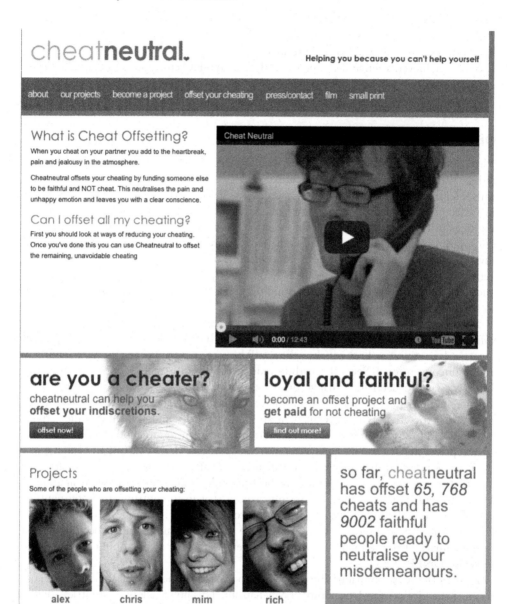

Figure 5.10 Cheat Neutral

Appendix 5.3
The Toxic Release Inventory and its effects

In 1988, the US government decided to adopt an innovative approach to environmental regulation by instituting a Toxic Release Inventory (TRI) requiring most major industrial plants to reveal the names and quantities of pollutants released to air, water and soil. The government then made this information freely available to the public in both print and electronic forms. The intent of this novel approach was to mobilize public pressure and "moral suasion" rather than government regulation to help reduce the release of pollution.

Thaler and Sunstein (2009) explicitly cite the TRI in their pathbreaking book *Nudge*, which explores the application of behavioral economic principles to many major current policy issues. A nudge is defined by the authors as follows:

> Any aspect of the choice architecture that alters people's behavior in a predictable way without forbidding any options or significantly changing their economic incentives. To count as a mere nudge, the intervention must be easy and cheap to avoid. Nudges are not mandates.
>
> (p. 6)

The general phrase used by the authors to describe this innovative approach to policy implementation is "libertarian paternalism." As Thaler and Sunstein conclude: "the Toxic Release Inventory may be the most unambiguous success story in all of environmental law." Why? Because "without mandating any behavioral change, the law has had massive beneficial effects." (The authors also hypothesize that a similar approach to global warming would work as well through the creation of a greenhouse gas inventory. There are reasons, however, to believe that the success of this approach with the TRI cannot be replicated with greenhouse gases because of the absence of any direct and obvious, localized deleterious effects that would mobilize local community pressure on industrial emitters.)

The positive impact of the TRI on conventional pollutants identified by Thaler and Sunstein has been supported by other authors, including Fung and O'Rourke (2000, p. 115), who state that the "TRI has achieved this regulatory success by creating a mechanism of 'populist maximin regulation'" (see also footnote 2 to this chapter). Grant (1997, p. 859) found that "states that have right-to-sue laws or that provide substantial funding for right-to-know programs have significantly lower rates of toxic emissions over time."

Fundamental to the rationale for the establishment of the TRI is the philosophical principle of "license to operate" – a concept which in some respects dates back to the origins of the international trading corporation in the 16th and 17th centuries, when European governments granted charters to such companies as the Hudson's Bay Company, the English and Dutch East India Companies, the Muscovy Company and the Royal African Company (Carlos and Nicholas 1988). In effect, these companies were granted a license to operate as long as they fulfilled some socially desirable purpose, and their survival was at the discretion of the government. The modern corporation is different in several important respects: it is theoretically immortal and has had many legal benefits conferred upon it that have traditionally been granted to individuals. Nevertheless, a corporation still runs the risk, albeit small, of losing its social license if it alienates a significant number of its key stakeholders, and the range of legally relevant stakeholders has grown in the last few decades (duPlessis 2011; OECD 2010a).

The most dramatic example of this loss of license is the Union Carbide Corporation, which was eventually swallowed by the Dow Corporation after the world's most devastating non-nuclear industrial accident in Bhopal, India, on December 2, 1984. This marked a sea change in the attitudes and behavior of many corporations toward environmental matters when they suddenly realized that such events could jeopardize not only their profits but also their continued existence. The increasing pressure on ecosystem services will change the expectations of important constituencies. A broad range of factors can affect a company's, or even an industry's, ability to conduct business in a successful manner. These include: failure to meet stakeholder expectations in general but, more specifically, failure to fully disclose the financial implications of a firm's environmental impacts; failure to provide transparency in ecosystem management; and failure to appreciate the risks of regulatory action, investor pressure and NGO and public boycotts or other media-based campaigns (see, for example, Repetto 2007). Several detailed reports have been published by business and governmental groups detailing the importance of ecosystem management to business (WBCSD 2009, 2010, 2011; UNEP 2001).

Case study: Sheldahl Inc. of Northfield, Minnesota

In 1991, the *Wall Street Journal* reported on the case of a small manufacturer of flexible electronic circuits for automobiles and computers. Situated in the college town of Northfield, Minnesota, the company had enjoyed a reputation as a solid corporate citizen. Its manufacturing plant generated no visible signs of pollution. This situation changed radically with the advent of the TRI. At some point, a local newspaper discovered via the TRI that the apparently innocuous plant was emitting almost 400 tons of methylene chloride (also called dichloromethane), deemed a probable human carcinogen. The ensuing community response convinced the company that its license to operate might be in jeopardy, and it promptly undertook to reduce its emissions of this toxic substance by 90% within two years by changing the mix of chemicals it used in the manufacturing process (*Wall Street Journal* January 2, 1991). Table 5.8 summarizes the TRI data for the plant for the years 1987 and 1994, prior to and after the change in technology.

It is obvious from this table that the principal change was a marked decrease in the offending pollutant with an accompanying increase in the output of toluene (another toxic pollutant), albeit at a lower quantity. This raises a paradoxical question: by substituting one toxic compound for another, is it possible to determine whether the company is lowering or raising the total environmental impact of its operations? Answering this question requires a metric which can measure the relative toxicity of varying pollutants. Fortunately, there are several risk-based metrics available to make such a comparison. The US EPA, for one, has developed Risk-Screening Environmental Indicators (RSEI) which

Table 5.8 Sheldahl Ltd. emissions 1987 and 1994

Air emissions from Sheldahl plant in Northfield, MN

Chemical	Stack or fugitive	1987 (lbs./yr.)	1994 (lbs./yr.)	1994 as % of 1987
1,1,1-Trichloroethane	STK	48,000	0	0
Acetone	STK	48,000	0	0
Ammonia	STK	29,000	7,500	26
Dichloromethane	**FUG**	**14,000**	**1,700**	**12**
Dichloromethane	**STK**	**780,000**	**15,300**	**2**
Freon 113	FUG	4,000	0	0
Freon 113	STK	50,000	0	0
Glycol Ethers	FUG	4,000	1,000	25
Glycol Ethers	STK	54,000	8,500	16
Methanol	STK	44,000	5,600	13
Methyl Ethyl Ketone	STK	84,000	20,400	24
Toluene	STK	9,000	24,200	269
Total		**1,168,000**	**84,200**	**7**

specifically address this problem (US EPA 2020a,b,c). In their description of this tool and accompanying software, the EPA (2020a, p. 1) states:

> EPA's Risk Screening Environmental Indicators (RSEI) is a screening-level, multi-media model that incorporates EPAs Toxics Release Inventory (TRI) information together with other data sources and risk factor concepts to assess the potential chronic human health impacts of TRI chemicals. To help provide context on the relative hazard and potential for risks posed by certain waste management activities of TRI chemicals (e.g., from releases to the environment), RSEI produces hazard estimates and unitless risk scores, which represent harm and relative risks to human health following chronic exposure to a TRI chemical. RSEI can be used to quickly and easily screen large amounts of chemicals and chemical emissions data from the TRI database, saving time and resources. RSEI is particularly useful for examining trends that compare potential relative risks from year to year, or for ranking and prioritizing chemicals, industry sectors, or geographic regions for strategic planning. In conjunction with other data sources and information, RSEI can ultimately be used to help policy makers, researchers, and communities establish priorities for further investigation and to look at changes in potential human health impacts over time. Using estimates of pounds of chemical releases to investigate potential health and environmental impacts is limited by the assumptions that all chemicals are equally toxic and that all people are equally exposed. Formal risk assessments are more accurate, but are complicated and time consuming to prepare, requiring detailed data that are not always available, and the results are often limited in scope and geographic area. The RSEI approach augments estimates of chemical pounds released with toxicity and exposure considerations, but does not address all of the potential factors that would have to be included in a full risk assessment. Thus, RSEI is not a stand-alone source

of information for making conclusions or decisions about the risks posed by any particular facility or environmental release of a TRI chemical.

In addition to the US EPA RSEI database, there are several other evaluative datasets, including:

1   Environmental Defense Fund (EDF) Scorecard Risk Scoring System (Hertwich et al. 2001);
2   Indiana Relative Chemical Hazard Score (IRCH), Indiana Clean Manufacturing Technology and Safe Materials Institute (Davis et al. 1994); and
3   US EPA – Waste Minimization Prioritization Tool (WMPT) (US EPA Office of Solid Waste 2000).

The Environmental Defense Fund's former scorecard (EDF n.d.) created an integrated evaluation tool which combines the results of these different risk measures to produce rankings for human health and ecological health effects. Table 5.9 summarizes the

Table 5.9 Toxicity scores for dichloromethane and toluene

	Dichloromethane	Toluene
Human health rankings		
Toxicity only – Ingestion toxicity weight (RSEI)	15	3
Toxicity only – Inhalation toxicity weight (RSEI)	3	5
Human health effects score (UTN)	5	2
Toxicity and persistence human health risk-screening score (WMPT)	6	n/a
Toxicity and exposure potential		
Cancer risk score – air releases (EDF)	0	n/a
Cancer risk score – water releases (EDF)	0	n/a
Non-cancer risk score – air releases (EDF)	7	1
Non-cancer risk score – water releases (EDF)	4	1
Worker exposure hazard score (IRCH)	24	18
Ecological health rankings		
Toxicity only ecological effects score (UTN)	2	5
Toxicity and persistence		
Environmental hazard value score (IRCH)	110	130
Ecological risk-screening score (WMPT)	6	n/a
Integrated environmental rankings		
Combined human and ecological scores		
Total hazard value score (IRCH)	30	29
Total hazard value score (UTN)	36	36

RSEI = US EPA risk-screening environmental indicators model
UTN = University of Tennessee Center for Clean Products and Clean Technologies Hazard Evaluation System
EDF = Environmental Defense Fund Risk Scoring System
IRCH = Indiana Pollution Prevention and Safe Materials Institute Pollution Prevention Progress Measurement System
WMPT = US EPA Office of Solid Waste – Waste Minimization Prioritization Tool

scorecard.org scores for the two key TRI-reported emissions from Sheldahl: toluene and dichloromethane. It does appear that Sheldahl responded to community sentiment by reducing many of its emissions of toxic compounds. However, while the release of the most contentious pollutant, dichloromethane, decreased by 98% from stack-specific sources and 88% for fugitive sources, the use of toluene increased by over 250%, and its integrated environmental ranking on the IRCH and University of Tennessee Total Hazard Value (Total UTN) scores is similar to that of dichloromethane. In sum, it is clear that these types of toxicity databases are indispensable in determining not only the direction and magnitude of toxic compound releases from changes in industrial processes but also the change in the total environmental burden of any specific industrial operation.

This issue of relative pollutant toxicity has been a challenge to the interpretation of the TRI list of major pollutant discharges. For example, Tables 5.10a and 5.10b list the leading pollutants by total discharge for the first TRI reporting year (1987) and 2018. In 1987, over half of the total output of pollutants was accounted for by one compound, sodium sulfate. In the Paper and Allied Products sector, 118 firms accounted for 29% of this output, and 340 firms in the Chemical and Allied Products sector accounted for 61%. It is noteworthy that one plant, owned by IMC Chemicals Inc., was responsible for 40% of all releases of sodium sulfate. The company discharged almost 1.85 million tons of this compound into a tailings pond on their property near Trona, in San Bernardino County, California. The magnitude of the discharges of sodium sulfate and their presence on the TRI list was ultimately deemed to be misleading, and the US EPA removed this chemical from the list in the following year as it was considered largely inert and harmless. When making comparisons between the total pollutant load on both lists, it is important to note that they are not strictly comparable since, over time, the TRI has expanded its list

Table 5.10a TRI – Top 10 releases 1987

Total releases – TRI – 1987	With Na_2SO_4		Without Na_2SO_4	
Chemical	Total releases (lbs.)	% of total	Total releases (lbs.)	% of total
Sodium sulfate (Na_2SO_4)	9,038,489,991	56.3	n/a	n/a
Ammonium sulfate (solution)	819,811,808	5.1	819,811,808	11.7
Hydrochloric acid	629,430,160	3.9	629,430,160	9.0
Methanol	475,580,381	3.0	475,580,381	6.8
Sulfuric acid	461,180,636	2.9	461,180,636	6.6
Ammonia	407,877,084	2.5	407,877,084	5.8
Toluene	374,224,061	2.3	374,224,061	5.3
Phosphoric acid	349,150,324	2.2	349,150,324	5.0
Acetone	257,737,211	1.6	257,737,211	3.7
Xylene (mixed isomers)	212,014,063	1.3	212,014,063	3.0
Methyl ethyl ketone	200,222,071	1.2	200,222,071	2.9
Other	2,824,016,241	17.6	2,824,016,241	40.3
Total	**16,049,734,031**	**100.0**	**7,011,244,040**	**100.0**

Table 5.10b TRI – Top 10 releases 2018

TRI – Largest releases by medium (2018)

	Air	
Chemical	*million lbs.*	*%*
Ammonia	120.4	20
Methanol	102.3	17
Sulfuric acid	66.2	11
n-Hexane	36.1	6
Hydrochloric acid	36.1	6
Styrene	30.1	5
All others	216.7	36
Total	**602.0**	**101**

Note: columns do not add precisely due to rounding errors

	Water		
Chemical	million lbs.	%	% of non-nitrate discharges
Nitrates	173.8	89	
Manganese	4.7	2	0.22
Ammonia	4.3	2	0.2
Methanol	3.2	2	0.15
Sodium Nitrite	1.9	1	0.09
Nitric Acid	1.7	1	0.08
Zinc	1.1	1	0.05
All others	4.5	2	0.21
Total	**195.31**	**100**	
	Land		
Chemical	**Million lbs.**	**%**	
Lead	822.4	32	
Zinc	565.4	22	
Manganese	231.3	9	
Arsenic	179.9	7	
Copper	179.9	7	
Barium	179.9	7	
All others	436.9	17	
Total	**2,570**		

Note: columns do not add precisely due to rounding errors

to include more pollutants, a larger number of industrial operations and lower emission cutoffs for inclusion.

As stated, the US EPA recognized that the interpretation of these data cannot be undertaken without consideration of relative toxicity. As such, the agency developed a toxicity weighting metric which combines a toxicity rating with the total quantity of pollutant release. There are two scales: one for cancer, the other for non-cancer-related health effects. In 2009, the EPA determined that two chemicals accounted for 92% of the total toxicity-weighted pounds of cancer effects: asbestos (78%) and arsenic and its compounds (14%). For non-cancer health effects, three chemicals accounted for 80% of the weighted total releases: manganese and its compounds (39%), arsenic and its compounds (21%) and lead and its compounds (20%). Arsenic appears on both lists because of its unusually toxic chemical properties (US EPA 2009a).

Easy access to toxicity data is available through EPA's websites entitled "Risk-Screening Environmental Indicators (RSEI) Model" and "Toxic Release Inventory (TRI) Program" with detailed and summary data for both industry and chemical. Table 5.11 summarizes the RSEI scores for both these categories.

In sum, the interpretation of the TRI data is complicated by at least seven factors: the aforementioned issue of relative toxicity; the persistence of the chemical in the environment; the form in which the chemical is released, which impacts the routes of exposure such as inhalation, ingestion and absorption; the potential for bioconcentration in the food chain (see Chapter 8); the type of disposal or release (whether to air, water, soil or underground injection); the type of off-site facility receiving the chemical and the efficiency of waste management practices; and the on-site waste management of the toxic chemical (US EPA 2009b).

Table 5.11 RSEI scores

RSEI scores			
By industry		By chemical	
Industry	% share		% share
Chemicals	33.3	Chromium and chromium compounds	40.4
Fabricated metals	21.4	Ethylene oxide	31.5
Transportation equipment	8.3	Cobalt and cobalt compounds	7.1
Other	7.8	Nickel and nickel compounds	5.0
Primary metals	7.1	Arsenic and arsenic compounds	2.1
Misc. manufacturing	5.6	Propyleneimine	1.5
Machinery	4.7	Chloroprene	1.4
Non-metallic mineral production	2.6	Benzene	1.0
Petroleum	2.1	Butadiene 1,3	1.0
Electric utilities	1.7	Trichloroethylene	0.8
Others	5.4	Other	8.2
Total	**100**	**Total**	**100**

Final observations concerning the TRI

The TRI not only influences decisions relating to the risk to license to operate, but it can also have a bearing on more short-term financial issues facing a corporation. It has been observed that banks and insurance companies are much less willing to insure or lend to companies who may be facing environmental risks associated with the releases of environmental contaminants. In a book entitled *Regulation through Revelation*, James T. Hamilton (2005) used regression analysis to explore the effect on stock prices of the release of TRI emission data. His results, based on event analysis, were quite dramatic:

> For companies that reported TRI data to the EPA, the average abnormal returns on the day this information was made public was negative and statistically significant. In terms of the dollar values of the abnormal returns, firms reporting TRI information lost on average $4.1 million in stock value on the first day the data were released. . . . The release of the TRI clearly provided new information to two communities: print journalists writing about pollution and investors concerned about the impact of pollution on financial performance. It remained to be seen how the information might be used by others, including the communities that contained facilities that generated TRI reports.
>
> (p. 74)

The findings reported in this book confirm the results of earlier research conducted by several other authors including Khanna et al. (1998) and Konar and Cohen (1997). Despite the apparently beneficial impact of information disclosure through the TRI, it is useful to look for any empirical evidence to support its relative effectiveness in reducing national pollutant releases. Few studies have directly addressed this question. A paper by Stephan et al. (2005) employed a survey instrument of 1,000 national manufacturing facilities to elicit their views on the role of the TRI in motivating pollutant reduction. Their findings were rather surprising, as they concluded that

> the role of the TRI as a motivator for community-level direct action seems to be fairly low. . . . Ultimately, the bottom line may come back to the anchor points for U.S. environmental policy: regulation and the threat of liability.
>
> (p. 14)

Only one other study found in the literature attempts to address this same question with a rigorous analytical methodology. Although based on a Canadian instrument similar to the TRI (called the National Pollution Release Inventory), there is reason to believe the findings of this study might apply to the US as well. In this study, Harrison and Antweiler (2003, p. 361) found that "the vast majority of reductions reported to the inventory to date were found not to be voluntary, as has often been assumed, but are, rather, the result of direct regulation of a relatively small number of polluters." The authors also identified three other unexpected findings: the growth of less visible waste streams through inter-media transfers (e.g. to land disposal and underground injection), the movement of wastes to other communities and the increasing toxicity of some waste streams despite overall reductions in quantities released.

Notes

1 The price elasticity of demand measures the response in quantity of a product demanded to changes in the price of the product. It is formally defined as:

$\%\Delta Q / \%\Delta P$, where Δ = change, Q = quantity of product demanded, P = product price.

2 "Maximin" is defined by the *Oxford English Dictionary* as "the largest of a set of minima" or "in Game Theory designating a strategy that maximizes the smallest gain that can be relied on by a participant in a game or other situation of conflict."

References

Atkinson, Scott E. and Donald H. Lewis (1974) "A cost-effectiveness analysis of alternative air quality control strategies," *Journal of Environmental Economics and Management*, 1, pp. 237–250.

Barde, Jean-Philippe and Nils Axel Braathen (2007) "Green tax reforms in OECD countries: An overview," Ch. 2 in Peter N. Nemetz (ed.) *Sustainable Resource Management: Reality or Illusion?*, Cheltenham: Edward Elgar, pp. 45–87.

Brown, Marilyn A. and Majid Ahmadi (2019) "Would a green new deal add or kill jobs?," *Scientific American*, December 17.

Canada's Ecofiscal Commission (2019) *Bridging the Gap: Real Options for Meeting Canada's 2030 GHG Target*, November.

Carlos, Ann M. and Stephen Nicholas (1988) "Giants of an earlier capitalism," *Business History Review*, 62(3), Autumn, pp. 398–419.

Chaulk, Amanda et al. (2011) "Mercury distribution and transport across the ocean-sea-ice-atmosphere interface in the Arctic ocean," *Environmental Science & Technology*, 45, pp. 1866–1872.

Clark, Colin W. (1973) "The economics of overexploitation," *Science*, 181, pp. 630–634.

Clark, Colin W. (1990) *Mathematical Bioeconomics: The Optimal Management of Renewable Resources* (2nd ed.), New York: Wiley Inter-Interscience, John Wiley and Sons, Inc.

Clark, Colin W., F.H. Clarke and Gordon R. Munro (1979) "The optimal exploitation of renewable resource stocks: Some problems of irreversible investment," *Econometrica*, 47, pp. 25–47.

Clark, Colin W. and Gordon R. Munro (1978) "Renewable resource management and extinction," *Journal of Environmental Economics and Management*, 5, pp. 198–205.

Coase, Ronald (1960) "The problem of social cost," *Journal of Law and Economics*, 3, October, pp. 1–44.

Conniff, Richard (2009) "The political history of cap and trade," *Smithsonian Magazine*, August.

Dales, John H. (1968) *Pollution, Property and Prices: An Essay in Policy-Making and Economics*, Toronto: University of Toronto Press.

Davis, G. et al. (1994) *UTN: Chemical Hazard Evaluation for Management Strategies: A Method for Ranking and Scoring Chemicals by Potential Human Health and Environmental Impacts*, Washington, DC: US EPA.

Dietz, Thomas et al. (2003) "The struggle to govern the commons," *Science*, 302, December 12, pp. 1907–1912, and supplementary material on line at www.sciencemag.org/cgi/content/full/302/5652/1907/.

duPlessis, Jean Jacques et al. (2011) *Principles of Contemporary Corporate Governance*, Cambridge: Cambridge University Press.

Environmental Defense Fund (EDF) (n.d.) "Moyers PBS report on toxics linked to www.scorecard.org website."

European Commission (2009) *EU Action against Climate Change: The EU Emissions Trading Scheme*.

European Union. *Free Allocation*, Climate Action. https://ec.europa.eu (accessed December 2020).

European Union. *Carbon Leakage*, Climate Action. https://ec.europa.eu (accessed December 2020).

Europe Environment Agency (2011) *Environmental Tax Reform in Europe: Implications for Income Distribution*, EEA Technical Report No. 16.

Fung, Archon and Dara O'Rourke (2000) "Reinventing environmental regulation from the grassroots up: Explaining and expanding the success of the toxics release inventory," *Environmental Management*, 25(2), pp. 115–127.

Grant, Don Sherman (1997) "Allowing citizen participation in environmental regulation: An empirical analysis of the effects of right-to-sue and right-to-know provisions on industry's toxic emissions," *Social Science Quarterly*, 78(4), December, pp. 859–873.

The Guardian (2010) "EU plans to clamp down on carbon trading scam," October 26.

Hamilton, James T. (2005) *Regulation Through Revelation: The Origins, Politics and Impacts of the Toxic Release Inventory Program*, Cambridge: Cambridge University Press.

Hardin, Garret (1968) "The tragedy of the commons," *Science*, 162, pp. 1243–1248.

Harrison, Kathryn (2019) "Lessons from British Columba's carbon tax," *Policy Options*, July 11.

Harrison, Kathryn and Werner Antweiler (2003) "Incentives for pollution abatement: regulation, regulatory threats, and non-governmental pressures," *Journal of Policy Analysis and Management*, 22(3), pp. 361–392.

Hertwich, E.G., S.F. Mateles, W.S. Pease and T.E. McKone (2001) "Human toxicity potentials for life cycle assessment and toxics release inventory risk screening," *Environmental Toxicology & Chemistry*, 20(4), pp. 928–939.

Indiana Clean Manufacturing Technology and Safe Materials Institute, Purdue University. IRCH: Indiana Relative Chemical Hazard Score. www.ecn.purdue.edu/CMTI/Pollution_Prevention_Progress_Measurement_Method/.

International Monetary Fund (2019) *Fiscal Monitor: How to Mitigate Climate Change*, October, Washington, DC: IMF.

Jaccard, Mark (2005) *Sustainable Fossil Fuels: The Unusual Suspect in the Quest for Clean and Enduring Energy*, Cambridge: Cambridge University Press.

Khanna, Madhu, Wilma Rose H. Quimio and Dora Bojilova (1998) "Toxics release information: A policy tool for environmental protection," *Journal of Environmental Economics and Management*, 36, pp. 243–266.

Konar, Shameek and Mark A. Cohen (1997) "Information as regulation: The effect of community right to know laws on toxic emissions," *Journal of Environmental Economics and Management*, 32, pp. 109–124.

Mani, Muthukumra and David Wheeler (1997) "In search of pollution havens? Dirty industry in the world economy, 1960–1995," *Workshop 3: Pollution Havens and Pollution Halos*, OECD Conference on FDI and the Environment, The Hague, 28–29 January, 1999.

Marcu, Andrei et al. (2020) *State of the EU ETS Report*, ERCST, BloombergNEF, UNICRAZ, Ecoact.

McLean, Brian J. (2007) "Emissions trading: US experience implementing multi-state cap and trade programs," in Peter N. Nemetz (ed.) *Sustainable Resource Management: Reality or Illusion?*, Cheltenham: Edward Elgar, pp. 22–41.

Montero, Juan-Pablo et al. (2002) "A market-based environmental policy experiment in Chile," *Journal of Law & Economics*, 45(1), April, pp. 267–287.

New York Times (1990) "Lawmakers agree on rules to reduce acid rain damage," October 22.

New York Times (2010) "Texas and E.P.A. clash over air pollution," June 11.

New York Times (2011) "In consumer behavior, signs of gas price Pinch," May 17.

Nuccitelli, Dana (2020) "The Trump EPA is vastly underestimating the cost of carbon dioxide pollution to society, new research finds," *Yale Climate Connections*, July 30.

Organization for Economic Co-operation and Development (OECD) (2010a) *Principles of Corporate Governance*, Paris: OECD.

Organization for Economic Co-operation and Development (OECD) (2010b) *Taxation, Innovation and the Environment*, Paris: OECD.

Ostrom, Elinor et al. (2002) *The Drama of the Commons*, Washington, DC: National Academy of Sciences.

Pigou, Arthur (1920) *The Economics of Welfare*, reprinted 2005, New York: Cosimo.

RECLAIM (Regional Clean Air Incentives Market) (2007) *2005 Annual Audit Report*, March. see also www.epa.gov/airmarkets/resource/docs/reclaimoverview.pdf.

Repetto, Robert (2007) "Better financial disclosure protects investors and the environment," Ch. 13 in Peter N. Nemetz (ed.) *Sustainable Resource Management: Reality or Illusion?*, Cheltenham: Edward Elgar, pp. 342–375.

Ricke, Katharine et al. (2018) "Country-level social cost of carbon," *Nature Climate Change*, September 24.

Scorecard.org website. http://scorecard.goodguide.com/.

Sierra Club of Canada (2008) *Voters Guide to the Climate Crisis.*

Steen et al. (2010) "Natural and anthropogenic atmospheric mercury in the European Arctic: A speciation study," *Atmos Chem Phys Discuss*, 10, pp. 27255–27281.

Stephan, Mark, Michael E. Kraft and Troy D. Abel (2005) "Information politics and environmental performance: The impact of the toxics release inventory on corporate decision making," paper prepared for delivery at the 2005 Annual Meeting of the American Political Science Association, Washington, DC, September 1–4.

Tax Foundation (2020) "Looking back on 30 years of carbon taxes in Sweden," Fiscal Fact No. 727, September.

Tax Foundation (2020) "Carbon Taxes in Europe," October 8.

Thaler, Richard and Cass Sunstein (2009) *Nudge: Improving Decisions about Health, Wealth and Happiness*, London: Penguin.

Tietenberg, T.H. (2006) *Emissions Trading: Principles and Practice*, Washington, DC: Resources For the Future.

United Nations Environment Programme (UNEP) (2001) *Buried Treasure: Uncovering the Business Case for Sustainability.*

United Nations Environment Programme (UNEP) (2007) *Global Environmental Outlook4 (GEO4) Environment for Development: Summary for Decision Makers.*

United Nations Environment Programme (UNEP) (2020) Emissions Gap Report.

US Environmental Protection Agency (EPA) (2000) "Office of solid waste and office of pollution prevention and toxics," *WMPT: Waste Minimization Prioritization Tool: Background Document for the Tier III PBT Chemical List.* Appendix A: WMPT Summary Spreadsheet. EPA, Washington, DC, July. www. epa.gov/epaoswer/hazwaste/minimize/chemlist.htm.

US Environmental Protection Agency (EPA) (2008) *Integrated Science Assessment for Particulate Matter.*

US Environmental Protection Agency (EPA) (2009a) *Toxics Release Inventory Summary.*

US Environmental Protection Agency (EPA) (2009b) "Toxics release inventory: Factors to consider."

US Environmental Protection Agency (EPA) (2020a) *EPA's Risk-Screening Environmental Indicators (RSEI) Methodology, RSEI Version 2.3.9*, Office of Pollution Prevention and Toxics, December, Washington, DC.

US Environmental Protection Agency (EPA) (2020b) "Join communities across the country. Use EPA's RSEI model to identify toxic releases that may require further evaluation and to plan for the future," June 18.

US Environmental Protection Agency (EPA) (2020c) "Office of pollution prevention and toxics," *RSEI: Risk-Screening Environmental Indicators Model: Version 2.1 (1988–2000 TRI reporting data)*, December. www.epa.gov/opptintr/rsei/index.html. Methodology described in Chapter 1: Introduction to EPAs Risk-Screening Environmental Indicators of the RSEI User's Manual. Values from Technical Appendix A. Available Toxicity Data for TRI Chemicals. (Appendix A last updated December 2002).

US Environmental Protection Agency (EPA) (2020d) Power plant emission trends.

Vancouver Sun (2020) "PM unveils green plan," December 12.

Wall Street Journal (1991) "Right to know: A U.S report spurs community action revealing polluters," January 2.

Wang, Pei et al. (2019) "Estimates of the social cost of carbon: A review based on meta-analysis," *Journal of Cleaner Production*, 209, pp. 1494–1507.

World Business Council on Sustainable Development (WBCSD) (2009) *Business and Ecosystems*, Geneva.

World Business Council on Sustainable Development (WBCSD) (2010) *Vision 2050*, Geneva.

World Business Council on Sustainable Development (WBCSD) (2011) *Guide to Corporate Ecosystem Valuation*, Geneva.

6 Cost-benefit analysis and measuring environmental benefits

Forestalling or reducing the consequences of pollution is not a cost-free exercise, and, as a result, any proposed policy or regulation should assess the relative benefits as well as costs. Commonly used by governments to choose between competing public projects, cost-benefit analysis (CBA) has been adopted as a useful conceptual framework for assessing policies and projects which have an environmental impact. The mathematical formulation of CBA is straightforward and is represented in the following equation for any given project:

$$NPV = (B_1 - C_1)/(1 + r) + (B_2 - C_2)/(1 + r)^2 \ldots (B_n - C_n)/(1 + r)^n$$

Where:

NPV = net present value

B_i = benefits of that project in period i

C_i = costs of that project in period i

r = discount rate per period

n = relevant time horizon

One of the common decision rules of CBA is to choose the project (or projects) with the highest NPV. The central principles of CBA analysis are: (1) all relevant costs and benefits of alternatives must be included and monetized and (2) all future costs and benefits must be discounted using an appropriate discount rate. There are conceptual challenges to CBA over issues related to intergenerational equity and the choice of an appropriate discount rate. Both of these concerns are addressed later in this chapter.

Quantifying costs and benefits

While costs of pollution control are relatively easy to estimate, as they are usually derived from the market-based prices of inputs such as equipment and labor, the estimation of environmental benefits poses a much more challenging task as the relevant values are rarely, if ever, captured in a market framework – i.e. they have no explicit prices since they are not traded.

Within a CBA framework, the convention for assessing the economics of pollution control is to define *costs* as those associated with controlling pollution and *benefits* as the value of the environmental damages avoided through the process of control. The

DOI: 10.4324/9781003170730-6

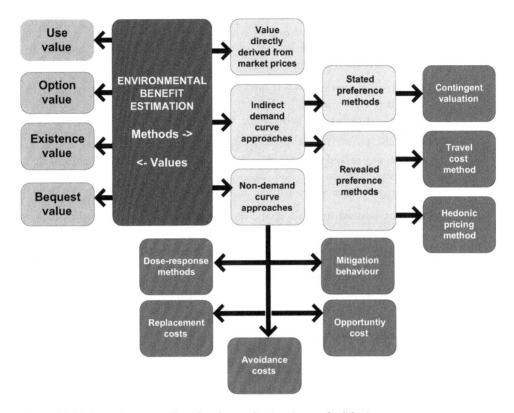

Figure 6.1 Major environmental benefit values and estimation methodologies

estimation of environmental benefits is one of the most intractable problems in the area of environmental/ecological economics and policy. Figure 6.1 depicts some of the major environmental benefit valuation and estimation methodologies. There are at least four separate types of value: (1) *use value* – derived from the actual use of the environment; (2) *option value* – value expressed through the option to use the environment in the future (i.e. the value of not foreclosing future options through development); (3) *existence value* – value associated with knowing that the environment is being preserved although the person concerned may not actually be using it directly; and a related value, (4) *bequest value* – a willingness to pay to preserve the environment for the benefit of one's descendants.

There are two general conceptual approaches to estimating benefits: market based and non-market based (also referred to as demand-curve based and non-demand-curve based respectively). The following is a brief typology of the alternative methodologies (see also Heal 2004; UK NEA 2011):

A   Non-demand-curve-based approaches

1   Dose-response methods
2   Replacement costs
3   Mitigation costs
4   Opportunity costs

B   Demand-curve approach

1   **Revealed preference methods** – where demand is revealed by examining individuals' purchases of market priced goods which are necessary in order to enjoy associated environmental goods.

i   **Travel cost method** – e.g. using the cost of travel to vacation spots to infer their environmental value

ii   **Hedonic pricing method** – e.g. using housing prices to determine the value of environmental variables

2   **Stated (or expressed) preference methods** – where demand is measured by examining individuals' stated, or expressed, preferences for environmental goods frequently elicited via surveys and/or questionnaires.

3   **Contingent valuation** – where the consumer is asked questions which allow the researcher to measure willingness to pay (WTP) for the preservation of environmental assets or willingness to accept (WTA) compensation for the loss of these assets.

Each of these techniques is described in turn with accompanying examples.

Non-demand-curve approaches

Dose-response methodology

This methodology is frequently used to estimate the extent of damage to human health from exposure to a pollutant. *Dose* refers to the amount of pollutant to which the individual is exposed, while *response* measures the extent of consequent human illness (ranging from degrees of morbidity to mortality). This type of analysis frequently requires the complementary use of clinical and epidemiological research and can be complicated by issues of causality and attribution. For example, while it is sometimes – although not always – relatively straightforward to associate workplace exposure to contaminants with subsequent human illness, this process is much more complex within the general public. Several steps are required – each fraught with conceptual difficulties: (1) ambient pollutant levels must be tied to specific emission sources, (2) human illness must be plausibly linked to a specific pollutant, (3) the pathways of exposure must be identified, (4) the pharmacokinetics of the specific interaction of the pollutant and the human body must be elucidated and, finally, (5) the human effects must be monetized. There are standard protocols for assigning dollar values to health effects, and a number of these are reviewed later in this chapter. Some of these protocols, such as those devoted to valuing the loss of life, are somewhat contentious and are discussed in Chapter 7.

Replacement cost methodology

This concept is based on the assumption that a damaged environmental good or service can be replaced by some anthropogenic substitute and that this substitute can be easily valued using current market prices for equipment, land and labor, etc. While simple in concept, there are certain complications associated with its implementation. Several examples illustrate this point.

The cost of lost pollination

There have been recent reports of massive die-offs of bee colonies (referred to as *colony collapse disorder, or CCD*) in the US and elsewhere in the world. It has been reported that US beekeepers lost 40% of honeybee colonies in 2019 (Bruckner et al. 2019). The scientific community was at first unsure of the cause of CCD as there appeared to be a number of causative factors, including stress, fungi and viruses. Conclusive evidence has emerged that pesticides known as neonicotinoids are the primary contributing factor to this serious ecological problem (Whitehorn et al. 2012; Woodcock 2016; CEH 2016). One hypothesis about the etiology of CCD is that an underlying cause may be hidden by secondary factors resulting from exposure to the primary agent. In this case, it has been postulated that one such mechanism is the weakening of the bee immune system by exposure to the pesticide, leading to subsequent vulnerability to secondary infections. This is analogous to the common medical practice of distinguishing between immediate and underlying causes of death. Other hypotheses attribute the resulting mortality to disruption of bee nest behavior, social networks and thermo regulation (Crall et al. 2018) or suppression of sperm production (Straub et al. 2016).

The magnitude of the bee colony collapse has forced a re-examination of the critical role these insects play in crop pollination. The number of crops so pollinated is large and includes forage and legumes, fruit, vegetables, oilseed crops and herbs and spices (Morse and Calderone 2000; Losey and Vaughn 2006; Klein et al. 2007; Stipp 2007). One estimate of the value of US crops which rely on honeybee pollination was $19 billion as of 2010 (Calderone 2012, supplementary material, S3, Tables S12–S14). (See Table 6.1.)

Table 6.1 Total crop value and value of honeybee-pollinated crops in the United States

Crop	Total crop value	Value of crops dependent on honeybee pollination	% of total crop value
	(million $)	*(million $)*	
Directly dependent			
Almond	2,839	2,839	100
Apple	2,221	1,999	90
Soybean	38,915	1,946	5
Cherry (sweet)	721	584	81
Blueberry (cultivated)	593	534	90
Sunflower	582	524	90
Orange	1,935	522	27
Watermelon	492	310	63
Peach	615	295	48
Avocado	322	290	90
Cranberry	316	285	90
Pear	382	240	63
Muskmelon (cantaloupe)	314	226	72
Canola	487	219	45
Grapefruit	286	206	72
Cotton (seed)	1,004	161	16

(Continued)

Table 6.1 (Continued)

Crop	Total crop value	Value of crops dependent on honeybee pollination	% of total crop value
	(million $)	(million $)	
Cucumber (fresh)	194	157	81
Cucumber (pickled)	185	149	81
Raspberry (all)	200	144	72
Tangerine (and mandarins)	276	124	45
Prune	150	94	63
Nectarine	129	62	48
Plum	78	49	63
Blueberry (wild)	51	46	90
Strawberry	2,245	45	2
Raspberry (red)	56	41	72
Grape	3,627	36	1
Muskmelon (honeydew)	50	36	72
Cherry (tart)	41	33	81
Apricot	47	27	56
Macadamia nuts	30	24	81
Blackberry	33	24	72
Kiwifruit	25	20	81
Squash	204	18	9
Peanut	901	18	2
Pumpkin	117	10	9
Lemon	381	8	2
Prune and plum	5	3	63
Tangelo	7	2	36
Raspberry (black)	2	2	72
Boysenberries	2	1	72
Olive	113	1	1
Rapeseed	1	1	90
Subtotal	**61,174**	**12,357**	**20**
Indirectly dependent			
Alfalfa	7,519	2,507	33
Onion	1,455	1,310	90
Cotton	7,318	1,171	16
Broccoli	649	584	90
Carrot	597	538	90
Celery	399	319	80
Cauliflower	247	223	90
Asparagus	91	82	90
Sugar beet	1,968	39	2
Carrot	30	27	90
Subtotal	**20,274**	**6,799**	**34**
Grand total	**81,448**	**19,155**	**24**

Source: Reproduced with permission of the author.

In an innovative study in South Africa, Allsopp et al. (2008) attempted to specifically measure the value of pollination of the Western Cape deciduous fruit industry by costing alternative methods to the traditional services provided by insects. These options include costly and labor-intensive methods such as aerial spraying and hand pollination. The resulting monetary values represent a significant proportion of the total crop value, reinforcing the conclusion that replacing services provided normally by nature for "free" can be a costly exercise. In contrast, Kasina et al. (2009) have used willingness to pay for pollination services in a study conducted in western Kenya. They found this analytical methodology preferable to revealed preference in light of the absence of markets for pollination in many developing countries.

In another study considering world agriculture as a whole, Gallai et al. (2009) estimated the total economic value of pollination at 153 billion Euros (approximately US$213 billion) and the potential loss of consumer surplus at between 190 and 310 billion Euros (approximately US$265–$425 billion). The authors add an important qualification, however:

> Although our results demonstrate the economic importance of insect pollinators, it cannot be considered a scenario since it does not take into account the strategic response of the market. Producers might have several levels of response strategies in interaction with the intermediate demands of the food supply chain. Moreover, the response of consumers faced to [sic] dramatic changes of relative prices would probably be more elaborate than the simple price elasticity can summarize. Short and long term reaction for each crop and in each region would probably be quite different.
>
> (p. 820)

The cost of lost wetlands

Wetlands are slowly disappearing in the US as the land is being developed for agricultural purposes, housing, etc. The question is whether it is possible and appropriate to use replacement cost methodology to estimate a value for wetland services. A very important function of wetlands is to filter out excess nutrients and toxics and other biodegradable chemicals from runoff. One possible approach to remedying this problem is to attempt to replace this natural ecosystem service with a human-constructed runoff-gathering system and filtration plant. In fact, an anthropogenic version of this type of ecosystem is used on a very small scale in some modern green buildings. If a large-scale version of this technological approach was possible, the replacement cost methodology could be employed to assign a value to lost wetland services. Table 6.2, drawn from a report of the UN's Millennium Ecosystem Assessment of 2005 entitled *Ecosystems and Human Well-Being: Wetlands and Water*, demonstrates that filtering is only one – albeit important – service provided by wetlands. Figure 6.2 (Lambert 2003) graphically displays the complex array of interdependent ecosystem services and economic values provided by fully functioning wetlands. The ineluctable conclusion from this table and figure is twofold: (1) the replacement cost methodology outlined prior which focuses solely on filtration benefits would seriously underestimate the value of the lost wetland, and (2), perhaps more importantly, replacing all these vital ecosystem services with anthropogenic counterparts would probably be impossible.

Table 6.2 Ecosystem services provided by or derived from wetlands

Service	Comments and examples
Provisioning	
Food	Production of fish, wild game, fruits and grains
Fresh water	Storage and retention of water for domestic, industrial and agricultural use
Fiber and fuel	Production of logs, fuelwood, peat, fodder
Biochemical	Extraction of medicines and materials from biota
Genetic materials	Genes for resistance to plant pathogens, ornamental species, etc.
Regulating	
Climate regulation	Source of and sink for greenhouse gases; influence local and regional temperature, precipitation and other climatic processes
Water regulation (hydrological flows)	Groundwater recharge/discharge
Water purification and waste treatment	Retention, recovery and removal of excess nutrients and other pollutants
Erosion regulation	Retention of soils and sediments
Natural hazard regulation	Flood control, storm protection
Pollination	Habitat for pollinators
Cultural	
Spiritual and inspirational	Source of inspiration; many religions attach spiritual and religious values to aspects of wetland ecosystems
Recreational	Opportunities for recreational activities
Aesthetic	Many people find beauty or aesthetic value in aspects of wetland ecosystems
Educational	Opportunities for formal and informal education and training
Supporting	
Soil formation	Sediment retention and accumulation of organic matter
Nutrient cycling	Storage, recycling, processing and acquisition of nutrients

Mitigation costing

Similar in concept to replacement cost methods, mitigation costing assigns value to ecosystem services by costing efforts to reduce or offset the negative effects of lost or compromised ecosystem services.

Opportunity cost

The opportunity cost methodology focuses on the value of goods and services lost by undertaking a specific course of action. Similar challenges emerge to those identified for replacement costing in measuring the value of all the foregone ecosystem services associated with degrading or destroying a wetlands area.

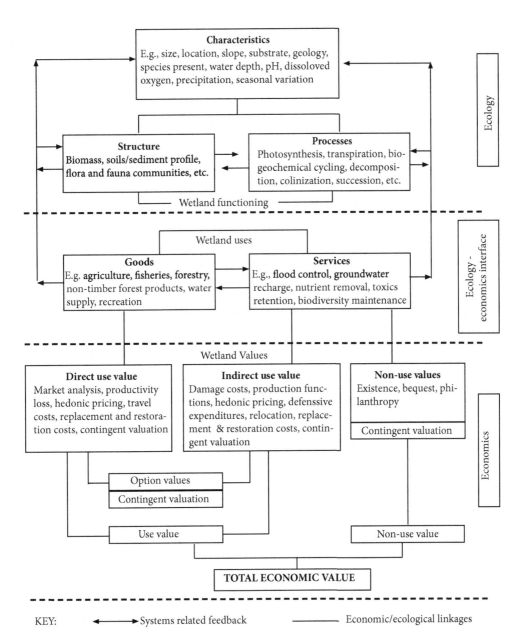

Figure 6.2 Connections among wetland functions, uses and values

Source: Reproduced with permission of the publisher.

Demand–curve approaches

Travel cost methodology (TCM)

The travel cost methodology is frequently used to assign a value to ecosystem amenities such as national parks or changes in recreational quality at these sites. Classified as a revealed preference method, the underlying assumption is relatively simple: the incurred costs of visiting a park (for example, the cost of gasoline used in travel to the site as well as an imputed value to travel time and any other incidental costs such as road tolls) in some way reflect the recreational value of a site. The data on number of visitors and their travel costs can be used with regression analysis to construct a surrogate demand curve for the recreational site from which a measure of total recreational value can be derived. The underlying principle is based on the concept of consumer surplus (CS) illustrated in Figure 6.3, where CS measures the benefit to a consumer, net of the sacrifice he/she has to make, from being able to buy a commodity at a particular price. It is widely used in cost-benefit analysis as an approximate measure of changes in consumer welfare. [fn 1] Graphically, it is the total (triangular) area ABC between the demand curve and price paid – i.e. it is the difference between the total perceived value (i.e. willingness to pay) and the actual price paid.

There are several variants of the travel cost methodology. The first and simplest, called the zonal travel model, estimates the value of the recreational site as a whole derived from average site visit data from predefined geographic zones around the site. The second variant (the individual travel cost approach) uses more disaggregated data based on information gleaned from individual surveys administered at the recreational site itself. The third approach, termed the random utility model (RUM), uses a more detailed and comprehensive statistical approach which permits the valuation of specific characteristics of the recreational site. An excellent example of the RUM model is described in Riera et al. (2011) in a study of Minorca beaches.

There are several conceptual complications associated with the TCM methodology: (1) time costs must be included, as ignoring the implicit cost of time spent traveling to a recreational site may underestimate the value of that site; however, some people enjoy traveling, so for them the journey itself may reflect a benefit rather than a cost; (2) where tourists

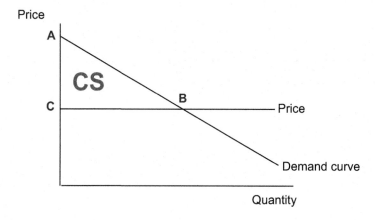

Figure 6.3 Consumer's surplus

undertake multiple visit journeys, it is not always simple to apportion travel costs among several recreational sites visited on the same trip; the only methodology which addresses this issue is the RUM model; (3) it can be difficult to differentiate between sites which are visited by people who choose one site in particular and sites which are visited by people who have little choice in sites (and, consequently, may value the site less); (4) TCM studies often omit visitors who have not incurred travel costs to reach the site because they live nearby; and (5) a particular challenge is associated with assigning a value when an individual or family values a site so highly that they make a decision to purchase a home nearby, thereby incurring low travel costs. This last qualification is particularly problematic as it implies an element of endogeneity to the problem of calculating an appropriate value. Bockstael and McConnell (2010), in their extensive theoretical discussion on revealed preference methodologies, identify several other conceptual challenges in applying TCM, especially the definition and construction of a theoretically defensible cost function.

Hedonic pricing methodology

A second major example of a revealed preference analytical technique, hedonic pricing attempts to measure the positive or negative contribution of environmental services to the market price of an asset, usually housing. The methodology is based on the assumption that the environmental effect will be a measurable residual after all other conventional factors contributing to housing prices are identified. This analysis is usually conducted in a regression analytic framework, and a typical formulation of the methodology may appear as follows:

> **House price =** f(# bedrooms, #baths, condition of structure, size of structure, zoning, land use, local development policies, type of neighborhood, lot size, access, *environment*), where: access is the distance to shops, workplace, etc., and environment is the residual value to be evaluated. A common approach is to look at two neighborhoods which are similar in many respects, allowing the analyst to control for extraneous variables.

Example #1: Valuing proximity to a greenway

Hamilton and Quayle (2002) studied how proximity to a greenway affects property values. The regression variables used by the authors included house age (in years), floor area (sq. ft.), prior sale price, lot size (sq. ft.), number of full baths, the total assessed value and the assessed value of the land only. They also included the variable of particular interest (physical proximity to a greenway) represented as a dichotomous variable (adjacent or near). The authors found a 10%–15% increase in economic value for proximity to a greenway after controlling for other factors such as age, location and other adjacent amenities.

Example #2: Valuing the economic impact of airport noise

Helmuth et al. (1997) studied the impact of airport runway noise associated with the SeaTac airport serving the Seattle-Tacoma region of Washington State. They used the following linear regression model:

$$Y = \alpha + \beta_1 X_1 + \beta_2 X_2 + \beta_3 X_3 + \beta_4 X_4 + \beta_5 X_5 + \beta_6 X_6 + \beta_7 X_7 + \beta_8 X_8 + \beta_9 X_9 + \beta_{10} X_{10}$$

where:

Y = assessed value of land and structures

X_1 = lot size (sq. ft.)

X_2 = structure size (sq. ft.)

X_3 = number of bedrooms

X_4 = number of baths

X_5 = distance from center of a jet flight track (east of runway 16/34R or west of runway 16/34L), measured in tenths of a mile

X_6 = a binary variable representing the city of Des Moines, WA

X_7 = a binary variable representing the city of Normandy Park, WA

X_8 = a binary variable representing the city of SeaTac, WA

X_9 = a binary variable representing unincorporated King County, WA

X_{10} = a binary variable representing the city of Tukwila, WA

Table 6.3 summarizes the results of their analysis. The average drop in house value attributable to local airport noise was in the range of 10%.

Some other useful examples of the application of this technique are used for evaluating road noise (Navrud 2011; Navrud and Strand 2011) and the quality of coral reefs in Hawaii (Brouwer et al. 2011).

Complexities with the application of this methodology

There are several complications with the hedonic pricing model: (1) the statistical challenge is to identify all relevant factors influencing housing and separate the effect of these influences on house prices, and (2) the method assumes that purchasers in the property market have the opportunity to select the combination of house features which they most prefer – an assumption which may be violated by personal income constraints.

The contingent valuation (CV) methodology

In contrast to the *revealed* preference techniques described prior, contingent valuation is a *stated* preference methodology. This method bypasses the need to refer to market prices

Table 6.3 Hedonic analysis of SeaTac airport noise

Community	Actual average assessed value of housing unit ($)	Estimated assessed value without airport ($)	Difference ($ loss from proximity to airport noise)
Burien	129,900	143,000	(13,100)
Des Moines	136,100	149,800	(13,700)
Federal Way	142,900	157,300	(14,400)
Normandy Park	173,600	191,100	(17,500)
Tukwila	122,400	134,800	(12,400)

and is perhaps the most frequently used method for evaluating environmental benefits. It asks individuals explicitly to place values upon environmental assets. The most commonly applied approach is to interview households either at the site of an environmental asset or at their homes and ask them what they are *willing to pay* for the preservation of that asset or what they are *willing to accept* in the form of compensation for the loss of the asset. One advantage of this approach is that it can be used to evaluate resources that people value the continued existence of but never personally visit.

Example: Measuring the benefits of reducing air pollution

Air pollution has been identified by numerous research studies conducted by governments and NGOs over the past few decades as significantly contributing to human illness and death. It is neither feasible nor economically desirable to reduce air pollution to zero levels. As a consequence, it is necessary to utilize a cost-benefit analysis to determine the optimal degree of reduction in ambient levels of air pollutants. This requires an assessment not only of the costs of abatement but also the monetized benefits associated with reduced damage to human health and other susceptible targets such as plants, animals, watercourses and buildings. In an early landmark study of the California South Coast Air Basin (Hall et al. 1992), the authors assessed a broad range of health effects attributable to ozone and particulate matter among the 12 million residents of the greater Los Angeles area. They found that the residents experienced ozone-related health symptoms on an average of 17 days per year and that particulate exposure led to an increased risk of death of 1/10,000 per year. They concluded that 1,600 lives a year could be saved by additional air pollution control, exclusive of the non-mortal health effects.

The central research question was whether the benefits from increasing air quality levels up to the National Ambient Air Quality Standards (NAAQS) outweighed the costs of pollution control. Negative economic impacts of air pollution were associated with medical costs and work loss, physical discomfort, inconvenience, fear and impact on others. Three economic measures were used to value pollution-related health effects: the cost of illness (COI), the willingness to pay (WTP) to avoid the health effects and the willingness to accept (WTA) compensation in order to tolerate the continuation of health symptoms. Table 6.4 summarizes their findings for the diverse range of health

Table 6.4 Adjusted daily values for air pollution symptoms in Los Angeles (1990 dollars)

Effect	Value ($)		
	Low	*Mid*	*High*
Cough	0.50	1.50	4.50
Headache	1.00	2.75	7.25
Eye irritation	0.75	1.75	4.00
Sore throat	1.00	2.00	4.25
Chest congestion	1.50	3.25	6.75
MRAD	14.50	23.00	37.25
MMSD	7.50	16.75	37.25
RAD	n/a	53.00	n/a

Source: Reproduced with permission of the publisher.

effects including cough, headache, eye irritation, sore throat, chest congestion, minor restricted activity days (MRAD), multiple minor symptom days (MMSD) and restricted activity days (RAD), including days missed from work, spent in bed or otherwise measurably constrained.

The total monetary value of the benefits of reducing ozone and particulates was estimated at $10 billion. This figure in and of itself cannot provide a guide to action without a comparison to the costs of achieving this level of control. The authors could find no comparable cost estimate for control but examined several related studies which suggested costs up to $13 billion. On the face of it, this would seem to imply that undertaking this level of air pollution reduction would be uneconomic from a social perspective. However, to quote the authors of the original study (Hall et al. 1992, p. 816):

> Attainment of the O_3 and PM_{10} NAAQS (National Ambient Air Quality Standards) requires control of both NOx and volatile organic compounds (VOCs), but these controls will lead simultaneously to attainment of the NO_2 NAAQS, improved visibility, reduced greenhouse gases, and reduced ecosystem effects. Ascribing all control costs to O_3 and PM_{10} overstates the costs of meeting these NAAQS standards.

In addition, the authors observed:

> In this study, no value is ascribed to improvements in visibility, protection of materials or vegetation, or prevention of chronic lung disease. Available information shows that important benefits (including preservation of lung function) are not yet quantifiable in dollars and that current benefit estimates are therefore likely to be underestimates.
>
> (p. 816)

Both these qualifications are illustrative of the fundamental point that cost-benefit analyses – which are critical to the determination of appropriate and economically justifiable public policy – must recognize and incorporate all relevant factors, for failure to do so will lead to socially inefficient policies. The import of this study is that when viewed from a systems perspective, the benefits of air pollution reduction incorporate beneficial outcomes apart from human health. Thus, the benefits clearly outweigh the costs. A series of more recent and inclusive studies have convincingly demonstrated the net benefits of air pollution reduction at the national level. (See Appendix 6.1 for a summary of the most important of these recent studies produced by the US EPA estimating the net benefits of the Clean Air Act over the period 1990–2020.)

Complexities associated with the contingent valuation method (CVM)

As with the other methodologies reviewed prior, there are significant conceptual difficulties associated with the use of CVM despite its common usage. These include the following:

1   *Understating WTP:* The hypothetical nature of CVM scenarios makes individuals' responses to them poor approximations of true value. In some cases, people will *free ride* – i.e. intentionally understating how much they were willing to pay if they thought they might have to actually pay. Conversely, one could argue that if the

individual viewed the question as purely hypothetical, he/she might overstate WTP in order to protect the resource.

2 ***Willingness to pay versus willingness to accept:*** Researchers have noticed a significant difference in responses when questions are framed in two different ways: "What are you willing to pay to receive this environmental asset?" versus "What are you willing to accept in compensation for giving up this environmental asset?" WTA has been found to be generally greater than WTP. There has been extensive debate in the economic literature over this discrepancy. Some have argued that this discrepancy is an artifact dependent on experimental design, while others have suggested that there is a legitimate and theoretically defensible explanation for this difference (Sayman and Onculer 2005; Plott and Zeiler 2005; Georgantzis and Navarro-Martinez 2010; Horowitz and McConnell 2002). Several reasons have been advanced for the continued discrepancy between these two measures: (1) there are psychological reasons to indicate that individuals feel the cost of a loss (WTA) more intensely than the benefit of a gain (WTP), which is consistent with the commonly held loss aversion, reference dependence and the endowment effect associated with Kahneman and Tversky's *prospect theory* (Kahneman and Tversky 1979; Rose and Masiero 2010; Kahneman et al. 1990); (2) because of *moral perceptions* relating to public goods, survey respondents will tend to have a higher WTA/WTP ratio than if the goods are ordinary private goods or money (Horowitz and McConnell 2002; Biel et al. 2011); and (3), related to the prior, there may be an income (or wealth) constraint which sets an upper bound to how much individuals are willing to pay (Alberini and Kahn 2006; Hanemann 1991). In this vein, the Harvard philosopher Michael Sandel (2012, p. 31) has argued that "willingness to pay for a good does not show who values it most highly. This is because market prices reflect the ability as well as the willingness to pay."

There may be another science-based explanation for the discrepancy between measures of WTA and WTP. Remarkable research results have been generated from innovative cross-disciplinary studies in the areas of economics, psychology and neurology under the general rubric of neuroeconomics (Glimcher et al. 2009). Scientists and social scientists have used diagnostic imaging of the brain (e.g. by functional magnetic resonance imaging – fMRI) to observe which portions of the brain are most active during a variety of decisions and emotional states (Levine 2011; Singer and Fehr 2005; Fehr et al. 2005). Using fMRI, for example, De Martino et al. (2009) found evidence to support Kahneman's theory of reference dependency (i.e. the endowment effect). The scientific support for a legitimate inherent difference between WTA and WTP is further enhanced by neurological imaging studies which suggests that emotional responses to losses occur in a separate part of the brain (such as the amygdala) from reward appreciation (see, for example, Lehrer 2009; Shiv et al. 2012; De Martino et al. 2010; Berridge and Kringelbach 2008). Under these circumstances, there may be no reason to assume that WTA would equal WTP.

Whether WTP or WTA is the appropriate measure depends largely on whether there is an increase or a decrease in an environmental good. The US EPA (2010) has concluded that WTP is the appropriate measure if an individual does not have the good in the baseline case or when an increase in the amount of the good is at issue. In contrast, WTA is the appropriate measure where the individual has the good in the baseline case or when a decrease in the amount of the good is at issue.

3   **Part-whole bias:** Individuals may produce inconsistent answers when asked how much they are willing to pay for either an entire ecosystem or its components. The values may bear no logical relationship to each other or may even exceed an individual's income or wealth. Consider the example of wildlife in a pond or lagoon in an urban setting as schematically illustrated by the nested Boolean diagram in Figure 6.4. A person answering a CVM survey designed to elicit his or her valuation of bird life may be presented with any of the following survey questions: (1) How much are you willing to pay for one type of duck (e.g. wood duck/ mallard/northern pintail/northern shoveler/American wigeon/greater scaup/harlequin duck/surf scoter/white-winged scoter/common goldeneye/Barrow's goldeneye/bufflehead/common merganser)? (2) How much are you willing to pay for one type of bird (e.g. swans/geese/herons/loons/grebes/ducks)? or (3) How much are you willing to pay for all the bird life? (For other examples, see Boyle et al. 1994; Bateman et al. 1997.)

4   **Vehicle bias:** Respondents may alter their WTP statements according to the specific payment vehicle chosen (e.g. charitable donations versus a tax). While individuals generally dislike paying taxes, many may feel that a tax would be more effective than relying on charitable funds to protect the environment.

5   **Starting point bias:** A phenomenon labeled by Kahneman and Tversky as *anchoring* may bias responses. Experiments have demonstrated that a survey question's choice of monetary starting point will have a major impact on a respondent's stated willingness to pay for an environmental amenity. For example, there is evidence to suggest that a survey respondent will choose a different value when faced with a suggested range from \$10–\$100 as opposed to \$100–\$1,000. Ariely (2008) suggests that the role of anchoring is even more insidious. He has demonstrated that even

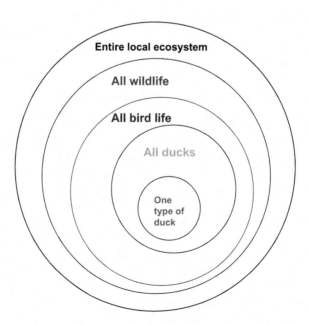

Figure 6.4 Wildlife subsets in example lake

asking survey participants to think of the last two digits of their social security number before making a choice about a totally unrelated matter will influence their decision.

6   ***Extrinsic vs. intrinsic motivation:***   One of the most interesting studies of the potential theoretical complexities in interpreting the results of CV studies emerges from research by Frey and Oberholzer-Gee (1997) on Swiss residents' response to offers of monetary compensation for accepting the siting of a nuclear waste repository in their community. The authors found that "while 50.8% of the respondents agreed to accept the nuclear waste repository without compensation, *the level of acceptance dropped to 24.6 percent* when compensation was offered" (p. 749, italics in original). The authors conclude that intrinsic motivation is partially destroyed when price incentives (i.e. extrinsic motivation) are introduced. These findings may call into question the relationship between monetary values derived from CV analysis and underlying public evaluation of certain projects where issues of social responsibility are in play.

Other methodologies

Several other methodologies have been used to estimate environmental benefits, including conjoint analysis, benefits transfer and production functions. Brief summaries of these techniques are presented in the following.

Conjoint analysis

A variant of contingent valuation, conjoint analysis (CA) has emerged from the marketing and consumer research literature but is easily transferable to the measurement of environmental benefits (Heal et al. 2004). In contrast to contingent valuation, where respondents are asked to assign a monetary value in either a WTP or WTA framework, conjoint analysis infers values by assessing the responses of individuals to a series of detailed choices. CA decomposes the object of choice into a set of attributes, thereby surpassing CVA in the richness of the choice set (Smith 2006). Stewart and Kahn (2006) suggest that CA can avoid some of the inherent bias which may afflict CVA, such as part-whole bias (see Figure 6.4) or the hypothetical nature of the questions, which can lead to intentional under- or overestimation of values. Conjoint analysis has several format variants: ranking, rating, graded-pair comparisons and dichotomous choices. The most commonly preferred format by economists is the last variant, which asks the respondent to indicate his/her preference among two or more scenarios. In a sense, this approach has some of the attributes of revealed preference.

By way of example, case studies of conjoint analysis are presented by Swallow et al. (1992), who analyze preferences about the location of a landfill site in Rhode Island, and Dohle et al. (2010), who focus on public preferences among attributes of mobile phone base stations in Switzerland.

Benefits transfer

Benefits transfer offers an alternative where the application of site-specific revealed or stated preference methodologies cannot be undertaken because of time or resource constraints. The normal procedure involves using monetary estimates from other similar cases and transferring them to the circumstances under study with or without modifications for any site-specific differences between off-site and target subject cases. Common examples entail the use of recreational values already derived in a different locale. (For other examples, see Morey et al. 2002; Smith et al. 2006.) There can be significant problems in guaranteeing the similarity of the source and target circumstances (Spash and Vatn 2006; Plummer 2009; Brouwer 2000; Barton 2002), in which case it may be more appropriate to employ a meta-analysis (e.g. Bergstrom and Taylor 2006; Thomassin and Johnston 2011) which relies on an average of multiple study values or a range bounded by one standard deviation above and below the average value.

Production functions

The production function methodology assumes that an environmental good or service serves as a factor input into a good whose market value is measurable (Heal et al. 2004, p. 113). A two-stage approach is required: first a linkage must be identified and specified between the underlying ecological resource or service and the marketed product or service; second, by holding other variables constant, the value of the ecological resource or services can be imputed from changes in the price of the marketed good or service and its effect on producer and consumer surplus. Heal et al. use an example of the impact of changes in wetland area on the abundance of crabs. The principal challenges in the application of this methodology are (1) assuring that all the relevant ecological-economic interactions have been identified correctly; (2) taking appropriate notice of the influence of market conditions and regulatory initiatives which will have an influence on the derived values; and (3) determining whether a static or dynamic model is more appropriate for capturing the relationship between the ecological good/services and the marketed product (Heal et al. 2004, p. 114).

General conclusions concerning economic valuation methodologies

There is a broader conceptual challenge with respect to valuation methodologies for environmental resources which rely on either direct or indirect assessment of individual monetary evaluations based on preferences. As Pascual et al. (2010) note, most methodologies in common use are grounded in an anthropocentric view of the world. This has been the subject of some debate, as some authors have suggested a viewpoint referred to as *deep ecology* which encompasses the inferred values of other living creatures who cohabit the world with the human species (de Steiguer 2006; Devall 1991; *Ecologist* 1988). Even if one adopts an anthropocentric view, however, the question arises as to what extent the values derived from preference methodologies – such as travel costing, hedonic pricing and contingent valuation – can capture the true economic value of the resource. In order to create legitimate estimates of true value, these methodologies must implicitly assume that the human subjects have access to all the relevant information, are science literate and are rational information processors. Each one of these prerequisites is contentious.

There are at least three types of errors which can arise from the failure to satisfy any one of these prerequisites: (1) incomplete scientific knowledge of system effects, linkages and *thresholds*, specifically (2) cumulative effects and (3) non-linearities. Brief examples of each type of potential error follow.

Incomplete scientific knowledge

In many cases, such information is unavailable to the general public or unknown until after a resource has been damaged or destroyed. Consider the value of *apex or keystone species*. (For more details on this and other scientific concepts and cases mentioned in this section, see Chapter 8.) For example, most people have a psychological distaste for sharks and little knowledge about *trophic cascades* associated with the loss of these apex predators. Any economic valuation derived by CV, for example, would grossly underestimate the economic value of this creature, even to humans. Similar cases include such disparate entities as forests (see Figure 1.2), wolves (see Figure 8.7) and salmon. By way of example, Cederholm et al. (2000, p. 15) list almost three dozen ocean, estuary and freshwater mammal, fish, insect, bird and vegetative species who are food web beneficiaries of Pacific salmon nutrients in the form of juvenile salmon, smolt, fry, eggs and adult salmon death before and after spawning.

Cumulative effects

A good example of potentially misleading economic assessments could stem from valuations placed on the loss of local wetlands. Any one wetland could have a marginal value less than the benefit of development and therefore not worth preserving. Yet the loss of many such wetlands could have a profound and devastating effect on species such as migratory birds, which rely on a network of wetlands on their flyways for survival. (See, for example, UNOPS n.d.) Other important examples of cumulative effects include biomagnification and bioaccumulation (see Chapter 8).

Non-linearities

Not infrequently, land development in wilderness areas impinges on or destroys wildlife habitat. It is not unreasonable to assume that reduction in wildlife numbers (such as deer) might be proportional to loss of habitat, and elicited values would reflect this assumption. However, the loss of even a small part of wildlife range can have an effect far out of proportion to its size because of the existence of a threshold effect. This *non-linear effect* can even lead to the total loss of a herd and a resulting economic effect much greater than the value elicited by contingent valuation (Dykstra 2004; Sinclair 2007).

It should be apparent from the previous discussion that each methodology for evaluating environmental benefits has limitations. A satisfactory resolution to this problem requires a hybrid approach which includes (1) *sensitivity analysis* and (2) *triangulation*, where several methods are used jointly to arrive at reasonable estimates of benefits.

This chapter concludes with two case studies (see Appendices 6.1 and 6.2) which demonstrate the value of a comprehensive analysis of environmental costs and benefits. The first is a US EPA assessment of the impact of the Air Pollution Control Act over the period 1990–2020; the second is a study conducted for the city of New York which attempted to value the ecosystem services associated with the city's water supply in order to assess the costs of two radically different alternatives.

Finally, it is worth noting that the use of cost-benefit analysis for the assessment of environmental effects is considered most appropriate in circumstances where there are marginal or incremental differences among options and a relatively short time horizon, such as a single generation. The utilization of CBA becomes more problematic when there are potentially major changes from the status quo and when such changes have an impact spanning several generations, such as climate change. This latter issue is particularly germane in the choice of discount rates and discussions of their relevance.

Discount rates

The determination of an appropriate discount rate is critical to the choice of an alternative project or course of action in CBA, and this poses some difficult conceptual issues. Figure 6.5 shows just how critical the discount rate can be by comparing the present value (PV) of $1 after x years at various rates. The higher the discount rate, the lower the PV of a dollar received in any future year. With a high enough discount rate (such as 18%), a dollar received after 25 years or more is worth virtually nothing. This has clear implications for decision-making among alternative projects which have markedly different temporal profiles of costs and benefits.

There are at least three types of discount rates: personal, corporate and social.

Personal discount rates assess individuals' temporal preferences with respect to costs and benefits. Different individuals may have radically divergent discount rates, and many of these may be high for the simple reason that human lives are finite. People generally prefer

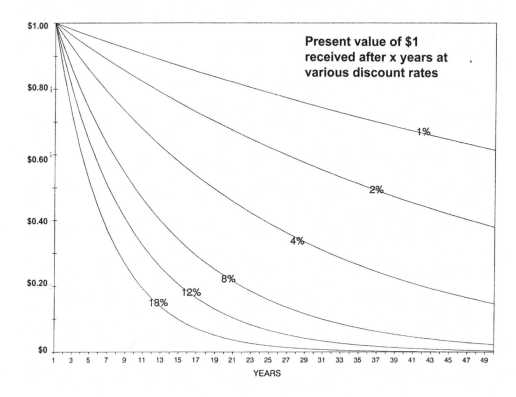

Figure 6.5 Present value at various discount rates

to realize benefits in the near, certain future than in the uncertain, more distant future. Several early studies found individual discount rates as high as 89%–300% in the context of consumer purchase decisions for energy-efficient appliances (Hausman 1979; Gately 1980).

Corporate discount rates. These rates are usually calculated as the weighted cost of capital to the firm, as this figure is used to make decisions about the timing and extent of capital investments. As these rates apply solely to private sector decisions made by companies in the pursuit of profit maximization, this poses a major challenge from a sustainability perspective, for there is no reason to believe that corporate time preferences are similar to those held by society in general.

Social discount rates. Since society is assumed to continue in existence indefinitely and some provision must be made for future generations (i.e. our children, and our children's children, etc.), governments and the society they represent will tend to have a longer view, and this is captured by a lower discount rate. [fn 2] At least two major challenges to sustainability emerge from contrasting corporate and social discount rates. First, since it is perfectly rational for a corporation to adopt a discount rate which is higher than the socially desirable rate, some private sector projects will be chosen that are either too early or too late, too small or too large or not desirable from a social perspective. These projects may include new plants and equipment, new processes or new products.

Second, given that the social discount rate is the most appropriate to adopt when making important public policy decisions which affect future generations, it is not clear what this rate should actually be. Governmental regulatory agencies in the United States and elsewhere have frequently adopted a social discount rate of 3%–4% in contrast to rates within the private sector, which may range from 10%–15%. A cost-benefit analysis with a sufficiently high discount rate – even 3% – could justify the destruction of a renewable resource which has existed from time immemorial and which could otherwise exist indefinitely into the future. Examples of this can be found in such areas as forestry and fisheries.

In the context of climate change, Brekke and Johnsson-Stenman (2008) argue for the use of a risk-free return, which they estimate for the United States at 0.4%. In fact, it has been hypothesized that any non-zero discount rate may jeopardize the welfare of future generations and that a zero discount rate must be adopted in some circumstances (Stern 2006). If one assumes that future generations may be worse off than ours – a not totally unreasonable assumption in light of the threats from global warming – then a negative discount rate may be appropriate. Both zero and negative rates pose unusual challenges for project evaluation.

These issues have not been resolved, but extensive research has been conducted on methods to address some of these concerns. Several authors have suggested that the use of a constant discount rate is inappropriate to deal with long-run major threats such as global warming and have proposed the use of *hyperbolic or quasi-hyperbolic* discounting (Harvey 1994; Ainslie 1991; Henderson and Bateman 1995; Laibson 1997). This approach is based on empirical evidence which suggests that many individuals actually use two implicit types of discounting: a high rate for short-term decisions, based on impulsive human instincts, versus a much lower, longer-term or planning rate for decisions in the future. Karp (2005) argues that the application of hyperbolic discounting to long-term issues of major import such as global warming would involve declining social discount rates as the time horizon is extended.

Current Approach

	Year 1	Year 2	Year 3	Year 4	Year 5	...	...	...	Year n
NPV0 =	$\dfrac{(B_1 - C_1)}{1 + r}$	$\dfrac{(B_2 - C_2)}{(1 + r)^2}$	$\dfrac{(B_3 - C_3)}{(1 + r)^3}$	$\dfrac{(B_4 - C_4)}{(1 + r)^4}$	$\dfrac{(B_5 - C_5)}{(1 + r)^5}$				$\dfrac{(B_n - C_n)}{(1 + r)^n}$

The Reality

	Year 1	Year 2	Year 3	Year 4	Year 5	Year 6	Year 7	...	Year n
NPV0 =	$\dfrac{(B_1 - C_1)}{1 + r}$	$\dfrac{(B_2 - C_2)}{(1 + r)^2}$	$\dfrac{(B_3 - C_3)}{(1 + r)^3}$	$\dfrac{(B_4 - C_4)}{(1 + r)^4}$	$\dfrac{(B_5 - C_5)}{(1 + r)^5}$				$\dfrac{(B_n - C_n)}{(1 + r)^n}$
NPV1 =		$\dfrac{(B_1 - C_1)}{1 + r}$	$\dfrac{(B_2 - C_2)}{(1 + r)^2}$	$\dfrac{(B_3 - C_3)}{(1 + r)^3}$	$\dfrac{(B_4 - C_4)}{(1 + r)^4}$	$\dfrac{(B_5 - C_5)}{(1 + r)^5}$			$\dfrac{(B_n - C_n)}{(1 + r)^n}$
NPV2 =			$\dfrac{(B_1 - C_1)}{1 + r}$	$\dfrac{(B_2 - C_2)}{(1 + r)^2}$	$\dfrac{(B_3 - C_3)}{(1 + r)^3}$	$\dfrac{(B_4 - C_4)}{(1 + r)^4}$	$\dfrac{(B_5 - C_5)}{(1 + r)^5}$		$\dfrac{(B_n - C_n)}{(1 + r)^n}$
			...						
									NPVn

The Proposal

	Year 1	Year 2	Year 3	Year 4	Year 5	...	...	...	Year n
NPV0* =	$\dfrac{\text{NPV1}}{1 + r}$	$\dfrac{\text{NPV2}}{(1 + r)^2}$	$\dfrac{\text{NPV3}}{(1 + r)^3}$	$\dfrac{\text{NPV4}}{(1 + r)^4}$	$\dfrac{\text{NPV5}}{(1 + r)^5}$	...	...	...	$\dfrac{\text{NPVn}}{(1 + r)^n}$

Figure 6.6 Alternative discounting methodology

Figure 6.6 presents another alternative to conventional *exponential discounting* from time period zero. The underlying approach of this hybrid (Sumaila 2004; Sumaila and Walters 2005) is that while we make a project decision now, the payoff will look different if such a decision were to be made in any subsequent year. This proposal suggests that such future valuations should be recognized and incorporated more explicitly into decisions today. According to Ainsworth and Sumaila:

> Under the intergenerational discounting approach, the NPV term considers the value of benefits received by the current generation (calculated at a standard discount rate) plus the value of benefits received by an annual influx of new stakeholders. These participants bring with them a renewed perspective on future earnings, partially reset-ting the discounting clock. The equation requires a standard annual discount factor and a discount factor to evaluate benefits destined for future generations.
>
> (Ainsworth and Sumaila 2005, p. 1106)

Prager and Shertzer (2006) provide a small clarification to the original formulation, emphasizing the distinction between the two types of discount rates: the future-genera-tional discount rate *per generation* and the future-generational discount rate *per year*.

In light of the complex theoretical issues surrounding the choice of an appropriate dis-count rate or system of rates, Helm (2009) has advanced the argument that the decisions our society faces today with respect to global climate change must transcend questions of discounting and focus instead on the existence and significance of *fat tails* (Taleb 2007; Weitzman 2009). This theory posits that the probability distribution of possible future negative outcomes from current GHG emissions contains a long right tail with non-zero probabilities of catastrophic consequences. In essence, the necessity to avoid these possible outcomes at all costs renders debate over the choice of discount rates essentially academic.

Another study which de-emphasizes the role of the discount rate in decisions concerning the response to possible effects of future climate change was authored by Sterner and Persson (2008). Drawing upon the work of Weitzman (2007), the authors argue that changing relative prices (specifically the rising relative prices of depleting environmental resources) may outweigh the importance of discount rates in motivating current public policy decisions on greenhouse gas abatement.

In sum, cost-benefit analysis remains an important part of the armory of decision methodologies available to policymakers, but it has been the subject of at least five major critiques. First, CBA was originally intended to compare public projects at the margin with relatively similar effects and timelines; it is inappropriate for making judgments about large-scale issues that affect future generations and the planet as a whole. Second, in parallel with this problem, conventional CBA's focus on efficiency and its utilitarian roots detracts from its ability to recognize or incorporate matters of distributional equity, whether cross-sectional or temporal. Third, CBA will invariably favor projects whose benefits can be more easily monetized despite the fact that some of the most pressing social issues and values are not easily quantified. Under these circumstances, the most appropriate course of action is to supplement this decision methodology with others which have compensatory strengths. One of these is multi-attribute decision-making (MADM), which is briefly described in Appendix 6.3. Fourth, there are serious concerns about the relevance of conventional cost-benefit analysis in circumstances where ecological systems may face major discontinuities or *tipping points*. The nature of this concern is explored in Chapters 8 and 10, which deal with key ecological concepts and risk analysis. And fifth, while CBA is claimed to be a value-free methodology able to make choices on the basis of objective assessments, several philosophical critiques have challenged the assumption of value neutrality (Copp and Levi 1982; Ackerman and Heinzerling 2004).

Final notes on evaluative methodologies

The aforementioned economic evaluation methodologies have continued to evolve with the increasing recognition of the critical importance of ecosystem services by both corporations and governments. In response to the perceived need for more advanced tools, several modeling efforts have been undertaken by universities and non-profit organizations. These models are specifically designed to permit the rigorous derivation of monetary estimates for ecosystems services at various levels of geographic scale. Foremost among these models are: (1) InVEST (InVEST website; Kareiva et al. 2011) from Stanford University, the University of Minnesota and the Nature Conservancy which utilizes a production function approach to estimation on a geographic information system (GIS) platform; (2) the ARIES (Artificial Intelligence for Ecosystem Services) project led by the Gund Institute at the University of Vermont (uvm.edu/gund) which utilizes the benefit transfer methodology; (3) the European Commission's TEEB (The Economics of Ecosystems and Biodiversity (TEEB 2010a, 2010b, teebweg.org); and (4) MIMES (Multiscale Integrated Models of Ecosystem Services) (see Nelson and Daily 2010).

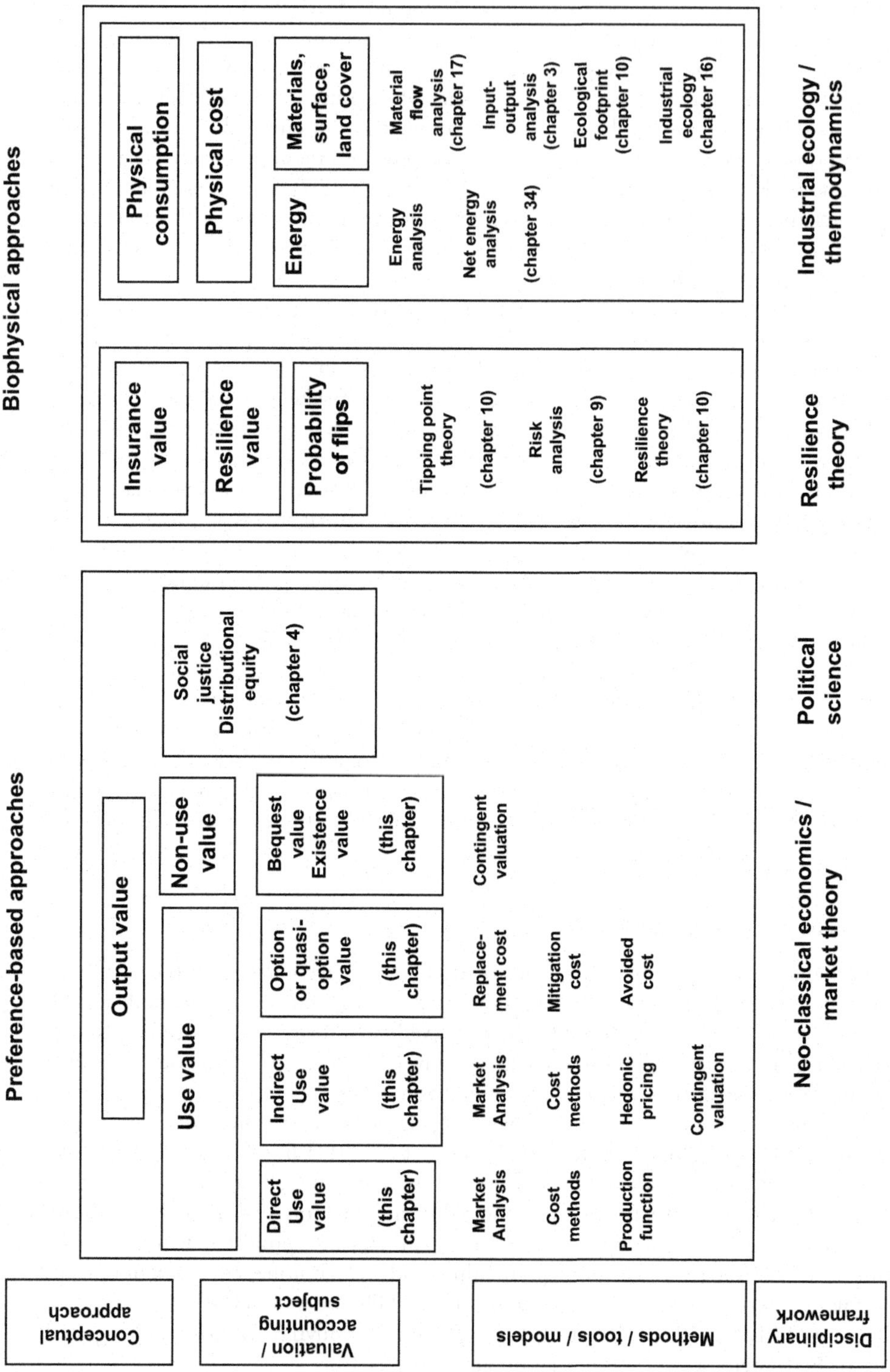

Figure 6.7 Alternative evaluation paradigms

Much of the previous discussion in this chapter relating to evaluative methodologies has been cast in terms of economic analysis – an approach common to policymakers and businesses in the industrialized world. In the view of Stewart and Kahn (2006, pp. 171–172), however, several of the most commonly used evaluative methodologies are ineffective in a developing world context. For example, the hedonic pricing model assumes the existence of perfect mobility where consumers are free to choose among housing options regardless of location. In addition, the authors doubt the value of information extracted from contingent valuation surveys when respondents have little or no experience of a market economy. Other more situation-appropriate methodologies may be preferable. By way of example, the authors cite a conjoint analysis study conducted in Latin America where respondents are presented with choice sets involving trade-offs between varying amounts of physical goods (such as diesel fuel and gasoline and access to health care and education) rather than hypothetical questions of CV analysis designed to elicit estimate of willingness to pay.

Another major issue revolves around the philosophical framework underlying most of the common evaluative methodologies; it is fundamentally anthropocentric, focusing on human preferences and utility – the language of modern economics. There is, however, another major paradigm which focuses on intrinsic ecological values, sometimes termed *biophysical evaluation*. In a comprehensive survey of the economics of valuing ecosystem services and biodiversity, Pascual et al. (2010) elaborated on the critical differences between preference-based and biophysical approaches. Figure 6.7, adapted from their analysis, classifies the principal evaluative methodologies under each of the two rubrics and indicates where each is discussed within this textbook. [fn 3]

Notes

1 In economics, total social welfare is composed of both consumer surplus and its mirror concept, producer surplus, measured as the area between the price line and supply curve. Producer surplus is a measure of the excess of what producers receive over the amount of money for which they are willing to sell their product.

2 The social discount rate is composed of two terms: the pure social time preference (or rate) plus the product of the growth rate of consumption and the elasticity of the marginal utility of consumption (Ramsay 1928). The UK Treasury (2003, Annex 6, p. 97) explains the rationale for the two components. The first is the rate at which individuals discount future consumption over present consumption on the assumption that no change in per capita consumption is expected. The second element is included,

if per capita consumption is expected to grow over time, reflecting the fact that these circumstances imply future consumption will be plentiful relative to the current position and thus have lower marginal utility. This effect is represented by the product of the annual growth in per capita consumption and the elasticity of marginal utility of consumption with respect to utility.

For further discussion of the social rate of discount related to climate change in particular, see Stern (2006, section 2A).

3   In their analysis, Pascual et al. (2010, p. 43) have adopted a specific definition of insurance value. To quote the authors:

> Currently, environmental economists interested in valuing resilience of ecosystems regard it not as a property but as natural capital (stock) yielding a "natural insurance" service (flow) which can be interpreted as a benefit amenable for inclusion in cost benefit analysis.

Appendix 6.1
Applying evaluation methodology – case study of the US Clean Air Act

Table 6.5 presents US EPA estimates of the distribution of a broad range of avoided health effects in 2020 as a result of the implementation of the Clean Air Act (US EPA 2011). Table 6.6 derives mean primary annual benefits for the years 2000, 2010 and 2020. The present value of total monetized benefits of the Clean Air Act as reported in Table 6.7 ranges from $1.4 to $35 trillion. By comparison, the value of direct compliance expenditures (i.e. costs) over the same period equals approximately $0.38 trillion, yielding a central benefit-cost ratio of 32:1.

Table 6.5 Health effects avoided via the US Clean Air Act (CAA)

Endpoint	Pollutant	Incidence			Valuation (million 2006$)		
		5th percentile	Mean	95th percentile	5th percentile	Mean	95th percentile
Mortality	Particulate matter (PM), Ozone	45,000	230,000	490,000	170,000	1,800,000	5,500,000
Morbidity							
Chronic bronchitis	PM	12,000	75,000	130,000	3,100	36,000	130,000
Non-fatal myocardial infarction	PM	80,000	200,000	300,000	6,200	21,000	48,000
Hospital admissions, respiratory	PM, Ozone	24,000	66,000	110,000	320	1,100	1,800
Hospital admissions, cardiovascular	PM	52,000	69,000	84,000	1,400	2,000	2,600
ER visits, respiratory	PM, Ozone	64,000	120,000	180,000	22	44	69
Acute bronchitis	PM	−7,000	180,000	340,000	−4	94	220
Lower respiratory symptoms	PM	1,200,000	2,300,000	3,300,000	18	42	76
Upper respiratory symptoms	PM	620,000	2,000,000	3,300,000	17	60	130

(Continued)

Table 6.5 (Continued)

Endpoint	Pollutant	Incidence			Valuation (million 2006$)		
		5th percentile	*Mean*	*95th percentile*	*5th percentile*	*Mean*	*95th percentile*
Asthma exacerbation	PM	270,000	2,400,000	6,700,000	15	130	390
Minor restricted activity days	PM, Ozone	91,000,000	110,000,000	140,000,000	3,800	6,700	10,000
Work loss days	PM	15,000,000	17,000,000	19,000,000	2,300	2,700	3,000
School loss days	Ozone	2,200,000	5,400,000	8,600,000	190	480	770
Outdoor worker productivity	Ozone	n/a	n/a	n/a	170	170	170

Source: US EPA 2011 pp. 5–26

Table 6.6 Annual monetized benefits of US CAA

Benefit category	Annual monetized benefits (million 2006$) by target year			Notes
	2000	*2010*	*2020*	
Heath effects				
PM mortality	710,000	1,200,000	1,700,000	PM mortality estimates based on Weibull distribution derived from Pope et al. (2002) and Laden et al. (2006); ozone mortality estimates based on pooled function
PM morbidity	27,000	46,000	68,000	
Ozone mortality	10,000	33,000	55,000	
Ozone morbidity	420	1,300	2,100	
Subtotal health effects	*750,000*	*1,300,000*	*1,900,000*	
Visibility				
Recreational	3,300	8,600	19,000	Recreational visibility only includes benefits in the regions analyzed in Chestnut and Rowe (1990) – i.e. California, the Southwest and the Southeast
Residential	1,000	25,000	48,000	
Subtotal visibility	*14,000*	*34,000*	*67,000*	
Agricultural and forest productivity	1,000	5,500	11,000	
Material damage	58	93	110	
Ecological	6.9	7.5	8.2	Reduced lake acidification benefits to recreational fishing
Total all categories	**770,000**	**1,300,000**	**2,000,000**	

Table 6.7 Annual estimates of benefits and costs of US CAA

	Annual estimates			Present value estimate
	2000	2010	2020	1990–2020
Monetized direct costs (millions 2006$):				
Low				
Central	20,000	53,000	65,000	380,000
High				
Monetized direct benefits (millions 2006$):				
Low	90,000	160,000	250,000	1,400,000
Central	770,000	1,300,000	2,000,000	12,000,000
High	2,300,000	3,800,000	5,700,000	35,000,000
Net benefits (millions 2006$):				
Low	70,000	110,000	190,000	1,000,000
Central	750,000	1,200,000	1,900,000	12,000,000
High	2,300,000	3,700,000	5,600,000	35,000,000
Benefit/cost ratio:				
Low	5 to 1	3 to 1	4 to 1	4 to 1
Central	39 to 1	25 to 1	31 to 1	32 to 1
High	115 to 1	72 to 1	88 to 1	92 to 1
Costs per premature mortality avoided (2006$):				
	180,000	330,000	280,000	not estimated

In its comprehensive study, the EPA (2011) makes several important qualifications which strengthen the already persuasive case for the net benefits of the Clean Air Act:

> The direct benefits of the Clean Air Act from 1970 to 1990 include reduced incidence of a number of adverse human health effects, improvements in visibility, and avoided damage to agricultural crops. Based on the assumptions employed, the estimated economic value of these benefits ranges from $5.6 to $49.4 trillion, in 1990 dollars, with a mean, or central tendency estimate, of $22.2 trillion. These estimates do not include a number of other potentially important benefits which could not be readily quantified, such as ecosystem changes and air toxics-related human health effects. The estimates are based on the assumption that correlations between increased air pollution exposures and adverse health outcomes found by epidemiological studies indicate causal relationships between the pollutant exposures and the adverse health effects.

Economy-wide modeling was also conducted to estimate the effect of the 1990 amendments on overall US economic growth and the economic welfare of American households. When some of the beneficial economic effects of clean air programs were incorporated along with the costs of these programs, economy-wide modeling projected net overall improvements in economic growth and welfare. These improvements are projected to occur because cleaner air leads to better health and productivity for American workers, as well as savings on medical expenses for air pollution–related health problems. The beneficial economic effects of these two improvements more than offset the costly effects across the economy of expenditures for pollution control.

Appendix 6.2
Placing a value on ecosystem services – case study of New York City's water supply

New York City has perennially faced the problem of guaranteeing an ample supply of clean water to its 8 million inhabitants. In the early 1990s, the US EPA introduced new requirements for public water systems that mandated either the construction of filtration systems for unfiltered sources or that the water supplied meet certain criteria in order to avoid filtration. The Catskill/Delaware watershed has provided clean water for New York City since 1915 without the need for filtering and had met 90% of the city's demands. In response to the new EPA requirement, city managers had two choices: (1) build a new filtration system or (2) introduce a comprehensive watershed protection program including land purchase, pollution reduction and conservation easements that would allow the natural ecosystems to purify the water.

It was estimated that the filtration plant would entail a capital expenditure of between $6 and $8 billion with annual operating costs in the range of $300–$500 million. In contrast, an innovative program to compensate private landholders in the watershed to reduce their environmental burden would cost only $1–$1.5 billion over a ten-year period (David Suzuki Foundation 2008; AWWA 2004; Perrot-Maitre and Davis 2001; Richmond et al. 2007; Heal 2004). This was clearly the desirable option, yet there were significant complications to pursuing this second alternative due to the need for an innovative financial model and because of the fragmented nature of land ownership and its diverse use within the watershed. For example, the city owned less than 10%, an additional 25% was devoted to state parks and the remaining 65% was under private ownership and devoted to small-scale forestry and agriculture. The major environmental concern focused on the potentially negative effects of 400 dairy and livestock farms which could threaten local waterways with runoff containing pathogens, nutrients and other pollutants. New York City adopted a broad array of instruments to pay for the second option, including the use of taxes, bonds and trust funds; compensation measures for landowners to adopt best management practices and improved forest management; and property transfer and purchase arrangements which entailed government acquisition and transfer of development rights, conservation easements and hydrologically sensitive land. Using a discount rate of 7% (the then current rate on New York City municipal bonds), New York derived a net present value for each alternative as presented in Table 6.8. With this discount rate, the NPV of the natural watershed filtration option was less than 8% of the combined capital and operating costs of a new filtration plant. The table also calculates the NPV of both options using an estimated social discount rate of 3%. The decision remains unchanged with this alternative rate.

Table 6.8 New York water supply options

$ million 30-year time horizon		NPV at 7%	Year											
			1	2	3	4	5	6	7	8	9	10	11	30
Watershed	Compensation payments	$878	$125	$125	$125	$125	$125	$125	$125	$125	$125	$125	$0	$0
Filtration plant	Capital	$7,000	$7,000												
	Operating	$4,590	$0	$400	$400	$400	$400	$400	$400	$400	$400	$400	$400	$400
	Total	$11,590													
	Difference at 7%	$10,712													
	Difference at 3%	$13,386													

Appendix 6.3
A brief overview of multi-attribute decision-making (MADM)

MADM has been employed to overcome some of the recognized deficiencies of CBA when decisions entail a broad range of social, ecological and economic issues. There are several variants of this type of decision methodology, but among the most common is the alternative-attributes matrix (AAM). In an AAM, the options or alternatives are arrayed on one axis, and the policy objectives and/or choice criteria are displayed on the other. Each cell of the matrix is filled with a qualitative or quantitative value. The challenge is how to evaluate these data in order to reach a decision, bearing in mind that, first, some criteria may be more important than others, and, second, information may range from a simple yes or no to a relative value scale from 0–10. A common methodological approach in an alternatives-attribute matrix is as follows: (1) for each criterion, assign a score (out of 100) for each policy option; (2) assign weights to each criterion; (3) multiply the criteria weights by the policy scores and sum for each policy alternative; and (4) finally choose the policy alternative with the highest score. Table 6.9 illustrates this process. In order to address any concerns among decision makers that the choice of weights may involve uncertainty or a certain degree of arbitrariness, sensitivity analysis may be employed to test for the robustness of the recommended option.

In certain circumstances, it may not be possible to enter a single value in a cell; uncertainty concerning values may necessitate the use of probability distributions. Microsoft Excel add-in software programs such as @RISK (Palisades Corp) and Crystal Ball (Oracle Corporation) allow the user to enter and evaluate different types of probability distributions in as many alternative-attribute cells as necessary. This involves a four-step process: (1) specifying the type of probability distribution for a cell, (2) entering the parameters of the distributions, (3) running the simulation which processes the model for n iterations (this is a type of Monte Carlo experiment), and (4) reporting the results of the Monte Carlo simulation as histograms along with the expected value and standard deviation. Cumulative probability distributions may also be generated. (See, for example, ADB 2002.)

Under certain circumstances, the decision makers may be unwilling or unable to force each variable to be expressed quantitatively. In its early work for NASA, the RAND Corporation developed a hybrid decision methodology which avoided some of the conceptual problems of reducing all data to a common metric. Table 6.10 reproduces the original problem addressed by this methodology: the choice of an astronaut's pressure suit for the US Apollo space mission. There were five design finalists, and the complexity of the choice process was due to a mix of quantitative and qualitative data as well as attributes with different levels of importance (MacCrimmon 1968). The suggested procedure was

Table 6.9 Alternative-attributes decision process

Step one	Alternatives – (scores out of 100)					
Attributes or criteria	I	II	III	IV	V	VI
A	80	40	50	75	40	10
B	25	60	60	35	60	100
C	0	40	90	65	30	20
D	60	40	15	10	70	70
E	40	60	90	25	40	40
F	40	10	5	85	90	75
G	55	40	20	15	10	100
H	50	20	50	75	40	20
I	60	40	25	75	60	70
J	0	10	30	60	90	5

Step two		Weighted alternatives					
Attributes or criteria	Criteria weights (out of 10)	I	II	III	IV	V	VI
A	1	80	40	50	75	40	10
B	5	125	300	300	175	300	500
C	9	0	360	810	585	270	180
D	2	120	80	30	20	140	140
E	5	200	300	450	125	200	200
F	7	280	70	35	595	630	525
G	7	385	280	140	105	70	700
H	5	250	100	250	375	200	100
I	4	240	160	100	300	240	280
J	8	0	80	240	480	720	40
	Total score	1680	1770	2405	2835	2810	2675
	Rank	6	5	4	1	2	3

to sequentially apply three separate decision techniques: (1) satisficing, (2) dominance and (3) lexicography.

Step one involved the application of the satisficing procedure; i.e. comparing the alternatives with the minimal attribute requirements of the decision maker. The purpose of this initial step was to reduce the number of admissible alternatives. For example, it was assumed that the basic requirements were: (1) average mobility, (2) average comfort, (3) three-hour life support capacity, (4) 3.7 psi pressurization, (5) 1,900 Btu/hr peak metabolic heat gain, (6) 30 km/sec primary flux meteoroid protection, (7) 250 Btu/hr maximum heat gain, and (8) 5% total ultraviolet radiation. (For "maximum thermal gain" and "total ultraviolet radiation," low values are preferred, while for the other six attributes, high values are preferred.) The result of this first step was that Design I was ruled out because of unsatisfactory life support and Design III was ruled out because of unsatisfactory mobility.

Table 6.10 Choices of five pressure suit designs for astronauts

Attribute	Alternative design				
	I	II	III	IV	V
Mobility	average to good	fair to average	poor to fair	fair to good	fair to average
Comfort	good, but perhaps minor waste management problems	good, but perhaps some minor hot and cold spots	good, no problems expected	average, minor pressure points expected	average, minor hot and cold spots expected
Life support (hr)	1 to 2	3 to 4	4 to 5	2 to 3	2 to 3
Pressurization (psi)	3.6–3.8	3.6–3.7	3.8–3.9	3.7–3.8	3.6–3.7
Peak metabolic temperature load (Btu/hr)	1,600–1,900	1,800–2,000	1,900–2,200	2,000–2,200	1,700–2,000
Primary flux meteoroid protection (km/sec)	25–30	30–35	30–35	27–32	25–32
Maximum thermal gain (Btu/hr)	180–240	210–230	150–170	230–270	230–260
Total ultraviolet radiation (%)	5 to 6	3 to 5	1 to 2	4 to 7	3 to 7

Step two involved the application of a dominance procedure. In this case, the maximum attribute value of II was at least as good as the corresponding minimum attribute value of V, and, in some cases, the attribute values of II were better than the corresponding values of V. The result was that Design V was weakly dominated by Design II; therefore, Design V was ruled out.

Finally, step three involved the application of the lexicographic procedure; only then did the decision maker require information about the relative importance of attributes in order to choose among the non-dominated, satisfactory alternatives. The result was the final choice of Design II over Design IV since it was assumed, with some justification, that life support was the most important attribute.

References

Ackerman, Frank and Lisa Heinzerling (2004) *Priceless: On Knowing the Price of Everything and the Value of Nothing*, New York: The New Press.

Alberini, Anna and James R. Kahn (eds.) (2006) *Handbook on Contingent Valuation*, Cheltenham: Edward Elgar.

Ainslie, George (1991) "Derivation of 'rational' economic behavior for hyperbolic discount curves," *American Economic Review*, May, pp. 334–340.

Ainsworth, C.H. and U.R. Sumaila (2005) "Intergenerational valuation of fisheries resources can justify long-term conservation: A case study in Atlantic cod (*Gadus morhua*)," *Canadian Journal of Fisheries and Aquatic Sciences*, pp. 1104–1110.

Allsopp, Mike H. et al. (2008) "Valuing insect pollination service with cost of replacement," *PLos One*, September, pp. 1–8.

American Water Works Association (AWWA) (2004) "Conserving forests to protect water," *OpFlow*, 30(5).

Ariely, Dan (2008) *Predictably Irrational: The Hidden Forces That Shape Our Decisions*, New York: Harper-Collins.

Artificial Intelligence for Ecosystem Service (ARIES) website (GUND Institute for Ecological Economics, University of Vermont). www.uvm.edu/giee/.

Asian Development Bank (ADB) (2002) *Handbook for Integrating Risk Analysis in the Economic Analysis of Projects*, Manila: ADB, May.

Barton, David N. (2002) "The transferability of benefit transfer: Contingent valuation of water quality improvements in Costa Rica," *Ecological Economics*, 42, pp. 147–164.

Bateman, Ian et al. (1997) "Does part-whole bias exist? An experimental investigation," *The Economic Journal*, 107, March, pp. 322–332.

Bergstrom, John C. and Laura O. Taylor (2006) "Using meta-analysis for benefits transfer: Theory and practice," *Ecological Economics*, pp. 351–360.

Berridge, Kent C. and Morten L. Kringelbach (2008) "Affective neuroscience of pleasure: Reward in humans and animal," *Psychopharmacology*, 199, pp. 457–480.

Biel, Anders et al. (2011) "The willingness to pay-willingness to accept gap revisited: The role of emotions and moral satisfaction," Working Papers in Economics, No. 497, April, University of Gothenburg.

Bockstael, Nancy E. and Kenneth E. McConnell (2010) *Environmental and Resources Valuation with Revealed Preferences*, Dordrecht: Springer.

Boyle, Kevin J. et al. (1994) "In investigation of part-whole biases in contingent-valuation studies," *Journal of Environmental Economics and Management*, 27, pp. 64–83.

Brekke, Kjell Arne and Olaf Johnsson-Stenman (2008) "The behavioural economics of climate change," *Oxford Review of Economic Policy*, 24(2), pp. 280–297.

Brouwer, Roy (2000) "Environmental value transfer: State of the art and future prospects," *Ecological Economics*, 32, pp. 137–152.

Brouwer, Roy et al. (2011) "A hedonic price model of coral reef quality in Hawaii," Ch. 3 in Jeff Bennett (ed.) *The International Handbook on Non-Market Environmental Valuation*, Cheltenham: Edward Elgar, pp. 37–59.

Bruckner et al. (2019) Honey bee colony losses 2018–2019. Preliminary Results, Bee Informed Partnership, June 19.

Calderone, Nicholas W. (2012) "Insect pollinated crops, insect pollinators and US agriculture: Trend analysis of aggregate data for the period 1992–2009," *PLoS One*, 7(5), May, 27 pages.

Cederholm, C.J. et al. (2000) "Pacific salmon and wildlife: Ecological contexts, relationships, and implications for management," Special Edition Technical Report, Washington Department of Fish and Wildlife, Olympia, Washington.

Centre for Ecology & Hydrology (CEH) (2016) New study/neonicotinoid insecticides linked to wild bee decline across England.

Chestnut, L.G. and R.D. Rowe (1990) Section B5 in NAPAP State of Science and Technology Report 27.

Copp, David and Edwin Levi (1982) "Value neutrality in the techniques of policy analysis: Risk and uncertainty," *Journal of Business Administration*, 13(1&2), pp. 161–190.

Crall, James D. et al. (2018) "Neonicotinoid exposure disrupts bumblebee nest behaviour, social networks, and thermoregulation," *Science*, November 9.

David Suzuki Foundation (2008) *Ontario's Wealth: Canada's Future: Appreciating the Value of the Greenbelt's Eco-Services*, Vancouver, BC: Suzuki Foundation.

De Martino, Benedetto, Colin F. Camerer and Ralph Adolphs (2010) "Amygdala damage eliminates monetary loss version," *PNAS*, 107(8), February 23, pp. 3788–3792.

De Martino, Benedetto et al. (2009) "The neurobiology of reference-dependent value computation," *The Journal of Neuroscience*, 29(2), March 25, pp. 3833–3842.

De Steiguer, Joseph Edward (2006) *The Origins of Modern Environmental Thought*, Tucson: University of Arizona Press.

Devall, B. (1991) "Deep ecology and radical environmentalism," *Society and Natural Resources*, 4(3), pp. 247–258.

Dohle, Simone et al. (2010) "Conjoint measurement of base station siting preferences," *Human and Ecological Risk Assessment*, 16, pp. 825–836.

Dykstra, P.R. (2004) "Thresholds in habitat supply: A review of the literature," *BC Ministry of Sustainable Resource Management*, Victoria, BC.

Ecologist (1988) 18(4/5), Special Deep Ecology issue.

The Economics of Ecosystems and Biodiversity (TEEB) website, UN Environment Programme, Geneva. www.teebweb.org/InformationMaterial/TEEBReports/tabid/1278/Default.aspx.

Fehr, Ernst et al. (2005) "Neuroeconomic foundations of trust and social preferences initial evidence," *American Economic Review*, 95(2), pp. 346–351.

Frey, Bruno S. and Felix Oberholzer-Gee (1997) "The cost of price incentives: An empirical analysis of motivation crowding out," *American Economic Review*, 87(4), September, pp. 746–755.

Gallai, Nicola et al. (2009) "Economic valuation of the vulnerability of world agriculture confronted with pollinator decline," *Ecological Economics*, pp. 810–821.

Gately, Dermot (1980) "Individual discount rates and the purchase and utilization of energy-using durables: Comment," *The Bell Journal of Economics*, 11(1), Spring, pp. 373–374.

Georgantzis, Nikolaos and Daniel Navarro-Martinez (2010) "Understanding the WTA-WTP gap through attitudes, feelings, uncertainty and personality," *Journal of Economic Psychology*, pp. 1–33.

Glimcher, Paul W. et al. (eds.) (2009) *Neuroeconomics: Decision Making and the Brain*, London: Academic Press.

Hall, Jane V. et al. (1992) "Valuing the health benefits of clean air," *Science*, February 14, pp. 812–817.

Hamilton, Stanley and Moura Quayle (2002) "Corridors of green: Impact of Riparian Suburban greenways on property values," in Peter N. Nemetz (ed.) *Bringing Business on Board: Sustainable Development and the B-School Curriculum*, Vancouver: JBA Press, pp. 365–390.

Hanemann, W. Michael (1991) "Willingness to pay and willingness to accept: How much can they differ?," *American Economic Review*, 81(3), June, pp. 635–647.

Harvey, Charles M. (1994) "The reasonableness of non-constant discounting," *Journal of Public Economics*, pp. 31–51.

Hausman, Jerry A. (1979) "Individual discount rates and the purchase and utilization of energy-using durables," *The Bell Journal of Economics*, 10(1), Spring, pp. 33–54.

Heal, Geoffrey M. et al. (2004) *Valuing Ecosystem Services: Toward Better Environmental Decision-Making*, Washington, DC: National Academy of Sciences.

Helm, Dieter (2009) "Climate-change policy: Why has so little been achieved?," Ch. 2 in Dieter Helm and Cameron Hepburn (eds.) *The Economics and Politics of Climate Change*, Oxford: Oxford University Press, pp. 9–35.

Helmuth, Obata + Kassabaum, Inc. and Raytheon Infrastructure Services, Inc. (1997) "SEA-TAC international airport impact mitigation study: Initial assessment and recommendations," February.

Henderson, Norman and Ian Bateman (1995) "Empirical and public choice evidence for hyperbolic social discount rates and the implications for intergenerational discounting," *Environmental and Resource Economics*, 5, pp. 413–423.

Horowitz, John K. and Kenneth E. McConnell (2002) "A review of WTA/WTP studies," *Journal of Environmental Economics and Management*, 44, pp. 426–447.

InVEST website. www.naturalcapitalproject.org. Stanford University.

Kahneman, Daniel and Amos Tversky (1979) "Prospect theory: An analysis of decision under risk," *Econometrica*, 47(2), March, pp. 263–291.

Kahneman, Daniel et al. (1990) "Experimental tests of the endowment effect and the Coase theorem," *Journal of Political Economy*, 98(6), pp. 1325–1348.

Kareiva, Peter et al. (2011) *Natural Capital: Theory and Practice of Mapping Ecosystem Services*, Oxford: Oxford University Press.

Karp, Larry (2005) "Global warming and hyperbolic discounting," *Journal of Public Economics*, 89, pp. 261–282.

Kasina, Muo J. et al. (2009) "Measuring economic value of crop pollination services: An empirical application of contingent valuation in Kakamega, Western Kenya," in Pushpam Kumar and Roldan Muradian (eds.) *Payment for Ecosystem Services*, Oxford: Oxford University Press, pp. 87–109.

Klein, Alexandra-Maria et al. (2007) "Importance of pollinators in changing landscapes for world crops," *Proceedings of the Royal Society B: Biological Sciences*, 274, pp. 303–313.

Laden, F., J. Schwartz et al. (2006) "Reduction in fine particulate air pollution and mortality: Extended follow-up of the Harvard six cities study," *American Journal of Respiratory and Critical Care Medicine*, 173, pp. 667–672.

Laibson, David (1997) "Golden eggs and hyperbolic discounting," *Quarterly Journal of Economics*, May, pp. 443–476.

Lambert, Alain (2003) "Economic valuation of wetlands: An important component of Wetland Management Strategies at the river basin scale," UNEP-SCS, May.

Lehrer, Jonah (2009) *How We Decide*, Boston: Mariner Books.

Levine, David K. (2011) "Neuroeconomics?," Department of Economics, Washington University, St. Louis, March 3.

Losey, John E. and Mace Vaughn (2006) "The economic value of ecological services provided by insects," *BioScience*, 56(4), April, pp. 311–323.

MacCrimmon, Kenneth R. (1968) *Decisionmaking among Multiple-Attribute Alternatives: A Survey and Consolidated Approach*, RAND Corporation, Santa Monica, CA.

Morey, Edward R. et al. (2002) "Estimating the benefits and costs to mountain bikers of changes in trail characteristics, access fees, and site closures: Choice experiments and benefits transfer," *Journal of Environmental Management*, 64, pp. 411–422.

Morse, Roger A. and Nicholas W. Calderone (2000) "The value of honey bees as pollinators of U.S crops in 2000," Cornell University, Ithaca, March.

Navrud, Stale (2011) "State-of-the-art in valuation of transportation noise," Presented at External Cots of Transport: Valuation of Travel Time and Traffic Noise, Charles University Environment Center, Prague, November 16.

Navrud, Stale and Jon Strand (2011) "Using hedonic pricing for estimating compensation payments for noise and other externalities from new roads," Ch. 2 in Jeff Bennett (ed.) *The International Handbook on Non-Market Environmental Valuation*, Cheltenham: Edward Elgar, pp. 14–36.

Nelson, Erik J. and Gretchen C. Daily (2010) "Modelling ecosystem services in terrestrial systems," *F1000 Biology Reports*, 2(53), July 22, 6 pages.

Oracle Corporation, Crystalball software. www.oracle.com/us/products/applications/crystalball/index.htm.

Palisade Corporation @Risk software. www.palisade.com/risk/.

Pascual, Unai et al. (2010) "The Economics of Valuing Ecosystem Services and Biodiversity (TEEB)," *Foundations* Ch 5, 133 pages.

Perrot-Maitre, Danielle and Patsy Davis (2001) "Case studies of markets and innovative financial mechanisms for water services from forests," *Forest Trends*, May, 48 pages.

Plott, Charles R. and Kathryn Zeiler (2005) "The willingness to pay-willingness to accept gap, the 'endowment effect', subject misconceptions, and experimental procedures for eliciting valuations," *American Economic Review*, 95(3), June, pp. 530–545.

Plummer, Mark L. (2009) "Assessing benefit transfer for the valuation of ecosystem services," *Frontiers of Ecology and Economics*, 7(1), pp. 38–45.

Pope, C.A., R.T. Burnett et al. (2002) "Lung cancer, cardiopulmonary mortality, and long-term exposure to fine particulate air pollution," *Journal of the American Medical Association*, 287(9), pp. 1132–1141.

Prager, Michael H. and Kyle W. Shertzer (2006) "Remembering the future: A commentary on 'Intergenerational discounting: A new intuitive approach'," *Ecological Economics*, 60, pp. 24–26.

Ramsay, F.P. (1928) "A mathematical theory of saving," *Economic Journal*, 38, pp. 543–559.

Richmond, Amy et al. (2007) "Valuing ecosystem services: A shadow price for net primary production," *Ecological Economics*, 64, pp. 454–462.

Riera, Pere et al. (2011) "Applying the travel cost methodology to Minorca beaches: Some policy results," Ch. 4 in Jeff Bennett (ed.) *The International Handbook on Non-Market Environmental Valuation*, Cheltenham: Edward Elgar, pp. 60–73.

Rose, John M. and Lorenzo Masiero (2010) "A comparison of the impacts of aspects of prospect theory on WTP/WTA estimated in preference and WTP/WTA space," *EJTIR*, 10(4), December, pp. 330–346.

Sandel, Michel (2012) *What Money Can't Buy: The Moral Limits of Markets*, London: Allen Lane.

Sayman, Serdar and Ayse Onculer (2005) "Effects of study design characteristics on the WTA-WTP disparity: A meta analytical framework," *Journal of Economic Psychology*, 26, pp. 289–312.

Shiv, Baba et al. (2012) "Investment behavior and the negative side of emotion," *Psychological Science*, 16(6), pp. 435–439.

Sinclair, Anthony R.E. (2007) "Is conservation a lost cause?," Ch. 8 in Peter N. Nemetz (ed.) *Sustainable Resource Management: Reality or Illusion?*, Cheltenham: Edward Elgar, pp. 217–238.

Singer, Tania and Ernst Fehr (2005) "The neuroeconomics of mind reading and empathy," *American Economic Review*, 95(2), May, pp. 340–345.

Smith, V. Kerry (2006) "Fifty years of contingent valuation," Chapter 2 in Anna Alberini and James R. Kahn (eds.) *Handbook on Contingent Valuation*, Cheltenham, UK: Edward Elgar, pp. 7–65.

Smith, V. Kerry et al. (2006) "Structural benefit transfer: An example using VSL estimates," *Ecological Economics*, 60, pp. 361–371.

Spash, Clive L. and Arild Vatn (2006) "Transferring environmental value estimates: Issues and alternatives," *Ecological Economics*, 60, pp. 279–388.

Stern, Nicholas (2006) *The Economics of Climate Change*, Cambridge: Cambridge University Press.

Sterner, Thomas and U. Martin Persson (2008) "An even Sterner review: Introducing relative prices into the discounting debate," Symposium: The Economics of Climate Change: The Stern Review and Its Critics, *Review of Environmental Economics and Policy*, 2(1), Winter, pp. 61–76.

Stewart, Steven and James R. Kahn (2006) "An introduction to choice modeling for non-market valuation," Chapter 7 in Anna Alberini and James R. Kahn (eds.) *Handbook on Contingent Valuation*, Cheltenham: Edward Elgar, pp. 153–176.

Stipp, D. (2007) "Flight of the honey bee," *Fortune*, 156(5), pp. 108–116.

Straub, Lars et al. (2016) "Neonicotinoids insecticides can serve as inadvertent insect contraceptives," *Proceedings Royal Society*, 283, p. 20160506.

Sumaila, Ussif Rashid (2004) "Intergenerational cost-benefit analysis and marine system restoration," *Fish and Fisheries*, 5, pp. 329–343.

Sumaila, Ussif Rashid and C. J. Walters (2005) "Intergenerational discounting: A new Intuitive approach," *Ecological Economics*, 52, pp. 135–142.

Swallow, Stephen K. et al. (1992) "Siting noxious facilities: An approach that integrates technical, economic, and political considerations," *Land Economics*, 68(3), pp. 283–301.

Taleb, Nassim Nicholas (2007) *The Black Swan: The Impact of the Highly Improbable*, New York: Random House.

TEEB (2010a) *TEEB: The Economics of Ecosystems and Biodiversity Report for Business: Executive Summary*.

TEEB (2010b) *TEEB: The Economics of Ecosystems and Biodiversity: Mainstreaming the Economics of Nature: A Synthesis of the Approach, Conclusions and Recommendations of TEEB*.

Thomassin, Paul J. and Robert J. Johnston (2011) "Evaluating benefit transfer for Canadian water quality improvements using US/Canada metadata: An application of international meta-analysis," Ch. 17 in Jeff Bennett (ed.) *The International Handbook on Non-Market Environmental Valuation*, Cheltenham: Edward Elgar, pp. 353–384.

United Kingdom (2011) *National Ecosystem Assessment* (NEA).

United Kingdom Treasury (2003) *The Green Book, Appraisal and Evaluation in Central Government*, London: Treasury Department.

United Nations Office for Project Services (UNOPS) (n.d.) *Protecting Migratory Waterbird Through Flyway Conservation*.

US Environmental Protection Agency (EPA) (2010) *Guidelines for Preparing Economic Analysis*.

US Environmental Protection Agency (EPA) (2011) *The Benefits and Costs of the Clean Air Act from 1970 to 1990*.

Weitzman, Martin L. (2007) "A review of the stern review of the economics of climate change," *Journal of Economic Literature*, 45, September, pp. 703–724.

Weitzman, Martin L. (2009) "On modeling and interpreting the economics of catastrophic climate change," *The Review of Economics and Statistics*, 91(1), pp. 1–19.

Whitehorn, Penelope R. et al. (2012) "Neonicotinoid pesticide reduces bumble bee colony growth and queen production," *Science*, 336, April 20, pp. 351–352.

Woodcock, Ben A. et al. (2016) "Impacts of neonicotinoid use on long-term population changes in wild bees in England," *Nature Communications*, 7, August 16, pp. 1–8.

7 Placing a value on human life

Any comprehensive assessment of the economic effects of major projects must address the thorny issue of valuing human life. This process raises three central questions: How does one measure the value of life? What are the ethical implications of doing so? And, ethically, should we attempt to attach a dollar value to human life itself? It is argued here that the question of whether we should attach a monetary value to life is basically irrelevant due to the fact that every public project entails some non-zero risk to human life. As a consequence, in making a choice among alternative projects, society is making an implicit judgement about the value of life. Making this value explicit leads to a more efficient, rational and equitable decision process.

One of the principal objections to this process of monetization is that life is sacrosanct and infinite in value; as a consequence, one cannot and must not attach a monetary value to it. If this were the case, society could not undertake any action at all because of the universality of non-zero risk to human life from all forms of human activity. What are the implications, then, of refusing to value life and therefore attaching a de facto value of zero to life? Consider the following choice between two alternatives:

Project A: net benefits of $10,000,000 with a risk to human life of x
or
Project B: net benefits of $11,000,000 with a risk to human life of x + y, where
 y > 0

If we value human life at zero (by refusing to attach a value to it), we will always choose Project B, even though it has a higher risk to human life – *regardless of the size of that risk*. Therefore, to make rational and equitable decisions, we have to be in a position to assess if the extra benefits are worth the extra risk to life. This generally requires valuing life.

Under US Executive Order 12291, issued by President Reagan in February 1981, federal government agencies were required to conduct risk-benefit analyses of proposed regulatory actions. The rationale was that "regulatory action shall not be undertaken unless the potential benefits to society from the regulation outweigh the potential costs to society." Incorporated in these risk-benefit studies are explicit or implicit values for life. In practice, values for human life under the Reagan administration varied markedly by federal government department. For example, the value for the Federal Aviation Administration (FAA) was $650,083, for the EPA $400,000–$7 million, for the Occupational Safety and Health Administration (OSHA) $2–$5 million and for the Office of Management and Budget $22,000. This last figure was both anomalous and contentious as it was intended

DOI: 10.4324/9781003170730-7

to estimate the value of life in proposed regulations to increase restrictions on asbestos. This value was based on a figure of $1 million per lost life but discounted over 40 years to represent the average latency period of mesothelioma, an asbestos-related cancer. It has been suggested that the logic behind this value was a result of political considerations driving science rather than the reverse.

More recent US federal government estimates include the US EPA at $9.1 million, the Food and Drug Administration (FDA) at $7.9 million and the Transportation Department at $9.6 million (*New York Times* February 16, 2011; US Department of Transportation August 8, 2016). In fact, a variety of methodologies have been suggested for the valuation of life. The challenge is to identify a measure which is both economically and ethically acceptable. Table 7.1 lists seven possible measures and the conceptual problems associated with each. Despite the ethical issues associated with the first option, it is commonly used in legal awards and settlements.

If each of these seven alternatives is philosophically unacceptable, one is left with no apparently defensible alternatives. One solution to this dilemma has been provided by the late Ezra Mishan (1971, 1972), an English economist who was a world-recognized expert on cost-benefit analysis. According to Mishan, ethical considerations demand that the

Table 7.1 Alternative proposals for valuing life

Proposals	Problems
1 Discounted Present Value (PV) of person's expected future earnings	Based on the principle of maximizing GDP as the only criterion; unequal treatment of people by gender, age, occupation, social status, extent of disabilities
2 Discounted PV of losses accruing to others as a result of a particular individual's death	Ignores feelings of potential victims; what about retired people?
3 Society makes implicit value judgments through the political process in investments	Inconsistent; not determined democratically
4 The insurance premium that a person is willing to pay	What if there is no beneficiary?
5 The chemical value of a body's constituents	Too little ($8.37, *New York Times* June 26, 1985) – 5 lbs. of calcium, 1.5 lbs. phosphorus, 9 oz. potassium, 6 oz. sulfur, 1 oz. magnesium, <1 oz. iron, copper and iodine; a more recent estimate places the value between $1.00 and $5.00 (Helmenstine 2020).
6 Infinity	Unworkable because all projects entail some risk to life
7 The going price for a contract murder	Hardly acceptable on ethical grounds; besides, it varies: $10,000 in NYC or $0 if it is for practice or to establish your credentials

value of human life should ultimately be determined by the person whose life is at risk. This value should be based on the minimum sum that a person is "willing to accept" in exchange for giving up his/her life. The question naturally arises as to how this proposal would work in practice. One could certainly not ask each individual how much money he/she is willing to accept to face certain death tomorrow. Mishan proposed a way around this dilemma. If a person is indifferent between (1) not assuming a particular risk and (2) assuming the risk along with a sum of money "V," then the sum "V" can be used to derive the relevant cost of the person being exposed to that risk. Consider the following example. Assume that a worker is in a high-risk industry where the risk of death is 1/10,000 per year. Assume also that the worker was offered another job where the risk is marginally higher (say, 2/10,000 per year) and is willing to do so for another $300 per year in pay. Then the implicit value that worker is putting on his/her life is: $300/0.0001 = $3,000,000. The problem this approach raises is that it is impractical for the government to ask everyone affected by a particular policy decision to go through a similar exercise as this process would be extremely time-consuming and expensive.

One possible solution to this problem is to approach it statistically by looking at the job choices made by large groups of people where one knows both the wages/salaries and risks associated with the jobs. Professor Kip Viscusi, an economist at Duke University, has attempted this large-group, statistical approach to valuing human life (Viscusi and Aldy 2002; Viscusi 2003). For example, if a certain job carries a fatality risk of 1 in every 10,000 workers in a year, and if workers are willing to face that risk for $300 in additional pay, then that group of workers values one member's life at $3 million ($300 × 10,000 workers). Viscusi's empirical results have ranged from a low of $600,000 per statistical life for workers in high-risk industries such as mining and oil rigging where the death rate is 1/1000/year to a high of $7–$10 million for white-collar workers.

There are at least four conceptual challenges to the application of Viscusi's theoretical approach: (1) society must be able to determine the relevant level of risk with some precision; (2) this information must be available to the worker; (3) society must be convinced that the worker understands the significance of the risk data; and (4) workers must have the freedom to choose, free of any external constraints, such as job availability. In sum, in order to operationalize this theory, one must assume: (1) a highly accurate method of determining risks; (2) a perfect market in information; (3) rational information processing by individuals; and (4) a perfect, smoothly functioning labor market. None of these conditions is usually satisfied in practice.

In 2010, the US EPA published a report which included a survey of over six dozen US and international studies which valued mortality risk reductions. This survey included both stated preference data and hedonic wage data. The values ranged from $0.04–$76 million per statistical life with an average of $9.24 million.

In an attempt to skirt the thorny issue of placing a value on life for use in a cost-benefit or risk-benefit analysis, an alternative approach has evolved known as the *cost of life saved* (CSX). This methodology is supposedly a type of cost-effectiveness analysis which examines the different values placed by society on life in different contexts and attempts to suggest an efficient reallocation of scare societal resources in order to save the most lives (Tengs et al. 1995; Morrall 2003). When one examines these implicit values, one sees vast differences. (See Figure 7.1.) There is one deficiency with this CSX graph, as lives are never "saved" per se, merely prolonged. So instead of net additional cost (in $) per life saved, we should consider the net additional cost (in $) per life-year saved. This dollar amount is calculated as the quotient of the cost per life saved and the average life

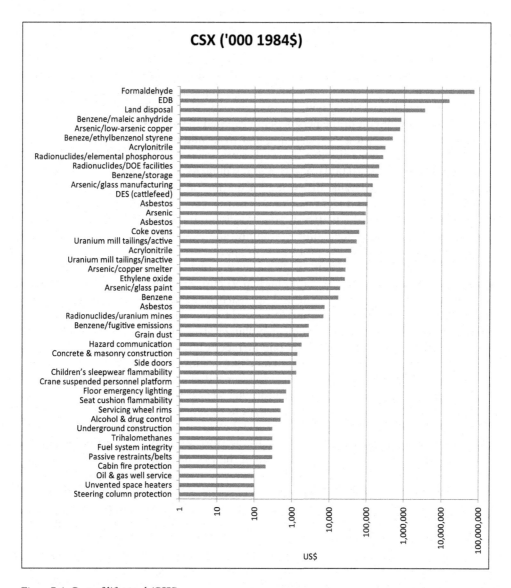

Figure 7.1 Cost of life saved (CSX)

expectancy gained by individuals whose lives are saved/prolonged. This type of revised calculation preserves the rank ordering of alternative regulations, but the risk values are significantly lower.

There are at least three conceptual problems with the CSX methodology. First, this methodology ignores risks other than human life and death (e.g. non-fatal health problems); second, counting life-years lost instead of lives lost discriminates against older people (i.e. a measure that saves the lives of the elderly/middle-aged is not as good as one which saves the lives of the middle-aged/young); and, third, CSX is basically cost-benefit analysis masquerading as cost-effectiveness. The critical assumption in CSX is that the benefits (i.e. the value of a life) are held constant and only the costs of saving or prolonging that life vary. That is, the critical assumption is that each and every human life is equivalent in value under all circumstances – society views the loss of one life in all circumstances in an equivalent manner (i.e. a risk is a risk).

However, we know this to be invalid. Individuals and society implicitly and explicitly place a value on human life which varies by time, place and type of risk. By way of example, in 2017, there were 37,150 vehicle accident deaths in the United States (Ward's Automotive Group 2019). Imagine an equivalent number of deaths from a series of medium-range commercial jets crashes *every day of the year* with an average loss of life of 102 people per crash (i.e. 365 × 102 = 37,230). Society is clearly not indifferent between these two scenarios. Figure 7.2 addresses this apparent anomaly by outlining the numerous characteristics of risks that cause them to be perceived or valued differently.

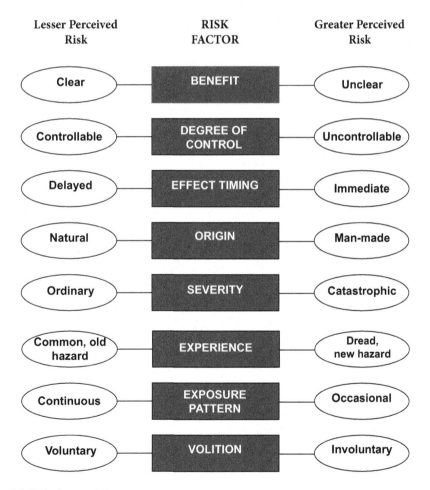

Figure 7.2 Risk characteristics

In conclusion, the practice of placing an economic value on human life seems like an inescapable necessity, yet most methods of so doing present either conceptual or empirical problems of implementation. The remedy is to choose one or more methods carefully, fully explain the assumptions therein and attempt to arrive at a reasonably robust estimate which is ethically defensible. Some progress in this direction has already been achieved by government agencies which assign values to life independent of gender, age or physical condition.

The most important distinction is between two radically different uses of this methodology: (1) government-based cost-benefit analyses which incorporate estimates of the value of human life with the express purpose of reducing the number of lives at risk and (2) those analyses which incorporate such estimates in order to justify policies which may endanger lives. Several well-known examples of the latter include corporate calculations concerning gas tank placement in the Ford Pinto, GM trucks and Boeing jetliners (Birsch and Fielder 1994; *New York Times* July 10, 1999; Negroni 2000). Perhaps the most notorious example of the dubious ethical application of this methodology is associated with a report prepared for the government of Czechoslovakia in 1999 by Philip Morris (Little 2000) and used to justify the sale and use of tobacco in that country. A brief summary of this report is provided in the Appendix 7.1 to this chapter.

Appendix 7.1
Philip Morris' report to the government of Czechoslovakia

In 1999, Philip Morris Ltd. commissioned a study to measure the budgetary implications of smoking in the Czech Republic (Arthur D. Little 2000). The specific aim of this report was to "determine whether costs imposed on public finance by smokers are offset by tobacco-related tax contributions and *external positive effects of smoking*" (p. 1; italics added). The last phrase was curious since, outside the confines of the tobacco industry, it is probably fair to say that there are few, if any, perceived positive effects of smoking. Table 7.2 summarizes Philip Morris' categories of both negative and positive results of smoking with their estimated monetary values. It is apparent that this report considers the shorter life expectancy of smokers as a benefit to the public treasury due to a reduction in health-care costs and pensions. Needless to say, Philip Morris attempted to remove this report from public circulation after the negative response to the macabre conclusions became apparent.

Table 7.2 Philip Morris' estimates of the monetary effects in smoking in the Czech Republic

Income and positive external effects	*21,463 mil CZK*
Savings on housing for elderly	28 mil CZK
Pension and social expenses due to early mortality	196 mil CZK
Health-care costs savings due to early mortality	968 mil CZK
Customs duty	354 mil CZK
Corporate income tax	747 mil CZK
Value-added tax	3,521 mil CZK
Excise tax	15,648 mil CZK
Smoking-related public finance costs	*15,647 mil CZK*
Fire-induced costs	49 mil CZK
Lost income tax due to higher mortality	1,367 mil CZK
Days out of work-related public finance costs	1,667 mil CZK
Environmental tobacco smoke-related health-care costs	1,142 mil CZK
Smoking (first-hand) related health-care costs	11,422 mil CZK
Net balance	**5,815 mil CZK**

References

Arthur D. Little (2000) "Public finance balance of smoking in the Czech republic," Report commissioned by Philip Morris CR.

Birsch, Douglas and John Fielder (1994) *The Ford Pinto Case*, New York: State University of New York Press.

Helmenstine, Anne Marie (2020) *How Much Are the Elements in You Worth?*, Thoughtco.

Mishan, Ezra (1971) *Cost-Benefit Analysis: An Introduction*, New York: Praeger Publishers.

Mishan, Ezra (1972) *Elements of Cost-Benefit Analysis*, London: George Allen & Unwin.

Morrall, John F. (2003) "Saving lives: A review of the record," *Journal of Risk and Uncertainty*, 27(3), pp. 221–237.

Negroni, Christine (2000) *Deadly Departure: Why the Experts Failed to Prevent the TWA Flight 800 Disaster and How It Could Happen Again*, New York: Cliff Street Books.

New York Times (1985) "Value of one life? From $8.37 to $10 million," June 26.

New York Times (1999) "Jury awards family $4.9B against GM," July 10.

New York Times (2011) "As U.S. agencies put more value on a life, businesses fret," February 16.

Tengs, Tammy O. et al. (1995) "Five-hundred life-saving interventions and their cost-effectiveness," *Risk Analysis*, 15(3), pp. 369–390.

US Department of Transportation (2016) "Guidance on treatment on the economic value of a statistical life," August 8.

Viscusi, W. Kip (2003) "The value of life: Estimates with risks by occupation and industry," Harvard John. M. Olin Center for Law, Economics, and Business, Discussion Paper No. 422, May.

Viscusi, W. Kip and Joseph E. Aldy (2002) "The value of a statistical life: A critical review of market estimates throughout the world," Harvard Law School [see also same title NBER 2003 WP 9487].

Ward's Automotive Group (2019) *Motor Vehicle Facts & Figures*, Southfield, MI: Ward's Automotive Group.

8 Some relevant ecological principles

Systems theory is an inherent part of sustainability within and across each of its three major pillars (ecology, economics and society), originally articulated by Elkington (1998) as the *triple bottom line*. The study of systems theory within ecology itself has enhanced and informed analysis within the spheres of economics and society by illustrating how principles which illuminate the understanding of one discipline have cross-disciplinary relevance.

Stability and resilience, non-linearities, thresholds and tipping points

One of the founders of ecological theory, C. S. Holling, was instrumental in elucidating concepts which have played a pivotal role in our modern understanding of the functioning of ecological systems and how they are influenced by anthropogenic behavior. Among the concepts developed by Holling are principles of stability and resilience, non-linearities, thresholds and tipping points.

Stable systems are systems which are not easily disturbed by shocks from their current state or path. In contrast, *resilient systems* are those which, if disturbed by shocks, tend to return to their previous state or path. Figure 8.1 presents one of Holling's classic representations of types of ecological systems (Holling 1973). In this model, there is a central *domain of attraction* (demarcated by the shaded area within the dashed line) where disturbances of sufficiently small magnitude move the system only temporarily away from the point of equilibrium. The system has a certain amount of resilience. However, with a sufficiently large shock, the system passes a *threshold* and jumps from one equilibrium state to another (i.e. there is a *non-linear response*). The crucial point is that this second state may be less desirable from a human perspective than the first.

In a major report on *Valuing Ecosystem Services*, the National Academy of Sciences (2004, pp. 137–138) highlighted the challenges facing conventional economic analysis in assessing thresholds. To quote:

> Severe disturbance of an aquatic ecosystem may lead to an abrupt, and possibly very substantial disruption in the supply of one or more ecological services. This "break" in supply is often referred to as a *threshold effect*. The problem for economic valuation is that before the threshold is reached, the marginal benefits associated with a particular ecological service may either be fairly constant or change in a fairly predictable

DOI: 10.4324/9781003170730-8

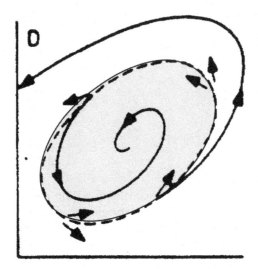

Figure 8.1 Holling's domain of attraction

manner with the provision of that service. However, once the threshold is reached, not only may there be a large "jump" in the value of an ecological service, but how the supply of the service changes may be less predictable. Such ecosystem threshold effects pose a considerable challenge, especially for ex ante economic valuation using revealed-preference methods – that is, when one wants to estimate the value of an ecological service that takes into account any potential threshold effects. Since such severe and abrupt changes have not been experienced, peoples' choices in response to them have not been observed.

In its simplest form, a non-linear response may appear as in Figure 8.2, which portrays the phase changes in water as it freezes or thaws. In this figure, S is a state variable (which may take at least two values: solid or liquid), and F is a forcing variable (e.g. T = water temperature in degrees Celsius). This figure addresses the critical question of whether such a sudden change at the threshold is reversible over some time period of interest. In this case, the answer is clearly yes. Water and ice change back and forth very quickly with modest changes in temperature.

What happens when one considers transformations of potential greater ecological consequence, such as possible changes in sea level driven by global warming? Figure 8.3 portrays the effect of two possible drivers of sea-level rise: (1) a steady expansion in volume due to warming and (2) a possible sudden increment in sea level driven by catastrophic loss of land-based Antarctic or Greenland ice sheets. In this figure, L = sea level and T = global temperature. The critical question is again one of reversibility, and, in this case, the answer is different. The figure contrasts the potentially rapid sea-level rise accompanying global warming with the slow reversal of this trend should there be a subsequent cooling trend. The point of inflection is often referred to as a *tipping point*, which, in layperson's terms, represents a sudden, non-linear and usually unfavorable change which is not reversible in the short to medium term.

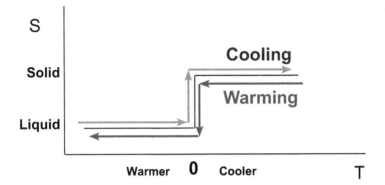

Figure 8.2 Phase change in water

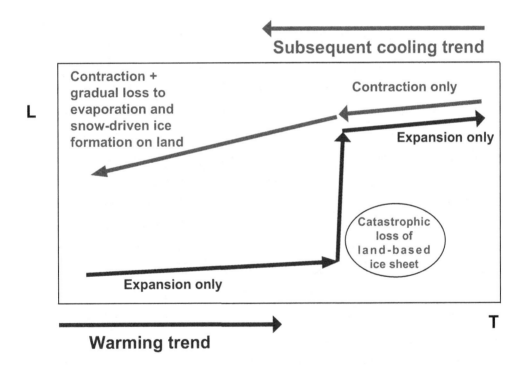

Figure 8.3 Tipping points in sea-level rise

A critical contributor to non-linear system dynamics are *feedback loops* which can be either negative or positive – or what Meadows (2008) has called *balancing* versus *accelerating* feedback. An archetypal example of a *negative feedback* system is the homeostatic system which regulates body temperature. There is a natural tendency to return to the equilibrium temperature of 98.6 degrees Fahrenheit (or 37 degrees Celsius) after any deviation – *as long as* this deviation is not too large (i.e. the temperature does not fall outside the domain of attraction which brings it back to normality).

In contrast, a *positive feedback* system can occur when a shock sets up a process where the system continues to move further away from the point of equilibrium, frequently at an increasing velocity (i.e. the response is non-linear). Recent greenhouse gas–related examples include melting Arctic ice and Siberian permafrost. In the former case, increasing global temperature reduces ice cover on the Arctic Ocean, thereby reducing its albedo (i.e. the capacity to reflect sunlight). As a consequence, the ocean absorbs more heat, and the melting of sea ice is accelerated. This process is self-reinforcing and non-linear. A similar mechanism is posited to exist in Siberia and other Arctic regions which have large areas of permafrost overlaying peat bogs (*Guardian* August 11, 2005; Ise et al. 2008). The concern is that global warming will melt the permafrost, releasing large quantities of entrained methane, which is 20 times more powerful than carbon dioxide as a greenhouse gas (Anthony et al. 2012; Pistone et al. 2014; IPCC 2014; Etminan et al. 2016; Chadburn et al. 2017; Herndon 2018). Research has also suggested the existence of potentially massive methane reservoirs beneath Antarctica which, if released by global warming, could also lead to a strong positive feedback loop on climate change (Wadham et al. 2012). While still the subject of ongoing scientific debate, these scenarios are non-zero-probability, potentially catastrophic events which could lead to a rapid and uncontrolled rise in global temperature, threatening many vulnerable parts of the world. Figure 8.4 illustrates a range of positive global feedback loops and their effect on global warming.

Recent studies of possible ecological tipping points include a broad range of examples across the globe, including the Amazon rainforest, the North Atlantic "conveyor" current, the Greenland ice sheet, the ozone hole, the Antarctic circumpolar current, the Sahara desert, the Tibetan plateau, the Asian monsoon, methane clathrates, ocean acidity levels, El Niño, the West Antarctic ice sheet and salinity valves (Broecker and Kunzig 2008; World Wildlife Fund and Allianz 2009; Zhang et al. 2020; Duffy et al. 2021). While many of these scenarios remain the subject of speculation with an indeterminate time frame, several local or regional ecological tipping phenomena have already been identified. Some of these examples concern sudden loss of forests in Alaska, the US Southwest and British Columbia (Kurz et al. 2008) due to predation by massive insect outbreaks attributed to the effects of global warming and the loss of fish species and their impact on ecosystems through *trophic cascades* (Estes et al. 2011; Eisenberg 2010; Terborgh and Estes 2010). Several illustrations of this phenomenon are presented later in this chapter. A well-documented case of a significant phase shift associated with a tipping point concerns coral reefs in the Caribbean. Hughes (1994) documents how overfishing, inter alia, led to a virtually total collapse of reefs near Jamaica and the emergence of an altered ecosystem dominated by fleshy macroalgae. This dramatic change has major impacts on ecotourism and other revenue streams associated with healthy coral reef–based ecosystems. (See also Pandolfi et al. 2011.)

A major study undertaken by Rockstrom et al. (2009a, 2009b) identified and attempted to quantify nine planetary boundaries that, if crossed, could lead to unacceptable environmental damage. The authors admitted the existence of a large degree of uncertainty in this initial research effort but were, nevertheless, able to draw a number of important conclusions. First, they estimated that three planetary boundaries had already been crossed (climate change measured as atmospheric CO_2 concentrations, the rate of biodiversity loss measured as the extinction rate per year and the nitrogen cycle measured as the amount of N_2 removed from the atmosphere for human use). In addition, it is estimated that our planet may be approaching boundaries for four others categories: global freshwater use, change in land use, ocean acidification and interference with the global phosphorous cycle.

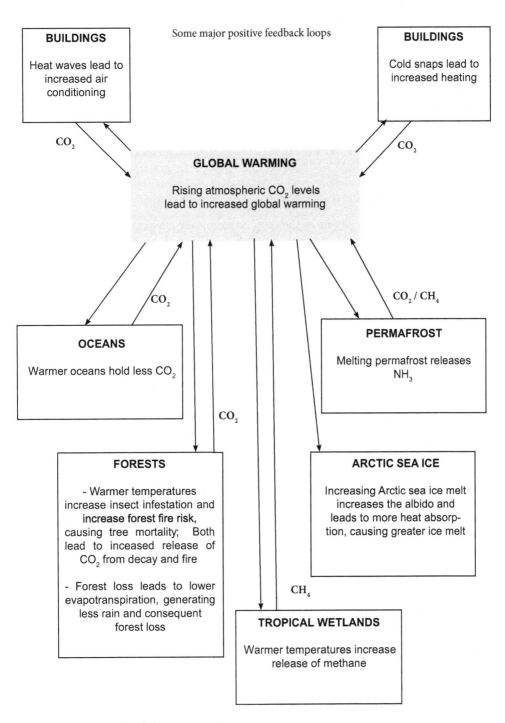

Figure 8.4 Positive feedback loops

From a business perspective, a critical question revolves around the economic effects of crossing a "tipping point." The ecological, economic and social effects of losing a *keystone species* or central system component such as a forest can be momentous. (See, for example, Figure 1.2.)

System boundaries and interdependencies

Central to the study of systems – be they in ecology, economics, business or society – is the correct definition of system boundaries. The following examples are based on ecology and some of the economic consequences thereof.

The case of US agriculture

US agriculture is considered one of the most economically efficient and productive agricultural systems in the world. But just how "efficient" is it? It all depends on where one draws the system boundary – both spatially and temporally. Figure 8.5 presents a schematic representation of the US agricultural system. If the analysis is confined solely to the

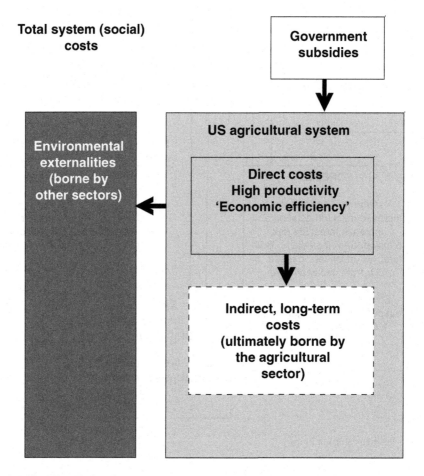

Figure 8.5 The US agricultural system

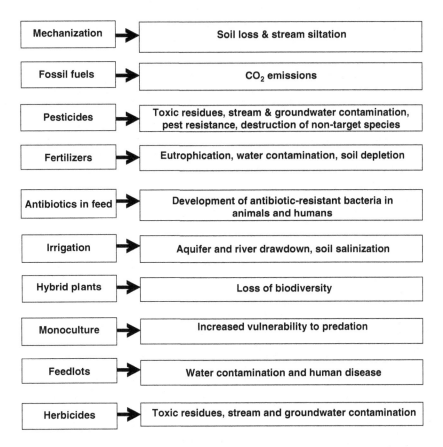

Mechanization	→	Soil loss & stream siltation
Fossil fuels	→	CO_2 emissions
Pesticides	→	Toxic residues, stream & groundwater contamination, pest resistance, destruction of non-target species
Fertilizers	→	Eutrophication, water contamination, soil depletion
Antibiotics in feed	→	Development of antibiotic-resistant bacteria in animals and humans
Irrigation	→	Aquifer and river drawdown, soil salinization
Hybrid plants	→	Loss of biodiversity
Monoculture	→	Increased vulnerability to predation
Feedlots	→	Water contamination and human disease
Herbicides	→	Toxic residues, stream and groundwater contamination

Figure 8.6 Externalities in modern US agriculture

direct costs of US farm output and its high productivity, the system can be considered highly efficient in a traditional sense. There are, however, three other system components which must be considered when calculating the total true (i.e. social) costs: (1) government subsidies; (2) indirect, long-term costs, ultimately borne by the agricultural sector but generally ignored or invisible in the short term; and (3) externalities, principally environmental, which are borne by other sectors. Figure 8.6 summarizes the major groups of uninternalized, agricultural externalities. Once this broader definition of system boundaries is adopted, the "efficiency" and indeed sustainability of US agriculture becomes debatable. The US farming system has been labeled "industrial agriculture" (Altieri 2007; Kimbrell 2002), which relies on massive inputs of energy both directly and indirectly for mechanization, irrigation and the production of herbicides, pesticides and fertilizer. Several studies have characterized the US diet as "eating oil" because of this massive reliance on the products of fossil energy (Green 1978; Pfeiffer 2006).

Other case studies

Systems are characterized by interdependencies, both obvious and counterintuitive. *Trophic levels* refer to the position in a food chain inhabited by an organism. *Trophic cascades* are the effects of additions or deletions of an apex predator (i.e. a predator at the top of a food chain) which ripple through and alter an ecosystem. Estes et al. (2011, p. 301) summarize the critical importance of this concept as follows:

> Until recently, large apex consumers were ubiquitous across the globe and had been for millions of years. The loss of these animals may be humankind's most pervasive influence on nature. Although such losses are widely viewed as an ethical and aesthetic problem, recent research reveals extensive cascading effects of their disappearance in marine, terrestrial, and freshwater ecosystems worldwide. This empirical work supports long-standing theory about the role of top-down forcing in ecosystems but also highlights the unanticipated impacts of trophic cascades on processes as diverse as the dynamics of disease, wildfire, carbon sequestration, invasive species, and biogeochemical cycles. These findings emphasize the urgent need for interdisciplinary research to forecast the effects of trophic downgrading on process, function, and resilience in global ecosystems.

In a typical food chain, each trophic level feeds on the level below and is fed upon by the level above. To understand the complexity of trophic cascades and system interdependencies, consider several recent examples drawn from the US Midwest, East Coast and Pacific regions. The underlying similarity in all these cases is the unexpected linkages which ultimately derive from our limited understanding of the complexity of ecosystems and our interactions with them.

The first example illustrates the unanticipated system effects of the controversial *reintroduction* of wolves into Yellowstone National Park. While the impact on domestic and farm animals was partially anticipated, little was known about the possible effect on fish and birdlife, if any. Figure 8.7 diagrams the rather complex chain of events which led to an increase in trout, yellow warbler and Lincoln's sparrow populations as an indirect result of the reintroduction of wolves (Beyer et al. 2007; Ripple and Beschta 2004, 2007).

Another study by Levi et al. (2012) describes the complex multistage process where the *loss* of wolves can ultimately lead to an increase in the incidence of Lyme disease.

Several additional examples illustrate the economic consequences of the loss and reintroduction of apex species. While changes in ecosystems are clearly of utmost importance to their functioning, casting these changes in economic terms increases the likelihood of a governmental or business response. The first such example, with unpredicted but tangible economic impacts on commercial fisheries, focuses on the loss of sharks off the East Coast of the United States. Sharks have largely been considered undesirable because of their tendency to predate on more valuable species and the occasional human. Myers et al. (2007) traced the trophic cascade associated with the loss of the shark as apex predator. The intentional and unintentional killing of 11 species of large sharks which typically feed on rays, skates and smaller sharks led to an explosion in the population of their prey, which was no longer under predator pressure. This, in turn, led to a massive predation of bay scallops, the next lower trophic level. The result was the total physical and economic collapse of the scallop fishery which had existed for over a century. To place this in context, the value of total scallop landings in the US over the period 2003–2007 was approximately $350 million (Stokesbury 2009).

In addition to the critical role of sharks as an apex species maintaining ecological balance within the complex food chain which they dominate, research has suggested that they have an economic value in and by themselves in the important growth area of ecotourism. A Pew-funded study (Vianna et al. 2010) conducted in the Pacific island state of Palau contrasted the value of a single shark sold on the market for food at US$108 with

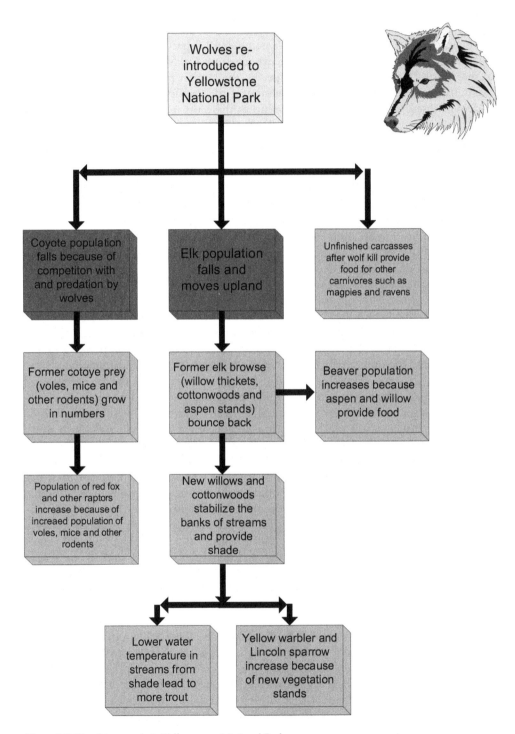

Figure 8.7 Trophic cascade in Yellowstone National Park

its lifetime value as a reef-based tourist attraction, which equaled US$179,000 in a single year or US$1.9 million over its lifetime.

The second example is also related to a commercial fishery with significant economic benefits: the Pacific salmon, whose range extends from California in the South to Alaska in the North. Considered a keystone species, the salmon play an essential role in the maintenance of a thriving ecosystem. Salmon of the Pacific Northwest and Alaska are under increased stress from global warming as these fish require relatively cool water temperatures in which to reproduce and thrive. The loss of this apex species would have a cascading and detrimental effect on a large array of mammals, insects and plants which rely on its central ecological role (Cederholm et al. 2000). Included among these are many creatures with tangible economic benefits from hunting or tourism, including the grizzly and black bear, bald eagle, Caspian tern, coon merganser, harlequin duck, killer whale and osprey, as well as 129 other mammals, birds, reptiles and amphibians.

The third and fourth examples are drawn from the Hawaiian Islands. In the early 1980s, the islands had to import milk powder from the US mainland because of unacceptably high levels of the pesticide heptachlor in the milk from local dairy herds. The question arose as to how milk became contaminated since there were strict rules in place to prevent the exposure of dairy cattle to toxic pesticides. The answer was that heptachlor was used on pineapple plants. The tops (or crowns) of these plants were cut off before processing and, following the dictum that "waste is lost profits," were fed to dairy cattle, generating additional revenue for pineapple growers. It was not immediately obvious that residual levels of heptachlor would be found in the pineapple crowns and that this pesticide would find its way into the milk supply because of the circuitous path of contamination.

The other example from the Hawaiian Islands is drawn from the late 1980s and 1990s. Biologists found strange tumors (non-malignant but life-threatening nevertheless) on green sea turtles off the island of Maui. (See Figure 8.8.) These tumors, which grow in soft tissue, can block the mouth, eyes and other vital areas, leading to death from starvation and related causes. Historically, turtles (up to four or five feet in length) have been revered as gods by the Hawaiians and made the subject of art and mythology. Subsequent to the discovery of these tumors, a book, entitled *Fire in the Turtle House* (Davidson 2003), was published outlining the nature of the problem and possible causes. The tumors were the result of infection by papilloma viruses, but three hypotheses emerged, all anthropogenic in origin: (1) immunosuppression from agricultural chemical runoff; (2) forced change in diet of the turtles as a result of agricultural runoff of nutrients and sediment, which destroys traditional food sources such as sea grasses and favors the growth of potentially toxic algae; and (3) global warming with increased nutrient and sediment loading, also shifting the diet of the turtles to more toxic food. The crucial scientific question was how to choose among these three possible explanations. In discriminating among hypotheses, it is important remember that correlation is a necessary but not sufficient condition for causality. Table 8.1 summarizes the three hypotheses and the observed recent decreasing trends in the prevalence of tumors. Each hypothesis has a driver which must be analyzed for consistency with the empirical evidence. In this case, global warming has been ruled out in favor of the decrease in agricultural activity. Only by conducting this type of analysis can plausible, but incorrect, hypotheses be eliminated. (See Van Houtan et al. 2010 for a more detailed description of the epidemiological underpinnings of this analysis.)

The final example is based on the re-emergence of sea otters in the Pacific Northwest coastal region of British Columbia. Gregr et al. (2020, p. 1243) describe how increased otter

Figure 8.8 Stricken sea turtle, Maui

Table 8.1 Alternative hypothesis for sea turtle pathogenesis

Hypothesis	Recent trends in tumors	Recent trends in hypothesized drivers	Consistency of hypotheses with recent trends in tumors
Immunosuppression from agricultural runoff	The incidence of this condition appears to have decreased in recent years (from personal observation) from about 25%–40% to about 10% now	Agricultural land is being increasingly displaced by residential vacation housing	**Consistent**
Forced change of diet from loss of traditional foods due to agricultural sediment runoff			
Global warming causing increased nutrient and sediment loading		Global warming is continuing	**Inconsistent**

populations have had a negative economic impact on invertebrate fisheries such as geoduck clams, Dungeness crabs and sea urchins, but this was more than offset by increases in finfish:

> Results suggest that sea otter presence yields 37% more total ecosystem biomass annually, increasing the value of finfish [+9.4 million Canadian dollars (CA$)], carbon sequestration (+2.2 million CA$), and ecotourism (+42.0 million CA$). To the extent that these benefits are realized, they will exceed the annual loss to invertebrate fisheries (−$7.3 million CA$). Recovery of keystone predators thus not only restores

ecosystems but can also affect a range of social, economic, and ecological benefits for associated communities.

Systems theory can also inform the discussion of the perceived benefits of eating locally, an idea which has received wide currency after the publication of the national bestseller *The 100-Mile Diet* (Smith and MacKinnon 2007). A key concept in this public debate is the concept of *food miles* – i.e. the distance food has to travel from point of production to point of consumption. Central to this calculation is the amount of energy expended (and associated greenhouse gases produced) in the transportation of this food. In general, the conclusion is that "local is better" since less energy is consumed – and fewer greenhouse gases are produced – in the transportation of the food.

A study from New Zealand critically re-examined this theory by analyzing the total system effects of transporting lamb from that country to the United Kingdom (Saunders et al. 2006). If one relies solely on food miles as the desideratum, clearly it makes more sense to consume domestically produced lamb in the UK. The gist of the New Zealand study is that food miles is an incomplete measure of environmental impact. It includes only the distance food travels and is misleading because it doesn't consider total energy use throughout the production process. In contrast, the New Zealand study takes a much broader view of the environmental impact of lamb and some other major food exports. The environmental impact calculations are based upon a *life-cycle assessment (LCA)* and include the energy use and CO_2 emissions associated with production and transport to the UK. This is a much more valid comparison than just distance traveled as it reflects differences in the two countries' production systems. Table 8.2 (Saunders et al. 2006) summarizes this system-wide re-analysis, which reveals the counterintuitive result that New Zealand lamb has a lower total energy and CO_2 profile than UK lamb even after transportation of imported lamb to the UK is factored into the analysis. Clearly, in order the assess the true overall effect and sustainability of a product, it is necessary to develop a methodology which looks at the problem from a systems perspective. Two major types of this approach are life-cycle analysis and the *ecological footprint*. The first is described in greater detail in Nemetz (2022), and the latter is discussed later in this chapter.

Revenge theory

In 1996, Edward Tenner of Harvard University published a book entitled *Why Things Bite Back: Technology and the Revenge of Unintended Consequences*. The central hypothesis advanced by Tenner was that we know very little about the complexity of systems (natural and even some man-made). As a consequence, any attempt to intervene in one location to fix a problem can lead to another totally unanticipated problem somewhere else. Through casual observation, it is possible to see a plethora of supporting examples of this persuasive theory.

One of the most famous is the story of malaria control in Borneo. While several variants of this tale have been related in the literature, the message is the same: unintended consequences, sometimes very serious, can emerge from what are considered benign interventions designed to cure major problems – in this case, a global disease that affects almost one-quarter of a billion people and kills almost a half million annually (WHO 2019). In the immediate postwar period, the World Health Organization encouraged the widespread use of DDT – considered a benign pesticide – for the control of malaria. Vast swaths of the third world, including Borneo, were sprayed with this chemical – with little understanding of its ultimate ecological effects. Figure 8.9 illustrates one of the cascades of totally unexpected consequences of this spraying (see, for example, Conway 1972). The

Table 8.2 Systems analysis of UK and New Zealand lamb

Item	Quantity (hectares)		Energy (MJ/ton carcass)		CO_2 emissions (kg CO_2/ton carcass)	
	NZ	UK	NZ	UK	NZ	UK
Direct						
Fuel, electricity and oil (l of diesel equiv)		128		17,156		1,116.9
Fuel use (l of diesel) (including contracting)	15.5		3,565		244.9	
Electricity use (kWh)	13.8		594		11.4	
Direct subtotal			**4,159**	**17,156**	**256.3**	**1116.9**
Indirect						
Nitrogen (kg)	5.7	76	1,953	16,147	90.1	807.4
Phosphorus (kg)	12.5	7	985	336	59.1	20.2
Potassium (kg)	0.5	15	29	498	1.7	29.9
Sulfur (kg)	12.3		323		19.4	
Lime (kg)	22.3	87	71	170	50.6	122.7
Agri-chemicals (l ai)	0.6	1.5	338	1,549	20.3	92.9
Concentrate (kg of dry matter)		681		7,432		457.5
Forage, fodder and bedding (kg grass silage)		271		1,319		76.5
Indirect subtotal			**3,699**	**27,451**	**241.2**	**1,607.1**
Capital						
Vehicles and machinery kg)	0.8		273		25.4	
Farm buildings (sq. mi.)	0.1	13.1	198	1,251	19.8	125.1
Fences (m)	1.9		194		17.5	
Stock water supply			66		3	
Capital subtotal			**731**	**1,251**	**65.7**	**125.1**
Total production			**8,589**	**45,858**	**563.2**	**2,849.1**
Yield (kg lamb carcass)	**190**	**308**				
Post-production						
Shipping NZ to UK (17,840 km)			2,030		124.9	
Total production energy input/ emissions			**10,619**	**45,858**	**688.1**	**2,849.1**

initial effect was a marked reduction in the number of mosquitoes and consequent incidence of malaria. However, the spraying of DDT, especially in residence huts, led to the mortality of both cats and small lizards, which controlled rats and caterpillars, respectively. This led, in turn, to a marked increase in the numbers of both these pests – the former carrying such diseases as plague and typhus and the latter feeding on thatched roofs, leading to roof collapse. Finally, through the process of Darwinian natural selection, the most resistant mosquitoes were able to reproduce. On balance, this initial attempt to eliminate malaria was counterproductive and ultimately led to the return of the disease accompanied by several other pests and diseases.

There are numerous, more recent examples of revenge theory – all the consequences of well-intentioned but ill-informed interventions as matters of public policy. They are summarized in Table 8.3. One of the best-known examples is China's now abandoned

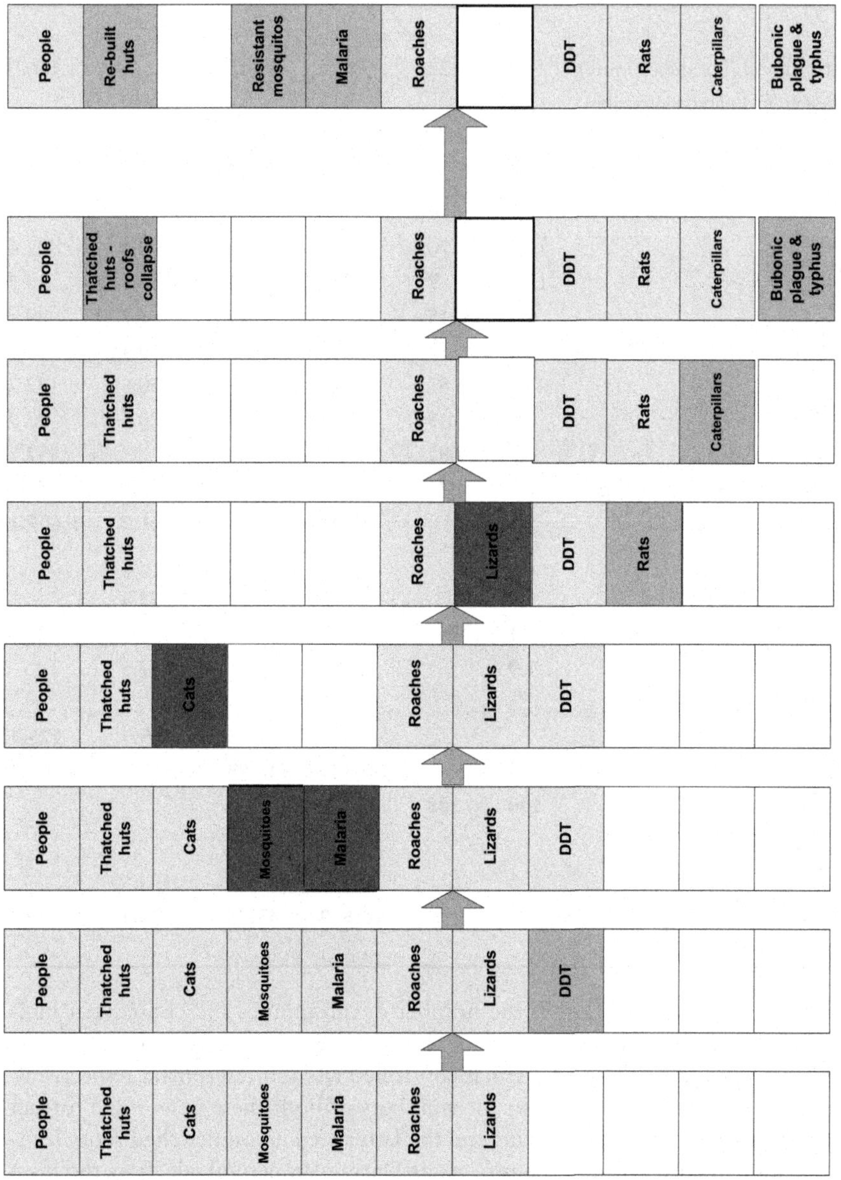

Figure 8.9 Consequences of DDT use in Borneo

Table 8.3 Examples of revenge theory

Revenge theory example	Original goal	Policy/action	Unintended consequence
Bangladesh drinking water	To find alternative sources to surface water contaminated with fecal coliform and other pollutants	Deep well drilling	Deep well water in Bangladesh contains arsenic, a known carcinogen
Mississippi River levees	To reduce the incidence of flooding	Installing and raising the levees	Levees trap sediment which would normally flow over the banks during flooding and restock local soils; to counter the rise of river levels from the build-up of silt, constant dredging is required along with levee raising; as levees become higher, there is a great risk of breeching and undermining
Lyme disease	To eliminate wolves	Wolf kills	Reduction in wolves led to explosion in deer population, which hosts Lyme vectors
China's population control policy	To control population growth	One-child policy	Rural populations, in particular, require male children for labor; female children are aborted or abandoned, leading to 30 million excess males known as "bare branches," with a potentially disruptive influence on social stability
Mad cow disease (MCD)	To find cheaper food and faster ways to fatten cattle	Adding animal by products (including spinal and neurological tissue) to the diet of cattle	Turning herbivores into carnivores has unintended effects, one of which is the inadvertent contamination of cattle feed with scrapie virus, leading to bovine spongiform encephalopathy (BSE) and possible transmission to humans in the form of Creutzfeldt-Jakob disease
Forest fire prevention	Desire to reduce forest fires, especially in national parks	Intensive effort to extinguish fires, even those from natural sources such as lightning	The interruption of the natural cycle of forest fires which can play a critical role in forest and ecosystem regeneration leads to the build-up of old trees and inflammable waste on the forest floor; when a spark starts a fire, there is a resulting conflagration because of the unnatural accumulation of flammable material
Greenhouse gases	To reduce GHG production and release	Policy adopted by the UN and European Union to pay producers in the third world to destroy HFC-23 (a potent greenhouse gas) produced as a byproduct of refrigerant gas manufacturing	Some factories have been established in China and India for the principal purpose of producing such gases in order to receive revenue for their destruction; the technological effect of such production processes is to make a net contribution to global greenhouse gas releases (*New York Times* August 8, 2012; *Nature* February 8, 2007)

one-child policy, devised in an attempt to control the multifaceted negative consequences – political, economic, social and ecological – of uncontrolled population growth
in a country whose population already exceeds 1.25 billion (World Bank 2011; Hudson
and Den Boer 2004). Another example is the attempt to encourage people to purchase
more energy-efficient commodities, such as cars and white goods. The method adopted
to encourage this switch in consumption patterns is absolutely critical. If attempted with
a sole reliance on increased efficiency standards without concomitant price increases for
energy, it is posited that the increased energy efficiency which ultimately saves consumers money can, in turn, be used to purchase other energy-using equipment. This novel
phenomenon – now labeled the *rebound effect* – was first anticipated in the 19th century by
the English economist Stanley Jevons (1865), who argued that increases in fuel efficiency
could ultimately lead to an increase rather than a decrease in its use. This phenomenon
has been subsequently referred to as the Jevons paradox. Originally concerned with coal,
the extent of the rebound effect remains a source of some debate today for all fossil fuels
(Saunders 2000; Alcott 2005; UKERC 2007; Herring and Sorrell 2009; Sorrell 2010; Gillingham et al. 2013).

One of the most graphic examples of revenge effects is associated with hydroelectricity –
long considered one of the most benign of all energy supply alternatives. As with all
energy sources, benefits come with associated costs, and large hydroelectric dams are
no exception (Scudder 2006; Goldsmith and Hildyard 1984; Ackermann et al. 1973).
The archetypal illustration of the law of unintended consequences is the Aswan High
Dam completed in Egypt in 1965. The benefits to this large but developing country
were substantial – in excess of 10,000 MW electricity capacity and conversion of over
700,000 acres from flood to canal irrigation, permitting double and triple cropping.
The construction costs exceeded US$1 billion but were expected to yield benefits many
times that in magnitude. It soon became apparent, however, that there were numerous
unanticipated externalities from the dramatic change in water flows and drastically
reduced sediment transport in the Nile River: (1) the loss of natural river water flushing
of salts from the soils of the fertile Nile delta, requiring the construction of an extensive
network of drainage tile systems costing $1 billion; (2) loss of soil-building and natural
fertilizing in the delta requiring chemical fertilization costing over $100 million per
year; (3) increased salinity and seawater intrusion in the delta; (4) increased coastal erosion; (5) increased river bank and bottom scouring, which threatened the integrity of
over 500 bridges built over the previous decade, requiring $250 million in mitigation
measures; (6) reduction in plankton and organic carbon levels in the eastern Mediterranean, which had traditionally sustained a large and productive sardine fishery; (7) less
water downstream because of evaporation and seepage; and (8) loss of dry periods
between floods which normally controlled the prevalence of water snails. These snails
carry schistosomiasis (or bilharziasis), a debilitating disease which affected a significant
proportion of the rural Egyptian population (Sterling 1973; Stanley and Warne 1993;
Vorosmarty and Sahagian 2000).

In a related manifestation of the revenge effect, a cascade of consequences affected
fisheries productivity off the mouth of the Nile delta in the decades following the
construction of the Aswan High Dam. First, the initial collapse in the fishery was
reversed in the late 1980s as the dual impact of fertilizer and sewage runoff produced a
surge in nutrient levels and fish populations. But the fishery declined once again from
increased levels of eutrophication (low oxygen) due to the accumulated impacts of the

aforementioned fertilizer and sewage discharges (Oczkowski and Nixon 2008; Oczkowski et al. 2009).

The most recent example of electricity-related revenge effects is associated with the world's largest hydroelectric installation on China's Yangtze River. The Three Gorges Dam, built at a cost of over US$24 billion to provide 20,000 MW of electricity and prevent the reoccurrence of historically devastating floods, has been deemed an environmental catastrophe. It not only required the displacement of 1.2 million people but also caused landslides, induced seismicity, created water pollution, reduced biodiversity, altered weather patterns, caused drops in downstream water tables with saltwater intrusions, led to jellyfish blooms and a rise in the number of cases of schistosomiasis (Hvistendahl 2008; *New York Times* May 19, 2011; *CNN* July 31, 2020).

In a controversial book entitled *Techno-Fix: Why Technology Won't Save Us or the Environment*, Huesemann and Huesemann (2011) detail the unintended consequences of technological advances in a broad range of areas including industrial agriculture, genetic engineering, automobiles, high-technology warfare and high-tech medicine.

Some other important ecosystem characteristics

As already noted, ecosystems are characterized by non-linear dynamics and tipping points. One related characteristic is the presence of lags. Figure 8.10 illustrates this phenomenon with the percolation of a soil disinfectant, 1,2-DCP, into groundwater long after spraying (Meadows et al. 1992, 2004). This phenomenon is of concern for the simple reason that

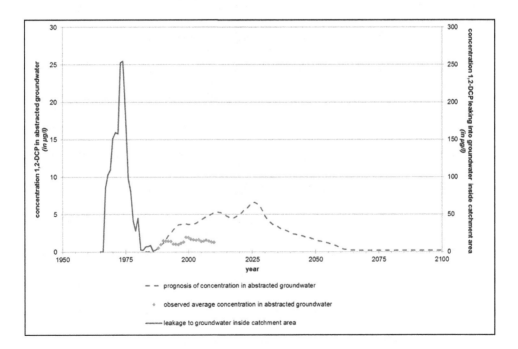

Figure 8.10 Ecological lags – 1,2-DCP

Source: Reproduced with permission of the author.

the deleterious effects may be neither anticipated nor immediately obvious. By the time these effects are manifested, reactive policies will be too late to stop the medium-term accumulation of physical – and ultimately economic – losses. Perhaps the most important form of lags is associated with global warming. NASA (accessed December 13, 2020) has estimated that even if all GHG emissions were to stop today, "the Earth's average temperature would climb another 0.6 degrees or so over the next several decades." This is due to the lengthy residence time of greenhouse gases in the atmosphere. For example, carbon can remain in the atmosphere for as long as 300–1,000 years (NASA October 9, 2019, p. 1). (See also Frolicher and Paynter 2015; Samset et al. 2020.)

Two other concepts are of particular relevance to global fauna, including humans – namely, *bioaccumulation* and *biomagnification* in food chains. Figure 8.11 demonstrates the

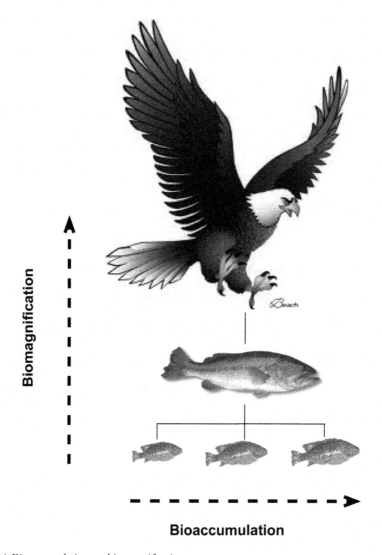

Figure 8.11 Bioaccumulation vs. biomagnification

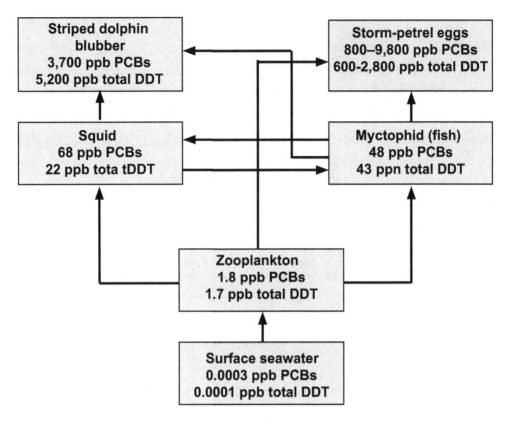

Figure 8.12 Biomagnification in a North Pacific food chain

different processes inherent in each of these concepts. Bioaccumulation represents the gradual accumulation of toxic chemicals in fish or animals as they age and grow, whereas biomagnification represents the increasing concentration of toxic chemicals as they rise through the food chain. Figure 8.12 illustrates how this process works by showing the dramatic increases in concentrations of organochlorines such as DDT and PCB in a North Pacific food chain, ranging from seven to eight orders of magnitude (based on data in Tanabe et al. 1984; Noble and Elliott 1986). What may appear to be a harmless concentration in seawater becomes potentially toxic at upper levels of the food chain – frequently animals consumed as food by humans. By way of example, the US EPA issued fish-eating guidelines in 2005 recommending that people not consume shark, sword-fish, king mackerel or tilefish because of bioaccumulated levels of mercury – a known neurotoxin.

There are, in fact, many pathways of human exposure to toxic chemicals aside from consumption of food products. Figure 8.13 is an EPA-generated flow diagram of the multiple routes of lead exposure from three major sources: air, soil and surface water and groundwater (US EPA 2006).

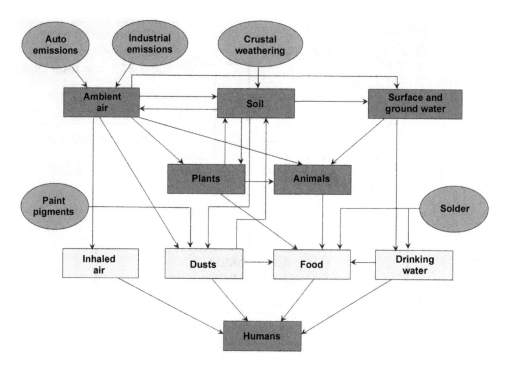

Figure 8.13 Principal pathways of lead exposure

The ecological footprint

While many of the aforementioned theories remain largely in the realm of scientific discourse, one concept which has gained wide currency among public agencies, NGOs and even the general public is that of *the ecological footprint*, which is an attempt to create a summary, system-level measure of the impact of human activity on the ecosystem (see the Global Footprint Network, www.footprintnetwork.org). The ecological footprint is a measure of the actual physical stocks of natural capital necessary to sustain a given human population within a given geographic region such as a city. It is sometimes expressed as a ratio; for example, if the ecological footprint of an urban area is 10.0, this implies that the land "consumed" by the urban region is ten times greater than that contained within its political boundaries. A full definition of the ecological footprint for a region – its EF or ACC (appropriated carrying capacity) – is the land (and water) area in various categories required exclusively by the people in this region (1) to continuously provide all the *resources* they currently consume and (2) to continuously absorb all the *wastes* they currently discharge. This land is either borrowed from the *past* (e.g. through the use of fossil fuels) or appropriated from the *future* (e.g. as contamination, plant growth reduction through reduced UV radiation, soil degradation, etc.) (see Rees 2007). In order to maintain consistency across all jurisdictions, the measure adopted for the ecological footprint is expressed as Gha, or global hectares, which measures the amount of biologically productive land with a productivity equal to the world average.

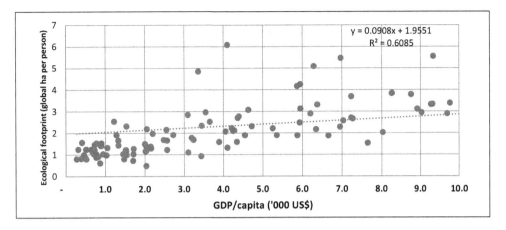

Figure 8.14 Ecological footprint vs. GDP

While the ecological footprint is frequently used to measure the impact of urbanization, it is also applicable to larger geographic areas such as regions or nations. The ratio of ecological footprint to national geographic area ranges from a high of 650:1 for Singapore to a low of 0.08:1 for Namibia with an overall average for all countries of approximatively 9.7. In general, the ecological footprint rises with national income, as illustrated in Figure 8.14 (F = 247.09 p = 3.4E-34; tstat = 15.72 p = 3.41E-34). The one outlier is the country of Luxembourg with the world's highest EF at 15.82.

Perhaps the most important level of EF analysis is at the global level, which measures the total impact of all human activity on our earthly environment. As the authors of the EF observe, the total land area of the earth is just over 13 billion ha, of which only 8.8 billion ha is productive cropland, pasture or forest. The most important observations flowing from this global-level EF analysis are that the industrialized world appropriates far more than its fair share of global carrying capacity, and if the third world were to achieve living standards comparable to those experienced in the first world, we would require several additional planet earths (World Wildlife Fund 2010). Figure 8.15 shows the trend in the global ecological footprint expressed as the equivalent number of earths. This value passed the 1.0 mark in 1970 and stood at 1.73 earths as of 2017.

The World Wildlife Fund (WWF) has formally incorporated EF analysis into its *Living Planet Reports*. Figures 8.16a and 8.16b, derived from the Global Footprint Network website, present the components of the ecological footprints of some of the wealthiest and poorest nations. As might be expected, the EF of most of the countries with the largest footprints is dominated by carbon emissions; the mix of components for most of the selected nations with low footprints is more varied except for those which have significant production of fossil fuels such as Brunei. Figure 8.17 shows the countries with the largest biocapacity surpluses and deficits.

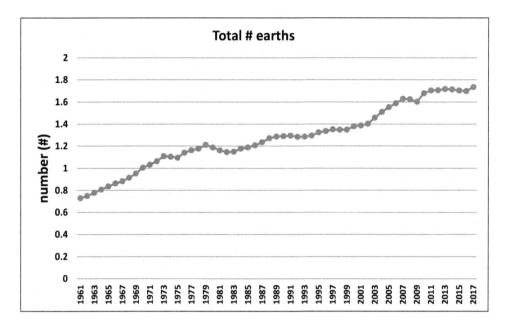

Figure 8.15 Global ecological footprint trends

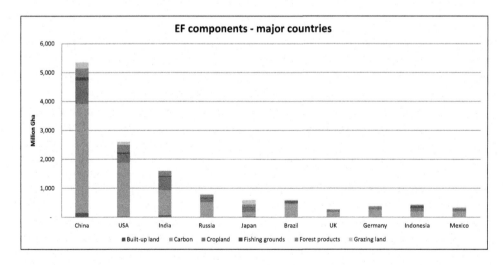

Figure 8.16a Components of ecological footprint in countries with the largest EF

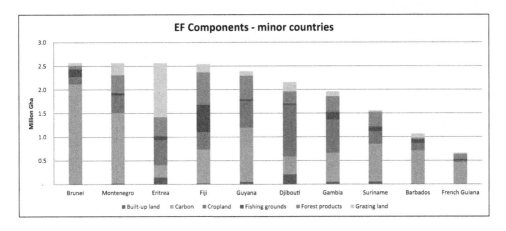

Figure 8.16b Components of ecological footprint in countries with low EF

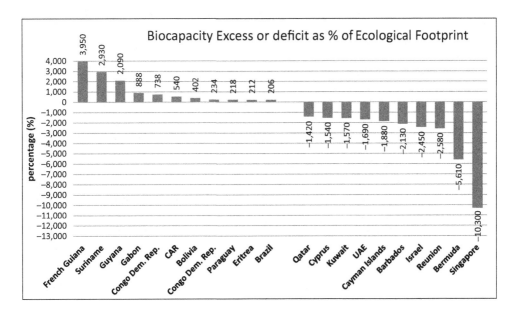

Figure 8.17 Biocapacity surplus and deficit

Finally, EF analysis can be used to assess the ecological impact (or sustainability) of commercial products. Wada (1993) used footprinting to compare the relative merits of hothouse and field-grown tomatoes. The rationale of the study was to critically examine the view of "technological optimists" that there are no practical constraints to food production and that "industrialized hydroponic greenhouse farming can increase agricultural output per hectare of land far beyond that of conventional field agriculture" (p. 1). The methodology used EF to convert energy inputs and embodied energy into their land equivalents in order to compare their appropriated carrying capacity. Table 8.4 contrasts

Table 8.4 Ecological footprint of BC tomato production

Ecological footprint of BC tomato production					
Variable	Units	Greenhouse A	Greenhouse B	Farm A	Farm B
Conventional economic measures					
Revenue	$1,000/ha/yr.	680	601	53	72
Profit	$1,000/ha/yr.	206	123	23	54
Growing area needed	ha/1,000 ton/yr.	2.02	2.29	17.84	12.14
Productivity of growing area	ton/ha/yr.	494	437	56	82
Ecological footprint results					
EF/ACC	ha/1,000 ton/yr.	919	765	56	43
Productivity of total EF land area	ton/ha/yr.	1.09	1.31	17.86	23.26

the conventional economic analysis of the two alternative growing processes with the EF results. While greenhouse cultivation produced much better economic results, the hydroponic greenhouse had an ecological footprint 14–21 times greater than a comparable field operation.

The conclusion of this study is particularly germane to the theoretical underpinnings of this textbook, which stress the need for a trans-economic systems perspective which incorporates elements of ecology and social values. To quote:

> This research reveals a conflict that is invisible to conventional economic analysis. Greenhouse farmers make a higher monetary profit per hectare of growing area than field farmers (from 2 to 9 times more). However, using the EF/ACC approach it becomes clear that greenhouse operations are not ecologically sound or sustainable. . . .This study shows that typical economic analysis does not necessarily lead to ecologically satisfactory conclusions. The underpricing of depletable energy, fertilizer, and other inputs to hydroponic production enables operators to profit while unconsciously appropriating the productive capacity of a landscape vastly larger than their own physical plant.
>
> (Wada 1993, p. 47)

In essence, national GDP accounts provide an incorrect and misleading signal with respect to sustainability, as many nations with increasing GDP have witnessed significant losses in their HPI. According to the New Economics Foundation: "the countries that are meant to represent successful development are some of the worst-performing in terms of sustainable well-being" (NEF 2009, p. 4). Included among these are China, India, the United States and many of the OECD countries.

A hopeful message from this analysis is that a middle-income country – Costa Rica – has the highest national Happy Planet Index (which includes measures of life expectancy, well-being, inequality of outcomes and the ecological footprint); their score is significantly greater than their richer counterparts, suggesting that high GDP per capita and economic growth are not prerequisites to sustainability.

In summary, the development of ecological footprinting has led to the emergence of similar and equally useful concepts in related types of analyses which can be applied to business, such as carbon footprinting and fishprinting, etc. (see Nemetz 2022).

The critical importance of biodiversity

Biodiversity is arguably the most important factor in ecosystem health, and it supports ecosystem function, resilience, redundancy, integrity and intactness. (See Dasgupta 2021.) SwissRe (2020a, p. 2; see also full report, SwissRe 2020b) has concluded:

> Over half (55%) of global GDP, equal to USD 41.7 trillion, is dependent on high-functioning biodiversity and ecosystem services. However, a staggering fifth of countries globally (20%) are at risk of their ecosystems collapsing due to a decline in biodiversity and related beneficial services.

The Convention on Biological Diversity (CBD) defines biodiversity as "the variability among living organisms from all sources including, inter alia, terrestrial, marine and other aquatic ecosystems and the ecological complexes of which they are part; this includes diversity within species, between species, and of ecosystems" (quoted in www.thegef.org). As Wilson (2016), one of the world's leading experts on ecology and biodiversity, observes: "biodiversity as a whole forms a shield protecting each of the species that together compose it, ourselves included. . . . As extinction mounts, biodiversity reaches a tipping point at which the ecosystem collapses." (p. 14)

Recent scientific research has demonstrated that the earth is currently undergoing its sixth mass extinction since the first such event approximately one-half billion years ago (Kolbert 2014). This crisis of ongoing extinction covers most living species, including marine and terrestrial life forms such as birds, mammals, insects, etc. (See also Diaz et al. 2019.) The decline is so severe that some scientists are warning that such losses, referred to as "biological annihilation" (Ceballos et al. 2017), threaten a catastrophic collapse of natural ecosystems (Sanchez-Bayo and Wyckhuys 2019; WWF 2018; Wilson 2016). Bradshaw et al. (2021, p. 6) "have summarized predictions of a ghastly future of mass extinction, declining health, and climate-disruption upheavals (including looming massive migrations) and resource conflicts this century."

Rosenberg et al. (2019) have reported on the loss of 3 billion birds in North America over the last 48 years, representing 29% of their 1970 abundance. The authors observe:

> Slowing the loss of biodiversity is one of the defining environmental challenges of the 21st century. Habitat loss, climate change, unregulated harvest, and other forms of human-caused mortality have contributed to a thousandfold increase in global extinctions in the Anthropocene compared to the presumed prehuman background rate, with profound effects on ecosystem functioning and services.
>
> (p. 120)

Comparable data for the United Kingdom have been reported by Burns et al. (2020). The Nature Conservancy is the coauthor of a study (2020) which has concluded that at least $700 billion is required to reverse the global biodiversity crisis. One of the most comprehensive efforts to track the state of biodiversity loss and its threat to the planet is provided by the World Wildlife Fund's *Living Planet Report*. The summary to their latest report (2020, p. 6) paints a grim picture:

> The global Living Planet Index continues to decline. It shows an average 68% decrease in population sizes of mammals, birds, amphibians, reptiles and fish between 1970 and 2016. A 94% decline in the LPI for the tropical subregions of the Americas is the largest fall observed in any part of the world. Why does this matter? It matters because biodiversity is fundamental to human life on Earth, and the evidence is unequivocal – it is being destroyed by us at a rate unprecedented in history. Since the industrial revolution, human activities have increasingly destroyed and degraded forests, grasslands, wetlands and other important ecosystems, threatening human well-being. Seventy-five percent of the Earth's ice-free land surface has already been significantly altered, most of the oceans are polluted, and more than 85% of the area of wetlands has been lost. Species population trends are important because they are a measure of overall ecosystem health. Measuring biodiversity, the variety of all living things, is complex, and there is no single measure that can capture all of the changes in this web of life. Nevertheless, the vast majority of indicators show net declines over recent decades. That's because in the last 50 years our world has been transformed by an explosion in global trade, consumption and human population growth, as well as an enormous move towards urbanisation. Until 1970, humanity's Ecological Footprint was smaller than the Earth's rate of regeneration. To feed and fuel our 21st century lifestyles, we are overusing the Earth's biocapacity by at least 56%.

Virtually all this loss in biodiversity is anthropogenic, and it has been estimated that 70% is due to agriculture (UNEP 2014). Future projections to 2050, short of major changes in agricultural systems, appear even worse (Williams et al. 2020, p. 314):

> The projected loss of millions of square kilometres of natural ecosystems to meet future demand for food, animal feed, fibre and bioenergy crops is likely to massively escalate threats to biodiversity. Reducing these threats requires a detailed knowledge of how and where they are likely to be most severe. We developed a geographically explicit model of future agricultural land clearance based on observed historical changes, and combined the outputs with species-specific habitat preferences for 19,859 species of terrestrial vertebrates. We project that 87.7% of these species will lose habitat to agricultural expansion by 2050, with 1,280 species projected to lose ≥25% of their habitat. Proactive policies targeting how, where, and what food is produced could reduce these threats, with a combination of approaches potentially preventing almost all these losses while contributing to healthier human diets. As international biodiversity targets are set to be updated in 2021, these results highlight the importance of proactive efforts to safeguard biodiversity by reducing demand for agricultural land.

While the livestock sector has received increased attention due to its direct and indirect contributions to greenhouse gases and water pollution, its contribution to the state of biodiversity is also noteworthy. The FAO (2020, p. xviii) has concluded that "livestock is either among the most harmful threats to biodiversity or necessary to maintain high nature value farmland." The purpose of the following section is to briefly review the contribution of the agricultural sector to this ecological crisis. Suffice it to say that the maintenance of a high level of biodiversity is absolutely essential for food and agriculture (Altieri 1999; FAO 2019). As Nakhauka (2009, p. 208) has stated: "Agricultural biodiversity is the first link in the food chain, developed and safeguarded by indigenous people throughout the world and it makes an essential contribution to feeding the world."

Agriculture and biodiversity

External effects: Sanchez-Bayo and Wyckhuys (2019) identify the main drivers of species decline in order of importance: (1) habitat loss and conversion to intensive agriculture and urbanization; (2) pollution, mainly by synthetic pesticides and fertilizers; (3) biological factors, including pathogens and introduced species; and (4) climate change. Clearly the two most important of these are intimately and directly linked to the practice of agriculture. Dudley and Alexander (2017) list four ways agriculture, in particular, drives biodiversity loss: (1) conversion of natural ecosystems into farms and ranches; (2) intensification of management in long-established cultural landscapes; (3) release of pollutants, including greenhouse gases; and (4) associated value chain impacts, including energy and transport use and food waste.

The adoption of monoculture practices has created vast "biological deserts" with grossly impaired ecosystems incapable of supporting traditional flora and fauna. The loss of beneficial insects and birds is particularly critical as it deprives the agricultural sector of natural pest control services, thereby increasing the reliance of the sector on human intervention with environmentally detrimental pesticides and herbicides. Monoculture also deprives the agricultural sector of ecosystem services provided by natural mixed vegetation, natural water flow and weed and pest control. Much newly created farmland has come at the expense of large natural forest areas in the developing world and entails the loss of all the vast array of vital ecosystem services they provide.

What is particularly disturbing is the rate at which insect and certain bird species are decreasing (Ceballos et al. 2017; Sanchez-Bayo and Wyckhuys 2019; Hallmann et al. 2017; CNRS 2018; Inger et al. 2015; Schwagerl 2016; Powney et al. 2019; MacPhail et al. 2019). Pimm et al. (2014, p. 987) state that "current rates of extinction are about 1000 times the likely background rate of extinction." The reasons are multifaceted and complex, although, as stated prior, the principal driver of this phenomenon is the agricultural sector. The speed at which these changes are occurring suggests that when appropriate remedial measures are identified and implemented, it may be too late to maintain the functioning of many of the earth's ecosystems.

Intrasectoral effects: Accompanying the loss of biodiversity resulting from agricultural production has been a similar loss within the agricultural sector itself driven by the necessities of modern industrial agriculture and the emergence of the agro-industrial sector. A relatively small number of crops account for a significant proportion of global terrestrial food production: sugar cane, maize (i.e. corn), wheat, rice and potatoes. In an attempt to increase yields of these and other major crops, there has been a concerted effort to develop selected plant variants at the expense of genetic biodiversity. Several studies from the scientific community have warned that this loss of diversity threatens the integrity and resilience of future food supply (Cardinale et al. 2012; Khoury et al. 2014; FAO n.d., 2019, IPBES 2019). Dewi and Gonzalez (2015, p. 1) state:

> Over the last two decades, 75% of the genetic diversity of agricultural crops has been lost; 100 to 1000-fold decrease over time. This phenomenon results in the decrease

of ecosystem abilities to provide food for people and decrease the function of other ecosystem services.

Figure 8.18 illustrates (Tomanio 2011) the decreased numbers of varieties of seeds of ten crops offered by commercial seed houses from 1903 to 1983. McMichael (2017, p. 249) concludes that "efficiency-driven culling of the ancient diversity of strains and types of many plant foods (such as potatoes, wheat and bananas) has lowered the resilience of agricultural systems and reduced options for the future."

Accompanying the decline in the variety of crops under cultivation has been a marked decrease in the nutritional value of many common foods, including protein, calcium, phosphorus, iron, riboflavin and ascorbic acid (*New York Times* September 15, 2015; Davis et al. 2004; Halweil 2007). Much of this decline has been attributed to the pursuit of increased crop yields representing a trade-off between yield and nutrient content. Efforts to offset recent declining marginal yields as the initial salutary impacts of the Green Revolution play out have frequently led to trade-offs with environmental sustainability, including land degradation, salinization, eutrophication, increased release of CH_4 and N_2O, groundwater pollution and loss of biodiversity (IAASTD 2008).

Fortunately, some major efforts have been undertaken to preserve a vast variety of seeds from around the world for future generations. The most notable of these efforts is the Svalbard Global Seed Vault, an underground storage facility established by the Norwegian government in 2008 on the remote Arctic island of Svalbard at a latitude of approximately 79 degrees north (Norway n.d.). Drawing on contributions from 23 international seed banks, 1 million seed samples are currently stored in this facility to act as a backstop against natural disasters, climate change or any anthropogenic activity which could lead to the loss of unique genetic information. Even this purportedly safe vault has not escaped the threat of global warming, however, as water from melting permafrost flooded the

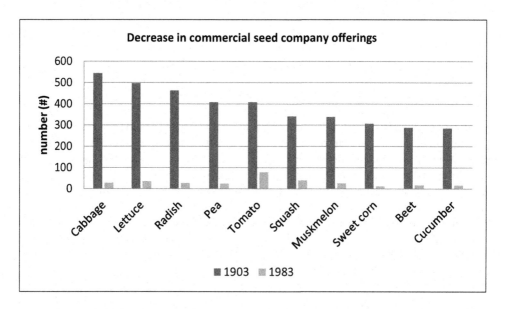

Figure 8.18 Decrease in variety of seeds

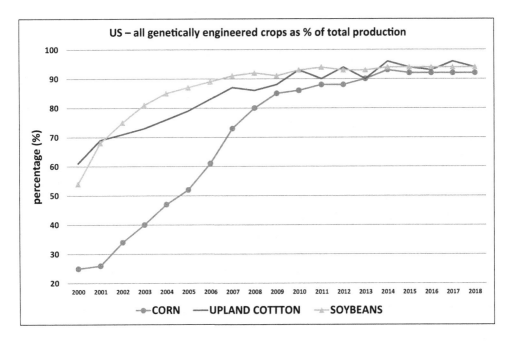

Figure 8.19 GMO crops in the US

entrance tunnel in 2017 (*Guardian* May 19, 2017). Whether the development of new seeds or reuse of ancient seeds will suffice to protect global food supplies is an open question in light of climate change.

Another major development within the last few decades has been the development of biotechnology in the form of genetic engineering and the creation of GMO (genetically modified organism) crops. The first of these technological innovations was Monsanto's Roundup Ready crops designed to tolerate the herbicide glyphosate. The motivation behind the development of GMOs is multifaceted and includes, inter alia, designing crops that have higher yields; resistance to pests, plant diseases or droughts; higher nutritional content; lower naturally occurring toxicants; or the ability to produce medicines (USDA n.d.). To date, however, the genetic modifications have focused on insect and herbicide resistance (NAS 2016). The use of GMO crops has expanded rapidly in the United States (Figure 8.19) focusing on three crops in particular – corn, cotton and soybeans – although much smaller crop initiatives include alfalfa, canola, sugar beets, potatoes, apples, squash and papaya (ISAAA 2017). The use of GMO crops has spread to many other nations, and the top ten countries ranked by million hectares planted are shown in Figure 8.20 (ISAAA 2017).

Despite the widespread adoption of genetically modified crops in Canada, the United States, Argentina, Brazil and Argentina, there is still significant hesitancy about this new technology in much of Europe (WHO 2014). While European countries generally allow the importation of GMO crops, more than half of EU countries have officially banned GMO crops (*New Scientist* 2015). These doubts are fostered by the unknown potential long-term detrimental effects on the food supply, birds, insects, human health and the genetic diversity of crops. The central issue is the application of the precautionary

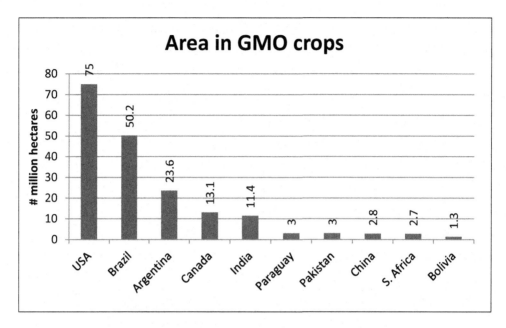

Figure 8.20 Top ten nations with GMO crops

principle. Despite the extraordinary promise of this technology, several red flags have been raised. These include findings that genetic modification has not accelerated crop yield or led to an overall reduction in the use of chemical pesticides (*New York Times* October 29 2016) and that there appears to be a decrease in wild bee abundance and pollination in GM fields compared to conventional and organic fields (Morandin and Winston 2006).

Of particular concern is the emerging dominance of a few large agribusinesses in the field of GM crops. While these large entities are engaged in the legitimate pursuit of profit, it is essential that private benefits accruing to these corporations are compatible with social welfare. A case study of this potential divergence is provided by Monsanto, one of the world's largest producers of GM seeds and now a subsidiary of the Bayer Corporation. Over the years, Monsanto gained a highly unfavorable reputation because of some of its products as well as its aggressive pursuit of small farmers in the court system whenever it thought its business model was under threat (Robin 2008; Barlett and Steele 2008). Society faces a difficult ethical choice between protecting corporate profits and the corporate practice of seeking, and often receiving, patent protection of products which are variants of those long considered part of the public domain. This is particularly critical in the realm of global food supply. Does the future security of food depend on increasing control by private corporations or the traditional model of open access?

A case in point is Monsanto's infamous sterile, or *terminator*, seeds, which forced farmers to buy seeds from the company every year. This development marked a radical transformation of the millennium–old model of farmers using their own seed to sow the following year's crops. Monsanto's corporate record undoubtedly contributed to its eventual demise as a separate corporate entity. During the process of assuming control over Monsanto, Bayer's CEO candidly admitted that "Monsanto's image does of course represent a major challenge for us, and it's not an aspect I wish to play down" (Reuters April 28, 2017). All these developments suggest that society has not invested the time or resources required to truly consider all the ramifications of the direction the agricultural sector is heading.

Parenthetically, it is worthwhile to note that while two of the UN's Sustainable Development Goals (#14 Life below Water and #15 Life on Land) are specifically tied to biodiversity, the maintenance of biodiversity is also essential to the direct achievement of many other SDGs (#1 Poverty, #2 Hunger, #3 Health and Well-Being, #6 Clean Water and Sanitation, #11 Sustainable Cites and Communities and #13 Climate) (IPBES 2019, p. 35). In fact, Blicharska et al. (2019) expand this analysis to include direct contributions to #7 (Affordable and Clean Energy), #8 (Decent Work and Economic Growth), #9 (Industry, Innovation and Infrastructure) and #12 (Responsible Consumption and Production). In addition, their analysis identifies the important indirect contributions of biodiversity to five other SDGs (#4 Quality Education; #5 Gender Equality; #10 Reduced Inequalities; #16 Peace, Justice and Strong Institutions; and #17 Partnerships for the Goals).

Finally, one of the major challenges to successfully addressing the loss of biodiversity is the difficulty of developing indicators due to the complex, multidimensional nature of biodiversity (Scholes and Biggs 2005). The principal threat to biodiversity comes from loss of habitat to agriculture and urban development. As such, early suggestions to measure biodiversity loss focused on a simple metric of extent of habitat destruction (Coady 2002). While useful as a first-pass approximation, this measure can miss the problems of habitat fragmentation and the non-linear response of many species to habitat loss. In an innovative attempt to address the complexities of biodiversity measurement, Scholes and Biggs (2005) developed a Biodiversity Intactness Index (BII), which has since been adopted in a number of subsequent research studies (Hill 2018, Alberta Biodiversity Monitoring Institute website).

The authors define their index as follows:

$$\text{BII} = (\Sigma_i \Sigma_j \Sigma_k R_{ij} A_{jk} I_{ijk}) / (\Sigma_i \Sigma_j \Sigma_k R_{ij} A_{jk})$$

Where:

I_{ijk} (population impact) is defined as the population of a species group I under land use activity k in ecosystem j

R_{ij} is richness (number of species) of taxon i in ecosystem j

A_{jk} = area of land use k in ecosystem j

The authors tested their methodology using a case study of Southern Africa, including South Africa, Namibia, Lesotho, Swaziland, Botswana, Zimbabwe and Mozambique. Their analysis included 4,650 estimates of I_{ijk} including five broad taxonomic groups (plants, mammals, birds, reptiles and amphibia), six ecosystem types (forest, savanna, grassland, shrubland, *fynbos* – a South African sclerophyllous thicket, and wetland) and an average of six land use activities (protected, moderate use, degraded, cultivated, plantation and urban) and eight functional types.

According to their findings (Scholes and Biggs 2005, p. 47):

> 84 +/−7% of the pre-colonial number of wild organisms persist in present-day southern Africa, despite greatly increased human demands on ecosystems over the past 300 years. In contrast, over 99% of the species persist, illustrating the insensitivity of indices based on extinction (changes in richness alone).

Despite the apparent deficiency of focusing solely on species extinction, Rounsevell et al. (2020) make a strong case for its use as a supplemental measure for the reason "that a comparable simple and measurable indicator is needed to support biodiversity policy with a specific and easily communicated target against which policy responses can be developed and tested" (p. 1193). They have chosen a target of "keeping described species extinctions to well below 20 per year over the next hundred across all major groups (fungi, plants, invertebrates, and vertebrates) and across all ecosystem types (marine, freshwater, and terrestrial)." While recognizing reliance on a single measure of the state of biodiversity, they offer the following rationale for its use:

> First, extinction fully incorporates the most fundamental aspect of biodiversity loss. Each species embodies distinct genetic diversity, usually shaped and developed over millions of years of independent evolution. The total body of extant species is the diversity of life on Earth. The extinction of a species represents an irreversible loss, a measurable reduction in the diversity of life on Earth, and is the ultimate concern for conservation. Although changes in species abundance or to ecological communities may be of equivalent concern, they are in principle, at least, reversible and recoverable. The extinction rate incorporates loss of species and of genetic diversity and there-fore two of the core components of the CBD [Convention on Biological Diversity] definition of biodiversity. Second, species extinction is widely understood and easy to communicate. There is widespread public concern about extinctions, as was demon-strated recently by the emphasis on the number of species at risk of extinction in the media coverage of the Intergovernmental Science-Policy Platform on Biodiversity and Ecosystem Services (IPBES) Global Assessment. There are collaborative networks recording the world's known and extinct species (www.gbif.org/what-is-gbif and www.catalogueoflife.org) and a program of work to catalog species close to extinc-tion and to monitor extinctions as they take place (www.iucnredlist. org).
>
> (Rounsevell et al. 2020, p. 1194)

Finally, it is worth noting that there has been a significant transformation in the nature and source of biodiversity loss with the increasing level of globalization. As Lenzen et al. (2012, p. 109) state:

> Historically, low-impact intrusion into species habitats arose from local demands for food, fuel and living space. However, in today's increasingly globalized economy, international trade chains accelerate habitat degradation far removed from the place of consumption. . . . We show that a significant number of species are threatened as a result of international trade along complex routes, and that, in particular, consumers in developed countries cause threats to species through their demand of commodities that are ultimately produced in developing countries.

Other studies have found similar results (Mayer et al. 2005; Muller n.d.; Moran et al. 2016), although Muller stresses that several international agreements contain clauses meant to lessen the ecological impacts of trade. Of particular interest is the innovative use of input-output analysis for international supply chains to track the impacts of trade on biodiversity. Moran et al. (2016) apply this methodology to a series of case studies, includ-ing nickel mining in New Caledonia, coltan from the Democratic Republic of Congo,

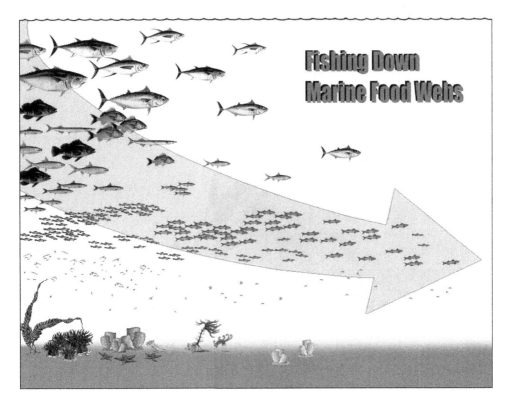

Figure 8.21 Fishing down the food web
Source: Reproduced with permission of the author.

cut flowers from Kenya and forestry practices in New Guinea. In all cases, the authors find a "clear link between a specific industry and biodiversity pressure" (p. 194).

There are numerous examples of local biodiversity being degraded or destroyed by access to international markets from what were formerly local or regional markets. Some of the most notable examples include: the impact on forest ecology and biodiversity in Russia as a result of timber exports to Finland and China (Mayer 2005); the emergence of palm oil plantations, particularly in Southeast Asia (IUCN n.d.); and soybean and cattle production in the Amazon (WWF 2014; Greenpeace 2020).

Within the marine environment, the most devastating impact on biodiversity has been what Pauly (1998) called "fishing down the food chain," where serial extraction of fish at higher trophic levels leads to reliance on progressively lower trophic levels (Figure 8.21). This is the product not only of increased domestic demand for fish but also the emergence of international fish fleets which both legally and illegally exploit the fisheries of developing nations (Sumaila et al. 2020; Intergovernmental Science-Policy Platform on Biodiversity and Ecosystem Services, IPBES 2019). For example, Lynam et al. (2006) and Belhabib et al. (2015) describe the profound ecosystem change which has occurred in the once highly productive Atlantic Ocean off Namibia as traditional fish stocks have entered a period of precipitous decline (Figure 8.22). There has been a

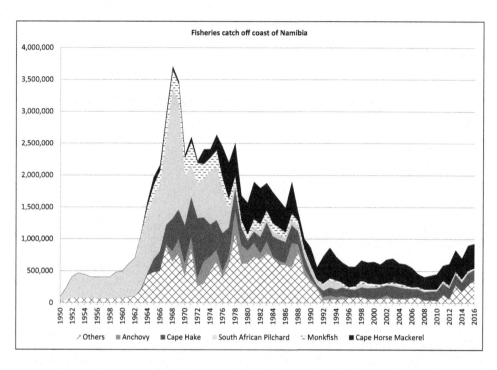

Figure 8.22 Fishing decline off Namibia

Source: Reproduced with permission of the author.

virtual explosion in the number of jellyfish to the point where their biomass (estimated at 12.2 MT) now far exceeds that of other species. The authors describe this transition as a "trophic dead end" as jellyfish – aside from having little value in the human food chain – have few natural predators. This example illustrates the absolute necessity of understanding the structure and processes of marine ecosystems as described by the innovative models *Ecosim, Ecopath* and *Ecospace*, developed at the University of British Columbia by Daniel Pauly and others (Christensen and Pauly 1992; Pauly et al. 2000; Christensen et al. 2000; Christensen and Walters 2004; Walters et al. 1997, 2000; Sumaila and Charles 2002). Once this transition to a jellyfish-dominated ecosystem has occurred, it may be very difficult or impossible to reverse by attempting to rebuild the stocks of higher-level pelagic fish for several reasons: first, jellyfish feed on fish eggs and larvae and are strong competitors for fish food; second, the concomitant overfishing of sardines off the coast of Namibia which feed on plankton has led to a bloom of plankton which, when dying, fall to the sea bottom. This produces an anoxic condition where low levels of oxygen lead to anaerobic decay with the resulting production of methane and hydrogen sulfide. This environment is highly unfavorable to most fish species. There are strong indications that a similar transition to a jellyfish-dominated ecosystem may also be occurring in other major fishing grounds such as the North Sea (Lynam et al. 2005; *New York Times* April 30, 2017; Sommer et al. 2002).

Namibia is not alone in experiencing increasing pressure on dwindling fish stocks. In light of the depletion of stocks in other oceans, foreign fishing fleets have capitalized on the availability of rich fishing grounds off much of West Africa either through illegal intrusion into African coastal waters or controversial intergovernmental agreements for access to the fisheries (AllAfrica.com 2012; Greenpeace 2015; *New York Times* April 30, 2017; Doumbouya et al. 2017).

In many of these cases, particularly with respect to renewable resources, the liquidation of national capital has been included in income from the sale of domestic products on international markets. This is clearly unsustainable and is tantamount to a firm selling its assets and treating these sales as part of its normal income stream.

In conclusion, one of the major challenges to successfully addressing the loss of biodiversity is not only the difficulty of developing indicators but also subsequently creating appropriate economic incentives to solve this formidable problem. The next chapter discusses several potential indicators and explores their economic application.

References

Ackermann, William C. et al. (1973) *Man-Made Lakes: Their Problems and Environmental Effects*, Washington, DC: American Geophysical Union.

Alberta Biodiversity Monitoring Institute (ABMI) (n.d.) "ABMI's intactness index," Measuring biodiversity. abmi.ca/home.html

Alcott, Blake (2005) "Jevons' Paradox," *Ecological Economics*, 54, pp. 9–21.

AllAfrica.com (2012) "Africa loses one million tonnes of fish yearly due to illegal fishing," October 25 [website].

Altieri, Miguel A. (1999) "The ecological role of biodiversity in agroecosystems," *Agriculture, Ecosystems and Environment*, 74, pp. 19–31.

Altieri, Miguel A. (2007) "Fatal harvest: Old and new dimensions of the ecological tragedy of modern agriculture," in Peter N. Nemetz (ed.) *Sustainable Resource Management: Reality or Illusion?*, Cheltenham: Edward Elgar, pp. 189–213.

Anthony, Katey M. Walter et al. (2012) "Geologic methane seeps along boundaries of Arctic permafrost thaw and melting glaciers," *Nature Geoscience*, May 20.

Barlett, Donald L. and James B. Steele (2008) "Monsanto's harvest of fear," *Vanity Fair*, May.

Belhabib, Dyhia et al. (2015) "A fishery tale: Namibian fisheries between 1950 and 2010," Working Paper #2015–65, Fisheries Centre, The University of British Columbia.

Beyer, Hawthorne L. et al. (2007) "Willow on Yellowstone's northern range: Evidence of a trophic cascade," *Ecological Applications*, 17(6), pp. 1563–1571.

Blicharska, Malgorzata et al. (2019) "Biodiversity's contributions to sustainable development," *Nature Sustainability*, 2, December, pp. 1083–1093.

Bradshaw, Corey J.A. et al. (2021) "Underestimating the challenges of avoiding a Ghastly future," *Frontiers in Conservation Science*, 1, article 615419.

Broecker, Wallace S. and Robert Kunzig (2008) *Fixing Climate: What Past Climate Changes Reveal about the Current Threat: And How to Counter It*, New York: Hill & Wang.

Burns, F. et al. (2020) *The State of the U.K.'s birds 2020*, The RSPB, BTO, WWT, DAERA, JNCC, NatureScot, NE and NRW, Sandy, Bedfordshire.

Cardinale, Bradley J. et al. (2012) "Biodiversity loss and its impact on humanity," *Nature*, 486, pp. 59–67.

Ceballos, Gerardo et al. (2017) "Biological annihilation via the ongoing sixth mass extinction signaled by vertebrate population losses and declines," *PNAS*, July 10.

Cederholm, C. Jeff et al. (2000) *Pacific Salmon and Wildlife: Ecological Contexts, Relationships, and Implications for Management*, Olympia, WA: Washington State Department of Fish and Wildlife.

Chadburn, S.E. et al. (2017) "An observation-based constraint on permafrost loss as a function of global warming," *Nature Climate Change*, 7, May, pp. 340–345.

Christensen, V. and D. Pauly (1992) "Ecopath II: A software for balancing steady-state ecosystem models and calculating network characteristics," *Ecological Modeling*, 61, pp. 169–185.

Christensen, V. and C.J. Walters (2004) "Ecopath with ecosim: Methods, capabilities and limitations," *Ecological Modelling*, 172(2–4), pp. 109–139.

Christensen, V., C. J. Walters and D. Pauly (2000) "Ecopath with ecosim: A user's guide," October 2000 Edition.

CNN (2020) "China's three Gorges Dam is one of the largest ever created: Was it worth it?," July 31.

CNRS News (2018) "Where have all the farmland birds gone?" April 19.

Coady, Linda (2002) "Iisaak: A new economic model for conservation-based forestry in coastal old growth forests British Columbia," in Peter N. Nemetz (ed.) *Bringing Business on Board: Sustainable Development and the B-School Curriculum*, Vancouver: JBA Press, pp. 561–575.

Conway, Gordon R. (1972) "Ecological aspects of pest control in Malaysia," in M. Taghi Farvar and John P. Milton (eds.) *The Careless Technology: Ecology and International Development*, Garden City, NY: Natural History Press, pp. 467–488.

Dasgupta, Partha (2021) *The Economics of Biodiversity: The Dasgupta Review*, London, UK: UK Treasury Department.

Davidson, Osha Gray (2003) *Fire in the Turtle House: The Green Sea Turtle and the Fate of the Ocean*, New York: Public Affairs.

Davis, Donald R. et al. (2004) "Changes in USDA food composition data for 43 garden crops, 1950–1999," *Journal of the American College of Nutrition*, 23(6).

Dewi, Gusti Ayu and Veronica Argelis Gonzalez (2015) "Conserving traditional seed crops diversity," GSDR brief.

Diaz, Sandra et al. (2019) "Pervasive human-driven decline of life on Earth points to the need for transformative change," *Science*, 366, December 13.

Doumbouya, Alkaly et al. (2017) "Assessing the effectiveness of monitoring control and surveillance of illegal fishing," *Frontiers in Marine Science*. The case of West Africa, 4, March, pp. 1–10, Article 50.

Dudley, Nigel and Sasha Alexander (2017) "Agriculture and biodiversity a review," *Biodiversity*, 18, pp. 2–3.

Duffy, Katharyn A. et al. (2021) "How close are we to the temperature tipping point of the terrestrial biosphere?," *Science Advances*, January 13.

Eisenberg, Cristina (2010) *The Wolf's Tooth: Keystone Predators, Trophic Cascades, and Biodiversity*, Washington: Island Press.

Elkington, John (1998) *Cannibals with Forks: The Triple Bottom Line of 21st Century Business*, Gabriola Island, BC: New Society Publishers.

Estes, James A. et al. (2011) "Trophic downgrading of planet earth," *Science*, July 15, pp. 301–306.

Etminan, M. et al. (2016) "Radiative forcing of carbon dioxide, methane, and nitrous oxide, a significant revision of the methane radiative forcing," *Geophysical Research Letters*, December 27.

Food and Agriculture Organization (FAO) (2019) *The State of the World's Biodiversity for Food and Agriculture*, Rome: FAO.

Food and Agriculture Organization (FAO) (2020) *Biodiversity and the Livestock Sector*.

Food and Agriculture Organization (FAO (n.d.) *What Is Happening to Agrobiodiversity?*

Frolicher, Thomas I. and David J. Paynter (2015) "Extending the relationship between global warming and cumulative carbon emissions to multi-millennial timescales," *Environmental Research Letters*, 10, p. 075002.

Gillingham, Kenneth et al. (2013) "The rebound effect is overplayed," *Nature*, January 24.

Goldsmith, Edward and Nicholas Hildyard (1984) *The Social & Environmental Effects of Large Dams*, San Francisco, CA: Sierra Club Books.

Green, Maurice B. (1978) *Eating Oil: Energy Use in Food Production*, Boulder, CO: Westview Press.

Greenpeace (2015) *Africa's Fisheries' Paradise at a Crossroads: Investigating Chinese Companies' Illegal Fishing Practices in West Africa*.

Greenpeace (2020) "How deforestation and cattle raising threaten biodiversity in Brazil," June 5.

Gregr, Edward J. et al. (2020) "Cascading social-ecological costs and benefits triggered by a recovering keystone predator," *Science*, 368, June 12, pp. 1243–1247.

Guardian (2005) "Warming hits 'tipping point'," August 11.

Guardian (2017) "Arctic stronghold of world's seeds flooded after permafrost melts," May 19.

Hallmann, Casper A. et al. (2017) "More than 75 percent decline over 27 years in total flying insect biomass in protected areas," *PLoS One*, October 18.

Halweil, Brian (2007) "Nutrient levels in US food supply eroded by pursuit of high yields," *Still No Free Lunch*, The Organic Center, September.

Happy Planet Index. website. www.happyplanetindex.org. [website based at The New Economics Foundation, London].

Herndon, Elizabeth M. (2018) "Permafrost slowly exhales methane," *Nature Climate Change*, April 8.

Herring, H. and S. Sorrell (2009) *Energy Efficiency and Sustainable Consumption: The Rebound Effect*, Houndmills, Basingstoke, Hampshire: Palgrave Macmillan.

Hill, Samantha et al. (2018) "Worldwide impacts of past and projected future land-use change on local species richness and the Biodiversity Intactness Index," preprint, May.

Holling, C.S. (1973) "Resilience and Stability of Ecological Systems," *Annual Review of Ecology and Systematics*, pp. 1–23.

Huesemann, Michael and Joyce Huesemann (2011) *Techno-Fix: Why Technology Won't Save Us or the Environment*, Gabriola Island, BC: New Society Publishers.

Hudson, Valerie and Andrea M. Den Boer (2004) *Bare Branches: The Security Implications of Asia's Surplus Male Population*, Cambridge, MA: MIT Press.

Hughes, Terence P. (1994) "Catastrophes, phase shifts, and large-scale degradation of a Caribbean coral reef," *Science*, 26, September 9, pp. 1547–1551.

Hvistendahl (2008) "China's three Gorges Dam: An environmental catastrophe?," *Scientific American*, March 25. scientificamerican.com.

Inger, Richard et al. (2015) "Common European birds are declining rapidly while less abundant species' numbers are rising," *Ecology Letters*, 18, pp. 28–36.

Intergovernmental Panel on Climate Change (IPCC) (2014) *Fifth Assessment Report*. AR5 Reports.

Intergovernmental Science-Policy Platform on Biodiversity and Ecosystem Services (IPBES) (2019) "Summary for policymakers of the global assessment report," May 29.

International Assessment of Agricultural Knowledge, Science and Technology for Development (IAASTD) (2008) "Global report chapter 1," *Context, Conceptual Framework and Sustainability Indicators*.

International Service for the Acquisition of Agro-Biotech Applications (ISAAA) (2017) "Biotech crop adoption surges as economic benefits accumulate in 22 years," *Global Status of Commercialized Biotech/GM Crops in 2017*.

International Union for Conservation of Nature (IUCN) (n.d.) *Palm Oil and Biodiversity*.

IPBES (2019) *The Global Assessment Report on Biodiversity and Ecosystem Services*.

Ise, Takeshi et al. (2008) "High sensitivity of peat decomposition to climate change through water-table feedback," *Nature Geoscience*, published online October 12.

Jevons, Stanley (1865) *The Coal Question*, reprinted 2012, Charleston, SC: Nabu Press.

Khoury, Colin K. (2014) "Increasing homogeneity in global food supplies and the implications for food security," *PNAS*, March 18.

Kimbrell, Andrew (ed.) (2002) *Fatal Harvest: The Tragedy of Industrial Agriculture*, Washington: Island Press.

Kolbert, Elizabeth (2014) *The Sixth Extinction: An Unnatural History*, New York: Henry Holt and Company.

Kurz, W.A. et al. (2008) "Mountain pine beetle and forest carbon feedback to climate change," *Nature*, 452, April 24, pp. 987–990.

Lenzen, M. et al. (2012) "International trade drives biodiversity threats in developing nations," *Nature*, June 7.

Levi, Tall et al. (2012) "Deer, predators, and the emergence of Lyme disease," *PNAS*, July 3.

Lynam, Christopher P. et al. (2005) "Evidence for impacts by jellyfish on North Sea herring recruitment," *Marine Ecology Progress*, 298, pp. 157–167.

Lynam, Christopher P. et al. (2006) "Jellyfish overtake fish in a heavily fished ecosystem," *Current Biology*, 16(13).

MacPhail, Victoria J. et al. (2019) "Incorporating citizen science museum specimens, and field work into the assessment of extinction risk of the American Bumble bee (Bombus pensylvanicus De Geer 1773) in Canada," *Journal of Insect Conservation*, April 17.

Mayer, Audrey L. et al. (2005) "Importing timber, exporting ecological impact," *Science*, April 15.

McMichael, Anthony J. et al. (2017) *Climate Change and the Health of Nations: Famines, Fevers, and the Fate of Populations*, Oxford: Oxford University Press.

Meadows, Donella (2008) *Thinking in Systems*, White River Junction, VT: Chelsea Green Publishing.

Meadows, Donella et al. (1992) *Beyond the Limits*, Post Mills, VT: Chelsea Green Publishing.

Meadows, Donella et al. (2004) *Limits to Growth: The 30-Year Update*, White River Junction, VT: Chelsea Green Publishing.

Moran, Daniel et al. (2016) "On the suitability of input-output analysis for calculating product-specific biodiversity footprints," *Ecological Indicators*, 60, pp. 192–201.

Morandin, Lora A. and Mark L. Winston (2006) "Pollinators provide economic incentive to preserve natural land in agroecosystems," April 5.

Muller, Manuel Ruiz (n.d.) "International trade and biodiversity: Complementarity or conflict?," Konrad Adenauer Stifung.

Myers, Ransom A. et al. (2007) "Cascading effects of the loss of Apex predatory sharks from a coastal ocean," *Science*, 31, pp. 1846–1850.

Nakhauka, Ekesa Beatrice (2009) "Agricultural biodiversity for food and nutrient security: The Kenyan experience," *International Journal of Biodiversity and Conservation*, 1(7), November, pp. 208–214.

NASA (2019) "The atmosphere: Getting a handle on carbon dioxide," October 9.

National Academy of Sciences (NAS) (2004) *Valuing Ecosystem Services: Toward Better Environmental Decision-Making*, Washington, DC.

National Academy of Sciences (NAS) (2016) *Genetically Engineered Crops: Experiences and Prospects*, Washington, DC: NAS.

Nature (2007) "Is the global carbon market working?," 445, February 8, pp. 595–596.

Nature Conservancy et al. (2020) "Closing the nature funding gap: A finance plan for the planet," September 14.

Nemetz, Peter N. (2022) *Corporate Strategy and Sustainability*, London: Routledge.

New Scientist (2015) "More than half of EU officially bans genetically modified crops," October 5.

New York Times (2011) "China admits problems with three Gorges Dam," May 19.

New York Times (2012) "Carbon credits gone awry raise output of harmful gas," August 8.

New York Times (2015) "A decline in the nutritional value of crops," September 15.

New York Times (2016) "Broken promises of GM crops," October 29.

New York Times (2017) "China's appetite pushes fisheries to the brink," April 30.

Noble, D.G. and J.E. Elliott (1986) "Environmental contaminants in Canadian seabirds, 1968–1985: Trends and effects," Canadian Wildlife Service Technical Report Series, No. 13, Ottawa.

The New Economics Foundation (NEF) (2009) *Happy Planet Index 2.0*, London, p. 4.

Norway (n.d.) "Svalbard global seed vault history," seedvault.no.

Oczkowski, Autumn and Scott Nixon (2008) "Increasing nutrient concentrations and the rise and fall of a coastal fishery: A review of data from the Nile Delta, Egypt," *Estuarine, Coastal and Shelf Science*, 77, pp. 309–319.

Oczkowski, Autumn et al. (2009) "Anthropogenic enhancement of Egypt's Mediterranean fishery," *Proceedings of the National Academy of Sciences*, 106(5), February 3, pp. 1364–1367.

Pandolfi, John M. et al. (2011) "Projecting coral reef futures under global warming and ocean acidification," *Science*, 333, July 22, pp. 418–422.

Pauly, Daniel, V. Christensen and C. Walters (2000) "Ecopath, ecosim, and ecospace as tools for evaluating ecosystem impact of fisheries," *ICES Journal of Marine Science*, 57, p. 697.

Pauly, Daniel et al. (1998) "Fishing down marine food webs," *Science*, 279, February 6.

Pfeiffer, Dale Allen (2006) *Eating Fossil Fuels: Oil, Food and the Coming Crisis in Agriculture*, Gabriola Island, BC: New Society Publishers.

Pimm, S.L. et al. (2014) "The biodiversity of species and their rates of extinction, distribution, and protection," *Science*, May 30.

Pistone, Kristina et al. (2014) "Observational determination of albedo decrease caused by vanishing Arctic sea ice," *PNAS*, March 4.

Powney, Gary D. et al. (2019) "Widespread losses of pollinating insects in Britain," *Nature Communications*, 10, p. 1018.

Rees, William (2007) "Is humanity fatally successful?," in Peter N. Nemetz (ed.) *Sustainable Resource Management: Reality or Illusion?*, Cheltenham: Edward Elgar, pp. 392–419.

Reuters (2017) "Bayer CEO says Monsanto's reputation is a 'major challenge'," April 28.

Ripple, William J. and Robert L. Beschta (2004) "Wolves, elk, willows, and trophic cascades in the upper Gallatin range of Southwestern Montana, USA," *Forest Ecology and Management*, 200, pp. 161–181.

Ripple, William J. and Robert L. Beschta (2007) "Restoring Yellowstone's aspen with wolves," *Biological Conservation*, 138, pp. 514–519.

Robin, Marie-Monique (2008) *The World According to Monsanto: Pollution, Corruption and the Control of Our Food Supply*, New York: The New Press.

Rockstrom, Johan et al. (2009a) "A safe operating space for humanity," *Nature*, 461, September 24, pp. 472–475.

Rockstrom, Johan et al. (2009b) "Planetary boundaries: Exploring the safe operating space for humanity," *Ecology and Science*, 14(2), p. 32. www.ecologyandociety.org/vol14/iss2/art32/.

Rosenberg, Kenneth V. et al. (2019) "Decline of the North American Avifauna," *Science*, October 4.

Rounsevell, Mark D.A. et al. (2020) "A biodiversity target based on species extinctions," *Science*, June 12.

Samset, B.H. et al. (2020) "Delayed emergence of a global temperature response after emission mitigation," *Nature Communications*, July 7.

Sanchez-Bayo, Francisco and Kris A.G. Wyckhuys (2019) "Worldwide decline of the entomofauna: A review of its drivers," *Biological Conservation*, 232, pp. 8–27.

Saunders, Carolie et al. (2006) *Food Miles: Comparative Energy/Emissions Performance of New Zealand's Agricultural Industry*, AERU, Lincoln University Research Report No. 285, July.

Saunders, Harry D. (2000) "A view from the macro side: Rebound, backfire and Khazoom-Brookes," *Energy Policy*, 28, pp. 439–449.

Scholes, R.J. and R. Biggs (2005) "A biodiversity intactness index," *Nature*, March 3.

Schwagerl, Christian (2016) "What's causing the sharp decline in insects, and why it matters," *Yale Environment 360*, July 6.

Scudder, Thayer (2006) *The Future of Large Dams*, London: Earthscan.

Smith, Alisa and J.B. MacKinnon (2007) *The 100-Mile Diet*, Toronto: Random House Canada.

Sommer, Ulrich et al. (2002) "Pelagic food web configurations at different levels of nutrient richness and their implications for the ratio fish production: Primary production," *Hydrobiologia*, 484, pp. 11–20.

Sorrell, Steven (2010) "Energy, economic growth and environmental sustainability: Five propositions," *Sustainability 2010*, 2, pp. 1784–1809.

Stanley, Danile Jean and Andrew G. Warne (1993) "Nile Delta: Recent geological evolution and human impact," *Science*, 260(5108), April 30, pp. 628–634.

Sterling, Claire (1973) "The trouble with superdams," in *Britannica Yearbook of Science and the Future, 1974*, Chicago: Encyclopedia Britannica, pp. 112–127.

Stokesbury, Kevin D.E. (2009) "SMAST cooperative scallop video survey and fisheries management," Department of Fisheries Oceanography, School for Marine Science and Technology, University of Massachusetts, February 2, PowerPoint presentation.

Sumaila, Ussif Rashid and Anthony T. Charles (2002) "Economic models of marine protected areas: An introduction," *Natural Resources Modeling*, 15(3), Fall.

Sumaila, Ussif Rashid et al. (2020) "Illicit trade in marine fish catch and its effects on ecosystems and people worldwide," *Science Advances*, February 26.

SwissRe (2020a) "Habitat, water security and air quality: new index reveals which sectors and countries are at risk from biodiversity loss," *Press Release*, September 23.

SwissRe Institute (2020b) *Biodiversity and Ecosystem Services. A business case for re/insurance*, Munich: SwissRe Institute.

Tanabe, Shinsuke et al. (1984) "Polychlorobiphenyls, SDDT, and hexachlorocyclohexane isomers in the Western North pacific ecosystem," *Archives of Environmental Contamination and Toxicology*, 13, pp. 731–738.

Tenner, Edward (1996) *Why Things Bite Back: Technology and the Revenge of Unintended Consequences*, New York: Alfred A. Knopf.

Terborgh, John and James A. Estes (2010) *Trophic Cascades: Predators, Prey and the Changing Dynamics of Nature*, Washington: Island Press.

Tomanio, John (2011) "graphic," https//thesocietypages.org/socimages/2011/07/19/loss-of-genetic-diversity-in-u-s-food-crops/.

UK Energy Research Centre (ERC) (2007) *The Rebound Effect: An Assessment of the Evidence for Economy-Wide Energy Savings from Improved Energy Efficiency*.

United Nations Environment Programme (UNEP) (2014) *Global Biodiversity Outlook 4*.

US Department of Agriculture (USDA) (n.d.) *Biotechnology FAQs*.

US Environmental Protection Agency (EPA) (2006) *Air Quality Criteria for Lead*, October.

Van Houtan, Kyle S., Stacy H. Hargrove and George H. Balazs (2010) "Land use, macroalgae, and a tumor-forming disease in marine turtles," *PLoS One*, 5(9), September, e1 2900, pp. 1–9.

Vianna, G.M.S. et al. (2010) *Wanted Dead or Alive? The Relative Value of Reef Sharks as a Fishery and an Ecotourism Asset in Palau*, University of Western Australia, Australian Government and Australian Institute for Marine Science.

Vorosmarty, Charles J. and Dork Sahagian (2000) "Anthropogenic disturbance of the terrestrial water cycle," *BioScience*, 50(9), pp. 753–765.

Wada, Y. (1993) "The appropriated carrying capacity of tomato production: Comparing the ecological footprints of hydroponic greenhouse and mechanized field operations," M.A. Thesis, University of British Columbia, School of Community and Regional Planning.

Wadham, J.L. et al. (2012) "Potential methane reservoirs beneath Antarctica," *Nature*, 488, August 30, pp. 633–637.

Walters, C., V. Christensen and D. Pauly (1997) "Structuring dynamic models of exploited ecosystems from trophic mass-balance assessments," *Reviews in Biology and Fisheries*, 7, pp. 139–272.

Walters, C., D. Pauly, V. Christensen and J.F. Kitchell (2000) "Representing density dependent consequences of life history strategies in aquatic ecosystems: EcoSim II," *Ecosystems*, 3, pp. 70–83.

Williams, David R. et al. (2020) "Proactive conservation to prevent habitat losses to agricultural expansion," *Nature Sustainability*, 4, December 21, pp. 314–322.

Wilson, Edward O. (2016) *Half-Earth: Our Plant's Fight for Life*, New York: Liveright Publishing Corporation.

World Bank (2011) *World Development Report 2012*, Washington, DC.

World Health Organization (WHO) (2014) *Frequently Asked Questions on Genetically Modified Foods*.

World Health Organization (WHO) (2019) *World Malaria Report*, Geneva.

World Wildlife Fund (WWF) (2010) *Living Planet Report*, Gland, Switzerland.

World Wildlife Fund (WWF) (2014) *The Growth of Soy: Impacts and Solutions*.

World Wildlife Fund WWF (2018) *Living Planet Report*.

World Wildlife Fund (WWF) (2020) *Living Planet Report*.

World Wildlife Fund and Allianz (2009) "Tyndall Centre," *Major Tipping Points in the Earth's Climate System and Consequences for the Insurance Sector*, Berlin, Germany.

www.footprintnetwork.org [website of Global Footprint Network, Oakland, CA].

Zhang, Peng et al. (2020) "Abrupt shift to hotter and drier climate over East Asia beyond the tipping point," *Science*, November 27.

9 A brief outline of ecological economics

One of the great strengths *and* weaknesses of environmental economics is its emergence from neo-classical economics – a discipline which grew and thrived largely in an era largely unaware of and unconcerned about environmental issues. Figure 9.1, familiar to all first-year economics students, captures the essence of the neo-classical economic model of the economy. It is basically a closed system with mutual exchanges between firms and households. Consumers provide their labor to producers, and they, in turn, sell the resulting goods back to consumers. As illustrated in Figure 9.2, environmental economics made a major addition to this model by adding another entity to this simple flowchart: the environment, which sits principally beside the producer's side and represents the repository for the waste generated by the industrial system of production. Table 9.1 lists the principal types of pollutants which have been the common focus of environmental economics. The goal is to internalize externalities in order to reduce economic inefficiency from a social perspective. The overall goal of maximizing economic growth to increase human

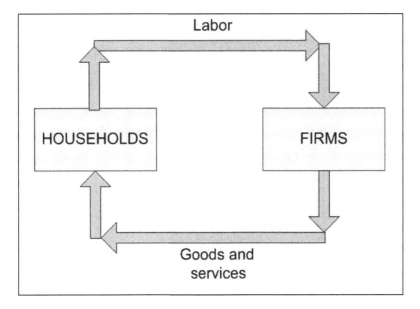

Figure 9.1 Neo-classical economics model

DOI: 10.4324/9781003170730-9

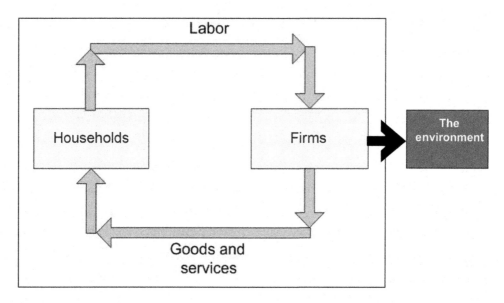

Figure 9.2 The environmental economics model

Table 9.1 Principal types of pollutants

Air	Smoke/particulates	Photochemical smog
	Noxious odors	Acid rain
		Pesticide deposition
		Heavy metal deposition
Water	Oil spills	Airborne deposition of pesticides and heavy metals
	Sewage discharge	Petroleum pollution
	Pesticide runoff	Forest runoff
	Fertilizer runoff	Urban runoff
	Heavy metal discharges	Agricultural runoff
	Suspended solids	
	Biochemical oxygen demand	
Soil	Toxic contamination	Erosion
	Municipal solid waste	Salinization
Radiation	Localized waste storage	Contamination from
	Contamination from nuclear accidents	nuclear accidents

welfare remains the central thrust. This is fundamentally neo–classical economics with minor modifications.

In contrast, Figure 9.3 captures the essence of the *ecological economics* model, which makes three major modifications to the environmental economics model: (1) waste products generated by both consumers and producers have a feedback loop, which means they have the capacity to negatively impact the production system from which they are generated; (2) there is a specific inclusion of certain natural resources as inputs, such as clean air, clean water and assimilative capacity; and (3) most importantly, there is an ecological system which includes at least 17 *ecological services*. The fundamental premise of this major conceptual revision is that the economic system is embedded in the ecological system, cannot function without it and is ultimately subject to the same laws and constraints which apply to natural systems.

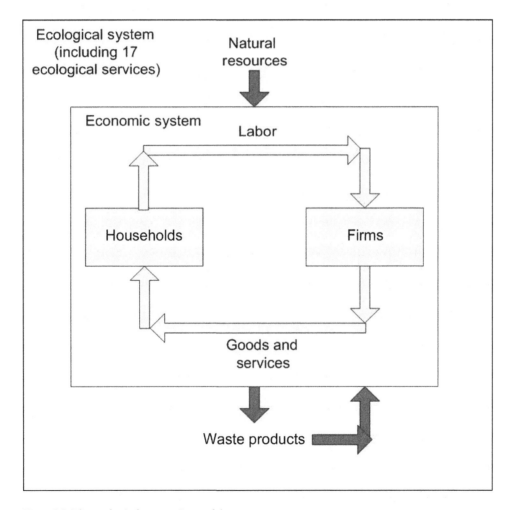

Figure 9.3 The ecological economics model

The import of this schematic is captured in the words of Herman Daly, a former senior economist of the World Bank and one of the founders of the new disciple of ecological economics. Daly states:

> It is interesting that so much should be at stake in a simple picture. Once you draw the boundary of the environment around the economy, you have implicitly admitted that the economy cannot expand forever. . . . The notion of an optimal scale for an activity is the very heart of microeconomics. Yet for the macro level, the aggregate of all microeconomic activities, there is no concept of an optimal scale. The notion that the macroeconomy could become too large relative to the ecosystem is simply absent from macroeconomic theory. The macroeconomy is supposed to grow forever. Since Gross National Product adds costs and benefits together instead of comparing them at the margin, we have no macro-level accounting by which an optimal scale could be identified. Beyond a certain scale, growth begins to destroy more values than it creates – economic growth gives way to an era of anti-economic growth. But GNP keeps rising, giving us no clue as to whether we have passed that critical point!
>
> (Daly 1999)

Figure 9.4, based on Daly's work, represents the transfer of the concept of optimal scale from micro- to macroeconomics (Daly 2005). Past the point of optimal production and consumption, we enter an area of what Daly terms *uneconomic growth*, where disutility exceeds utility and humankind may face a potential ecological and economic catastrophe. This critical problem is confounded by the fact that it is not clear at which point this transfer will occur. One of the most persuasive articulations of the dilemma we face was voiced by Ronald Colman (2007, p. 427), who stated:

> Scientists recognize that the only biological organism that has unlimited growth as its dogma is the cancer cell, the apparent model for our conventional economic theory. By contrast, the natural world thrives on balance and equilibrium, and recognizes inherent limits to growth. The cancer analogy is apt, because the path of limitless growth is profoundly self-destructive. No matter how many cars we have in the driveway or how many possessions we accumulate, the environment will not tolerate the growth illusion even if we fail to see through it.

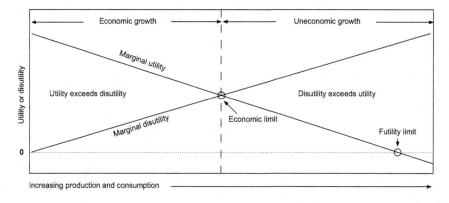

Figure 9.4 Daly on macroeconomic optimality

Source: Reproduced with permission of Jan Christiansen.

One of the principal challenges posed by ecological economics is that it forces us to examine the specific interlinkages and interdependencies of our economic and ecological systems. What does the ecological system provide that we need? There are at least four components: (1) a natural resource base, including both renewable and non-renewable resources; note that "renewable" may be a misnomer as it is just as easy, if not easier, to deplete a renewable as a non-renewable resource base; (2) a set of natural goods, such as landscape and amenity resources; (3) a waste assimilation capacity which is finite in extent; and (4) most importantly, a life support system. Quintin Cronk (2003), formerly of London's world-renowned Kew Gardens, has provided a tongue-in-cheek version of this issue which is reproduced in Figure 9.5. The total bill amounts to the staggering average figure of $33 trillion, with a range of between $16 and 54 trillion. Where does this figure come from?

In 1997, a multidisciplinary research team composed of scientists and social scientists under the leadership of Robert Costanza et al. (1997) published a landmark article in the leading English-language scientific journal, *Nature*. The article, "The Value of the World's Ecosystem Services and Natural Capital," was the first major and comprehensive effort to attach a dollar figure to the ecological services which sustain the planet. To place this total estimated value of $33 trillion in context, the global gross national product in that year was estimated at $18 trillion. The calculation was accomplished by aggregating estimates across 17 ecosystem services for 16 *biomes* (see Table 9.2).

The study by Costanza et al. (1997) was a meta-analysis which relied largely on extracting economic estimates from dozens of studies using a broad range of analytical methodologies. A short list of the estimation methods used is provided in Table 9.3, with some of the most commonly used methodologies highlighted in bold. Chapter 6 describes in more detail how some of these methodologies are used in practice. The authors recognized that the value of some ecosystem services will be infinite (i.e. no life would be possible on earth without them). As a consequence, Costanza et al. (1997) focused on changes in incremental value from the goods and services provided by existing natural capital resources. Costanza et al. (2014) subsequently updated these estimates to 2011. Their revised estimate for total ecosystem services was $124.8 trillion per year in 2007US$ based on a change in both unit values and area (Table 9.4). Their estimate based on change in unit values only was $145 trillion. They were then able to estimate the annual loss of ecoservices at $4.3–$20.2 trillion depending on whether they used updated unit ecosystem service values and changes to biomes areas or only changes to unit values. They added the following caveat concerning the interpretation of these data:

> Global estimates expressed in monetary accounting units, such as this, are useful to highlight the magnitude of eco-services, but have no specific decision-making context. However, the underlying data and models can be applied at multiple scales to assess changes resulting from various scenarios and policies. We emphasize that valuation of eco-services (in whatever units) is not the same as commodification or privatization. Many eco-services are best considered public goods or common pool resources, so conventional markets are often not the best institutional frameworks to manage them. However, these services must be (and are being) valued, and we need new, common asset institutions to better take these values into account.

(p. 153)

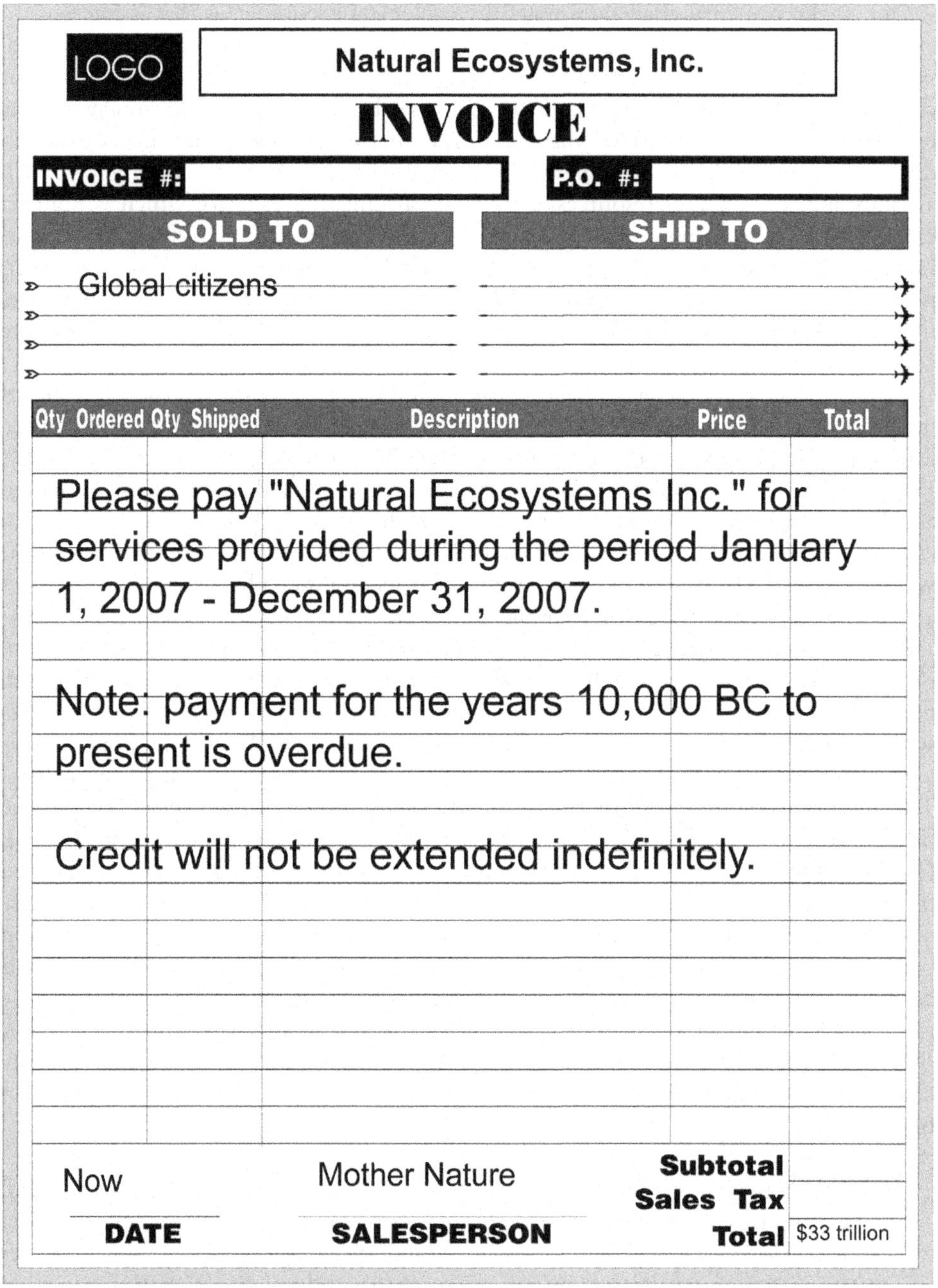

LOGO	Natural Ecosystems, Inc.

INVOICE

INVOICE #: ☐   **P.O. #:** ☐

SOLD TO	SHIP TO
➣ Global citizens	➤
➣	➤
➣	➤
➣	➤

Qty Ordered	Qty Shipped	Description	Price	Total

Please pay "Natural Ecosystems Inc." for services provided during the period January 1, 2007 - December 31, 2007.

Note: payment for the years 10,000 BC to present is overdue.

Credit will not be extended indefinitely.

Now	Mother Nature	Subtotal	
		Sales Tax	
DATE	**SALESPERSON**	**Total**	$33 trillion

Figure 9.5 Nature's bill for ecosystem services

Table 9.2 Ecosystem services and biomes

Ecosystem services	Biomes
Nutrient cycling	**Marine**
Cultural	Open ocean
Waste treatment	Coastal
Disturbance regulation	Estuaries
Water supply	Seagrass/algae beds
Food production	Coral reefs
Gas regulation	Shelf
Water regulation	**Terrestrial**
Recreation	Forest
Raw materials	Tropical
Climate regulation	Temperate/boreal
Erosion control	Grass/rangelands
Biological control	Wetlands
Habitat/refugia	Tidal marsh mangroves
Pollination	Swamps/floodplains
Genetic resources	Lakes and rivers
Soil formation	Desert
	Tundra
	Ice/rock
	Cropland
	Urban

Table 9.3 Analytical methodologies for estimating ecosystem values

Donations	Price of alternatives
Energy analysis	Productivity effects
Expenditures	Property value
External costs	Real estate value
Gross revenues	Regional income
Hedonic demand	**Replacement cost**
Marginal cost of reduction	Revenues
Marginal value	Shadow price
Market value	Substitution cost
Net income	Surrogate market price
Net rent	**TCM – travel cost methodology**
Net revenue	TEV – total enterprise value
NPV current expenditures	Treatment costs
Opportunity cost	TVM – time value of money
Option value	**WTP – willingness to pay**
Preservation payments	**(contingent valuation)**

Table 9.4 Revised estimates of value of ecosystem services 2011

Biome	Aggregate global flow value in 2011
	Trillion 2007 US$/yr.
Marine	49.7
Open ocean	21.9
Coastal	27.7
Estuaries	5.2
Seagrass/algae beds	6.8
Coral reefs	9.9
Shelf	5.9
Terrestrial	75.1
Forest	16.2
Tropical	6.8
Temperate/boreal	9.4
Grass/rangelands	18.4
Wetlands	26.4
Tidal Marsh/mangrove	24.8
Swamps/floodplains	1.5
Lakes/rivers	2.5
Desert	
Tundra	
Ice/rock	
Cropland	9.3
Urban	2.3
Total	**124.8**

Figure 9.6, drawn from the UN's Millennium Ecosystem Assessment (2005, p. 6), provides a graphical summary of the earth's ecosystems and some of the major services they provide. (See Appendix 9.1 for a study on the value of North America's boreal forests and Appendix 9.2 for the application of this theory to third world shrimp cultivation.)

As an addendum to this estimate of the value of global ecological services, UNEP commissioned a report published in October 2010 which attempted to estimate the annual environmental *costs* from global human activity. The report arrived at an estimate of $6.6 trillion (UNEP 2010).

Comparing environmental and ecological economics

Table 9.5 summarizes the critical differences between environmental and ecological economics. It has been commonly assumed that while the theoretical interpretations of distribution and scale differ markedly between the two fields, the basic neo–classical concept of allocative efficiency [fn 1] remains the same in both areas. In fact, it can be argued that this accepted theory is incorrect and that ecological economics brings a critically

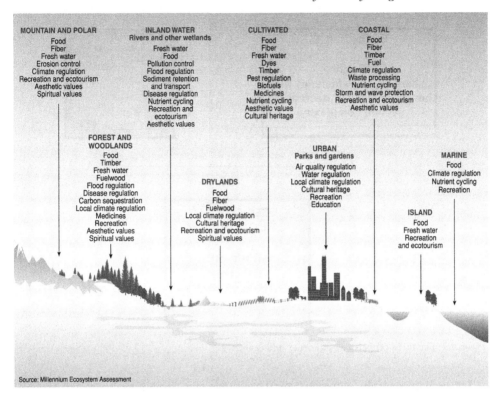

Source: Millennium Ecosystem Assessment

Figure 9.6 Ecosystem services

Table 9.5 Comparing environmental and ecological economics

	Environmental economics	*Ecological economics*
Allocative efficiency	Principal focus	Accepted theory
Distribution	Secondary focus (essentially left to the political process)	Prominent focus (both intra- and intergenerational)
Scale (macro level)	The more, the better	Central – i.e. the physical volume of throughput – concept of optimality

important modification (called *resilience*) borrowed from the field of ecology to the concept of allocative efficiency. Resilience refers to the ability of natural systems to rebound from shocks. As illustrated in Figure 9.7, the problem posed by focusing solely on the traditional definition of allocative efficiency is that it may be achieved by decreasing system resilience. There is a trade-off between efficiency and resilience, and ecological economics specifically recognizes this distinction. (See, for example, Goerner et al. 2009.) Consider two simple examples drawn from the fields of ecology and economics: advanced agricultural production and the global trading and financial system.

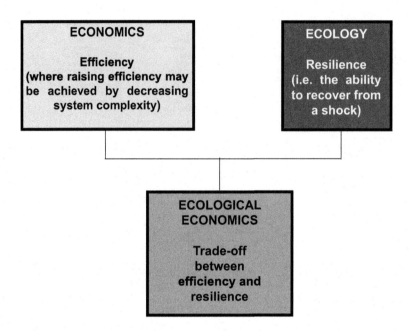

Figure 9.7 The trade-off between efficiency and resilience

The modern agricultural system typical of US farming – and often referred to as *industrial agriculture* – has achieved extraordinary levels of productivity, creating vast surpluses of food available for both domestic and international consumption. One of the principal characteristics of industrial agriculture that contributes to its productivity is a reliance on monoculture. This highly efficient system of agricultural production relies on a cropping protocol which has little, if any, resilience. It is highly vulnerable to insect attacks and plant diseases. As such, economic efficiency – narrowly defined to exclude systemic considerations – is achieved at the expense of resilience.

One can argue that a similar sacrifice of resilience for the sake of efficiency has been achieved through the use of just-in-time inventory control, as such systems are extremely vulnerable to breakdowns at any point in the supply chain. (See Chapter 11.) But perhaps the most important example of the critical trade-off is the inherent characteristics of the vast and complex international systems of trading and finance, often referred to as globalization. These highly efficient institutions and processes for the movement of large amounts of goods and services as well the concomitant vast daily financial flows which make this possible are also extremely vulnerable to system shocks. Examples in the last two decades (including, inter alia, the Mexican peso crisis of 1994–1995, the 1997 Asian financial crisis and the subprime market meltdown of 2008 and its sequelae) demonstrate how the consequences of events which in previous times could be geographically isolated now have the capacity to threaten the functioning of the entire global financial system.

The challenge posed by Daly's reconceptualization of our modern economic systems

There is a fundamental paradox at the center of our modern capitalist system. The perceived success or failure of this system is measured by the extent of economic growth, yet it is this growth that is ultimately unsustainable in a closed ecological system such as the planet earth. The theoretical solution to this critical problem is to achieve development without a concomitant increase in the growth of energy and material throughput. This is a meta-version of the delinkage challenge posed by the growth of carbon emissions along with gross domestic product. As discussed in Chapters 3 and 5, this type of delinkage appears to be beyond our grasp, at least at the planetary level – which is clearly the most critical level.

Over the past few decades, there have been numerous books articulating conceptualizations of alternative economic systems under the rubrics of steady state, zero growth and degrowth (Daly 1973, 1991, 2014; Victor 2019; Jackson 2009; Heinberg 2011; Rubin 2012; Czech 2013; D'Alisa et al. 2015; Washington and Twomey 2016; Pilling 2018).

Steady-state economics

In many respects, this concept is associated largely with the work of Herman Daly, former senior economist of the World Bank. He provides the following definition of the term "steady-state economy" (Daly 2014, p. 78):

> A steady-state economy is one that develops qualitatively (by improvement in science, technology and ethics) without growing quantitatively in physical dimensions; it lives on a diet – a constant metabolic flow of resources from depletion to pollution (the entropic throughput) maintained at a level that is within the assimilative and regenerative capacities of the ecosystem of which the economy is a subsystem.

He has proposed ten measures which are key components of a transition to a steady-state economy (pp. 78–86):

1 Cap-auction-trade systems for basic resources
2 Ecological tax reform, involving a shift in the tax base from labor and capital and toward resources extracted from nature and returned to nature in the form of pollution
3 Limit the range of inequality in income distribution
4 Free up the length of the working day, week and year
5 Re-regulate international commerce, moving away from free trade, free capital mobility and globalization.
6 Downgrade the World Trade Organization, World Bank and International Monetary Fund to something like Keynes's original plan for a multilateral payments clearing union
7 Move away from fractional reserve banking toward a system of 100% reserve requirements
8 Stop treating the scarce as if it were non-scarce (e.g. the atmosphere, electromagnetic spectrum and public lands), and the non-scarce (e.g. the non-rival commonwealth of knowledge and information) as if it were scarce
9 Stabilize population
10 Reform national accounts

Despite the fact that some of these proposals would seem radical to mainstream economists, Daly observes (p. 86):

The conceptual change in vision from the norm of a growth economy to that of a steady-state economy is radical, but the policies advocated are subject to gradual application. . . . These measures are based on the impeccably conservative institutions of private property and decentralized market allocation. The policies advocated simply recognize that: (1) private property loses its legitimacy if too unequally distributed; (2) markets lose their legitimacy if prices do not tell the truth about opportunity costs; and (3) that the macroeconomy becomes as absurdity if its scale is required to grow beyond the biophysical limits of the earth.

Two questions come immediately to mind: (1) is the necessity of growth required in a capitalist system and unique to such a system, and (2) how realistic is it to expect that a transition to a steady state is feasible in the near- to medium-term future?

With respect to the first question, the growth imperative is not confined to modern capitalist systems. Communist economies face the same imperative to grow in order to maintain and/or increase the living standards of their citizens. Lawn (2011, p. 1) makes the argument that a steady-state economy is perfectly compatible with capitalism. He observes:

A capitalist system can exist in a wide variety of forms. Unfortunately, many observers fail to recognize that the current "growth imperative" is the result of capitalist systems everywhere being institutionally designed to grow. They need not be designed this way to survive and thrive. Indeed, because continued growth is both existentially undesirable and ecologically unsustainable, redesigning capitalist systems through the introduction of Daly-like institutions would prove to be capitalism's savior. What's more, it would constitute humankind's best hope of achieving sustainable development.

The second question is not easily answered. Even if renewable energy were to replace fossil fuels, the pressures of increasing population and wealth would continue to drive the extraction of increasing quantities of renewable and non-renewable resources, with their unsustainable impact on global ecosystems. The response of techno-optimists is that continued advances in technology would allow us to transition from an economy which depends quantity to one that is focused on quality. There are several outstanding examples of this type of transition, including Anderson's model of focusing on services provided by goods rather than goods per se and the development of the modern information economy with accompanying technology (2007). One need only visit the poorer nations of Africa to see how the advent of cellular phone networks has revolutionized the economy and society, which previously had limited ground-based phone networks. The existence of these new networks has brought about a revolution in local market economies where women in the workforce, particularly in rural areas, can now bypass traditional local and constrictive financial trading institutions and deal directly with a global market.

The emergence of the information age has also had a profound impact on our economic systems, creating a much more efficient system of production, communication and trade. Questions have been raised, however, about the proposed shift from the paperless office to electronic records. The global production of paper and cardboard has continued to rise despite the technological revolution of digital storage (VDP 2021). And the predicted savings in energy associated with the production of paper have been at least partially offset by the enormous energy requirements associated with data storage. It has been reported that the internet will use a fifth of all the world's electricity by 2025, but some analysts feel that technological advances will significantly reduce this percentage in the future through increased efficiency and conversion to renewable power sources (McKenzie 2021). Despite the promise of technology, questions remain as to whether technology advices will be fast enough to offset the world's increased demands for material throughput and if such developments will entail *revenge effects* that offset any benefits the technology might offer.

Degrowth

Degrowth is an emerging concept which shares many critical characterizes with steady-state economics but entails a broader philosophical rationale. Kallis et al. (2015, pp. 3–4) provide a summary description of this concept:

> Degrowth signifies, first and foremost, a critique of growth. It calls for the decolonization of public debate from the idiom of economism and for the abolishment of economic growth as a social objective. Beyond that, degrowth signifies also a desired direction, one in which societies will use fewer natural resources and will organize and live differently than today. "Sharing", "simplicity", "conviviality", "care" and the "commons" are primary significations of what this society might look like. Usually, degrowth is associated with the idea that smaller can be beautiful. Ecological economists define degrowth as an equitable downscaling of production and consumption that will reduce societies' throughput of energy and raw materials. However, our emphasis here is on different, not only less. Degrowth signifies a society with a smaller metabolism, but more importantly, a society with a metabolism which has a different structure and serves new functions. Degrowth does not call for doing less of the same. The object this is not to make an elephant leaner, but to turn an elephant into a snail. In a degrowth society everything will be different: different activities, different forms and uses of energy, different relations, different gender roles, different allocations of time between paid and non-paid work, different relations with a non-human world. . . . Degrowth is not the same as negative GDP growth. Still, a reduction in GDP, as currently counted, is a likely outcome of actions promoted in the name of degrowth. A green, caring and communal economy is likely to secure the good life, but unlikely to increase gross domestic activity two or three percent per year.

The concept of degrowth is clearly an aspirational goal and, like a steady-state economy, raises critical questions over the timing, feasibility and acceptability of its realization.

Monetizing biodiversity and ecosystem services

Biodiversity markets have been defined as "any payment for the protection, restoration, or management of biodiversity. Just a small sample includes: biodiversity offsets, conservation easements, certified biodiversity-friendly products and services, bioprospecting, payments for biodiversity management, hunting permits, and eco-tourism" (Ecosystemmarketplace 2009, p. 1). Of these, the mechanism which has achieved the widest adoption is biodiversity offsets. There are three types of such offsets: one-off, payments-in-lieu and biobanking. The OECD (2016, pp. 52–53) describes these as follows:

One-off offsets are undertaken by the developer themselves or by a third-party provider on their behalf, often a conservation NGO. . . . The biobanking approach relies on pre-existing offsets that are established in anticipation of future development impacts on biodiversity from which developers can purchase offsets directly. Biobanks are a repository of existing offset credits where each credit represents a quantified gain in biodiversity resulting from actions to restore, establish, enhance and/or preserve biodiversity. Biobanks have been established by both the public and private sector. . . . Payments in-lieu is an approach to biodiversity offsetting whereby regulatory agencies levy fees on developers for causing adverse impacts to biodiversity. The regulatory agency then arranges for the collected fees to be spent on compensatory biodiversity conservation in a subsequent process.

Kormos et al. (2015, p. 10) report that conservation banks are "the state of the art of biodiversity offsetting in the US." They conclude:

Conservation banks have many advantages over PRM [permitee responsible mitigation]. Certainly one of the advantages to a developer for choosing to buy credits from a bank rather than PRM is that developers often do not have in-house expertise on mitigation and offsetting and therefore the ability to pass the responsibility of managing an offset site for species conservation to a third party can be attractive. This transfer of responsibility also allows passing the liability for the success of the mitigation from the developer to the conservation bank sponsor. Another attraction is that the permitting time is often reduced and mitigation costs can be more predictable, and often less than PRM.

(p. 10)

The OECD reported in 2016 that at least 56 countries had laws or policies that specifically required biodiversity offsets or some form of compensatory conservation. At that time, more than 100 biodiversity offset programs were currently operating globally. In fact, the OECD has been among the most prolific organizations advancing the economic and business case for biodiversity (e.g. OECD 2001, 2002, 2003, 2004, 2016, 2017, 2018, 2019).

A strong case has already been made that corporate attention to this subject is good for risk reduction and ultimately the bottom line (Earthwatch 2000, n.d.; Earthwatch et al., 2002; F&C Management Ltd. 2004; GRI 2007; Bishop et al. 2008; IUCN 2004; OECD 2001, 2002, 2003, 2004, 2019; Secretariat of the Convention on Biological Diversity 2010; BBOP 2018). For example, Earthwatch (n.d.) lists some of the major components of a business case for a corporate biodiversity-related strategy: managing risks, facilitating legal compliance with new regulations and legislation, improving reputation, attracting and retaining staff, financial benefits from cutting costs, avoiding fines and enhancing sales opportunities from green credentials, gaining and retaining investment, retaining the license to operate, securing sustainable supply chains and demonstrating a commitment to corporate social responsibility. In addition, there are profitable opportunities for new businesses, including: (1) environmental consulting for the design of offsets as well as consulting for project developers, (2) brokers who bring together demanders and suppliers, (3) registration and certification agents and developers, (4) financial service providers offering loans and insurance and (5) biodiversity offsets offered by landowners (Global Nature Fund and the German Environmental Aid c2013, p. 15).

A more recent report by the OECD (2019) has provided an estimate of global financial flows for biodiversity (see Table 9.6), and a 2018 report by ecosystemmarketplace (Forest

Table 9.6 Estimated finance flows for biodiversity

Type of finance Public	Amount per year	Notes
Domestic budget	47 governments: US$48.96 billion in 2015; Ireland – 250 million Euros per year (average 2010–2015); European Union – 11 billion Euros in 2015	Includes ODA (official development assistance) in some cases; methods are not harmonized; EU covers central budget (direct and indirect expenditures)
ODA = Official development assistance – bilateral	US$7.83 billion in 2017	Commitments, current prices
ODA = Official development assistance – multilateral	US$2.56 billion in 2017	Commitments, current prices
OOF = Other official flows	US$145 million in 2017	Bilateral and multilateral; reporting is limited
Multilateral development banks	Not available	
Debt-for-nature swaps	US$900 million	Possible double counting with ODA?
(Other) biodiversity funds		More than 120 biodiversity-relevant funds identified; very little data available on finance
Biodiversity-relevant positive subsidies	US$0.89 billion 2012–2016 average	Current prices
Potentially beneficial flows from government support to agriculture	2.6 billion Euros (OECD countries)	Includes US Conservation Reserve Program (CRP), which is also included in the PES (payments for ecosystem services) estimate following
Private		
Philanthropy/foundations	US$380 million in 2017	Commitments, current prices (biodiversity marker); based on 14 foundations
Payments for ecosystem services (PES)	US$12 billion	10 large PES programs
Biodiversity offsets	US$4.8 billion in 2016	
Biodiversity-relevant fees and charges	US$2.29 billion (2012–2016 average)	Current prices
Impact investing for "conservation" – i.e. conservation assets under management	US$6.84 billion (assets under management) in 2017	Based on survey of 226 impact investors
Private equity and debt finance	n/a	e.g. Mirova Althelia

Notes: adding these numbers would likely lead to significant double counting in some cases; green/blue bonds can be part of impact investment; bonds can also be issued by public issuers – i.e. sovereign bonds

Trends 2018) provided an initial estimate of 62.7 million Euros as the transacted value of offsets by compensatory mitigation type over the period 2011–2015. The value of one-off offsets dwarfed the size of both financial compensation and banking.

While the public sector has a dominant role in offsetting through the regulatory process, a number of major private sector initiatives have been undertaken to create and maintain a market in biodiversity values. For example, British-based Canopy Capital established a template for investment in ecosystem services including biodiversity (www.canopycapital.co.uk), and a major NGO-corporate collaboration has been established under the rubric of BBOP (Business and Biodiversity Offsets Programme (www.bbop.forest-trends.org and Forest Trends et al. 2009a). Initiated by Forest Trends, Conservation International and the Wildlife Conservation Society, this organization has an advisory board from a large group of international agencies, NGOs and a diverse range of corporate sponsors such as Anglo America, Newmont, Sherritt, Alcoa, Rio Tinto, Shell Oil, etc. The BBOP program provides extensive documentation to assist corporations in participating in this emerging market, including a biodiversity offset cost-benefit handbook (Forest Trends 2009b), biodiversity offset design handbook (Forest Trends 2009c), biodiversity offset implementation handbook (Forest Trends 2009d) and extensive in-depth case studies from the US (Forest Trends 2009e), Ghana (Forest Trends 2009f), Madagascar (Forest Trends 2009g), etc.

Many of these studies and initiatives appear to be concerned with companies engaging in activities which endanger biodiversity. As a consequence, they fund the creation of biodiversity reserves or activities on- or off-site in order to compensate for this damage. The opportunities a corporation might be able to capitalize on are threefold: (1) offering companies who are reducing biodiversity as a result of their business activities a distant off-site opportunity to offset, (2) offering companies who are engaging in some other form of environmentally detrimental activity the opportunity to "cross offset," or (3) offering companies and other investors an opportunity to invest in biodiversity credits for other reasons – goodwill, desire to protect and preserve the environment, etc.

A number of issues are associated with the design and implementation of biodiversity offsets. By way of example, Bull et al. (2013) list the following challenges in designing appropriate offsetting programs:

- Currency – choosing metrics for measuring biodiversity
- No net loss – defining requirements for demonstrating no net loss of biodiversity
- Equivalence – demonstrating equivalence between biodiversity losses and gains
- Longevity – defining how long offset schemes should endure
- Time lag – deciding whether to allow a temporal gap between development and offset gains
- Uncertainty – managing for uncertainties throughout the offset process
- Reversibility – defining how reversible development impacts might be
- Thresholds – defining threshold biodiversity values beyond which offsets are not acceptable

Koh et al. (2019, p. 679) present a typology of offset policies and assess how well they perform in practice in six countries in relation to their ideal type. They conclude that "government, contrary to received wisdom, plays a key role not just in enforcing mandatory policies but also in determining the supply and demand of biodiversity units, supervising the transaction or granting legitimacy to the compensation site."

There are several additional considerations before undertaking biodiversity offsetting. The first is that such offsets should be the option of last resort after attempting other approaches in the mitigation hierarchy. This hierarchy

> determines that impacts on nature and landscape must be (a) avoided, (b) minimized, (c) restored as far as possible, and that (d) residual impacts have to be compensated (obligatory biodiversity offsets). The "residual impact on biodiversity" refers to the damage remaining after all efforts of avoiding, minimising and restoring. It is this impact which eventually has to be subjected to compensation measures.
>
> (GNF/GEA c2014, p. 11)

In fact, the process is further constrained by the potential irreplaceability of biodiversity. To quote the same report (p. 19):

> The effectiveness of biodiversity offsets is limited and not every impact can be adequately compensated. The laws and regulations define clear ecological limits determining in which cases an impact may not take place, since it could not be compensated by any adequate compensatory measure. This includes for example the loss of species facing extinction, which cannot be compensated by any compensation measure.

Because the market for biodiversity is a subset of the larger concept of paying for ecosystem services, this, in turn, offers the prospect for this component in a new, more broadly focused sustainability instrument focused on habitat management.

Payment for ecosystem services

Payment for ecosystem services can be defined as a "voluntary and conditional agreement between a provider and a buyer on a well-defined ecosystem service or land use" (GNF/GEA c2013). There are two fundamental requirements: (1) additionality – i.e. the undertaking must be new or additional and not one that would be implemented anyway – and (2) conditionality – i.e. the project requires remuneration. There are five types of PES schemes: public payment schemes for private landowners, formal markets with open trading, self-organized private deals, tax incentives and certification programs (Elisha 2019). Despite the fact that these mechanisms are available for both private and public implementation, in general most of these programs have tended to be undertaken by government or non-governmental organizations. The report by the Global Nature Fund and German Environmental Aid (GNF/GEA c2013, p. 31) lists the following reasons why the adoption rate from the private sector is generally low:

> (1) Lack of direct demand for ecosystem services in the region; (2) The ecosystem services required for the production are available free of charge for companies at the level of quality or quantity desired; (3) The cost of launching a PES programme is substantially higher than the value of the required natural capital. This can be the case because there is no substitute or the natural capital is highly relevant for the company; (4) It is relatively easy for the company to relocate the ecosystem service or to move its own production to a new location; and (5) Companies are uncertain if other actors might not negatively impact the natural capital (rights of use and access ae insufficiently safeguarded).

The report also explains why services are frequently bundled together (p. 28):

> Instead of only offering one ecosystem service (e.g. CO_2 capture) in a PES pro-
> gramme, it is also possible to bundle and offer multiple ecosystem services (e.g. CO_2
> capture and erosion protection). The most important reason for offering multiple
> ecosystem services in a bundle is that PES programmes which only focus on one
> ecosystem service run the risk that other ecosystem services are negatively affected. A
> tree plantation, for example, can store a lot of CO_2, but perhaps it does not have any
> positive impact on biodiversity, or maybe even a negative one. An advantage of the
> bundled PES is reducing fixed costs and transaction costs. Also, an ecosystem service
> for which there is no willingness to pay can be co-financed that way: via the so-called
> "piggy-backing method."

The OECD (2010, pp. 16–17) lists 12 criteria that are required to enhance environmental and cost-effectiveness in a PES program: perverse incentives such market distortions in the form of subsidies must be removed; property rights must be clearly defined;
PES goals and objectives must also be defined; a program requires a robust monitoring
and reporting framework; buyers must be identified and sufficient long-term sources of
financing must be ensured; sellers and target ecosystem service benefits must be identified;
baseline and target payments to ecosystem services must be established that are at risk of
loss or in order to enhance their provision; payments must be differentiated based on the
opportunity costs of ecosystem service provision; bundling or layering multiple ecosystem
services should be considered; potential leakage must be addressed where the provision of
services in one location increases pressure for conversion in another; permanence must be
ensured; and performance-based payments must be delivered and adequate enforcement
is essential. The cumulative burden of all these requirements provides yet another impetus
for government involvement. Such involvement is typically focused on forest and watershed management, health and preservation.

Finally, the UNDP (n.d.) identifies the principal risks and challenges of PES-based
programs:

Pros

- Flexible instrument compared to command and control regulation, allowing high
  customization to local circumstances.
- Behavioural changes are promoted with positive incentives rather than coercion,
  more likely leading to transformational change.
- PES can help to correct market failures by pricing conservation efforts.
- PES provide opportunities for cash income in rural areas where poverty might be
  concentrated.
- Rural communities can benefit from increased knowledge of sustainable resource
  use practices that are usually connected to PES through the provision of training
  and technical assistance.

Cons

- The economic valuation of ecosystem is a difficult and still costly process, despite
  innovations in techniques and technology. (See also Boerema et al. 2016.)

- PES implementation might be costly due to the specifics of design, negotiation and implementation of the programme.
- PES are not designed to reduce poverty but primarily to offer economic incentives to foster the conservation of ecosystem services. Additional measures need to be enforced to make PES pro poor.
- The efficacy of PES implementation is partially connected to the availability of data on land property, which is a known challenge in many developing countries.
- PES might result in limiting the flexibility of local government and communities in making decisions on their own development particularly where easements or long-term contracts specify a narrow range of alternatives.

Risks

- Failure to monitor the effectiveness of the compensation schemes, including risks of not fulfilling the performance condition.
- Risks associated with the enforcement of property rights. For example, illegal logging or land appropriation will undermine the ability of a landholder to protect the ecosystem. Changes in land management rules and regulations may also have a significant impact on ecosystem service delivery and the PES.
- Leakage can occur when the provision of ecosystem in one location increases pressure for conversion in another.
- Unintended perverse incentives that negatively affect biodiversity, for example, farmers are paid to plant nonnative tree species.
- Regressive distributional outcomes, especially, when limiting access to resources and land to impoverished communities. Elites might capture the largest income provided through PES.
- Corruption and abuses. Like other public subsidies, PES schemes are vulnerable to corruption practices that might divert resources.
- Uncontrolled liabilities. The Government might incur in commitments for conservation payments beyond its budget due to flawed legal arrangements or lack of coordination, putting the whole financial sustainability of the programme at risk.

PES schemes can be undertaken at local, regional or international levels. One of the most convincing demonstration of a regional program was New York City's payment for upstate ecosystem services as an alternative to a massive new capital expenditure program (as described in Chapter 6, Appendix 9.2). At the international level, the most successful undertaking is that sponsored by the Costa Rican government. As described by the Organization of American States (n.d., p. 1):

> Costa Rica is one of the pioneer countries where PES schemes have been successful at a national scale. The Environmental Services Payments Program was launched by The National Financing Fund (FONAFIFO) in 1997 to benefit small and medium-sized landowners whose included forests are suitable for forestry activities, with the aim of promoting the conservation and recovery of the country's forest cover. The ESPP program started investing US$ 14 million in payments for environmental services, which resulted in: reforestation of 6,500 ha, sustainable management of 10,000 ha of natural forests and, the preservation of 79,000 ha of private natural forests. PES in Costa Rica provides subsidies to farmers for plantations and agroforestry systems.

Table 9.7 Costa Rica payment for ecosystem services

Environmental service	Primary forest			Secondary forest		
$/hectare	*min*	*med*	*max*	*min*	*med*	*max*
Carbon sequestration	19	38	57	14.63	29.26	43.89
Protection of water	2.5	5	7.5	1.25	2.5	3.75
Biodiversity protection	5	10	15	3.75	7.5	11.25
Ecosystem protection	2.5	5	7.5	1.25	2.5	3.75
Total	29	58	87	20.88	41.76	62.64

Source: Reproduced with permission of the publisher.

The tax on fossil fuels is the main source of funding (80%), and the other 20% comes from international sale of carbon from public protected areas.

This undertaking was an essential response by the government to reverse the high rates of deforestation that had occurred during the 1970 and 1980 driven by cheap credit for cattle, land-titling laws that rewarded deforestation and rapid expansion of the road system (UNFCCC n.d.) Funding for the government program is provided by the government's fuel tax and water charge coupled with Certificates of Conservation of Biodiversity, carbon credits and alliances with the private sector.

The government of Costa Rica compensates landowners for four environmental services, of which biodiversity is one (Castro et al. 2000). (See Table 9.7.) An OECD study in 2010 of global PES markets across all sectors – e.g. forestry, agriculture, water resources, etc. – identified over 300 programs with a value in excess of US$6.5 billion (OECD 2010). More recent estimates place the global value at between US$10 and US$12 billion (OECD 2018, 2019). This is considered a minimum estimate as there is no comprehensive OECD database of these projects as of yet.

Summary and conclusion

The field of ecological economics is still in its infancy, and major conceptual advances are being made annually. There are, however, at least four basic points of consensus in ecological economics. As summarized by Costanza et al. (1997), they are: (1) the earth is a thermodynamically closed and non-materially growing system, which implies that there are limits to biophysical throughput of resources; (2) the future goal is a sustainable planet with a high quality of life for all its inhabitants (humans and other species), which includes both the present and future generations; (3) a complex system, such as the earth, where fundamental uncertainty is large and irreducible and certain process are irreversible, requires a fundamentally *precautionary* stance (see Chapter 10); and (4) institutions and management should be proactive rather than reactive and should result in simple, adaptive and implementable policies based on a sophisticated understanding of the underlying systems which fully acknowledges their inherent uncertainties. In light of this new focus on ecosystem services, the central question which arises concerns their significance for business, and this challenge is specifically addressed in a companion book (Nemetz 2022).

Appendix 9.1
Valuing ecosystem services of North America's boreal forest

Figure 9.8 illustrates the extent of the disappearance of global boreal forests over the past 8,000 years. Stretching from Alaska eastward through northern Europe and all the way to Siberia, these forests are considered among the most productive and important on the earth's surface, yet the absence of any explicit valuation of their ecosystem services precludes any rational cost-benefit analysis of the degree to which this vast resource base should be transformed for human development. A study by the Pembina Institute (Anielski and Wilson 2005) entailed the creation of a Boreal Ecosystem Wealth Accounting System (BEWAS) in an attempt to identify, inventory and measure the full economic value of the ecological goods and services provided just by Canada's portion of this forest. Table 9.8 presents a summary of the findings. One important and innovative technique was to compare the net market value of boreal natural capital extraction (at $CDN37.8 billion) with the total non-market value of boreal ecosystem services (at $93.2 billion). The ratio of non-market to market values is approximately 2.5:1, reinforcing the critical conclusion that omitting these more comprehensive economic estimates from development plans could lead to seriously distorted and economically inefficient decisions.

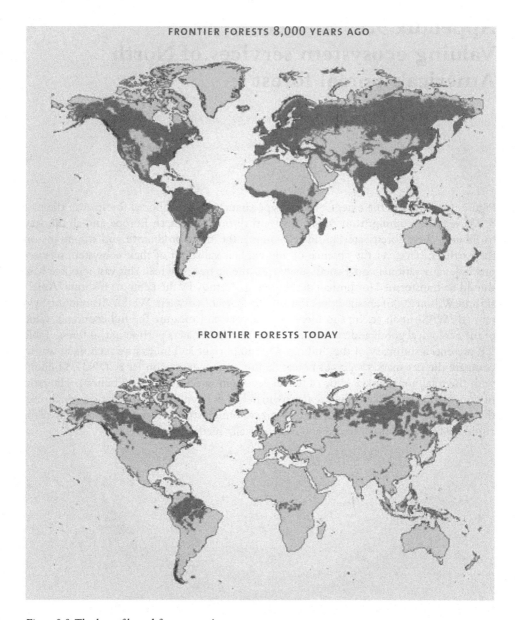

Figure 9.8 The loss of boreal forest over time

Source: Anielski and Wilson 2005, p. 90, reproduced with permission of the Canadian Boreal Initiative.

Table 9.8 Summary of natural capital economic values for Canada's boreal region

Boreal ecosystem wealth natural capital accounts	Values and costs *
Forests	
Market values:	
Estimated market value of forestry-related GDP in the boreal region (est. 2002)	$14.9 billion
Costs:	
Estimated cost of carbon emissions from forest industry activity in the boreal region (deduction against forestry-related GDP)	$150 million
Non-market values:	
Value of pest control services by birds	$5.4 billion
Nature-related activities	$4.5 billion
Annual net carbon sequestration (excludes peatlands)	1.85 billion
Subsistence value for Aboriginal peoples	$575 million
Non-timber forest products	$79 million
Watershed service (i.e. municipal water use)	$18 million
Passive conservation value	$12 million
Wetlands and peatlands	
Non-market values:	
Flood control and water filtering by peatlands only	$77.0 billion
Flood control, water filtering and biodiversity value by non-peatland wetlands	$3.4 billion
Estimated annual replacement cost value of peatlands sequestering carbon	$383 million
Minerals and subsoil assets	
Market values:	
GDP from mining and oil and gas industrial activities in the boreal region (est. 2002)	$14.5 billion
Costs:	
Federal government expenditures as estimated subsidies to oil and gas sector in the boreal region	$541 million
Government expenditures as estimated subsidies to mining sector in the boreal region	$474 million
Water resources	
Market values:	
GDP for hydroelectric generation from dams and reservoirs in the Boreal Shield ecozone (est. 2002)	$19.5 billion
Waste production (emissions to air, land and water)	
Costs:	
Estimated air pollution costs to human health	$9.9 billion
Total market values (forestry, mining, oil and gas activity and hydroelectric generation)	$48.9 billion
Less cost of pollution and subsidies:	
Air pollution costs	−$9.9 billion
Government subsidies to mining sector	−$474 million
Federal government subsidies to oil and gas sector	−$541 million
Forest sector carbon emission costs	−$150 million
Net market value of boreal natural capital extraction	$37.8 billion
Total market value of boreal ecosystem services	$93.2 billion
Ratio of non-market to market values	2.5

* Monetary economic values and regrettable costs (at CDN 2002 $ per annum)

Appendix 9.2
Case study of Thai shrimp farming

The importance of valuing ecosystem services is graphically illustrated by research on the global loss of mangrove forests and their associated ecosystem services in both hemispheres (Aburto-Oropeza et al. 2008). Thailand's exports of crustaceans have been increasing exponentially since the mid-1970s (UN Comtrade database) to meet market demand in the industrialized countries, particularly the United States. This new and profitable application of aquaculture has come at the expense of vast areas of mangrove swamps which have been cut down to make way for shrimp ponds. The amount of mangrove globally lost to aquaculture, logging, use of wood for fuel and charcoal production, diseases and storms has varied from 35%–80% by country (UNEP et al. 2006); in Thailand alone, the loss has ranged from 50%–65% due to shrimp aquaculture (Thorton et al. 2003). There are several major consequences of the replacement of mangroves with fish ponds: the exposure of coastal areas to erosion, flooding, increased storm damage, altered natural drainage patterns, increased salt intrusion and removal of critical habitats for aquatic and terrestrial species. The impacts of mangrove forest loss were clearly illustrated during the devastating 2004 tsunami that completely eradicated countless coastal villages and killed up to 250,000 people in Southeast Asia.

The business model for shrimp farming makes good economic sense to a private entrepreneur. While the yield from the ponds may last for only five to ten years, generally followed by abandonment of the land, there is a positive net present value to this investment. Once one area has been ecologically devastated, the business can move to a new unspoiled area and repeat the process. Sathirathai and Barbier (2004) conducted a detailed analysis of the economics of this type of undertaking and found that private returns are high. Figure 9.9 illustrates the simple economics of the private benefits of this business. In this representation, the net benefits from shrimp production dwarf the value of the direct benefits derived from the mangroves, such as a small yield of timber and non-timber products which are terminated once the shrimp fishery begins.

This private sector orientation seriously misrepresents the underlying social costs and benefits of shrimp production as it does not formally account for the value of a standing mangrove forest. Sathirathai and Barbier attempt to value the mangrove ecosystem services, including coastline protection and what they term "offshore fishery linkages." This latter term refers to the food and shelter provided to fish as they grow. Also included in their calculation are the external costs of water pollution. Figure 9.10 recasts the economic analysis by comparing the private cost and social cost models. It is clear that once ecosystem services are monetized, what has appeared to be a desirable

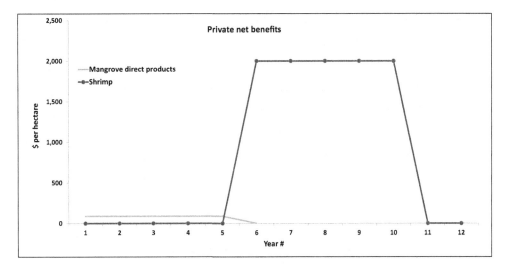

Figure 9.9 Private net benefits from shrimp production in Thailand

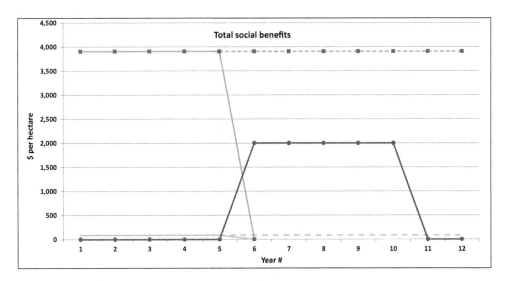

Figure 9.10 Comparing private and social net benefits from shrimp

business venture is not economic from a societal perspective, as the indefinite stream of indirect mangrove benefits are lost as well as the much smaller direct benefits. The benefits identified by the authors are lower bound estimates, as they have omitted important mangrove-related benefits such as tourism, carbon fixation, option value and non-use values.

Note

1   Allocative efficiency, another term for Pareto efficiency, is the cornerstone of neo-classical economic theory. To quote Brander (2006, p. 18):

> Pareto efficiency is a broader concept of efficiency than is management efficiency. It requires management efficiency as a necessary condition, but requires additional conditions as well. Ultimately, however, the concept of Pareto efficiency refers fundamentally to the absence of waste. If a situation is Pareto inefficient, it means it is possible to improve the welfare of at least one person without harming anyone else, and it would be wasteful not to do so. Pareto inefficiency means that potential human welfare is being wasted.

References

Aburto-Oropeza, Octavio et al. (2008) "Mangroves in the Gulf of California increase fishery yields," *Proceedings of the National Academy of Sciences*, 105(30), July 29, pp. 10456–10459.

Anderson, Ray (2007) "Mid-course correction: toward a sustainable enterprise," Chapter 3 in Peter N. Nemetz (ed.) *Sustainable Resource Management. Reality or Illusion?* Cheltenham, UK: Edward Elgar, pp. 88–114.

Anielski, Mark and Sara Wilson (2005) *Counting Canada's Natural Capital: Assessing the Real Value of Canada's Boreal Ecosystems*, Calgary, AB: Pembina Institute.

Bishop, Joshua et al. (2008) *Building Biodiversity: Business*, London and Gland, Switzerland: Shell Oil and International Union for Conservation of Nature (IUNC).

Boerema, Annelies et al. (2016) "Are ecosystem services adequately quantified?," *Journal of Applied Ecology*, 54, pp. 358–370.

Brander, James A. (2006) *Government Policy toward Business* (4th ed.), Mississauga, ON: John Wiley & Sons.

Bull, Joseph W. et al. (2013) "Biodiversity offsets in theory and practice," *Oryx*, 47, July.

Business and Biodiversity Offsets Programme (BBOP) (2018) *Business Planning for Biodiversity Net Gain: A Roadmap, Forest Trends*, Washington, DC: Forest Trends and the Wildlife Conservation Society.

Castro, Rene et al. (2000) "The Costa Rican experience with market instruments to mitigate climate change and conserve biodiversity," *Environmental Monitoring and Assessment*, 61, pp. 75–92.

Colman, Ronald (2007) "Measuring genuine progress," in Peter N. Nemetz (ed.) *Sustainable Resource Management: Reality or Illusion?*, Cheltenham: Edward Elgar.

Costanza, Robert et al. (1997) "The value of the world's ecosystem services and natural capital," *Nature*, 387, May 15, pp. 253–260, and supplementary material.

Costanza, Robert et al. (2014) "Changes in the global value of ecosystem services," *Global Environmental Change*, 26, pp. 152–158.

Cronk, Quintin (2003) "The thin green line: Plants and the future of humanity," Address to the Vancouver Institute, University of British Columbia, Vancouver, BC, November 22.

Czech, Brian (2013) *Supply Shock: Economic Growth at the Crossroads and the Steady State Solution*, Gabriola Island, BC: New Society Publishers.

D'Alisa, Giacomo et al. (eds.) (2015) *Degrowth: A Vocabulary for a New Era*, London: Routledge.

Daly, Herman E. (ed.) (1973) *Toward a Steady-State Economy*, San Francisco, CA: W.H. Freeman and Company.

Daly, Herman E. (1991) *Steady-State Economics* (2nd ed.), Washington, DC: Island Press.

Daly, Herman E. (1999) *Ecological Economics and the Ecology of Economics: Essays in Criticism*, Cheltenham: Edward Elgar.

Daly, Herman E. (2005) "Economics in a full world," *Scientific American*, September, pp. 100–107.

Daly, Herman E. (2014) *From Uneconomic Growth to a Steady-State Economy*, Cheltenham, UK: Edward Elgar.

Earthwatch (2000) *Case Studies in Business & Biodiversity*, Oxford.

Earthwatch (n.d.) *Engaging Businesses With Biodiversity: Guidelines for Local Biodiversity Partnerships*, Oxford.

Earthwatch, International Union for Conservation of Nature (IUCN) and World Business Council for Sustainable Development (2002) *Business & Biodiversity: The Handbook for Corporate Action*, Oxford.

Ecosystemmarktplace (2009) *State of Biodiversity Markets: Offset and Compensation Programs Worldwide*, Washington, DC. www.ecosystemmarketplace.com

Elisha, Benjamin (2019) "Payment for ecosystem services: An important tool in conservation," *Environment*, December 18.

F&C Management Ltd. (2004) *Is Biodiversity a Material Risk for Companies? An Assessment of the Exposure of FTSE Sectors to Biodiversity Risk*, Edinburgh, UK.

Forest Trends (2018) *Voluntary Carbon Markets Insights: 2018 Outlook and First-Quarter Trends*, Washington, DC: Forest Trends, August.

Forest Trends, Conservation International and Wildlife Conservation Society (2009a) *Business, Biodiversity Offsets and BBOP: An Overview*, Washington, DC: Forest Trends.

Forest Trends, Conservation International and Wildlife Conservation Society (2009b) *Biodiversity Offset Cost-Benefit Handbook*, Washington, DC: Forest Trends.

Forest Trends, Conservation International and Wildlife Conservation Society (2009c) *Biodiversity Offset Design Handbook*, Washington, DC: Forest Trends.

Forest Trends, Conservation International and Wildlife Conservation Society (2009d) *Biodiversity Offset Implementation Handbook*, Washington, DC: Forest Trends.

Forest Trends, Conservation International and Wildlife Conservation Society (2009e) *BBOP Pilot Project Case Study: Bainbridge Island*, Washington, DC: Forest Trends.

Forest Trends, Conservation International and Wildlife Conservation Society (2009f) *BBOP Pilot Project Case Study: The Ambatovy Project*, Washington, DC: Forest Trends.

Forest Trends, Conservation International and Wildlife Conservation Society (2009g) *BBOP Pilot Project Case Study: Akyem Gold Mining Project, Eastern Region, Ghana*, Washington, DC: Forest Trends.

Global Nature Fund and the German Environmental Aid (GNF/GEA) (c2013) *Markets for Natural Capital: Status Quo and Prospects*, naturalcapitalmarkets.org.

Global Reporting Initiative (GRI) (2007) *Biodiversity: A GRI Reporting Resource*, Amsterdam: GRI.

Goerner, Sally J. et al. (2009) "Quantifying economics sustainability: Implications for free-enterprise theory, policy and practice," *Ecological Economics*, 69, pp. 76–81.

Heinberg, Richard (2011) *The End of Growth: Adapting to Our New Economic Reality*, Gabriola Island, BC: New Society Publishers.

International Union for Conservation of Nature (IUCN) (2004) *Biodiversity Offsets: Views, Experience, and the Business Case*, Gland, Switzerland: IUCN.

Jackson, Tim (2009) *Prosperity without Growth: Economics for a Finite Planet*, London: Earthscan.

Kallis, Giorgos et al. (2015) "Degrowth," Introduction in D'Alisa, Giacomo et al. (eds.) *Degrowth: A Vocabulary for a New Era*, London: Routledge.

Koh, Niak Sian et al. (2019) "How much of a market is involved in a biodiversity offset? A typology of biodiversity offset policies," *Journal of Environmental Management*, 232, pp. 679–691.

Kormos, Rebecca et al. (2015) *Biodiversity Offsetting in the United States: Lesson Learned on Maximizing Their Ecological Contribution*, Cambridge, UK: Fauna & Floral International

Lawn, Philip (2011) "Is steady-state capitalism viable? A review of the issues and an answer in the affirmative," *Annals of the New York Academy of Sciences*, 1219, pp. 1–25.

McKenzie, James (2021) "Powering the beast: Why we shouldn't worry about the Internet's rising electricity consumption," *Physicsworld*, January 13.

Nemetz, Peter N. (2022) *Corporate Strategy and Sustainability*, London: Routledge.

Organization for Economic Co-operation and Development (OECD) (2001) *Valuation of Biodiversity Benefits. Selected Studies*, Paris: OECD.

Organization for Economic Co-operation and Development (OECD) (2002) *Handbook of Biodiversity Valuation: A Guide for Policy Makers*, Paris: OECD.

Organization for Economic Co-operation and Development (OECD) (2003) *Harnessing Markets for Biodiversity: Towards Conservation and Sustainable Use*, Paris: OECD.

Organization for Economic Co-operation and Development (OECD) (2004) *Handbook of Market Creation for Biodiversity: Issues in Implementation*, Paris: OECD.

Organization for Economic Co-operation and Development (OECD) (2010) *Paying for Biodiversity: Enhancing the Cost-Effectiveness of Payments for Ecosystem Services*, Paris: OECD.

Organization for Economic Co-operation and Development (OECD) (2016) *Biodiversity Offsets: Effective Design and Implementation*, Paris: OECD.

Organization for Economic Co-operation and Development (OECD) (2017) *The Political Economy of Biodiversity Policy Reform*, Paris: OECD.

Organization for Economic Co-operation and Development (OECD) (2018) *Tracking Economic Instruments and Finance for Biodiversity*, Paris: OECD.

Organization for Economic Co-operation and Development (OECD) (2019) *Biodiversity: Finance and the Economic Case for Action*, Paris: OECD.

Organization of American States (OAS) Department of Sustainable Development (n.d.) "National Payment for Environmental Services Programs," Costa Rica.

Pilling, David (2018) *The Growth Delusion*, London: Bloomsbury.

Rubin, Jeff (2012) *The End of Growth: But Is That All Bad?*, Toronto: Random House Canada.

Sathirathai, Suthawan and Edward B. Barbier (2004) "Comparative returns of mangroves for shrimp farming and local direct and indirect uses in Surat Thani Province," in B. Barbier and Suthawan Sathirathai (eds.) *Shrimp Farming and Mangrove Loss in Thailand*, Cheltenham, UK: Edward Elgar. [See also Sathirathai, Suthawan and Edward B. Barbier (2001) "Valuing mangrove conservation in Southern Thailand," *Contemporary Economic Policy*, 19(2), April, pp. 109–122].

Secretariat of the Convention on Biological Diversity (CBD) (2010) *Global Biodiversity Outlook 3*, Montreal: CBD.

Thorton, Coralie et al. (2003) "From wetlands to wastelands: Impact of shrimp farming," Environmental Justice Foundation, London. www.ejfoundation.org

UN Comtrade database. http://comtrade.un.org/db/

UN Development Programme (UNDP) (n.d.) Financing Solutions for Sustainable Development. "Payment for Ecosystems Services."

UN Environment Programme (UNEP) (2010) *Universal Ownership. Why environmental externalities matter to institutional investors*, Finance Initiative, PRI. Nairobi, Kenya: UNEP.

UN Environment Programme (UNEP) et al. (2006) *In the Front Line: Shoreline Protection and Other Ecosystem Services from Mangroves and Coral Reefs*, Nairobi, Kenya: UNEP.

UN Framework Convention on Climate Change (FCCC) (n.d.) *Climate Change*.

UN Millennium Ecosystem Assessment (2005) *Living Beyond Our Means. Natural Assets and Human Well-Being. Statement from the Board*, Nairobi, Kenya: UNEP.

Verband Deutscher Papierfabriken e.V. (VDP) (2021) *Papier Kompass*, Bonn: VDP.

Victor, Peter A. (2019) *Managing without Growth: Slower by Design, Not Disaster* (2nd ed.), Cheltenham, UK: Edward Elgar.

Washington, Haydn and Paul Twomey (eds.) (2016) *A Future beyond Growth: Towards a Steady State Economy*, London: Earthscan.

www.fscoax.org/principal.htm [website for Greenpeace International].

www.maweb.org [Millennium Ecosystem Assessment website].

www.teebweb.org [website for The Economics of Ecosystems and Biodiversity].

10 Risk analysis and the precautionary principle

Because risks are ubiquitous, risk analysis is a common tool used by government, business and individuals, whether consciously or not. Risk (R) is defined as the product of accident consequences (C) and accident probability (P): i.e. (R) = C × P. For example, if the probability of an accident is 10^{-1}/year, and the average number of deaths per accident is 100, then the risk is $1/10 \times 100 = 10$ deaths/year. The discussion in this chapter focuses on technological risk and the threat to human health and life, rather than financial risk.

One of the most controversial public pronouncements on the subject of risk was enunciated by the former secretary of defense under the Bush administration, Donald Rumsfeld (2002), when he stated in the context of dangers in Iraq (CBS News November 9, 2006):

> Reports that say that something hasn't happened are always interesting to me, because as we know, there are known knowns; there are things we know we know. We also know there are known unknowns; that is to say we know there are some things we do not know. But there are also unknown unknowns – the ones we don't know we don't know.

While the public and press were perplexed by this apparently bizarre statement, in fact, Rumsfeld had enunciated a fundamental principle of risk analysis.

Table 10.1 presents some crucial concepts and terminology in the field of risk analysis. Note their correspondence to the speech given by Rumsfeld. This table builds upon the work of Frank Knight (1921) by dividing the nature of risks into four categories: (1) Certainty – which is not technically risk per se – where we are aware of the consequences of an event or decision and know that consequence is certain to occur: i.e. its probability is 1.0. (2) Risk – where the consequences of an event or decision are known but not with precision. In this case, a probability distribution is used to define the outcomes. (3) Uncertainty – a situation where the consequences are known but the probability of occurrence is unknown. (4) "Wicked" problems – a series of outcomes that society does not even know the existence of, let alone their probability. Table 10.2, drawn from a study commissioned by the European Environment Agency (Harremoes 2001), provides an example of each category.

The concept of risk can be used effectively in informing both governmental and corporate decision-making. The World Economic Forum (WEF) (2020) has produced a report which focuses on the broad range of global risks facing both public and private sector decision makers. Figure 10.1 places these multifaceted risks, many of which are environmentally related, in an impact-likelihood framework. Of particular usefulness to

DOI: 10.4324/9781003170730-10

Table 10.1 Some risk analysis terminology

	Consequences (single or multiple)	Probability of occurrence
Certainty	Known	1
Risk	Known	Probability distribution
Uncertainty	Known	Unknown
"Wicked" problems	Unknown	Unknown

Table 10.2 Examples of categories in risk analysis

	Case study examples
Risk	*Known impacts and known probabilities:* e.g. **asbestos** causing respiratory disease, lung disease and mesothelioma
Uncertainty	*Known impacts and unknown probabilities:* e.g. **antibiotics in animal feed** and development of bacterial resistance
Ignorance or "wicked" problems	*Unknown impacts and therefore unknown probabilities:* e.g. surprises of **CFCs** and their destruction of the ozone layer

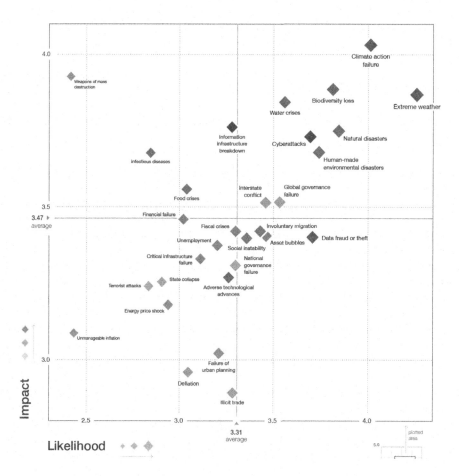

Figure 10.1 Global risks matrix

	Negligible	Marginal	Serious	Very serious
Frequent	IV	II	I	I
Probable	IV	III	II	I
Occcasional	V	IV	III	II
Remote	V	V	IV	III

Figure 10.2 Risk matrix

corporate decision-making is a risk matrix which subdivides, or decomposes, the consequences and frequency of outcomes, as illustrated in Figure 10.2. Each cell in the matrix
is given a color to signify its importance or potential threat to corporate operations and
profitability. Figure 10.3 applies example numerical data to demonstrate how this matrix
could be operationalized. The critical nature of the results progresses from the lower left
of the matrix – where results are considered unambiguously acceptable – to the upper
right, where results are progressively more stringent: acceptable with controls, undesirable,
highly undesirable and totally unacceptable. While it may seem intuitively obvious that a
firm would wish to minimize its risks, there is frequently a linkage between opportunities
and risks, inducing firms to balance potential gains and losses in light of their degree of
risk tolerance or aversion.

Probabilistic risk assessment

A central methodology in risk analysis is probabilistic risk assessment (PRA), which measures the probability and severity of major threats to human life, safety and the environment. PRA is of particular usefulness today because of complex modern technologies and
their capabilities to cause a large degree of damage – either accidentally or intentionally.
Examples of PRA include studies of hydroelectric dams, nuclear power plants, chemical

	Injury or illness $2K–$10K OR damage $0.1–$1M	Injury or illness $10K–$200K OR damage $1–$10M	Permanent disability or illness $200K–$1M OR damage $10–$100M	Death or total disability >$1M OR damage >$100M
> 10⁻¹	Acceptable as is	Highly undesirable	Unacceptable	Unacceptable
10⁻¹–10⁻²	Acceptable as is	Undesirable	Highly undesirable	Unacceptable
10⁻²–10⁻³	Acceptable as is	Acceptable with controls	Undesirable	Highly undesirable
10⁻³–10⁻⁴	Acceptable as is	Acceptable as is	Acceptable with controls	Undesirable

Figure 10.3 Risk matrix with possible values

factories, etc. There are a number of ways to derive probability estimates used in this type of analysis:

1   **The actuarial method** is used in cases where there is substantial recorded experience and the accident probability can be determined directly from these data.
2   **Fault trees** start with the definition of the undesired event whose probability is to be determined, and the analysis works backward to examine all possible contributory causes (US NRC 1981). Figure 10.4 illustrates a highly simplified fault tree which depicts the possible precursors to the release of radioactive wastes to the biosphere (McGrath 1974). The final probability can be computed from the probabilities assigned to each of the preceding risk factors. The US Nuclear Regulatory Commission (NRC) has produced numerous studies utilizing fault tree analysis to estimate the probability of both minor and major accident sequences at US reactors. One of the first and most detailed of these was the *Reactor Safety Study: An Assessment of Accident Risk in U.S. Commercial Nuclear Power Plants* (WASH-1400), which established baselines for subsequent analyses (US NRC 1975). While this was a

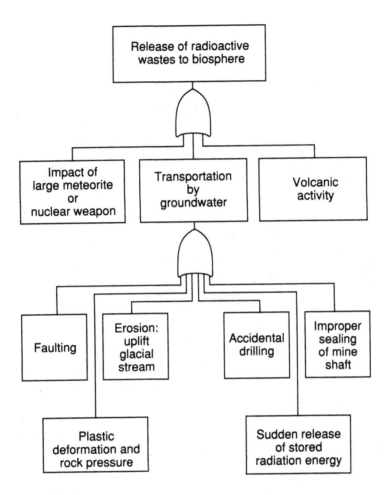

Figure 10.4 Example fault tree

generic study, some subsequent reports attempted to generate risk estimates on a plant-specific basis (US NRC 1991). The findings of these reports indicated a marked disparity in potential system risk depending upon, inter alia, susceptibility to flooding, proximity to geological faults and high population density. Because much of the data used to construct fault trees is the result of expert opinion, which is subjective in nature, and because such uncertainties can be compounded by the serial multiplication of probabilities throughout the fault tree, the results can have a significant degree of imprecision. This issue has been particularly contentious with respect to the US NRC's estimates of serious reactor accidents such as core melts (US NRC 1978; Lochbaum 2011; Cochran 2011). This type of problem was graphically illustrated by the 2011 Fukushima reactor accident in Japan, where the sequence of events which led to the catastrophic meltdowns in four nuclear reactors had been totally unanticipated.

3   **Event trees** are similar to fault trees, but the logic is used in reverse – i.e. the event tree starts with an initiating event and asks to what states of the system it might lead.

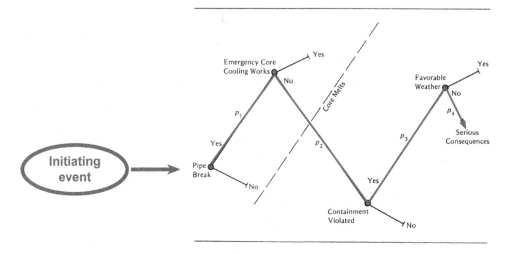

Figure 10.5 Example event tree

Source: Reproduced with permission of the publisher.

Figure 10.5 is a highly simplified version of the most probable sequence for a catastrophic failure in a nuclear pressurized water reactor (PWR) (Crouch and Wilson 1980; Wilson and Crouch 1982). The overall probability of the accident is the product of all probabilities along the branches of the tree. In this example, probabilities are derived from a number of sources, including actuarial data on pipe breaks and unfavorable weather from past experience and expert opinion where a sufficiently accurate actuarial database cannot be constructed. There are two basic assumptions in event tree analysis: (1) the analysis is assumed to be complete – i.e. the event trees calculated include all possible accident paths, or at least all those with a major contribution to risk – and (2) the probabilities are assumed unrelated to one another (e.g. that p_1, p_2, p_3, and p_4 are, in fact, independent). If interdependencies are known, they can be formally incorporated into the analysis. The validity of PRA can be compromised by the existence of unknown correlation between paths, commonly referred to as *common mode failures*. Two archetypal examples of this type of failure are the 1975 accident at the Tennessee Valley Authority's Browns Ferry nuclear reactor accident in Alabama (US NRC 1975) and the March 2011 Fukushima reactor accident in Japan. In the first case, when a worker used a candle to check for air leaks in the basement of the reactor building, the flame ignited a tray of plastic-coated cables, burning through all of them. It turned out that multiple system power cables had been routed through this one tray, leading to the simultaneous disabling of supposedly independent safety systems.

In the second case, Japan's Fukushima reactors had been designed to sustain the shock from an earthquake event and had an independent diesel back-up power system outside the reactor building to provide emergency power in the case that power was lost. The unanticipated common mode failure on March 11, 2011, was the combined effect of (1) the direct earthquake shock to the reactor, which disabled the primary power source, and (2) the indirect effect of the earthquake, which induced a tsunami. The resulting massive ocean wave breached protective seawalls, inundating and disabling the diesel power units located close to the shore at too low an elevation.

Risk-benefit analysis (RBA)

Risk-benefit analysis combines probabilistic risk assessment and cost-benefit analysis in social decision-making. This methodology received a major impetus in February 1981 when US president Ronald Reagan issued Executive Order 12291 (subsequently modified by President Clinton), which required federal government agencies to conduct risk-benefit analyses of proposed regulatory actions. The stated rationale was that "regulatory action shall not be undertaken unless the potential benefits to society from the regulation outweigh the potential costs to society" (US Archives 1981). Figure 10.6 presents an idealized model of RBA which a government agency would be expected to employ in determining whether a given project or undertaking was worth pursuing. RBA is principally a modification of CBA to explicitly account for risk. Cost-benefit analysis entails the discounting of a stream of anticipated costs and benefits which can be subject to some uncertainty. In those cases, expected values (EV) of outcomes are generally used, where EV is the summation of the products of probability and consequences across all outcomes. In risk-benefit analysis, there are at least two major differences: (1) the "costs" may entail risks to health and life of plants, animals or ecosystems; and (2) the outcomes and their probabilities are much less certain (e.g. uncertainty and "wickedness"). In such circumstances, it is common practice to use wide uncertainty bands or safety factors. There are at least two major generic uses of RBA in the public sector: (1) before introducing a new product (such as a pesticide) with *known benefits but uncertain costs*; or (2) before introducing a new regulation (such as tightening a pollution standard inside or outside a factory) with *known costs but uncertain benefits*.

Aside from the problems associated with measuring and predicting risk, there are several other major complexities once questions of risk enter the arena of public decision-making: (1) the perception of risk, (2) the valuation of risk and (3) the manner in which the risk is calculated or framed.

The objective measurable risk of an accident (if such an objective measurement is possible) is not necessarily equivalent to perceived risk by the public. Consider the empirical data in Figure 10.7 comparing the perceptions of experts and the general public (Lichtenstein et al. 1978). There is a clear bias in the discrepancy between the perception of the public and that of experts, who frequently base their assessments on empirical data. The general pattern is one of public overestimation of high-visibility, high-dread but rare events and underestimation of conventional, more frequent events. There are several explanations for this deviation. For example, the media tend to focus on rare events which elicit a high emotional response from the public (Lichtenstein et al. 1978).

The underlying question is whether differences in public attitudes toward the severity of risk are due to ignorance – which can be corrected with education – or a legitimate aspect of public values to be considered in social decision-making (Schrader-Frechette 1991). There are numerous characteristics of risks that cause them to be perceived and/or valued differently, as illustrated in Figure 7.2. The timing and magnitude of risks appear to play an important role in their assessment by the general public, as illustrated by the different public reaction to frequent automobile accidents and rare airplane disasters described in Chapter 7. From a simple risk perspective, the examples given are equivalent. In each of the scenarios, the same number of people die per year, yet it is clear that the public would react quite differently in each case. In fact, the chances are that public travel by airplane would fall significantly after as few as three or four crashes in succession. Why should this be so? The answer is based on the aforementioned characteristics of risk

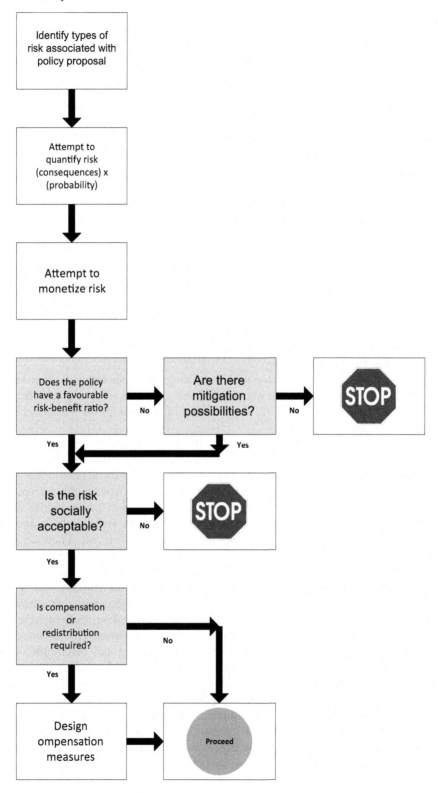

Figure 10.6 Idealized model of RBA

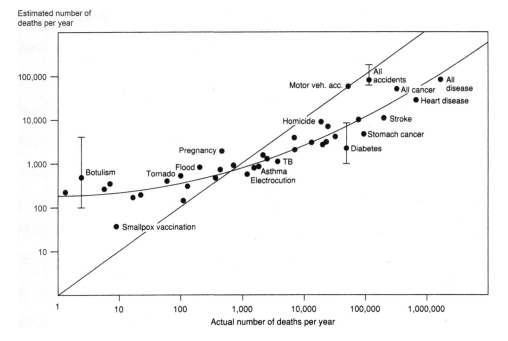

Estimated number of deaths per year

Figure 10.7 Risk perception by experts vs. the lay public

Source: Licchtenstein et al. 1978, reproduced with the permission of Cambridge University Press.

which elicit different public reactions. In this case, they include: (1) a dread factor; (2) a control factor – people tend to assign a greater risk to flying because of a lack of control, as opposed to a common, and erroneous, sense that they can control the risk of accidents in an automobile because they are driving; and (3) a frequency factor – automobile accidents are common and taken for granted while airplane accidents are not.

Regardless of whether these perceptions are considered rational, there is one additional factor which appears to have unambiguous legitimacy. Rare accidents with large numbers of injuries or fatalities pose a greater risk to the fabric of a society – whether it be a local community or the nation as a whole. This is one manifestation of the *zero-infinity dilemma* where the expected value of an accident may be low but the consequence predominates. A cogent example is the rare occurrence of nuclear reactor accidents. At least one public agency (the US Nuclear Regulatory Commission) has incorporated this non-linear public perception of risks into its decision-making. Called the *alpha model*, the methodology constructs what is termed the *equivalent social cost*, defined as (Frequency) × (Consequences)$^\alpha$, where the exponent on the consequences term $a > 1$. One of the examples used by the NRC to illustrate the application of this methodology recognizes the important perceptual difference between early deaths after a nuclear accident compared to deaths from the delayed onset of radiation-induced cancer. In the NRC model, the social costs for delayed cancer deaths have a value of 1.0, but the social costs for early deaths have a value of 1.2. Even such an apparently low exponent as 1.2 can have a major impact on the value of the equivalent social cost if the consequences (in this case, deaths) are large in number (Griesmeyer and Okrent 1981; Okrent et al. 1981).

The alpha model presaged the emergence of radically new thinking in the area of public sector decision-making in the face of low-probability/high-consequence events. The traditional rational choice model assumes that governments will calculate the expected values of possible events (i.e. probability × consequence) and choose the option with the highest net benefits. The underlying assumption is that because of their size and long-term view, governments can be risk neutral in decisions which affect society as a whole. With the emergence of ecological scenarios that include rare but possibly catastrophic consequences, the calculus of decision-making has evolved. In probabilistic terms, such events are called fat tails, referring to the extreme right tail of the probability distribution of outcomes. Taleb (2007) has termed these *black swans*, and such phenomena are not uncommon and are found in such diverse areas as flood insurance claims, crop loss, natural disasters, hospital discharge bills, finance and nuclear power (Cooke and Nieboer 2011; Mandelbrot and Hudson 2004). Weitzman (2009, p. 1) was among the first to develop econometric models of climate change. He concluded that "the economic consequences of fat-tailed structural uncertainty (along with unsureness about high-temperature damages) can readily outweigh the effects of discounting in climate change policy analysis." In the context of climate change, Kousky et al. (2009, p. 1) observed:

> Catastrophes are of particular concern because, while an exact quantification is not possible, the most extreme adverse impacts from climate change (e.g. the worst 1% of scenarios) may account for a large portion of expected losses. Consequently, focusing primarily on more likely or anticipated (albeit serious) outcomes may miss much of the problem in terms of risks from climate change.

The framing of risk calculations also entails significant complexities. The critical importance of the issue of *framing* was first recognized by Kahneman and Tversky in their seminal work on the rationality (or lack thereof) of the human mind in perceptions and decision-making (Tversky and Kahneman 1974, 1981; Kahneman et al. 1982). Consider the simple question of which mode of travel is riskier: cars or airplanes. Many people have a pathological fear of flying and are convinced that aircraft travel is inherently much riskier than travel by automobile. Table 10.3 presents comparative data for both travel modes for two years: 2007 and 2018. On a simple calculation of number of *deaths per billion passenger miles* in both years, the risk of death from driving far outweighs the risk of flying in commercial aircraft. In contrast, if one calculates the number of *deaths per billion hours of travel*, the same marked disparity in risk appears in 2007, a very safe year for flying, but for 2018, when 555 people were killed in commercial airplane crashes, the ratios are quite similar. These calculations are sensitive to the assumed average speed of both modes of transport; nevertheless, the framing chosen to portray the relative risks is clearly an important consideration. These comparisons might be quite different if the much less safe accident record of all air flights, including general aviation, were to be included.

In another example of the importance of framing, Slovic and Weber (2002) describe nine ways that fatality risks associated with chemical manufacturing can be measured: (1) deaths per million people in the population, (2) deaths per million people within x miles of the source of exposure, (3) deaths per unit of concentration, (4) deaths per facility, (5) deaths per ton of air toxics released, (6) deaths per ton of air toxics absorbed by people, (7) deaths per ton of chemical produced, (8) deaths per million dollars of product

Table 10.3 Comparative risk data for automotive and airplane travel 2001 vs. 2007 in the US

Comparative risk data for automobiles and airplanes in the United States	Automobiles	Airplanes	
2018			
# deaths	36,560	555	555
Billion passenger miles	4,849.00	730.43	730.43
# deaths per billion passenger miles	7.54	0.760	0.760
Assumed average speed	32.00	350.00	500.00
Therefore # billion hours of travel	151.53	2.09	1.46
# deaths per billion hours of travel	241.27	265.94	379.92
2007			
# deaths	43,100	1	1
Billion passenger miles	2,640.60	607.50	607.50
# deaths per billion passenger miles	16.32	0.002	0.002
Assumed average speed	27.60	350.00	300.00
Therefore # billion hours of travel	95.67	1.74	2.03
# deaths per billion hours of travel	450.49	0.58	0.49

produced and (9) reduction in life expectancy associated with exposure to the hazard. The authors cite a major report by the National Research Council (Stern and Fineberg 1996, p. 52) when they observe:

> Every way of summarizing deaths embodies its own set of values. For example, reduction in life expectancy treats deaths of young people as more important than deaths of older people, who have less life expectancy to lose. Simply counting fatalities treats deaths of the old and the young as equivalent; it also treats as equivalent deaths that come immediately after mishaps and deaths that follow painful and debilitating disease. Also in the case of delayed illness or death, a simple count of adverse outcomes places no value on what happens to exposed people who may spend years living in daily fear of illness, even if they do not die from the hazard. Using number of deaths as the summary indicator of risk implies that it is as important to prevent deaths of people who engage in activity by choice as it is to prevent deaths of those who bear its effects unwillingly. Thus, the death of a motorcyclist in an accident is given the same weight as the death of the pedestrian hit by the motorcycle. It also implies that it is as important to protect people who have been benefiting from a risky activity or technology as it is to protect those who get no benefit from it. One can easily imagine a range of arguments to justify different kinds of unequal weightings for different kinds of deaths, but to arrive at any selection requires a judgment about which deaths one considers most undesirable. To treat all deaths as equal also involves a judgment.

Appendix 10.1 presents two classic examples of how framing can have a transformative influence on risk perception and response thereto.

Pathologies of PRA and RBA

Despite the powerful tools that both PRA and RBA bring to decision-making, there are numerous conceptual difficulties, or pathologies, with both methodologies that, on balance, suggest a more modest and supplementary role for these tools in public decision-making rather than one of preeminence. Figure 10.8 has recast Figure 9.6 to portray the presence and potential role of each of these issues. There are several types of pathologies which can afflict PRA and RBA (Fairley 1977): (1) not assigning probabilities to credible threats which are difficult to quantify, (2) inadequate treatment of multiple risks and possible synergistic effects, (3) not choosing the most appropriate measure of risk, (4) common mode failures, (5) past analytical errors or oversights in the data, (6) not determining the correct dose-response relationships, (7) inability to anticipate all accident scenarios and (8) inaccurate estimation of probabilities of anticipated accident scenarios (esp. underestimates). Each of these is reviewed briefly in the following.

PRA Pathology #1: Not assigning probabilities to credible but difficult-to-quantify risks

Estimates of the "probability" of an accident must include, explicitly or implicitly, contributions from all possible accident sources. Consider a simple game of five-card stud poker and ask what is the probability of seeing at least one royal flush in a single round of play (Fairley 1977). Assume specifically that one hand is dealt and there are four players, each of whom receives five cards. Using simple combinatorial arithmetic, the probability is 1 in 162,338. Now consider recasting this problem as occurring in an environment where you do not know the other players or their background. The probability of seeing at least one royal flush in the poker hand depends on two probabilities: the probability of the royal flush appearing naturally plus the probability of the royal flush appearing dishonestly. The probability of the royal flush appearing naturally is known (1/162,338), but the probability of it appearing dishonestly is unknown. However, under the circumstances of playing with complete strangers, the chance of it appearing dishonestly may be greater than it appearing naturally. Therefore, a subjectively assessed probability of it appearing dishonestly, roughly set at 1/10,000, for example, swamps the natural probability: $p = 1/162,338 + 1/10,000 = $ approximately 1/10,000.

The message from this simple exercise is that not assigning probabilities to credible but difficult-to-quantify risks is a potentially significant pathology of PRA. Estimates of the "probability" of an accident must include, explicitly or implicitly, contributions from all possible sources of an accident. Real-world examples of this type of potential error are associated with terrorism and threats to public facilities such as nuclear power reactors. The US Nuclear Regulatory Commission's first comprehensive assessment of risks to nuclear power plants, called WASH-1400 (US NRC 1975), did not include flooding and sabotage, yet (1) flooding appears to be a potentially significant contributor to risk at some sites since nuclear plants must be located near ample supplies of water for cooling; and (2) there seems to be little basis for justifying the probability of sabotage by terrorists as being small compared to the estimated frequency of a core melt accident (i.e. WASH-1400's estimate of 1 in 20,000 per reactor-year). (See also Jaczko 2019; Allison 2004.)

Another cogent example is proved by the infamous terrorist attack on the World Trade Center on September 11, 2001. Table 10.4 speculates how an insurer might assess potential risks in the period prior to the attack. This is an archetypical example of a "wicked" problem where the event was totally unanticipated yet the consequences were enormous.

PATHOLOGIES OF FORMAL RISK -BENEFIT ANALYSIS

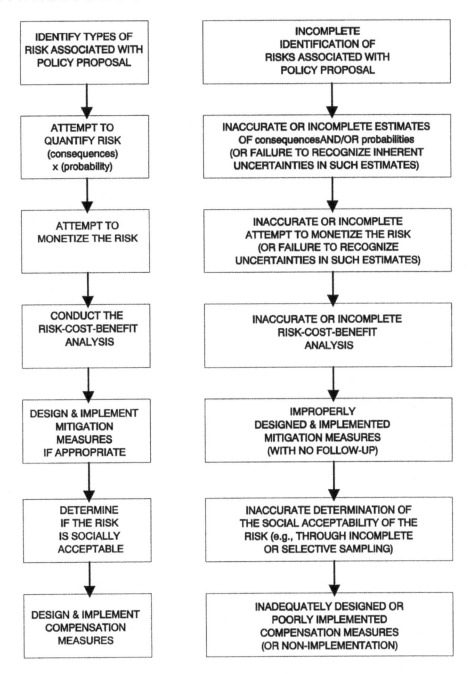

Figure 10.8 Possible pathologies of RBA

Table 10.4 Assumed insurer assessment ex ante 9-11

Event	Probability	Consequences for the World Trade Center
Hurricane	Low	None
Earthquake	Very low	Very low
Conventional explosives	Low	Low
Aircraft impact – Empire State Building experience, July 28, 1945, B-25 bomber, $1 million damage, 14 dead	Low	Low
Suitcase atomic bomb	Very low	Very high
Large jet aircraft – like September 11, 2001	Unanticipated	Very high
Other?		

PRA Pathology #2: Multiple risk exposure

Almost all risk analyses focus on the probability and consequences of single threats such as chemicals with potential mutagenic, teratogenic or carcinogenic properties. However, the population is rarely exposed to single risk sources. The general pattern is exposure to a multitude of chemical agents which may act additively, synergistically or antagonistically. Consider the example in Table 10.5 of the super-additive risk of esophageal cancer from the combined exposure of tobacco and alcohol, a not infrequent pattern of behavior (Olsen 1983, p. 223). The importance of this synergistic reaction (where the combined risk is greater than the sum of the individual risks) is graphically portrayed in Figure 10.9.

PRA Pathology #3: Choosing the right measure of risk

See the example cited prior in Table 10.3 which compares the risk of driving and flying using two different measures: deaths per billion passenger miles versus deaths per billion hours of travel.

PRA Pathology #4: Common mode failures

As described prior, event tree/fault tree analysis is built on the assumption of the independence of branches. Where interdependence can be identified, it is included. Some general

Table 10.5 Super-additive risk of tobacco and alcohol consumption

		Tobacco (g/day)				Adjusted for tobacco
		0 to 9	10 to 19	20 to 29	30+	
Alcohol (g/day)	0 to 39	1.0	3.0	4.2	12.0	1.0
	40 to 79	8.2	5.9	11.3	46.1	3.9
	80 to 119	11.9	22.7	18.0	159.3	8.0
	120+	37.4	53.0	77.8	240.7	17.6
Adjusted for alcohol		1.0	1.2	1.5	7.9	

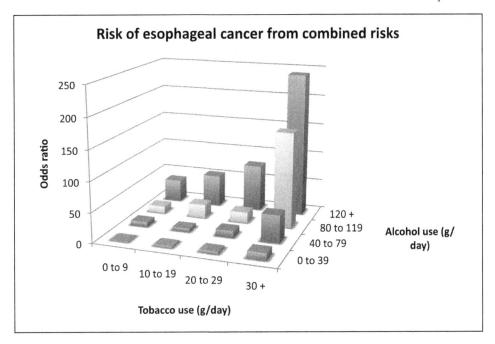

Figure 10.9 Synergistic effects of alcohol and tobacco use on risk of esophageal cancer

types of examples of events which can trigger common mode failure are flooding and earthquakes. Two of the best examples of common mode failures resulting from errors in engineering design were the aforementioned 1975 accident at Browns Ferry nuclear reactor in the United States and the Fukushima nuclear disaster in 2011.

PRA Pathology #5: Choosing the correct dose-response function

This function measures damage to human health in response to a given dose of pollutant. There are several major uncertainties associated with the construction of meaningful dose-response functions. For example, the effects of short-term acute doses of pollutants can be measured reasonably well; however, it is much more difficult to measure the effects of long-term, chronic pollution exposure. Most observational datasets are based on high dosage levels within an occupational setting, and it is therefore necessary to extrapolate back to infer the shape of the dose-response function at low levels of exposure. Figure 10.10 depicts some alternative functions. There are at least two major characteristics of these functions (convexity/concavity; threshold/no threshold) which can have a profound impact on the choice of the appropriate response to a particular pollutant. Figure 10.11 provides an example of the regulatory confusion surrounding the status of saccharin as a possible carcinogen prior to the conclusion that this compound did not, in fact, pose a risk of cancer (US HHS 2011). Two conceptual issues bedeviled this analysis: first, the choice of an appropriate biological model of carcinogenesis and, second, the method of extrapolating the dose response of test rats to humans. When these two factors were taken into consideration, the estimated risk of cancer from a given dose of saccharin

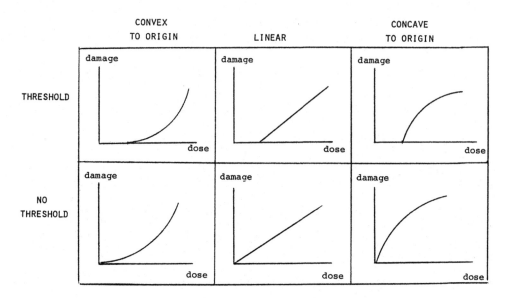

Figure 10.10 Alternative dose-response functions

varied by almost seven orders of magnitude – obviously rendering impossible a scientifi-cally defensible regulation.

PRA Pathology #6: Past analytical errors or oversights in the data

Post–World War II radiation standards were initially based on epidemiological data drawn from cancer victims who initially survived the atomic bombs dropped on Hiroshima and Nagasaki. Subsequent discovery of major errors in the calculation of gamma ray and neutron radiation forced a major re-examination of these standards. In deriving the dose-response functions which measure the level of cancer risk associated with a given level of radiation exposure, it was assumed that a large group of workers in a Mitsubishi steel factory in Nagasaki had been standing outside the factory. The Mitsubishi building was made of steel and concrete and contained heavy machinery. However, many of the workers were actually inside the factory and shielded from much of the radiation (*Science* 1981). Figure 10.12 is a schematic representation of the error and its consequences for the standard-setting process. The recalibration of the estimated dose received by the workers shifted the dose-response function up and to the left, thereby necessitating a revision of standards.

PRA Pathology #7: The inability to anticipate all accident scenarios

Two examples illustrate this pathology. The first was the existence of operator error in the near meltdown of the Three Mile Island nuclear reactor in Pennsylvania in 1979 (Stephens 1980; Report of the President's Commission 1979). This case was particularly instruc-tive in the re-examination of assumptions considering the normal operation of modern

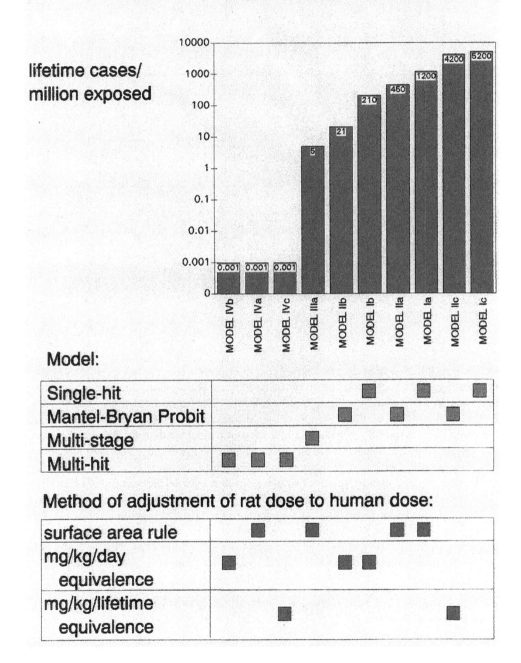

Figure 10.11 Alternative human cancer risk models from saccharin ingestion

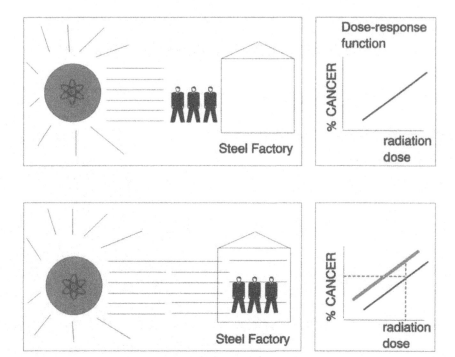

Figure 10.12 Radiation exposure in Nagasaki

technology. It highlighted the critical problem of understanding the nature of the human-machine interface and human behavior in conditions of boredom, disease, fatigue, stress, deviation from standard operating procedures, etc. The second example was the catastrophic failure of cargo doors on DC-10 jet airlines in the 1970s. Unlike other aircraft, the cargo door of the DC-10 was designed to open out rather than in. The first problem was revealed in 1972, when American Airlines Flight 96 lost its aft cargo door after take-off from Detroit. On Flight 96, airport employees had forced the door shut, weakening the locking pin and causing the door to blow out as it reached altitude. In 1974, another DC-10, owned by Turkish Airlines, crashed into a forest shortly after leaving Orly Airport in Paris and killed 346. A modified seating configuration on the Turkish aircraft caused its control cables to be severed when the cargo door was lost, rendering the aircraft uncontrollable (Fielder and Birsch 1992). The design team which built the DC-10 was unable to identify these scenarios as possible risks despite conducting an a priori risk analysis.

PRA Pathology #8: Inaccurate estimation of probabilities of anticipated accident scenarios (esp. underestimates)

There is a fundamental problem in assigning probabilities to accidents which might be anticipated but have not yet occurred. A number of examples of this pathology have emerged from the nuclear power industry. For example, a small-break loss of coolant accident (LOCA) occurred at the Ginna nuclear plant near Rochester, New York, on January 25, 1982 (*New York Times* February 13, 1982). Based on data in WASH-1400, the

NRC's comprehensive risk analysis, this type of accident should happen about once every 40 years in the US with 75 operating reactors (i.e. once per every 3,000 reactor-years). In the five-year period 1975–1982, there were four accidents of this type. In another case, the NRC had calculated that the simultaneous failure of two independent systems to prevent a core meltdown would occur with a probability of 1/17,000 per year, yet it happened twice in four days at two reactors in New Jersey in 1991 (*New York Times* March 29, 2011). Although the events in both these cases were not technically inconsistent with the original probabilistic estimates, it is much more likely that there were errors in the original risk analysis.

This discussion concludes with a brief description of two monumental failures of risk analysis to predict the nature and extent of the risks involved: the Chernobyl nuclear catastrophe of 1986 and the *Challenger* space shuttle disaster of the same year.

The Chernobyl nuclear disaster

On April 29, 1986, the *New York Times* headlined the Soviet announcement of a major accident at one of its nuclear power plants in the Ukraine. The subsequent massive release of radioactive material spread throughout western Europe, prompting major restrictions on the consumption of certain food products. It is unclear if a formal PRA had ever been conducted prior to the accident, but if it had, it would have provided no indication of the probability or consequences of the accident. Figure 10.13 illustrates what a risk analysis might have looked at and what it would have missed given the state of the science at the time. None of the seven major events or consequences was, or could have been, anticipated in a formal risk analysis (Nemetz 2022). Despite the uniqueness of the Soviet reactor design, this is a sobering message for risk assessments of other currently operating reactors worldwide. (See also Medvedev 1989.)

The Challenger space shuttle disaster

An equally problematic risk analysis was revealed by the US's most devastating space accident: the loss of the *Challenger* spacecraft on January 28 1986. In this case, NASA had carried out an extensive risk analysis prior to the accident and calculated the risk of disaster at 1 in 10,000. This implied that NASA could launch a space shuttle every day for 25 years and not expect any equipment-based disaster. The renowned Caltech physicist Richard Feynman was appointed by the US government to lead the investigation of the disaster (Feynman 1986; Feynman and Leighton 2001). He examined the historical data and found that of 2,900 solid rocket boosters launched, the number which failed was 121, yielding a failure ratio of 1 in 24. It is ironic but statistically meaningless that the shuttle exploded on its 25th flight. As brilliantly described in his post-mortem of the accident, Edward Tufte (1997) of Yale University graphically demonstrated how NASA had misinterpreted its own data by graphing the historical record in a manner which was totally misleading. When Tufte reconceptualized and replotted the graphical information, the risk of the misguided launch became painfully obvious. Tufte's work is a brilliant example of the critical role that good or bad graphical information can play in decision-making.

In sum, while PRA and RBA are powerful tools for the interpretation of risk, their use must be tempered by a realization of their inherent conceptual flaws. In a manner similar to CBA, these methodologies can and should be used to inform the decision-making process but cannot act as a sole guide to the choice of alternatives, especially those with major potential impacts on human health and the global ecosystem.

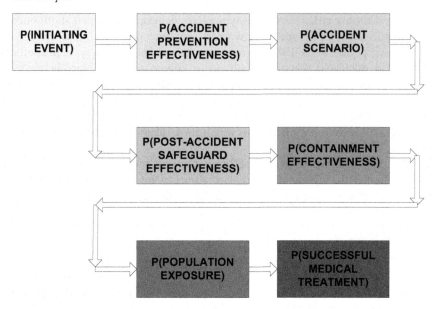

1.	Initiating event	Operator error - UNANTICIPATED
2.	Accident prevention	Failure of control rod reinsertion - UNANTICIPATED
3.	Accident mode	Steam explosion + core disintegration - UNANTICIPATED
4.	Post-accident safeguard	Lack of effectiveness water pool for steam - UNANTICIPATED
5.	Containment	Inability to contain steam explosion - UNANTICIPATED
6.	Population exposure	Wind dispersion patterns - UNANTICIPATED
7.	Medical treatment success	Poor success of bone marrow transplants - UNANTICIPATED

Figure 10.13 Pathologies of PRA in the Chernobyl nuclear accident

The precautionary principle

In light of the complexities associated with risk analysis and the diverse range of threats faced by modern society, especially catastrophic outcomes in fat tails, the challenge is to find a decision rule which can help protect the ecosystem and current and future generations of humanity. The *precautionary principle* is one such rule. Simply stated, it is based on the premise that we live in an uncertain world and that society cannot wait for definitive scientific proof of a potential threat before acting if that threat is both large and credible. The underlying theory is based on scientific principles largely associated with the work of ecologists such as C. S. Holling. (See discussion in Chapter 8.) Holling has demonstrated that ecosystems are non-linear and when under stress do not necessarily adjust slowly and steadily but may jump suddenly between alternative equilibrium states, some much less hospitable for human activity than others. The import of this theory is that by the time one recognizes or begins to feel the tangible effects of certain types of ecological threats, it may be too late to forestall or reverse the negative effects.

Variations of the precautionary principle have already been incorporated into legislation and regulation in several countries within the OECD – mostly in Europe but also in the United States.

Table 10.6 lists major examples of this principle in some international treaties and agreements (Harremoes et al. 2001), and Tickner et al. (n.d.) list 12 other such international

Table 10.6 Some examples of the precautionary principle in international treaties and agreements

Year	Treaty	Key wording
1987	**Montreal Protocol on Substances that Deplete the Ozone Layer**	Parties to this protocol . . . determined to protect the ozone layer by taking **precautionary measures** to control equitably total global emissions of substances that deplete it.
1990	**Third North Sea Conference**	The participants . . . will continue to apply the **precautionary principle**, that is to take action to avoid potentially damaging impacts of substances that are persistent, toxic, and liable to bioaccumulate even where there is no scientific evidence to prove a causal link between emissions and effects.
1987	**London Declaration (Protection of the North Sea)**	Accepting that, in order to protect the North Sea from possibly damaging effects of the most dangerous substances, a precautionary approach is necessary which may require action to control inputs of such substances even before a causal link has been established by absolutely clear scientific evidence.
1992	**The Rio Declaration on Environment and Development**	In order to protect the environment, the Precautionary Approach shall be widely applied by states according to their capabilities. Where there are threats of serious or irreversible damage, lack of full scientific certainty shall not be used as a reason for postponing cost-effective measures to prevent environmental degradation.
1992	**Framework Convention on Climate Change**	The parties should take **precautionary measures** to anticipate, prevent or minimise the causes of climate change and mitigate its adverse effects. Where there are threats of serious or irreversible damage, lack of full scientific certainty should not be used as a reason for postponing such measures, taking into account that policies and measures to deal with climate change should be cost-effective so as to ensure global benefits at the lowest possible cost.
1992	**Treaty on European Union (Maastricht Treaty)**	Community policy on the environment . . . shall be based on the **precautionary principle** and on the principles that preventive actions should be taken, that the environmental damage should as a priority be rectified at source and that the polluter shall pay.
2000	**Cartagena Protocol on Biosafety**	In accordance with the **precautionary approach** the objective of this Protocol is to contribute to ensuring an adequate level of protection in the field of the safe transfer, handling and use of living modified organisms resulting from modern biotechnology that may have adverse effects on the conservation and sustainable use of biological diversity, taking also into account risks to human health, and specifically focussing on transboundary movements.
2000	**EU communication on the Precautionary Principle**	The precautionary principle applies where scientific evidence is insufficient, inconclusive or uncertain and preliminary scientific evaluation indicates that there are reasonable grounds for concern that the potentially dangerous effects on the environment, human, animal or plant health may be inconsistent with the high level of protection chosen by the EU.
2001	**Stockholm Convention on Persistent Organic Pollutants (POPs)**	Precaution, including transparency and public participation, is operationalised throughout the treaty, with explicit reference in the preamble, objective, provisions for adding POPs and determination of best available technologies. The objective states: Mindful of the **Precautionary Approach** as set forth in Principle 15 of the Rio Declaration on Environment and Development, the objective of this Convention is to protect human health and the environment from persistent organic pollutants.

Table 10.7 Some US examples of the precautionary principle

Issue	Precautionary prevention
Food safety (carcinogenic additives)	The Delaney Clause in the Food, Drug and Cosmetics Act, 1957–1996, which banned animal carcinogens from the human food chain
Food safety (BSE)	A ban on the use of scrapie-infected sheep and goat meat in the animal and human food chain in the early 1970s, which may have helped the United States avoid BSE (mad cow disease)
Environmental safety (CFCs)	A ban on the use of CFCs in aerosols in 1977, several years before similar action in most of Europe
Public health (DES)	A ban on the use of diethylstilbestrol (DES) as a growth promoter in beef, 1972–1979, nearly 10 years before the EU ban in 1987

agreements. Table 10.7 cites four examples of its application in the US (UNESCO 2005; Harremoes et al. 2001).

Perhaps the most important distinction with respect to the application of the precautionary principle rests with the divergent approach to the introduction of new chemical compounds in Europe and the United States (Gold and Wagner 2020). The US Toxic Substances Chemical Act (TSCA) "does not require companies to test chemicals before they notify EPA of their intent to manufacture the chemicals" (US GAO 2006, p. 2). To the Government Accountability Office – an independent branch of the US Congress – this provides "only limited assurance that health and environmental risks are identified." In contrast, a European Union program entitled REACH (Registration, Evaluation and Authorization of Chemicals) reverses the onus of proof. In contrasting the two disparate approaches to chemical regulation, the US GAO (2007, p. 2) concludes:

> TSCA places the burden of proof on EPA to demonstrate that a chemical poses a risk to human health or the environment before EPA can regulate its production or use, while REACH generally places a burden on chemical companies to ensure that chemicals do not pose such risks or that measures are identified for handling chemicals safely.

Despite this apparent contrast between the United States and European regulatory approaches toward the introduction of new chemicals, Wiener and Rogers (2002) have argued that the use of the precautionary principle is less an issue of geography than one of circumstance. They identify cases in which either Europe or the US has taken a more proactive role:

> Sometimes the EU is more precautionary than the US (such as regarding hormones in beef), while sometimes the US is more precautionary than the EU (such as regarding mad cow disease in blood). Thus, neither the EU nor the US can claim to be categorically 'more precautionary' than the other. The real pattern is complex and risk-specific.
>
> (p. 317)

The issue of potential risks related to industrial chemicals is particularly important as there are in excess of 144,000 such chemicals currently in use in the world today

(Phys.org February 7, 2017), and their production increased from 1 million tons in 1930 to over 2.3 billion tons by 2017, and their value is expected to double from 3.47 Euros in 2017 to 6.6 trillion Euros in 2030 (UNEP 2019). A US EPA report (1998) on the availability of data concerning potential chemical hazards reported that 2,863 organic chemicals (i.e. excluding polymers and inorganic chemicals) were either produced or imported at or above 1 million pounds per year in the United States. The report observed:

> EPA's analysis found that no basic toxicity information, i.e. neither human health nor environmental toxicity, is publicly available for 43% of the high volume chemicals manufactured in the US and that a full set of basic toxicity information is available for only 7% of these chemicals. The lack of availability of basic toxicity information on most high volume chemicals is a serious issue.
>
> (p. 2)

A more recent article found that

> only about 15% of premanufacture notifications for new chemicals submitted to EPA include any health or safety data at all and EPA's own statistics show that only 10% of the new chemicals entering commerce between 1979 and 2016 involved restrictions or testing orders.
>
> (Gold and Wagner 2020)

The impact of chemicals on human health has led to the emergence of an entirely new field of research: environmental neuroscience, which studies the potentially multifaceted impact of chemicals on brain function and pathogenesis (NAS 2020b).

There are at least three major classes of chemicals in the last several decades which entail unknown but potentially significant risks to human health and the environment and are, as a consequence, candidates for the application of the precaution principle: plastics, endocrine mimickers and nanomaterials.

Plastics (and particularly microplastics): Geyer et al. (2017, p. 1) have estimated that

> 8300 million metric tons (Mt) as [sic] of virgin plastics have been produced [from 1950] to date. As of 2015, approximately 6300 Mt of plastic waste had been generated, around 9% of which had been recycled, 12% was incinerated, and 79% was accumulated in landfills or the natural environment. If current production and waste management trends continue, roughly 12,000 Mt of plastic waste will be in landfills or in the natural environment by 2050.

Plastics have become a central part of modern manufacturing, and they are ubiquitous. The United Nations reports that as many as 51 trillion microplastic particles litter the sea – representing 500 times more than the number of stars in our galaxy (UN News February 23, 2017). Borrelle et al. (2020) have concluded that the predicted growth in plastic waste exceeds effort to mitigate plastic pollution. Table 10.8 lists the extraordinary range of occurrences of plastics in the world today. Most plastics do not biodegrade and continue to accumulate in the environment, posing a threat of unknown magnitude to human health and the functioning of ecosystems (*Lancet* 2017; Prata et al. 2020). Given the extraordinary range and quantity of plastic pollution and its largely but potentially enormous impact, this represents an archetypal example of massive uninternalized externalities.

Table 10.8 The ubiquitous nature of plastics

Location	Scientific references
Foodwebs and ecosystems in general	D'Souza et al. (2020),Rillig and Lehmann (2020)
Human food chains/diet	Liebezeit and Liebezeit (2014), Cox et al. (2019), NEXUS3 et al. (2019), Conto et al. (2020)
Human organs	WebMD (2020), Ramsperger et al. (2020)
Bivalves and mussels	Li et al. (2018), Van Cauwenberghe and Janssen (2014)
Human stool	Liebmann et al. (2018)
Tap water and bottled water	Tyree and Morrison (2018), WHO (2019)
Groundwater	Panno et al. (2019)
Rain water	Brahney et al. (2020)
Ocean surface, shorelines, sediments and deep water and seabed	Jambeck et al. (2015), Brandon et al. (2019), Browne et al. (2011), Barrett et al. (2020), Martin et al. (2020), Pabortsava and Lampitt (2020), Mohrig (2020)
Rivers	Woodward et al, 2021
Birds	Kane et al. (2020), D'Souza et al. (2020)
Marine mammals	Nelms et al. (2019), WWF (2018)
Ocean fish and mariculture	Wieczorek et al. (2018), Lusher et al. (2013), Zhang et al. (2020)
Insects	Windsor et al. (2019)
Mountains and remote regions	Allen et al. (2019), Evangeliou et al. (2020), *Science* (June 11, 2020a); *Guardian* (November 20, 2020)
Arctic ocean and sea ice and organisms	Peeken et al. (2018), Cozar et al. (2017), Hallanger and Gabrielsen (2018)
Snow	Bergmann et al. (2019)
Microbes	Zhang et al. (2020), Yang et al. (2020), *Science* (September 11, 2020b)

Endocrine mimickers: According to the US NIH (n.d., p. 1),

> Many chemicals, both natural and man-made, may mimic or interfere with the body's hormones, known as the endocrine system. Called endocrine disruptors, these chemicals are linked with developmental, reproductive, brain, immune, and other problems. Endocrine disruptors are found in many everyday products, including some plastic bottles and containers, liners of metal food cans, detergents, flame retardants, food, toys, cosmetics, and pesticides. Some endocrine-disrupting chemicals are slow to break down in the environment. That characteristic makes them potentially hazardous over time. Endocrine disrupting chemicals cause adverse effects in animals. But limited scientific information exists on potential health problems in humans. Because people are typically exposed to multiple endocrine disruptors at the same time, assessing public health effects is difficult.

Common endocrine disruptors include bisphenol A (BPA), dioxin, perfluoroalkyl and polyfluoroalkyl substances (PFAS) most commonly associated with the production of Teflon, phthalates, phytoestrogens, polybrominated diphenyl ethers (PBDE), polychlorinated biphenyls (PCBs) and triclosan. In 2012, the European Environment Agency strongly recommended the adoption of a precautionary principle with respect to the introduction and use of chemicals with endocrine-disrupting properties in light of their potentially devastating impact on hormonal systems within humans and other animal species.

Nanomaterials: While present in the environment since the earth's formation, only recently has this natural background of nanomaterials been supplemented by human-engineered counterparts for use in medicine, electronics, energy, water and food production (Hochella et al. 2019). They are generally in the range of millionths of a millimeter in size (i.e. nanometer size). The challenge is identifying and quantifying the risk to human health and the environment due to the proliferation of these anthropogenic materials. One review study on exposure to workers found that certain types of nanoparticles may impact the immunological system and cause inflammation of the lungs, signs of asthma, interstitial fibrosis, genotoxicity and possible human cancer (Pietroiusti et al. 2018). There is a clear need to extend our understanding of the biological and pharmacological properties and effects of these substances to create a clearer picture of the risk-benefit trade-offs in the general population. Valued at $1.055 trillion in 2013, the global nanotechnology-enabled market was expected to grow to $3.4 trillion by 2018 (NAS 2016, 2020a).

The application of the precautionary principle is not an arbitrary exercise but one which must follow strict rules of logic and proof. Table 10.9 provides a quick summary of varying levels of proof required by several national and international bodies with respect to the precautionary principle (Harremoes et al. 2001). To demonstrate the usefulness of the principle, in 2001, the European Environmental Agency published a landmark study which re-examined the history of 14 controversial cases – many involving the introduction of new chemicals – from the late 1800s to this century (Harremoes et al. 2001). Included among these case studies were major public policy and regulatory decisions concerning fisheries, radiation, benzene, asbestos, PCBs, halocarbons, the drug DES, antimicrobials such as antibiotics added to animal feed as growth promoters, sulfur dioxide, the gasoline additive Methyl tert-butyl ether (MTBE), Great Lakes contamination, tributyltin (TBT) antifoulants, estrogen mimickers and mad cow disease. It was concluded that in many of the cases: (1) "early warnings," and even "loud and late" warnings, were clearly ignored; (2) the scope of hazard appraisal was too narrow; and (3) regulatory actions were taken without sufficient consideration of alternatives or the conditions necessary for their successful implementation in the real world. A second edition was published by the European Environment Agency (2013) covering leaded gasoline, perchloroethylene, mercury, beryllium, tobacco, vinyl chloride, the pesticide dibromochloropropane (DBCP), BPA and DDT.

To exemplify the type of failure the precautionary principle is designed to address, Table 10.10 provides a timeline of the stop-and-go nature of the historical regulatory

Table 10.9 Various examples of evidentiary proof

Verbal description	Examples
"Beyond all reasonable doubt"	Criminal law; Swedish chemical law, 1973 (for evidence of "safety" from manufacturers)
"Balance of evidence"	Intergovernmental Panel on Climate Change, 1995 and 2001
"Reasonable grounds for concern"	European Commission communication on the precautionary principle
"Scientific suspicion of risk"	Swedish chemical law, 1973, for evidence required for regulators to take precautionary action on potential harm from substances

Table 10.10 Timeline of regulatory actions relating to growth promoters

1970s	Concerns about growth promoters' safety, as DES confirmed a human carcinogen	CAUTION
1972	Peakal publishes that DES likely to affect a wide range of species in the environment (wildlife) but this was ignored until the late 1980s	CAUTION
1972	DES banned as a hormone growth promoter in the United States	STOP
1974	Use of DES reinstated in the United States	GO
1976	US Food and Drug Administration (FDA) sets the minimum detectable level of DES	STOP
1979	DES banned again on the grounds of the impossibility of identifying levels below which it would not be carcinogenic	STOP
1982	EU expert working group (Lamming Committee) concludes that some growth promoters are safe	GO
1985	First EU ban is adopted, ignoring results from the Lamming Committee because the scope of their assessments had not been broad enough	STOP
1987	Lamming Committee disbanded by EU and their results were not published	
1988	Ban of several growth promoters throughout the EU based on uncertainty of their effects on humans	STOP
1988	WHO/FAO Joint Expert Committee on Food, using standard risk assessment, reaches same conclusions as Lamming Committee	GO
1989	EU ban extended to other growth promoters and to imports from third world countries	STOP
1989	Pimenta Report finds illegal use of growth promoters in some Member States	GO
1989-96	USA takes unilateral retaliatory measures on EC exports	STOP
1995	European Commission organises an international conference on growth promoters and meat production where uncertainties remain regarding effects on the immune system, endocrine system and cancer	GO
1999	The EU Scientific Committee on Veterinary Measures Relating to Public Health publishes a report concluding that no threshold can be defined for six growth promoters	CAUTION
2000	International workshop on hormones and endocrine disrupters in food and water confirms impacts on the environment (wildlife) of veterinary drugs	CAUTION
2001	EU still suffers from sanction to its exports of around EUR 160 million per year	GO

response around hormones as growth promoters in the last several decades (Harremoes et al. 2001).

The original EEA report concluded with 12 major recommendations:

1 Acknowledge uncertainty and risk in technology appraisal and public policy-making.
2 Provide adequate long-term environmental and health monitoring and research into early warnings.
3 Identify and work to reduce "blind spots" and gaps in scientific knowledge.
4 Identify and reduce interdisciplinary obstacles to learning.
5 Account for real-world conditions in regulatory appraisal.
6 Scrutinize the claimed justifications and benefits alongside the potential risks.
7 Evaluate a range of alternative options for meeting needs alongside the option under appraisal, and promote more robust, diverse and adaptable technologies so as to minimize the costs of surprises and maximize the benefits of innovation.
8 Use "lay" and local knowledge as well as relevant specialist expertise in the appraisal.
9 Account for assumptions and values of different social groups.
10 Maintain regulatory independence from interested parties while retaining an inclusive approach to information and opinion gathering.
11 Identify and reduce institutional obstacles to learning and action.
12 Avoid "paralysis by analysis" by acting to reduce potential harm when there are reasonable grounds for concern.

Table 10.11, based on Harremoes et al. (2001), illustrates how the precautionary principle could be applied to the three major categories and examples of risk identified in

Table 10.11 Examples of the application of the precautionary principle to major risk categories

Situation	State and dates of knowledge	Examples of action
Risk	"Known" impacts, "known" probabilities – e.g. asbestos causing respiratory disease, lung and mesothelioma cancer	**Prevention:** action taken to reduce known risks – e.g. eliminate exposure to asbestos dust
Uncertainty	"Known" impacts, "unknown" probabilities – e.g. antibiotics in animal feed and associated human resistance to those antibiotics	**Precautionary prevention:** action taken to reduce potential hazards – e.g. reduce/eliminate human exposure to antibiotics in animal feed
Ignorance or "wicked" problems	"Unknown" impacts and therefore "unknown" probabilities – e.g. the "surprises" of CFCs and ozone layer damage prior to 1974; asbestos mesothelioma cancer	**Precaution:** action taken to anticipate, identify and reduce the impact of "surprises" – e.g. use of properties of chemicals such as persistence or bioaccumulation as "predictors" of potential harm; use of the broadest possible sources of information, including long-term monitoring; promotion of robust, diverse and adaptable technologies and social arrangements to meet needs, with fewer technological "monopolies" such as asbestos and CFCs

Table 10.2. Two additional studies by Raffensperger and Tickner (1999) and Tickner (2002) provide numerous examples where the principle has been applied in a diverse range of industries and countries. Perhaps the most persuasive use of the precautionary principle is in the area of global warming. (See Appendix 10.2.)

Despite these diverse applications of the precautionary principle, some decision makers, policy analysts and businesspeople have expressed concern that the general principle is too imprecise to permit an economically efficient determination of the appropriate timing and magnitude of anticipatory action (Marchant and Mossman 2004). In contrast to these concerns, Pittinger and Bishop (1999, p. 960) from Procter & Gamble stated:

> Neither the practice of risk assessment nor the elements of the precautionary principle are "new" or "revolutionary." For decades, they have been important elements in the design, manufacture and marketing of new consumer products. They also have long been embodied in the frameworks used to regulate the introduction of new products, globally. Due precaution is entirely consistent with sound, cost-effective management of the risks and uncertainties inherent in new technologies.

In response to the concern over issues of operationalizing what appears to be a vague principle, numerous researchers have proposed several methodologies which can bring analytical rigor to the study and application of the precautionary principle (see, for example, Sandin 1999; Sandin and Hansson 2002; Varas and Xepapadeas 2010). The continuing debate over the principle sometimes loses sight of the fact that it is not a "one size fits all" approach which may hamper the development of potentially useful new technologies and products but is instead a more nuanced concept with several dimensions. Cameron (2006) and others (Cooney 2005, Cooney and Dickson 2005; Peterson 2006; Wiener and Rogers 2002) have identified three distinct versions (weak, moderate and strong) of the precautionary principle, each tied closely to different evidentiary standards. To quote Cameron (2006, pp. 12–13):

Weak version

The weak version is the least restrictive and allows preventive measures to be taken in the face of uncertainty, but does not require them. To satisfy the threshold of harm, there must be some evidence relating to both the likelihood of occurrence and the severity of consequences. Some, but not all, require consideration of the costs of precautionary measures. Weak formulations do not preclude weighing benefits against the costs. Factors other than scientific uncertainty, including economic considerations, may provide legitimate grounds for postponing action. Under weak formulations, the requirement to justify the need for action (the burden of proof) generally falls on those advocating precautionary action. No mention is made of assignment of liability for environmental harm.

Moderate version

In moderate versions of the principle, the presence of an uncertain threat is a positive basis for action, once it has been established that a sufficiently serious threat exists. Usually, there is no requirement for proposed precautionary measures to be assessed against other factors such as economic or social costs. The trigger for action may be less rigorously defined, for example, as "potential damage", rather than as "serious or irreversible" damage as in the weak version. Liability is not mentioned and the burden of proof generally remains with those advocating precautionary action.

Strong version

Strong versions of the principle differ from the weak and moderate versions in reversing the burden of proof. Strong versions justify or require precautionary measures and some also establish liability for environmental harm, which is effectively a strong form of "polluter pays". Reversal of proof requires those proposing an activity to prove that the product, process or technology is sufficiently "safe" before approval is granted. Requiring proof of "no environmental harm" before any action proceeds implies the public is not prepared to accept any environmental risk, no matter what economic or social benefits may arise. At the extreme, such a requirement could involve bans and prohibitions on entire classes of potentially threatening activities or substances.

There is clearly a continuum, from weak to strong, along which the various forms of the precautionary principle may apply. Shamir et al. (2007) have linked two locations on this continuum, in particular, to accepted rules of evidence: the midpoint is equivalent to "the balance of probabilities" concept typical of civil litigation, while the strong point is equivalent to the criminal law's use of "beyond a reasonable doubt." The fundamental challenge is determining which point on the continuum (i.e. which degree of precaution) is appropriate for any given problem. The incorrect placement of any particular problem on this continuum can lead, in extremis, to one of two pathologies: suppression of a course of action which has net benefits to society or accession to a course of action which poses a serious threat. There is a clear need for a rigorous analytical methodology which can address and resolve this ambiguity. *Fuzzy logic* may offer such a solution.

Originally conceived by Professor Lofti Zadeh (1965, 1973), formerly of the University of California, Berkeley, fuzzy logic is a system for "describing the vagueness of the real world" (Kosko and Isaka 1993). In contrast to conventional Boolean sets, where an object is either in a set or not, "a fuzzy set is a class of objects with a continuum of grades of membership. Such a set is characterized by a membership (characteristics) function which assigns to each object a grade of membership ranging from zero and one" (Zadeh 1965, p. 338). Fuzzy logic is a system which uses such sets to arrive at analytically rigorous solutions to apparently imprecise problems by "1) use of so-called 'linguistic' variable in place of or in addition to numerical variables; 2) characterization of simple relations between variables by fuzzy conditional statements; and 3) characterization of complex relationships by fuzzy algorithms" (Zadeh 1973, p. 28).

Numerous studies have already been published on how the concept of fuzzy logic can be applied to the precautionary principle (see, for example, Jablonowski 2006; Shamir et al. 2007; Cameron and Peloso 2001, 2005; Takacs 2010; Marusich 2004). Perhaps the clearest explanation and application of fuzzy logic to the precautionary principle is the work by Shamir et al. (2007).

In conclusion, the essence and importance of the comments of the former US secretary of defense, Donald Rumsfeld, about "unknown unknowns" has been echoed in books by prominent scientists and economists, including Benoit Mandelbrot and Richard L. Hudson's *The (Mis)Behavior of Markets: A Fractal View of Financial Turmoil* (2004), Nassim Taleb's

The Black Swan: The Impact of the Highly Improbable (2007) and John Quiggin's *Zombie Economics: How Dead Ideas Still Walk Among Us* (2010). To quote Quiggin (p. 70):

> The implications [of these types of events] are profound. One is that in environments where surprises are likely to be unfavorable, it makes sense to apply a precautionary principle to decision-making. In such environments, we should prefer simple and easily understood choices to those that are complex and poorly understood, even when the complex option appears to offer greater net benefits.

A brief note on risk-risk trade-offs and the precautionary principle

One of the principal challenges to the use the precautionary principle has been the emergence of the concept of *risk-risk trade-offs*. Simply stated, this theory states that any action or policy to curtail or prevent the use of a product or technology motivated by the desire to reduce potential risks by invoking the precautionary principle must be tempered by the consideration of the risks associated with abandoning or not adopting such technology. Clearly enunciated in a book by Graham et al. (1997) entitled *Risk vs. Risk: Tradeoffs in Protecting Health and the Environment*, the theory has been applied to several case studies by other authors. Marchant and Mossman (2004) examine the use of the precautionary principle in the European Union courts, focusing, by way of example, on the use of antibiotics in animal feed. This is a controversial subject which has received a large degree of scientific scrutiny. Antimicrobials are used to promote rapid animal growth and counteract natural forces which increase the likelihood of bacterial infection in animals due to their artificially high stocking density in a feedlot environment. Mathematical epidemiological models of disease spread (Anderson and May 1979; May and Anderson 1979) identify density as one of the critical determining factors in the development of epidemics and their spread and endurance. There is strong evidence that one of the major causes of emerging bacterial resistance to antibiotics is overuse of these pharmaceuticals in both livestock and aquaculture (Mellon et al. 2001; AAM 2002; FAO 2006; FAO-WHO-OIE 2007; Pew Commission on Industrial Food Animal Production 2008; Hawkey and Jones 2009; US HHS 2010; Davis et al. 2015; Neyea et al. 2012; Pereira et al. 2014; Tang et al. 2017; OIE 2018). The position advanced by Marchant and Mossman is that discontinuance of the use of these drugs in current modes of livestock production poses a greater threat than their continued use because of the increased chances that human consumers will be exposed to a greater level of bacteria from the food production system. This risk trade-off is part of a generic argument which presumably could apply in other cases where the precautionary principle is being considered.

However, there is a logical fallacy with the argument advanced in this particular case study because of an incorrect definition of system boundaries. In essence, the argument is that the current system of livestock production achieves significant economic efficiencies but has some inherent risks which require offsetting actions such as the use of antibiotics. Cessation of this preventative measure will expose consumers to the inherent system risk. The implicit assumption – and logical pitfall – is that the current system of meat production is a given and that no other alternatives are possible or economically desirable. If one expands the range of alternatives to include range-fed rather than feedlot-based production systems, then a comprehensive life-cycle systems analysis which recognizes and incorporates all externalities might suggest that the feedlot system is less economically efficient from a societal perspective than the alternative. This issue is part of the larger debate over the costs and benefits of what has been termed *industrial agriculture* (Kimbrell 2002).

The logical conclusion is that any situation with a potential risk–risk trade-off should be considered on a case-by-case basis with a clear delineation of the appropriate system boundaries to avoid the logical inconsistencies inherent in too narrow an analysis of alternatives.

Appendix 10.1
Two classic examples of risk framing

In the first example, Daniel Kahneman and Amos Tversky and Kahneman (1981, p. 453) ask two separate groups of respondents how they would respond to one of the following scenarios.

> Problem 1: Imagine that the U.S. is preparing for the outbreak of an unusual Asian disease, which is expected to kill 600 people. Two alternative programs to combat the disease have been proposed. Assume that the exact scientific estimate of the consequences of the programs are as follows: If Program A is adopted, 200 people will be saved. If Program B is adopted, there is a 1/3 probability that 600 people will be saved, and 2/3 probability that no people will be saved. Which of the two programs would you favour?
>
> Problem 2: If Program C is adopted, 400 people will die. If Program D is adopted, there is a 1/3 probability that nobody will die, and 2/3 probability that 600 people will die. Which of the two programs would you favour?

In test after test of these scenarios, the authors found a consistent pattern. Program A is overwhelmingly preferred to B. According to the authors (p. 453), "The majority choice in this problem is risk averse: the prospect of certainly saving 200 lives is more attractive than a risky prospect of equal expected value; that is, a one-in-three chance of saving 600 lives." However, Program D is overwhelmingly preferred to C. The authors state that "the majority choice in problem 2 is risk taking: the certain death of 400 people is less acceptable than the two-in-three chance that 600 will die" (p. 453). The authors conclude:

> The preferences in problems 1 and 2 illustrate a common pattern: choices involving gains are often risk averse and choices involving losses are often risk taking. However, it is easy to see that the two problems are effectively identical. The only difference between them is that the outcomes are described in [the first choice] . . . by the number of lives saved, and in [the second choice] . . . by the number of lives lost. Inconsistent responses . . . arise from the conjunction of a framing *effect* with contradictory attitudes toward risks involving gains and losses.
>
> (1981, p. 453)

Kahneman and Tversky state:

> We have considered a variety of examples in which a decision, a preference or an emotional reaction was controlled by factors that may appear irrelevant or inconsequential.

The difficulty people have in maintaining a comprehensive view of consequences and their susceptibility to the vagaries of framing are examples of such impediments. The descriptive study of preferences also presents challenges to the theory of rational choice because it is often far from clear whether the effects of decision weights, reference points, framing and regret should be treated as errors or biases or whether they should be accepted as valid elements of human experience.

(1982, p. 173)

The second example is equally macabre and addresses the issue of how individuals might respond when they have the opportunity to influence some else's impending death (Greene et al. 2001). Again, two slightly different questions are asked of two randomly selected groups: QUESTION A: A runaway trolley is hurtling toward five people. They will all be killed – unless you throw a switch that will steer the trolley onto a spur, where it will kill just one other person instead of five. Should you throw the switch? QUESTION B: A runaway trolley is hurtling toward five people. You are standing next to a large stranger on a footbridge that arches over the tracks. The only way to save the five is to push the stranger off the bridge onto the tracks below; it is certain that he will die, but his heavy body will stop the trolley, saving the five others. Should you push the stranger to his death?

A vast majority of people say yes to Question A, according to moral philosophers and psychologists who have posed the question over many years. It is morally acceptable to throw the switch to save five innocent lives at the expense of one. But most people say no to Question B; in this case, it is morally wrong to kill one person to save five.

After many years of debate, moral philosophers have never been able to arrive at a set of principles to explain why people treat the two situations differently. There appears to be no rational explanation for the difference.

The study by Greene et al. (2001) relies on functional magnetic imaging of the brain while subjects are making their choice of action. The runaway trolley study finds that the two trolley car problem formulations engage different parts of the brain. In Choice A, the idea of throwing a switch is impersonal; it is processed by a location in the neocortex that deals mainly with memory, part of the cognitive processing part of the brain. In Choice B, by contrast, the notion of personally pushing a stranger to his death activates the limbic region of the brain that deals with emotions, temporarily suppressing the memory areas. The conclusion is that issues of moral judgment contain both rational and emotional components. The degree to which either emotion or rationality will be dominant depends in part on the nature of the moral dilemma, especially the difference between what have been called "moral personal" (i.e. "up close and personal") situations and "moral impersonal" situations.

Appendix 10.2
The precautionary principle and global warming

While a near universal consensus has emerged among members of the scientific community that global warming is occurring and that it is anthropogenic, there are some doubters left in the general public, and this theme has been adopted by certain special interest groups who face the loss of business revenue from any measures undertaken to reverse the emission of carbon dioxide and other greenhouse gases (Bowen 2008; Michaels 2008; Dyer 2009; Hoggan 2009; Pooley 2010; Oreskes and Conway 2010; *Guardian* June 12, 2019). It can be demonstrated, however, that it is ultimately in the interest of even non-believers to recognize and act against the threat of global warming. Consider Table 10.12, which analyzes the global warming problem using Von Neumann and Morgenstern game theory (1953). In this representation of the standard two-person game theoretic, Player #1 is society in general, and Player #2 represents nature.

The table presents a simple 2 × 2 decision matrix which represents two states of nature (global warming is/is not occurring) and two possible courses of action (act/not act). Each of the four matrix cells entails markedly different "payoffs." Given the enormous costs of non-response to global warming, a "maximin" strategy is warranted, where society (here denoted as Player #1) chooses a course of action which minimizes potential losses. Acting on the assumption that global warming is occurring may entail significant opportunity costs if global warming is not occurring but avoids the potentially catastrophic consequences of not acting if global warming is actually occurring.

Up until recently, there were no reasonable estimates of the benefits or costs available to attach to this matrix. In October 2006, a pathbreaking study commissioned by the prime minister and chancellor of the exchequer in the United Kingdom was published. It was – and remains – the most exhaustive and comprehensive analysis of the economics of global climate change. Organized by Sir Nicholas Stern, head of the Government Economic Service and former chief economist of the World Bank, the report was portentous yet essentially optimistic. According to Stern (2007, p. vi): "There is still time to avoid the worst impacts of climate change, if we take strong action now." One of the most important outcomes of the Stern Report (2007) was the ability to, for the first time, assign credible numbers to both benefits and costs of attempts to control the process of global warming. Table 10.13 recasts the decision matrix in terms of actual economic projections with the focus on the costs of ignoring and addressing climate change. To place these data in context, global GDP at the time of the Stern Report's publication in 2006 was estimated at US$48 trillion. It is clear from this analysis that even if the probability of global

Table 10.12 Von Neumann and Morgenstern game theoretic approach to global warming

		Player #2 (in this case, unknown states of nature)	
		Global warming is NOT occurring	Global warming is occurring
Player #1 (in this case, society) possible actions	We assume global warming is occurring and act on it	Generally unproductive investment **COSTS**: signficant **BENEFITS**: marginal	**COSTS**:1% of global GDP /year **BENEFITS**: we can slow or possibly reverse damage
	We assume global warming is NOT occurring and do nothing	**COSTS**: none **BENEFITS**: none	**COSTS**: between $6 trillion and 20% of global GDP **BENEFITS**: none

warming is deemed to be unlikely (i.e. with a low probability of occurrence), it is still rational behavior to engage in avoidance behavior because of the extraordinary costs of not acting should global warming actually occur. Parenthetically, it should be noted that Stern's maximum estimated GDP loss of 20% (Stern 2007, p. 162) associated with massive climate change may be overly sanguine in light of the fact that China has admitted that environmental despoliation costs it as much as 10% of its GDP (China.org.cn 2012; see also World Bank 2007).

Some researchers have even considered Stern's estimates of GDP loss as overly optimistic. Sterner and Persson (2008) observe that Stern's calculations are based on an assumed deviation from a continuing economic growth path which remains positive despite the potential negative effects of increasing greenhouse gas emissions. Citing the work of Weitzman (2007) and the non-zero probability of catastrophic climate change, Sterner and Persson suggest the possibility of global climate change making us "significantly worse off" (2008, p. 63) than we are today. This possibility suggests an even more rigorous application of the precautionary principle with respect to this global threat.

Table 10.13 Table 10.12 with Stern's estimates

		Player #2 (in this case, unknown states of nature)	
		Global warming is NOT occurring	Global warming is occurring
Player #1 (in this case, society) possible actions	**We assume global warming is occurring and act on it**	Generally unproductive investment **COSTS:** 1% of global GDP /year.	**COSTS:**1% of global GDP /year
	We assume global warming is NOT occurring and do nothing	**COSTS:** none	**COSTS: between $6 trillion and 20% of global GDP**

References

Allen, Steve et al. (2019) "Atmospheric transport and deposition of microplastics in a remote mountain catchment," *Nature Geoscience*, April 15.

Allison, Graham (2004) *Nuclear Terrorism. The Ultimate Preventable Catastrophe*, New York: Henry Holt.

American Academy of Microbiology (AAM) (2002) *The Role of Antibiotics in Agriculture*, Washington, DC: AAM.

Anderson, Roy M. and Robert M. May (1979) "Population biology of infectious diseases: Part I," *Nature*, 280, August 2, pp. 361–367.

Barrett, Justine et al. (2020) "Microplastic pollution in deep-sea sediments from the Great Australian Bight," *Frontiers in Marine Science*, October 5.

Bergmann, Melanie et al. (2019) "White and wonderful? Microplastics previal in snow from the Alps to the Arctic," *Science Advances*, 5(8), August 14, eaax1157.

Borrelle, Stephanie B. et al. (2020) "Predicted growth in plastic waste exceeds efforts to mitigate plastic pollution," *Science*, September 18.

Bowen, Mark (2008) *Censoring Science: Inside the Political Attack on Dr. James Hansen and the Truth of Global Warming*, New York: Dutton.

Brahney, Janice et al. (2020) "Plastic rain in protected areas of the United States," *Science*, June 12.

Brandon, Jennifer A. et al. (2019) "Mulitdecadal increase in plastic particles in coastal ocean sediments," *Science Advances*, September 4.

Browne, Mark Anthony et al. (2011) "Accumulation of microplastic on shorelines worldwide: Sources and sinks," *Environmental Science & Technology*, 45, pp. 9175–9179.

Cameron, Enrico and Gain Francesco Peloso (2001) "An application of fuzzy logic to the assessment of aquifer's pollution potential," *Environmental Geology*, 40, pp. 1305–1315.

Cameron, Enrico and Gain Francesco Peloso (2005) "Risk management and the precautionary principle: A fuzzy logic model," *Risk Analysis*, 25(4), pp. 901–911.

Cameron, Linda (2006) "Environmental risk management in New Zealand: Is there scope to apply a more generic framework?," New Zealand Treasury Policy Perspectives Paper 06/06, July.

CBS News (2006) "Known knowns, known unknowns and unknown unknowns: A retrospective," November 9.

China.org.cn (2012) "Economic losses from pollution account for 10% of GDP" (accessed May 1).

Cochran, Thomas B. (2011) "Statement of Thomas B. Cochran, Ph.D. on the Fukushima Nuclear Disaster and its implications for U.S. Nuclear Power Reactors," Joint Hearings of the Subcommittee on Clean Air and Nuclear Safety and the Committee on Environment and Public Works, United States Senate, April 12, New York: Natural Resources Defense Council (NRDC).

Conto, Gea Olivieri et al. (2020) "Micro-and nanoparticles in edible fruit and vegetables," *Environmental Research*, 187, p. 109677.

Cooke, Roger M. and Daan Nieboer (2011) *Heavy-Tailed Distributions: Data, Diagnostics, and New Developments*, Washington, DC: Resources for the Future, DP 11–19, March.

Cooney, Rosie (2005) "From promise to practicalities: The precautionary principle on biodiversity conservation and sustainable use," in Rosie Cooney and Barney Dickson (eds.) *Biodiversity and the Precautionary Principle: Risk and Uncertainty in Conservation and Sustainable Use*, London: Earthscan, pp. 3–17.

Cooney, Rosie and Barney Dickson (eds.) (2005) *Biodiversity & The Precautionary Principle: Risk and Uncertainty in Conservation and Sustainable Use*, London: Earthscan.

Cox, Kieran D. et al. (2019) "Human consumption of microplastics," *Environmental Science & Technology*, in press.

Cozar, Andres et al. (2017) "The Arctic Ocean as a dead end for floating plastics in the North Atlantic branch of the thermohaline circulation," *Science Advances*, April 19.

Crouch, Edmund and Richard Wilson (1980) "Estimates of risks," in Peter N. Nemetz (ed.) *Resource Policy: International Perspectives*, Montreal: Institute for Research on Public Policy, pp. 299–318.

Davis, Gregg et al. (2015) "Intermingled Klebsiella pneumoniae Populations Between Retail Meats and Human Urinary Tract Infections," *Clinical Infectious Diseases*, 61, September 15, pp. 892–899.

D'Souza, Joseph M. et al. (2020) "Food web transfer of plastics to an apex riverine predator," *Global Change Biology*, April 18.

Dyer, Gwynne (2009) *Climate Wars*, Toronto: Vintage.

European Environment Agency (EEA) (2012) *The Impacts of Endocrine Disruptors on Wildlife, People and Their Environments*. The Weybridge+15 (1996–2011) report.

European Environment Agency (EEA) (2013) *Late Lessons for Early Warnings: Science, Precaution, Innovation*, Report No 1.

Evangeliou, N. et al. (2020) "Atmospheric transport is a major pathway of microplastics to remote regions," *Nature Communications*, 11, pp. 1–11.

Fairley, William B. (1977) "Evaluating the 'small' probability of a catastrophic accident from the marine transportation liquefied natural gas," in William B. Fairley and Frederick Mosteller (eds.) *Statistics and Public Policy*, Reading, MA: Addison-Wesley, pp. 331–354.

FAO-WHO-OIE (2007) *Joint FAO/WHO/OIE Expert Meeting on Critically Important Antimicrobials*, 26–30 November, Rome.

Feynman, Richard (1986) Appendix F to *Report of the Presidential Commission on the Space Shuttle Challenger Disaster*.

Feynman, Richard and Ralph Leighton (2001) *What Do You Care What Other People Think? Further Adventures of a Curious Character*, New York: W.W. Norton & Co.

Fielder, John H. and Douglas Birsch (eds.) (1992) *The DC-10 Case: A Study in Applied Ethics, Technology and Society*, New York: State University of New York Press.

Food and Agriculture Organization (FAO) (2006) *Livestock's Long Shadow: Environmental Issues and Options*, Rome: United Nations.

Geyer, Roland et al. (2017) "Production, use and fate of all plastics ever made," *Science Advances*, July 19.

Gold, Steve C. and Wendy E. Wagner (2020) "Filling gaps in science exposes gaps in chemical regulation," *Science*, 368(6495), June 5, pp. 1066–1068.

Graham, John D. et al. (1997) *Risk vs. Risk: Tradeoffs in Protecting Health and the Environment*, Cambridge, MA: Harvard University Press.

Greene, Joshua D. et al. (2001) "An fMRI investigation of emotional engagement in moral judgment," *Science*, 293, September 14, pp. 2105–2108.

Griesmeyer, J. Michael and David Okrent (1981) "Risk management and decision rules for light water reactors," *Risk Analysis*, 1(2), pp. 121–136.

Guardian (2019) "Revealed: Mobil sought to fight environmental regulation, documents show," June 12.

Guardian (2020) "Microplastic pollution found near summit of Mount Everest," November 20.

Hallanger, Ingeborg G. and Geir W. Gabrielsen (2018) *Plastic in the European Arctic*, Tromso, Norway: Norwegian Polar Institute.

Harremoes, Poul et al. (2001) *Late Lesson from Early Warnings: The Precautionary Principle 1896–2000*, Copenhagen, Denmark: European Environment Agency.

Hawkey, Peter M. and Annie M. Jones (2009) "The changing epidemiology of resistance," *Journal of Antimicrobial Chemotherapy*, 64(Suppl. I), pp. i3–i10.

Hochella, Michael F. et al. (2019) "Nanomaterials impact on Earth system," *Science*, March 29.

Hoggan, James (2009) *Climate Cover-Up: The Crusade to Deny Global Warming*, Vancouver: Greystone.

Jablonowski, Mark (2006) *Precautionary Risk Management*, New York: Palgrave Macmillan.

Jaczko, Gregory B. (2019) *Confessions of a Rogue Nuclear Regulator*, New York: Simon & Schuster.

Jambeck, Jenna R. et al. (2015) "Plastic waste in inputs from land into the ocean," *Science*, February 13.

Kahneman, Daniel, P. Slovic and A. Tversky (1982) *Judgment under Uncertainty: Heuristics and Biases*, New York: Cambridge University Press.

Kahneman, Daniel and Amos Tversky (1981) "The framing of decisions and the psychology of choice," *Science*, 211, January 30, pp. 453–458.

Kahneman, Daniel and Amos Tversky (1982) "The psychology of preferences," *Scientific American*, January 30, pp. 160–173.

Kane, Ian A. et al. (2020) "Seafloor microplastic hotspots controlled by deep-sea circulation," *Science*, April 30.

Kimbrell, Andrew (ed.) (2002) *Fatal Harvest: The Tragedy of Industrial Agriculture*, Washington, DC: Island Press.

Knight, Frank (1921) *Risk, Uncertainty and Profit*, [reprinted in 2010 Kissimee, FL: Signalman Publishing].

Kosko, Bart and Satoru Isaka (1993) "Fuzzy logic," *Scientific American*, July, pp. 76–81.

Kousky, Carolyn et al. (2009) "Responding to threats of climate change mega-catastrophes," Kennedy School, Harvard University, October 19.

Lancet (2017) "Microplastics and human health: An urgent problem," October.

Li, Jiana et al. (2018) "Microplastics in mussels sampled from coastal water and supermarkets in the United Kingdom," *Environmental Pollution*, 241, pp. 35–44.

Lichtenstein, S., P. Slovic, B. Fischhoff, M. Layman and B. Combs (1978) "Judged frequency of lethal events," *Journal of Experimental Psychology: Human Learning and Memory*, 4, pp. 551–578.

Liebezeit, Gerd and Elisabeth Liebezeit (2014) "Synthetic particles as contaminants in German beers," *Food Additives & Contaminants Part A*, August 11.

Liebmann, Bettina et al. (2018) "Assessment of microplastic concentrations in human stool – preliminary results of a prospective study," Poster, International Conference on Emerging Contaminants (EMCON), Oslo, 25–28 June.

Lochbaum, David (2011) *The NRC and Nuclear Plant Safety in 2010: A Brighter Spotlight Needed*, Cambridge, MA: Union of Concerned Scientists.

Lusher, A.L. et al. (2013) "Occurrence of microplastics in the gastrointestinal tract of pelagic and demersal fish from the English Channel," *Marine Pollution Bulletin*, 67, pp. 94–99.

Mandelbrot, Benoit and Richard L. Hudson (2004) *The (Mis)Behavior of Markets: A Fractal View of Financial Turmoil*, New York: Basic Books.

Marchant, G. and K. Mossman (2004) *Arbitrary and Capricious: The Precautionary Principle in the European Union Courts*, Washington, DC: AEI Press.

Martin, C. et al. (2020) "Exponential increase of plastic burial in mangrove sediments as a major plastic source," *Science Advances*, 6, October 28, eaaz5593.

Marusich, Lourdes Juarez (2004) *The Application of Fuzzy logic Analysis to Assessing the Significance of Environmental Impacts: Case Studies from Mexico and Canada*, Ottawa: Canadian Environmental Assessment Agency.

May, Robert M. and Roy M. Anderson (1979) "Population biology of infectious diseases: Part II," *Nature*, 28, August 9, pp. 455–461.

McGrath, P.E. (1974) "Radioactive Waste Management: Potentials and Hazards from a Risk Point of View," Report EURFNR-1204 (KFK 1992), US-EURATOM Fast Reactor Exchange Program, Karlsruhe, Germany.

Medvedev, Grigori (1989) *The Truth about Chernobyl*, New York: Basic Books.

Mellon, Margaret et al. (2001) *Hogging It: Estimates of Antimicrobial Abuse in Livestock*, Cambridge, MA: Union of Concerned Scientists, January.

Michaels, David (2008) *Doubt Is Their Product: How Industry's Assault on Science Threaten Your Health*, Oxford: Oxford University Press.

Mohrig, David (2020) "Deep-ocean seafloor islands of plastic," *Science*, June 5.

National Academy of Sciences (NAS) (2016) *Triennial Review of the National Nanotechnology Initiative*, Washington, DC: NAS.

National Academy of Sciences (NAS) (2020a) *A Quadrennial Review of the National Nanotechnology Initiative*, Washington DC: NAS.

National Academy of Sciences (NAS) (2020b) *Environmental Neuroscience*, Washington. DC: NAS.

National Institutes of Health (NIH) (n.d.) "Endocrine disruptors," Bethesda, MD.

Nelms, S.E. et al. (2019) "Microplastics in marine mammals stranded around the British coast: Ubiquitous but transitory," *Scientific Reports*, January 31.

Nemetz, Peter N. (2022) *Unsustainable World: Are We Losing the Battle to Save Our Planet?* New York: Routledge.

New York Times (1982) "Added damage bars reopening of Ginna Plant," February 13.

New York Times (2011) "When all isn't enough to stop a catastrophe," March 29.

NEXUS3 et al. (2019) "Plastic waste poisons Indonesia's food chain," November.

Neyea, Castillo et al. (2012) "Antimicrobial-resistant bacteria: An unrecognized work-related risk in food animal production," *Safety and Heath at Work*, 3, pp. 85–91.

OIE (World Organization for Animal Health) (2018) *OIE Annual Report on Antimicrobial Agents Intended for Use in Animals*, Paris.

Okrent, D. et al. (1981) "Industrial Risks," *Proceedings of the Royal Society of London A*, 376, pp. 133–149.

Olsen, J. (1983) "Epidemiological approach to assessment of combined effects: Theoretical background," in World Health Organization (WHO) (ed.) *Health Aspects of Chemical Safety: Combined Exposures to Chemicals*, Interim Document 11, Geneva: WHO, pp. 211–225.

Oreskes, Naomi and Erik M. Conway (2010) *Merchants of Doubt: How a Handful of Scientists Obscured the Truth on Issues from Tobacco Smoke to Global Warming*, New York: Bloomsbury Press.

Pabortsava, Katsiaryna and Richard S. Lampitt (2020) "High concentrations of plastic hidden beneath the surface of the Atlantic Ocean," *Nature Communications*, 11, August 18, pp. 1–11.

Panno, Samuel et al. (2019) "Microplastic contamination in karst groundwater systems," *Groundwater*, March–April.

Peeken, Ilka et al. (2018) "Arctic sea ice is an important temporal sink and means of transport for microplastic," *Nature Communications*, April 24.

Pereira, R.V. et al. (2014) "Effect of on-farm use of antimicrobial drugs on resistance in fecal *Escherichia coli* of preweaned dairy calves," *Journal of Dairy Science*, 97, pp. 7644–7654.

Peterson, Deborah C. (2006) "Precaution: Principles and practice in Australian environments and natural resource management," Presidential address, 50th Annual Australian Agricultural and Resource Economics Society Conference, Manly, New South Wales, February 8–10.

Pew Commission on Industrial Food Animal Production (2008) *Putting Meat on the Table: Industrial Farm Animal Production in America*, Washington, DC: Pew Charitable Trusts.

Phys.org (2017) "Scientists categorize Earth as 'toxic planet'," February 7.

Pietroiusti, Antonio et al. (2018) "Nanomaterial exposure, toxicity, and impact on human health," *WIREs Nanomedicine and Nanobiotechnology*, February 23.

Pittinger, Charles A. and William E. Bishop (1999) "Unraveling the chimera: A corporate view of the precautionary principle," *Human and Ecological Risk Assessment*, 5(5), pp. 951–962.

Pooley, Eric (2010) *The Climate War: True Believers, Power Brokers, and the Fight to Save the Earth*, New York: Hyperion.

Prata, Joana Correia et al. (2020) "Environment exposure to microplastics: an overview on possible human health effects," *Science of the Total Environment*, 702, 134455, pp. 1–9.

Quiggin, John (2010) *Zombie Economics: How Dead Ideas Still Walk among Us*, Princeton, NJ: Princeton University Press.

Raffensperger, Carolyn and Joel Tickner (1999) *Protecting Public Health and the Environment: Implementing the Precautionary Principle*, Washington, DC: Island Press.

Ramsperger, A.F.R.M. et al. (2020) "Environmental exposure enhances the internalization of microplastic particles into cells," *Science Advances*, December 9.

Registration, Evaluation, Authorisation and Restriction of Chemicals (REACH). http://ec.europa.eu/environment/chemicals/reach/reach_intro.htm.

Report of the President's Commission on the Accident at Three Mile Island. The Need for Change: The Legacy of TMI (1979) New York: Pergamon Press.

Rillig, Matthias and Anika Lehmann (2020) "Microplastic in terrestrial ecosystems," *Science*, June 26.

Rumsfeld, Donald (2002) "News conference transcript," February 12. www.defense.gov/Transcripts/Transcript.aspx?TranscriptID=2636.

Sandin, Per (1999) "Dimensions of the precautionary principle," *Human and Ecological Risk Assessment*, 5(5), pp. 889–907.

Sandin, Per and Sven Ove Hansson (2002) "The default value approach to the precautionary principle," *Human and Ecological Risk Assessment*, 8(3), pp. 463–471.

Schrader-Frechette, K.S. (1991) *Risk and Rationality: Philosophical Foundations for Populist Reforms*, Berkeley, CA: University of California Press.

Science (1981) "Japanese A-bomb data will be revised," October 2, pp. 31–32.

Science (2020a) "Plastic dust is blowing into U.S. national Parks: More than 100 tons each year," June 11.

Science (2020b) "Microplastic's role in antibiotic resistance," September 11.

Shamir, Mirit et al. (2007) "The application of fuzzy logic to the precautionary principle," *Artificial Intelligence and Law*, 15, pp. 411–427.

Slovic, Paul and Elke U. Weber (2002) "Perceptions of risk posed by extreme events," Conference paper for "Risk Management Strategies in an Uncertain World," Palisades, New York, April 12–13.

Stephens, Mark (1980) *Three Mile Island*, New York: Random House.

Stern, Nicholas (2007) *The Economics of Climate Change*, London: Cabinet Office – HM Treasury.

Stern, Paul C. and Harvey V. Fineberg (eds.) (1996) *Understanding Risk: Informing Decisions in a Democratic Society*, Washington, DC: US NRC Committee on Risk Characterization.

Sterner, Thomas and U. Martin Persson (2008) "An even sterner review: Introducing relative prices into the discounting debate," *Review of Environmental Economics and Policy*, 2(1), Winter, pp. 61–76.

Takacs, Marta (2010) "Multilevel fuzzy approach to the risk of disaster management," *Acta Polytechnica Hungerica*, 7(4), pp. 91–102.

Taleb, Nassim Nicholas (2007) *The Black Swan: The Impact of the Highly Improbable*, New York: Random House.

Tang, Karen L. et al. (2017) "Restricting the use of antibiotics in food-producing animals and its associations with antibiotic resistance in food-producing animals and human beings: A systematic review and meta-analysis," *The Lancet*, 1, November, pp. e316–e327.

Tickner, Joel A. (ed.) (2002) *Precaution: Environmental Science and Preventive Public Policy*, Washington, DC: Island Press.

Tickner, Joel A., Carolyn Raffensperger and Nancy Myers (n.d.) "The precautionary principle in action: A handbook," Written for the Science and Environmental Health Network.

Tufte, Edward (1997) *Visual Explanations*, Cheshire, CT: Graphics Press.

Tversky, Amos and Daniel Kahneman (1974) "Judgment under uncertainty: Heuristics and biases," *Science*, 185(4157), pp. 1124–1131.

Tversky, Amos and Daniel Kahneman (1981) "The framing of decisions and the psychology of choice," *Science*, 211(4481), pp. 453–458.

Tyree, Chris and Dan Morrison (2018) "Invisibles: the plastic inside us," Orbmedia.org.faqs.

UN News (2017) "'Turn the tide on plastic' urges UN, as microplastics in the seas now outnumber stars in our galaxy," February 23.

UNEP (2019) *Global Chemicals Outlook II, From Legacies to Innovative Solutions*, Synthesis Report, Nairobi, Kenya.

UNESCO (2005) *The Precautionary Principle*, Paris: UNESCO.

US Department of Health and Human Services (US HHS), Food and Drug Administration and Center for Veterinary Medicine (2010) *The Judicious Use of Medically Important Antimicrobial Drugs in Food-Producing Animals*, June 28.

US Department of Health and Human Services (US HHS), Public Health Services and National Toxicology Program (2011) "Report on carcinogens review group actions on the nomination of saccharin for delisting from the report on carcinogens," in *Report on Carcinogens* (12th ed.), pp. 467–469, Washington, DC: US HHS.

US Environmental Protection Agency (EPA) (1998) *Chemical Hazard Data Availability Study*, Office of Pollution Prevention and Toxics, April.

US General Accountability Office (GAO) (2006) *Chemical Regulation. Actions Are Need to Improve the Effectiveness of EPA's Chemical Review Program*, August 2, Washington, DC: US GAO.

US General Accountability Office (GAO) (2007) *Chemical Regulation Comparison of U.S. and Recently Enacted European Union Approaches to Protect Against the Risks of Toxic Chemicals*, Washington, DC: US GAO.

US National Archives Office (1981) *Text of Executive Order 12291*, Washington, DC: NAO.

US Nuclear Regulatory Commission (NRC) (1975) *Reactor Safety Study: An Assessment of Accident Risks in U.S. Commercial Nuclear Power Plants* (WASH-1400).

US Nuclear Regulatory Commission (NRC) (1978) *Risk Assessment Review Group Report to the U.S. Nuclear Regulatory Commission*, H.W. Lewis et al., Rockville, MD: US NRC.

US Nuclear Regulatory Commission (NRC) (1981) *Fault Tree Handbook*, Rockville, MD: US NRC.

US Nuclear Regulatory Commission (NRC) (1991) *Severe Accident Risks: An Assessment for Five U.S. Nuclear Power Plants*, Rockville, MD: US NRC.

Van Cauwenberghe, Lisbeth and Colin R. Janssen (2014) "Microplastics in bivalves cultured for human consumption," *Environmental Pollution*, 193, pp. 65–70.

Varas, Giannis and Anastasios Xepapadeas (2010) "Model uncertainty, ambiguity and the precautionary principle: Implications for biodiversity management," *Environmental and Resource Economics*, 45, pp. 379–404.

Von Neumann, John and Oskar Morgenstern (1953) *Theory of Games and Economic Behavior*, Princeton, NJ: Princeton University Press.

WebMD (2020) "Autopsies show microplastics in major human organs," August 17.

Weitzman, Martin L. (2007) "A review of the stern review on the economics of climate change," *Journal of Economic Literature*, 45, September, pp. 703–724.

Weitzman, Martin L. (2009) "On modeling and interpreting the economics of catastrophic climate change," *Review of Economic and Statistics*, 91(1), pp. 1–19.

Wieczorek, Alina M. et al. (2018) "Frequency of microplastics in mesopelagic fishes from the Northwest Atlantic," *Frontiers in Marine Science*, 5, February, Article 39.

Wiener, Jonathan B. and Michael D. Rogers (2002) "Comparing precaution in the United States and Europe," *Journal of Risk Research*, 5(4), pp. 317–349.

Wilson, Richard and Edmund Crouch (1982) *Risk/Benefit Analysis*, Cambridge, MA: Ballinger Publishing.

Windsor, Fredric M. et al. (2019) "Microplastic ingestion by riverine macroinvertebrates," *Science of the Total Environment*, 646, pp. 68–74.

Woodward, Jamie et al. (2021) "Acute riverine microplastic contamination due to avoidable releases of untreated wastewater," *Nature Sustainability*, May 13.

World Bank (2007) *Cost of Pollution in China: Economic Estimates of Physical Damages*, Washington, DC: World Bank.

World Economic Forum (WEF) (2020) *Global Risks 2020*, Geneva: An Initiative of the Risk Response Network.

World Health Organization (WHO) (2019) *Microplastics in Drinking Water*, Geneva: WHO.

World Wildlife Fund Australia (2018) "Plastic in our oceans is killing marine mammals," October 11.

Yang, Yuyi et al. (2020) "Microplastics provide new microbial niches in aquatic environments," *Applied Microbiology and Biotechnology*, 104, pp. 6501–6511.

Zadeh, Lofti (1965) "Fuzzy sets," *Information and Control*, 8, pp. 338–353.

Zadeh, Lofti (1973) "Outline of a new approach to the analysis of complex systems and decision processes," *IEEE Trans. Systems, Man and Cybernetics*, 2, pp. 28–44.

Zhang, Yuxuan et al. (2020) "Potential risks of microplastic combined with superbugs: Enrichment of antibiotic resistant bacteria on the surface of microplastics in mariculture system," *Ecotoxicology and Environmental Safety*, January 15.

11 Pandemics and sustainability

Humanity has been afflicted with disease throughout history, but especially following the agricultural revolution of 10,000 years ago and the subsequent dramatic transformation in human economic, social and political institutions. Driving the emergence of these new diseases, which were largely absent from hunter-gatherer societies (see Chapter 2), were such factors as the domestication of animals and settlement patterns involving increased population density. Much has been written about the role that disease has played in human history (Cartwright and Biddiss 1972; Cohen 1989; Nikiforuk 1991; McNeill 1998; Cantor 2001; Oldstone 2010; Harrison 2012; Shah 2016; Skwarecki 2016; Snowden 2020). In many cases, the impact has been dramatic, determining the outcome of battles and the fate of nations and empires (Winegard 2019). An archetypal example is provided by the vicissitudes of the Roman Empire over its long history – influenced, to no small degree, by disease and climate change (Harper 2017). While epidemics are relatively common in the historical record, pandemics have had the most dramatic results. The black death of the 14th century was responsible for as many as 200 million deaths, killing as much as one-third of the world's population (Meacham 2020). This momentous event is posited to have destroyed the old feudal order and begun the long transition into modernity (Johnson and Mueller 2002; Alfani 2020).

Prior to the emergence of COVID-19 in 2019–2020, the most recent global experience of pandemics dated to the Spanish flu, which afflicted a world exhausted from World War I. It affected as much as one-third of the global population, with estimates of mortality ranging as high as 50–100 million (Johnson and Mueller 2002; Hagemann 2020). As of the writing of this book, the official estimate of global COVID-19 cases has reached over 167 million with over 3.47 million deaths (World Health Organization accessed May 25, 2021). However, WHO has expressed the opinion that the real toll of this disease could be as high as 6–8 million cases due to widespread underreporting (The Hill May 21, 2021). One example, in particular, is illustrative of this problem of underreporting. The *New York Times* (May 25, 2021) has conducted its own study of Indian epidemiological data with the help of experts where official case numbers suggest 26.9 million reported cases with 307,231 deaths. *The Times* has created three additional scenarios: a conservative scenario, a more likely scenario and a worse scenario. In this last scenario, cases are estimated as 700.7 million with 4.2 million fatalities.

Not all countries have been impacted to the same degree by COVID-19. For example, while the United States has approximately 4% of the world's population, it has experienced 20% of the cases and 17% of the deaths (World Health Organization, accessed May 25, 2021). The effects of this virus have been devastating, affecting all spheres of

DOI: 10.4324/9781003170730-11

human activity. The impacts have had a major impact on international trade (WTO 2020) and have been particularly severe among developing nations (World Bank 2020a; Egger et al. 2021), with the cumulative effects of COVID-19, conflict and climate change leading to a reversal in gains in poverty eradication for the first time in a generation (World Bank 2020b). While the developed nations have more resilience than their southern counterparts, none has escaped the economic, social and political impacts of the virus. For example, the US Congressional Budget Office (2020) has projected that over an 11-year time horizon, the US could lose as much as $7.9 trillion in GDP. Socially and politically, many industrialized nations have experienced the rise of right-wing extremism, threatening the post–World War II democratic consensus. In the United States, the pandemic is considered a contributing factor to the change in government during the federal election of November 2020.

Table 11.1 is an initial summary of some of the most important effects of this most recent pandemic, understanding that data are incomplete and much remains to be

Table 11.1 The potential multifaceted effects of COVID-19

Area of concern	Immediate impact	Immediate effect on sustainability			Possible medium- to long-term effects
		Ecological	Economic	Social	
Mass transit	Pronounced reduction in use and shift to alternative modes of transport	−	−	−	Slow recovery
Automobile use	Overall reduced use	+	−		Probable recovery of use post-COVID
Air travel	Reduced use	+	−		Probable recovery post-COVID for pleasure, but less so for business with increase in video conferencing and virtual meetings
Retail trade	Reduced employment and bankruptcies	+	−	−	Slow and partial recovery of in-person shopping in light of replacement by e-commerce (e.g. online shopping) and mega-retailers like Amazon
Employment	Down, especially among women and minorities; increased stress and health risks for essential workers		−	−	Slow recovery, although some jobs are gone forever and certain groups remain at disadvantage
Trade and supply chains	Disrupted	+	−		Potential disruption in manufacturing due to delays in sourcing parts and materials; increase in domestic sourcing
Creative arts – theaters, movies, concerts, museums, art galleries	Reduced attendance and bankruptcies		−	−	Some will not survive or recover as digital access increases

Table 11.1 (Continued)

Area of concern	Immediate impact	Immediate effect on sustainability			Possible medium- to long-term effects
		Ecological	Economic	Social	
Social gatherings – weddings, funerals, parties	Smaller and fewer in number		−	−	Eventual recovery
Sporting events	Fewer events and smaller in-person events		−	−	Eventual recovery
Religious gatherings	Fewer events and smaller in-person events			−	Eventual recovery
Outdoor recreation sector	Restricted to local activities and some bankruptcies, lower stress on outdoor facilities	+	−	−	Full recovery but may be delayed; potential overuse of local areas and resources
Educational sector	Reduced number and size of in-person classes; fewer teaching opportunities; some institutions encounter significant fiscal shortfalls		−	−	Probable return to full attendance despite parallel online learning but lost opportunities with potential lifelong effects for affected cohorts
Fossil fuel use	Reduced	+	+/−		May not achieve previous levels because of changing competitive environment for alternative fuels leading to changing energy industry structure, but atmospheric levels of CO_2 will continue to rise for some time even with severe cutbacks in fossil fuel use
Greenhouse gases	Reduced	+	+		May recover if return to business as usual
Air pollution	Reduced	+	+		May recover if return to business as usual
Ambient noise	Reduced	+			May recover if return to business as usual
Restaurants and cafes	Low patronage and bankruptcies		−	−	Many will be permanently out of business
Mental health	Increased levels of stress, anxiety and depression and worsening of some personality disorders		−	−	Long road to recovery, increased resource needs

(Continued)

Table 11.1 (Continued)

Area of concern	Immediate impact	Immediate effect on sustainability			Possible medium- to long-term effects
		Ecological	Economic	Social	
General health	Other illnesses receive less attention; fewer inoculations, postponed surgeries, premature deaths		−	−	Only partial recovery for those affected and possible long-term negative effects on personal and public health
Family relationships	Potential for increased family bonding but also potential for increased spousal and child abuse			+/−	Permanent benefits as well as damage
Urban structure	Less traffic and more people seek suburban and exurban space and isolation	+/−	+/−	+/−	Loss of inhabitants and working population may be difficult to reverse but potential increase in liveability through urban redesign; lower conurban density may lead to greater infrastructure requirements; possible revitalization of rural areas
Work environment	Increased work at home but less social contact, less commuting and increased office space vacancies; greater level of job satisfaction and efficiency	+	+/−	−	May represent a permanent change accompanied by digital communication
Tourism and ecotourism	Reduced tourism accompanied by major fiscal impacts on airlines, charter buses, cruise companies, travel agents and tour groups and the ecotourism sector	+/−	−	−	Less stress on many local environments but loss of jobs for locals and fewer funds for conservation and ecological protection
Personal and household finances	Increased levels of poverty, loss of homes and poorer diet		−	−	Long-term detrimental personal financial consequences and more limited future opportunities
Health-care sector	Increasing stress on limited resources, with greater need for vaccines, public health education and resources to overcome backlog in diagnostic and surgical procedures		−	−	Possible future employment opportunities and remuneration due to increased funding of public health, but possible long-term system recovery

learned as the pandemic plays out. Fortunately, at this point, it appears that the virus may be facing eventual control through the initiation of rules on social distancing, mask wearing, personal sanitation measures in the form of hand washing, avoidance of large social gatherings and the development of vaccines at unprecedented speed. Foremost among the responses of the medical community has been a series of scientific breakthroughs which have led to the development of non-traditional treatments such as messenger RNA (mRNA) vaccines to complement more traditional vaccines based on viral DNA (*Science* December 16, 2020a). These new vaccine types may hold the promise of a rapid and effective medical response to new virus variants which evolve from a continuous process of mutation.

Table 11.1 is constructed as follows: column 1 identifies the affected sector, column 2 describes the immediate impact of the virus, column 3 attempts to assess its effect on the three components of sustainability and column 4 speculates on the possible medium- to long-term effects in each area.

As stated prior, this table is a work in progress and must await the continuing development of events and consequences. It is necessarily speculative, but certain general observations can be made at this point. First, the foremost question is whether human society – involving government, business and individuals – will seize this opportunity to create new economic, political and social structures more consistent with the goal of achieving global sustainability. This process will entail a complex mix of policies, instruments and technologies, many of which already exist, but some that do not. (See Chapter 12.) There is considerable inertia in all these areas, and the achievement of this goal is by no means certain.

Second, and equally important, is the strong possibility that pandemics will be a reoccurring feature of our global society (Settele et al. 2020; UNEP 2020; The Guardian 2020a; 2020b, 2020c, 2020d; Snowden 2020). A scientific consensus is emerging that several fundamental changes at the global level are possible drivers of this, including continued increases in population and urbanization, increased wealth and its concomitant need for great material inputs, intensification of animal husbandry in the developing world (e.g. *Science* June 29, 2020b) as well as factory farming in the developed world (e.g. Pew Commission on Industrial Farm Animal Production 2008; Munnink et al. 2020) and increased interaction of humans with currently remote or undeveloped natural environment, which exposes the population to a wide range of localized and relatively dormant viruses through the process of economic development. While the current rapid global transportation networks increase the speed and capacity for dispersion of disease, this is merely a modern manifestation of the historical role of commerce and trade in the spread of diseases (Harrison 2012). Several candidates of such emerging viruses include, inter alia, Ebola, SARS, MERS, Zika, chikungunya, Avian influenza, Nipah, dengue and Marburg, but the potential reservoir of latent or dormant viruses which could pose a significant threat to human health may number in the hundreds or more (Watsa and WDSFG 2020; see also Walters 2003; Quammen 2012).

Over the past half century, the developed world has been lulled into a sense of security through the widespread adoption of certain critical public health measures such as the provision of clean water and the separation of sanitary and drinking water sources and their disposal. Adding to this complacency has been a reliance on antibiotics to cure many bacterial diseases once considered fatal. This optimistic view is being challenged by the widescale development of antibiotic resistance propelled largely by overuse and misuse among both the human population and the agricultural sector (US HHS 2010; Davis et al.

2011 and 2015; Neyra et al. 2012; Pereira et al. 2014; Tang et al. 2017; Hall et al. 2018; OIE-WOAH 2018; Who 2020). Despite the widespread toll of COVID-19, some epidemiologists and virologists feel that future rates of mortality could be significantly higher with localized or as yet undiscovered emerging viruses (Snowden 2020). As Snowden (2020, p. 7) states:

> Many of the central features of a global modern society continue to render the world acutely vulnerable to the challenge of pandemic disease. The experience of SARS and Ebola – the two major "dress rehearsal" of the new century – serve as a sobering reminder that our public health and biomedicine defences are porous. Prominent features of modernity – population growth, climate change, rapid means of transportation, the proliferation of megacities, with inadequate urban infrastructure, warfare, persistent poverty, and widening social inequalities – maintain the risk.

The one note of optimism in this regard is that the optimal strategy for a successful virus is to maximize the opportunity for reproduction, transmission and ultimate survival. As a general principle, viruses which are too lethal run the risk of killing their host before there is a chance to be transmitted to a new host (Christakis 2020). On balance, this provides only modest solace for a civilization which faces large numbers of sick and dying people.

The prospect of future pandemics suggests that some of the changes that have occurred in response to the current pandemic may become a more common and prevalent characteristic of our societies. Not all these changes will necessarily be negative, particularly if they lead to a world of great sustainability. Within the business sector, we may experience what Joseph Schumpeter has termed "creative destruction," where forces that cause the demise of some companies and industries may open up opportunities for new and innovative models of business.

There has been, and may continue to be, significant opportunity costs associated with future pandemics and our responses to them. For example, the varied scarce resources devoted to combating and treating COVID-9 have led to reductions in progress against other diseases. These effects may be manifested in reduced inoculations, delayed surgeries, premature deaths and other public health measures with insufficient funding. Much of the developing world has been characterized by serious underfunding of public health measures and institutions, but a similar problem affects the developed world as well. For over three decades, Laurie Garrett (1994, 2000) has been warning of the chronic underfunding of public health, and we are suffering the consequence of this profound lapse in social and economic priorities. Harrison (2012, p. xvi) concludes:

> Public health measures are best understood as unstable compromises between disparate and sometimes conflicting interests. Governments have always balanced the prospect of infection against the losses that may result from curtailment of commerce.

This profound dilemma has been recognized globally today in the difficult political, social and economic decisions around lockdowns and curfews intended to slow the spread of COVID-19. COVID-19 has been called an "SOS signal for the human enterprise," (*Guardian* 2020e), and unless we abandon a business-as-usual model, the continued acceleration of climate change will facilitate the generation and spread of new pandemics (NPR March 24, 2020).

References

Alfani, Guido (2020) "The economic consequence of large-scale pandemics: Lessons from the history of plague in Europe and the Mediterranean," University of Warwick, April 27.

Cantor, Norman F. (2001) *In the Wake of the Plague: The Black Death and the World It Made*, New York: Simon & Schuster.

Cartwright, Frederick F. and Michael D. Biddiss (1972) *Disease and History*, New York: Dorset Press.

Christakis, Nicholas A. (2020) *Apollo's Arrow: The Profound and Enduring Impact of Coronavirus*, New York: Little, Brown Spark.

Cohen, Mark Nathan (1989) *Health and the Rise of Civilization*, New Haven, CT: Yale University Press.

Davis, Meghan F. et al. (2011) "An ecological perspective on U.S. industrial poultry production-the role of anthropogenic ecosystems on the emergence of drug-resistant bacteria from agricultural environments," *Current Opinion in Microbiology*, 14, pp. 244–250.

Davis, Gregg S. et al. (2015) "Intermingled *Klebsiella pneumoniae* populations between retail meats and human urinary tract infections," *Clinical Infectious Diseases*, September 15, Volume 61, pp. 892-899.

Egger, Dennis et al. (2021) "Falling living standards during the COVID-19 crisis: Quantitative evidence from nine developing countries," *Science*, February 5.

Garrett, Laurie (1994) *The Coming Plague: Newly Emerging Diseases in a World Out of Balance*, New York: Farrar, Straus and Giroux.

Garrett, Laurie (2000) *Betrayal of Trust: The Collapse of Global Public Health*, New York: Hyperion.

Guardian (2020a) "'Tip of the iceberg': Is our destruction of nature responsible for COVID-19?," March 18.

Guardian (2020b) "Halt destruction of nature or suffer even worse pandemics, say world's top scientists," April 27.

Guardian (2020c) "'Promiscuous treatment of nature' will lead to more pandemics: Scientists," May 7.

Guardian (2020d) "Pandemics result from destruction of nature, say UN and WHO," June 17.

Guardian (2020e) "Coronavirus is an 'SOS signal for the human enterprise'," June 5.

Hagemann, Hannah (2020) "The 1918 flu pandemic was brutal, killing more than 50 million people worldwide," *NPR*, April 2.

Hall, William et al. (2018) *Superbugs: An Arms Race against Bacteria*, Cambridge, MA: Harvard University Press.

Harper, Kyle (2017) "How climate change and disease helped the fall of Rome," Aeon, December 15.

Harrison, Mark (2012) *Contagion: How Commerce Has Spread Disease*, New Haven, CT: Yale University Press.

The Hill (2021) "WHO: COVID-19 deaths likely two to three times higher than reported," May 21.

Johnson, Niall P.A.S. and Juergen Mueller (2002) "Updating the accounts: Global mortality of the 1918–1920 'Spanish' influenza pandemic," *Bulletin of the History of Medicine*, 76, pp. 105–115.

McNeill, William H. (1998) *Plagues and People*, New York: Anchor Books.

Meacham, Jon (2020) "Pandemics of the past," *New York Times*, May 7.

Munnink, Bas B. Oude et al. (2020) "Transmission of SARS-Co-V-2 on mink farms between humans and mink and back to humans," *Science*, November 10.

National Public Radio (NPR) (2020) "How climate change increases our risk for pandemics," March 24.

New York Times (2021) "Just how big could India's true Covid toll be?" May 25.

Neyra, Ricardo Castillo et al. (2012) "Antimicrobial-resistant bacteria: An unrecognized work-related risk in food animal production," *Safety and Health at Work*, 3, pp. 85–91.

Nikiforuk, Andrew (1991) *The Fourth Horseman: A Short History of Plagues, Scourges and Emerging Viruses*, Toronto: Penguin.

Oldstone, Michael B.A. (2010) *Viruses, Plagues, & History*, Oxford: Oxford University Press.

Pereira, R.V. et al. (2014) "Effect of on-farm use of antimicrobial drugs on resistance in fecal Escherichia coli of preweaned dairy calves," *Journal of Dairy Science*, 97, pp. 7644–7654.

Pew Commission on Industrial Farm Animal Production (2008) *Putting Meat on the Table: Industrial Farm Animal Production in America*, Philadelphia, PA: Pew Charitable Trusts.

Quammen, David (2012) *Spillover: Animal Infections and the Next Human Pandemic*, New York: Norton.

Science (2020a) "Messenger RNA gave us a COVID-19 vaccine: Will it treat diseases, too?," December 16.

Science (2020b) "Swine flu strain with human pandemic potential increasingly found in pigs in China," June 29.

Settele, Josef et al. (2020) "IPBES guest article: COVID-10 stimulus measures must save lives, protect livelihoods, and safeguard nature to reduce the risk of future pandemics," April 27.

Shah, Sonia (2016) *Pandemic*, New York: Sara Crichton Books.

Skwarecki, Beth (2016) *Outbreak! 50 Tales of Epidemics That Terrorized the World*, Avon, MA: Adams Media.

Snowden, Frank M. (2020) *Epidemics and Society: From the Black Death to the Present*, New Haven, CT: Yale University Press.

Tang, Karen L. et al. (2017) "Restricting the use of antibiotics in food-producing animals and its associations with antibiotic resistance in food-producing animals and human beings: A systematic review and meta-analysis," November.

United Nations Environment Programme (UNEP) et al. (2020) *Preventing the Next Pandemic: Zoonotic Disease and How to Break the Chain of Transmission*, Nairobi: UNEP.

US Congressional Budget Office (CBO) (2020) "Re: Comparison of CBO's May 2020 interim projections of gross domestic product and its January 2020 baseline projections," Letter to the Honorable Charles E. Schumer.

US Department of Health and Human Services (US HHS), Food and Drug Administration and Center for Veterinary Medicine (2010) *The Judicious Use of Medically Important Antimicrobial Drugs in Food-Producing Animals*, June 28.

Walters, Mark Jerome (2003) *Six Modern Plagues and How We Are Causing Them*, Washington, DC: Island Press.

Watsa, Mrinalini and Wildlife Disease Surveillance Focus Group (WDSFG) (2020) "Rigorous wildlife disease surveillance," *Science*, July 10.

Winegard, Timothy C. (2019) *The Mosquito. A Human History of Our Deadliest Predator*, Toronto: Allen Lane.

World Bank (2020a) Brief, Understanding Poverty/Topics/Poverty, June 8.

World Bank (2020b) *Reversal of Fortune: Poverty and Share Prosperity*, Washington, DC: World Bank.

World Health Organization (WHO) (2020) "Antibiotic resistance: Key facts," July 31.

World Health Organization *Coronavirus (COVID-19) Dashboard* (accessed May 25, 2021).

World Organization for Animal Health (OIE) (2018) "Annual report on antimicrobial agents intended for use in animals: 3rd report."

World Trade Organization (WTO) (2020) "WTO goods barometer flashes red as COVID-19 disrupts world trade," May 20.

12 The path forward

In light of the existential threat posed by climate change, a multitude of economic, political and technological responses have been generated by governments, corporations and non-governmental organizations under the rubric of *mitigation* and *adaptation*. In essence, the former represents addressing the causes of the problem rather than dealing with its effects while the latter addresses the effect but not the cause of the problem. In fact, the distinction between these two approaches is not always clear cut, and several actions might fall under either of these rubrics (WRI 2020). Figure 12.1 summarizes the diverse range of supply- and demand-side approaches to the reduction of greenhouse gases. (See also IPCC 1996; Pacala and Socolow 2004, 2006.)

Economic instruments provide a powerful weapon in the form of market forces in the attempt to first achieve net zero (i.e. releasing no more carbon than is removed from the atmosphere by natural or man-made activity) and ultimately to achieve de facto decarbonization of the economy. But such instruments cannot operate in isolation. What is required is a radical transformation in the organization of production and consumption in the modern industrial economy. Several related proposals attempt to conceptualize this goal. Among the first was the work of the late Ray Anderson, CEO of Interface Carpets, one of the globe's leading corporations in the goal to achieve sustainability in the business sector. His conceptualization of the prototypical sustainable corporation of the future is presented in Figure 12.2 and entails several key elements: zero waste; benign emissions; renewable energy; closed loop recycling; resource efficient transportation; a "sensitivity hookup" which includes service to the community and closer relations with employees, suppliers and customers; and a redesign of commerce itself which entails the acceptance of entirely new notions of economics, especially prices that reflect full costs. It means shifting emphasis from simply selling products to providing services and, thus, a commitment to downstream distribution, installation, maintenance and recycling. These are all aimed at forming cradle-to-cradle relationships with customers and suppliers – relationships based on delivering the services their products provide in lieu of the products themselves (Anderson 2007).

A similar approach has been generated by McDonough and Braungart, who proposed what they call the "Next Industrial Revolution" (1998, 2002). They have proposed a transformation away from our current linear, once-through "cradle-to-grave" production system, which is profoundly inefficient and generates massive amounts of waste. The fundamental thrust of the innovation proposed by McDonough and Braungart is to redesign our production systems so they mimic nature where there is no waste per se, where virtually all byproducts of natural production – with the exception of energy – are recycled

DOI: 10.4324/9781003170730-12

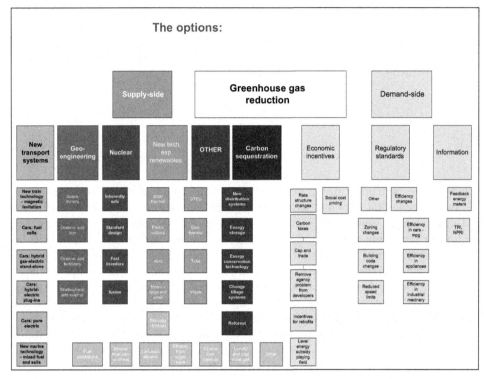

Figure 12.1 Supply- and demand-side approaches to reducing GHGs

into nutrients for the production of other organisms. The industrial challenge is to alter the design process of modern industrial products so their waste products can be recycled into two streams: what the authors call "biological nutrients" and "technical nutrients." There is a key distinction between these two waste streams: the first can re-enter the ecosystem without synthetic or toxic components and are thus able to be recycled without altering or contaminating natural cycles; in contrast, the second are recycled in closed loop systems with the production process so that no toxics are released into the environment. This is the essence of the "cradle-to-cradle" system.

The essence of what Anderson and McDonough and Braungart proposed has been incorporated in to the modern movement toward a *circular economy*, championed by the Ellen MacArthur Foundation (n.d.). According to Stahel (2016, p. 435):

A "circular economy" would turn goods that are at the end of their service life into resources for others, closing loops in industrial ecosystems and minimizing waste. It would change economic logic because it replaces production with sufficiency: reuse what you can, recycle what cannot be reused, repair what is broken, remanufacture what cannot be repaired. A study of seven European nations found that a shift to a circular economy would reduce each nation's greenhouse gas emissions by up to 70% and grow its workforce by about 4%! – the ultimate low-carbon economy.

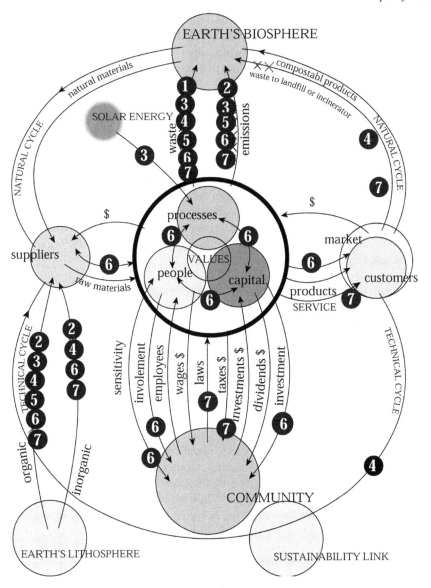

LINK #	DESCRIPTION
1	Zero waste
2	Benign emissions
3	Renewable energy
4	Closing the loop
5	Resource-efficient transportation
6	Sensitivity hookup-service to community, closer relations among stakeholders
7	Redesign of commerce itself

Figure 12.2 Anderson's conceptualization of the archetypal sustainable corporation

Source: Reproduced with permission of the author.

According to the Ellen MacArthur Foundation (n.d.), a number of factors indicate that the traditional linear model of production (i.e. "cradle-to-grave") is being challenged: economic losses and structural waste, price risks, supply risk, natural systems degradation, regulatory trends, advances in technology, acceptance of alternative business models and urbanization.

But despite the emerging recognition of this imperative by governments and many corporations, a recent report (Circle Economy 2018, p. 11) has found that the world economy is only 9.1% circular. A major reason for this shortfall is resource extraction, which has increased 12-fold between 1900 and 2015. According to Circle Economy:

> Increased and accelerated material use is to a large extent driven by rising prosperity levels globally. Whist elevating people out of poverty is a desirable, even essential outcome, the associated material use is not. The circular economy has a key role to play in decoupling growth from material extraction, thereby creating the conditions for sustainable development to deliver more prosperity for a larger population, but with diminishing use of primary resources.

As the advantages of economic instruments were reviewed earlier in this book, and the corporate strategic response is the subject of a companion volume (Nemetz 2022a), this chapter briefly summarizes the issues relating to the costs and risks of four major supply-side responses: nuclear power, geoengineering, carbon capture and storage and renewable energy. (More detailed analysis is provided in Nemetz 2022b) A short note is also provided on the unique challenges posed by climate change to global food supplies.

Nuclear power

No form of energy provision elicits such strong emotions as nuclear power. The industry is established in at least 30 countries with 443 operating reactors as of the end of 2019; 54 rectors are currently under construction, and another 78 are planned (IAEA 2020). Nuclear power is considered by some as the only feasible means of meeting future energy demand without generating greenhouse gases. While the *operation* of nuclear reactors generates no carbon dioxide, an assessment of nuclear power's total contribution to climate change requires the measurement of carbon dioxide production from the construction and operation of all facilities and equipment used in the nuclear fuel cycle. In fact, only this type of comprehensive systems analysis will reveal the differences among all alternative energy sources, be they nuclear, fossil or renewable.

Emotions run strong on both sides of this debate, and it is noteworthy that the environmental movement is split, with some environmental non-governmental organizations (ENGOs) now suggesting that nuclear power may be an acceptable transition source of power while other longer-term solutions are identified and implemented. Nuclear power accounted for about 10% of total global electricity production in 2020 (WNA 2020), but the importance of nuclear power in a nation's overall power production varies markedly by country. While nuclear power contributes 20.2% of all US electricity production, it represents 76.2% and 75.2% of Lithuania's and France's total electricity output respectively.

The United States opened its first commercial reactor in 1957, following closely on the heels of the United Kingdom. The first years of the new nuclear power era were filled with optimism, as characterized by the remark of Lewis Strauss, then chairman of the US Atomic Energy Commission, that electricity from nuclear reactors would be "too cheap to meter" (Strauss 1954). The construction of nuclear reactors in the United States largely came to a halt with the last commercial reactor to go critical in 1997. The reasons are multifaceted and complex and, in many respects, represent the challenges facing the growth or even survival of the industry today. In essence, the critical issue is one of risk, and these risks include: reactor design, operation safety and technological, security, environmental, waste disposal and financial factors. Of all these issues, one of the most pressing risks which has influenced the development of nuclear power, particularly in the United States, has been financial.

Several factors, in particular, have been cited as reasons for the cessation of most nuclear power construction in the United States. First is what is termed NIMBY, or the "not in my backyard" phenomenon, where local citizens object to the placement of reactors in or near their neighborhoods, slowing down the process of regulatory approval. Even more important has been the escalation of costs associated with the construction of the reactors themselves. As safety standards have become stricter, builders face increasing costs. A major part of this problem is that each reactor is essentially unique; there has been no single template for reactor construction in the United States. This makes the entire process, from initial design to final completion, much more costly. One remedy for this problem is to adopt the French system, where a standardized design is used throughout the country, thereby significantly reducing the time and cost of construction. This approach is characterized by a trade-off between efficiency and resilience. The downside of a uniform design and lack of diversity is that if an unexpected and serious problem is found in one reactor, it may affect all, thereby transforming localized risk into *systemic risk*, with all its attendant cost consequences.

The issue of the cost of nuclear power in comparison with other power sources is controversial due to several technology-specific issues which affect nuclear power. First, the use of market prices may distort the comparison of alternative electricity production technologies. The nuclear industry has been the recipient of significant subsidies, tilting the playing field, including the establishment of a ceiling on liability established by the US Price-Anderson Nuclear Industries Indemnity Act of 1957, which caps the level of private sector liability from an accident at $12.6 billion (US NRC n.d.). Sovacool (2011) has estimated the combined property and health cost of 105 nuclear accidents from 1952 to 2011 at $176.9 billion. The federal government has also provided loan guarantees, funds for reactor decommissioning and experimental waste storage facilities. In addition to these de facto subsidies, the cost of the initial development of modern PWR reactors was absorbed by military expenditures associated with the development of ship-based, nuclear propulsion systems. Where nuclear accidents have occurred, such as Fukushima, it is estimated that the decommissioning process could take 40 years or more (*New York Times* December 21, 2011). This entails both long-term disposal of highly radioactive material and short- to medium-term challenges of dealing with such things as large quantities of water used to cool the melted reactors (BBC September 10, 2019). A similar litany of decommissioning challenges for Chernobyl could take as long or longer.

In one half-serious, half-tongue-in-cheek comment about the financial problems facing the industry, Koplow (2011, p. 1) has observed:

> Subsidies to the nuclear fuel cycle have often exceeded the value of the power produced. This means that buying power on the open market and giving it away for free would have been less costly than subsidizing the construction and operation of nuclear power plants. Subsidies to new reactors are on a similar path.

In conclusion, a joint declaration by eight European non-nuclear countries on May 25, 2011 (Austria et al. 2011, p. 1) concluded that "the risks of nuclear power outweigh any potential benefit [and] . . . nuclear power is not compatible with the concept of sustainable development and . . . does not provide a viable option to combat climate change." On balance, the summation of all the enumerated costs and risks associated with nuclear power represents a serious challenge to proposals to adopt atomic energy as a bridge to a sustainable energy future.

Geoengineering

The concept of geoengineering encompasses a range of major interventions in the global ecosystem founded on the assumption that increasing GHG production is a given and cannot be reduced significantly. There are two basic variants of this technology: (1) carbon dioxide removal (CDR) from the atmosphere and (2) solar radiation management (SRM), which entails reflecting solar radiation back into space. This relatively new area of engineering has come under intense scrutiny over the last decade, with a broad diversity of scientific assessments ranging from resigned acceptance through counseling caution to severe criticism (Crutzen 2006; Kunzig 2008; Dean 2008; Royal Society of the United Kingdom 2009; Robock 2008; *Scientific American* 2008; Hegerl and Soloman 2009; Blackstock et al. 2009; Keith 2010; Fleming 2010; Kintisch 2010; Parkinson 2010; Pielke 2010; US GAO 2011; Hamilton 2013; Keller et al. 2014; Cusack et al. 2014; *Earth's Future* 2016; Trisos et al. 2018; Proctor et al. 2018; Irvine et al. 2019). The nature of the scientific criticism rests on four critical concerns: first, there is a fundamental uncertainty about the effectiveness of these techniques; second, if some of these techniques work, they would have to be continued for the indefinite future, for failure to do so would lead to a potentially catastrophic surge in greenhouse gases; third, many of these technological solutions would fail to address, or would contribute to, equally serious problems such as the acidification of the world's oceans (UNEP 2010); and fourth, most of these technologies entail unacceptable levels of risk since our knowledge of the complex functioning of ecosystems remains seriously incomplete. Table 12.1 summarizes some of the most prominent of the recent proposals and their inherent risks. By proposing to conduct experiments on grand scale which impacts the entire global ecosystem, humankind is running the risk of fat tail (Weitzman 2009) or zero-infinity events (i.e. possibly low-probability events with massive consequences). With only one earth, a failed experiment of this magnitude could be disastrous. As such, it may be safer to consider a technology that is a version of something that already exists, such as carbon capture and storage.

Carbon capture and storage

One potential technology that has received a great deal of international attention is carbon capture and storage (CCS), also referred to as CCUS (carbon capture, utilization and storage) (IPCC 2005). There are two general approaches: recovery of CO_2 from flue gases or directly from the atmosphere. Several flue-gas recovery projects are currently in operation worldwide, associated with power plants and fertilizer and steel production, as well as oil sands and biofuel (Carbonbrief 2014; Carbon Capture & Storage Association n.d.). In the energy sector, the carbon dioxide is generally injected into underground fossil fuel reservoirs to promote recovery of oil and natural gas. Some research has suggested, however, that this practice is, in fact, net CO_2 additive (Sekera and Lichtenberger

Table 12.1 Geoengineering and its risks

Solar radiation management (SRM)	Risks
Injecting sulfate aerosols into the stratosphere	Potentially large hydrological effects, including, in extremis, megadroughts. Can also lead to reduced precipitation, soil moisture, and river flow at regional levels. Can lead to accelerated destruction of the ozone cycle. Can alter the carbon cycle. Could shift atmospheric optical properties from blue toward whitish. Would attenuate little of global agricultural danger from climate change. Could make oceans more acidic. Would allow atmospheric GHG concentrations to continue increasing.
Cloud brightening at sea	Potentially large regional changes in precipitation, evaporation and runoff.
Sea-based injection of sea water aerosol into the atmosphere	Some effects could be similar to the first two proposals.
Giant reflectors in orbit	Would require constant monitoring and maintenance, depending on the number and size of the reflectors. Depending on the size, misalignment could have large unanticipated consequences, including unknown effects on ocean currents, temperature, precipitation and wind.
Cloud seeding	Similar effects to cloud brightening at sea.
General risks for SRM	No reduction in CO_2 production, thereby leading to continued acidification of the entire ocean biological chain. This would threaten sea life and oxygen production. Less insolation for photosynthesis and solar energy production. Continual upkeep required to forestall sudden cessation, which could lead to rapid climate warming in a short period of time. Must be maintained indefinitely. No experimental proof of concept.

Carbon dioxide removal (CDR)	Risks
Iron fertilization of the ocean	Could potentially disrupt the ocean food web and biogeochemical cycles. Could lead to anoxic conditions in large regions of the ocean, leading to methane production. Could potentially lead to increased acidification of deep ocean.
Pumping CO_2 into subsea geological formations	Any loss of CO_2 from such formations would accelerate ocean acidification, leading to potentially catastrophic consequences for both marine and land-based life.
Pumping CO_2 into underground geological formations (CCS)	See discussion of carbon capture and storage (CCS) in text.
Capturing CO_2 from the air and subsequent sequestration	Likely to be much less efficient and more expensive that CO_2 capture from concentrated point sources. Faces many of the same issues as CCS.
Afforestation/reforestation	Would require a massive reversal in current accelerating trends in deforestation, especially in the developing world. Potential loss of agricultural land.
Irrigation of desert regions to promote vegetative growth	Significant new requirements for scarce water resources. An increase in biological productivity in desert regions could have negative effects on productivity elsewhere because of induced changes in atmospheric circulation and precipitation and temperature patterns.
Converting roofs and pavements to a light, reflective color	Would have to be of an extraordinarily large scale, entailing massive costs and logistical issues.
Genetic crop modification	Potentially unanticipated effects on food production.

(2020). In other industrial sectors, the carbon is captured at the point of emission and then injected into the earth, where the goal is to isolate the gas indefinitely. Dowell et al. (2017, p. 243) argue that carbon utilization in industries outside the oil and gas industry is a "costly distraction, financially and politically, from the real task of mitigation," and "it is highly improbable the chemical conversion of CO_2 will account for more than 1% of the mitigation challenge."

Several critical criteria must be met before flue-gas recovery can be considered a viable solution at the global level. First, the technology would only be useful for large single-point emission sources and inappropriate for distributed or fugitive sources. Second, there must be reasonably proximate favorable geological formations for carbon dioxide injection. Third, the costs must be a relatively small proportion of the total cost of energy production. And, finally, there must be some assurance that the geological formations designed to contain the injected CO_2 are stable and able to hold the gas indefinitely.

One report (Thomson 2009) concluded that "by one estimate the United States would have to construct 300,000 injection wells at a cost of $3 trillion by 2030 just to keep emissions at 2005 levels." Smil (2010) has calculated that governments will have to construct CO_2 infrastructure about twice the size of the world's crude oil industry just to bury 25% of the world's emissions. These scale-up issues pose among the most imposing challenges to this technology even if other scientific questions were to be resolved satisfactorily.

A fundamental uncertainty remains about the ultimate effectiveness and safety of such a system. It is not known with any certainty how long the CO_2 would stay underground; if it were to escape, the consequence could be an environmental crisis of potentially greater magnitude than the original problem. This type of risk is an archetypal example of revenge theory. A US EPA study (2008) has stressed the multitude of scientific uncertainties associated with CCS, focusing on the vulnerability of the geological system to unanticipated migration, leakage, undesirable pressure changes and the possible negative consequences of system failure on human, plant and animal life.

While research continues into the scientific and economic feasibility of this technology, fewer than two dozen commercial-scale facilities are in operation, and several high-profile projects in the United States, Britain and Canada have been cancelled in the last decade (New Scientist 2011; Globe and Mail 2012; The Guardian 2011; *New York Times* 2011a, 2011b, 2011c, 2012a, 2012b). While this technology may prove viable in the future, its recent track record and current level of uncertainty suggest that any corporate or governmental plans to rely extensively on this technology for carbon dioxide control entail an unacceptable risk (Kirchsteiger 2008; Wilday et al. 2011; Rochon et al. 2008; Smil 2010). A report from the National Academy of Sciences (2019, p. 4) cautions:

> Negative emissions technologies are best viewed as a component of the mitigation portfolio, rather than a way to decrease atmospheric concentrations of carbon dioxide only after anthropogenic emissions have been eliminated. . . . The committee recognizes that there is a possibility that large negative emissions in the future could result in a moral hazard, by reducing humanity's will to cut emissions in the near term. Reducing emissions is vital to addressing the climate problem.

This view is echoed by Anderson and Peters (2016, p. 183), who conclude that reliance on negative-emission concepts locks in humankind's carbon addiction: "negative-emission technologies are not an insurance policy, but rather an unjust and high-stakes gamble."

In light of the economic and technological challenges facing the direct recovery of CO_2 from combustion sources, a second major approach has been proposed: the direct removal of carbon dioxide from the atmosphere. Broecker and Kunzig (2008, p. 211) conclude that "we cannot solve the CO_2 problem without tacking small and mobile sources, right now Lackner and Wright's invention [scrubbing the gas directly from the air] offers the only hope." (See The Earth Institute, Columbia University n.d.) A major step toward the achievement of viable direct air capture and storage (DACS) (Mulligan et al. 2018) has been achieved by several demonstration projects (BBC News June 7, 2018, April 3, 2019; Keith et al. 2018). However, this potential solution must still overcome some of the fundamental challenges which face flue-gas recovery: scale-up, number of global units required to achieve significant levels of atmospheric CO_2 reduction, energy inputs required, cost and the issue of carbon dioxide disposition.

Hansen et al. (2017, pp. 577–578) have concluded:

> Continued high fossil fuel emissions today place a burden on young people to undertake massive technological CO_2 extraction if they are to limit climate change and its consequences. Proposed methods of extraction such as bioenergy with carbon capture and storage (BECCS) or air capture of CO_2 have minimal estimated costs of USD 89–535 trillion this century and also have large risks and uncertain feasibility. Continued high fossil fuel emissions unarguably sentences young people to either a massive, implausible cleanup or growing deleterious climate impacts or both.

In contrast to these high-tech solutions with their attendant risks, Griscom et al. (2017) have provided a comprehensive analysis of 20 "natural climate solutions" (NCS) which increase carbon storage and/or avoid greenhouse gas emissions through conservation, restoration and improved management practices across global forests, wetlands, grasslands and agricultural lands. According to the authors (p. 11645):

> We show that NCS can provide over one-third of the cost-effective climate mitigation needed between now and 2030 to stabilize warming to below 2 °C. Alongside aggressive fossil fuel emissions reductions, NCS offer a powerful set of options for nations to deliver on the Paris Climate Agreement while improving soil productivity, cleaning our air and water, and maintaining biodiversity.

Renewable energy sources

While nuclear power is considered by many as a transition fuel away from reliance on fossil fuels, it is generally agreed that the ultimate goal must be to convert global energy use to renewable sources. The principal advantage of such fuels is their zero net operational contribution to the global GHG burden. Included in the list of renewables are such diverse sources as hydropower, solar thermal, solar photovoltaic, geothermal, wind, biogas, solid and liquid biomass, tidal, wave power, ocean thermal gradients and municipal and industrial waste. Virtually all these renewable sources, with the exception of tidal power and geothermal energy, are directly or indirectly the result of solar insolation. While some renewable technologies are under continued development, others, such as wind, falling water and biomass, have been in use for centuries.

Global renewable installed energy capacity has grown dramatically from 1,136 GW in 2009 to 2,533 GW in 2019, with China accounting for 30% and the United States

second with 10% of total global capacity, according to the International Renewable
Energy Agency (IRENA 2020a, 2020b). Despite China's leading role in the production
of renewable energy, coal still accounted for 68.6% of China's primary energy production
in 2019 (China 2020). In 2018, two-thirds of new global electricity-generating capacity
was renewable (IEA 2019a, 2019b, 2019c), and in 2020, the 27 members of the European Union for the first time produced more electricity from renewables than fossil fuels
(Agora and Ember 2020). As of 2019, 11.41% of all global primary energy came from
renewables excluding traditional sources (Oxford University OWID 2020), and the World
Bank (WDI 2019) has reported that as of 2015, 22.85% of all electricity produced globally
came from renewables, including hydropower.

While the broad range of alternatives offers the prospect of making a major contribution to global energy supply in the mid to distant future, there are several critical issues
which affect their development and application: (1) short-term, on-demand availability;
(2) lack of efficient electricity storage media; (3) distance from markets and integration
into existing grids; (4) current per kW costs; (5) externalities of conventional energy
sources; (6) climatic feedback effects; and (7) scale-up time for a renewable energy economy. (A more detailed discussion of renewables is provided by Nemetz 2022b).

One of the longstanding criticisms of renewable power sources, especially from the
established fossil fuel and nuclear power sectors, has been the supposed cost disadvantage of renewables. One of the principal arguments against the expanded deployment of
renewables has been their costs compared to conventional energy sources such as coal,
oil, natural gas and nuclear. However, the cost of renewables has undergone a major shift
within the last decade. Most renewable technologies have been moving rapidly down the
learning curve and, with the benefit of extensive R&D and economies of scale, have been
able to realize substantial decreases in per unit cost of electricity (IRENA 2019). The
International Energy Agency (IEA 2018; see also IEA 2020 and IEA/NEA 2020) reports
that since 2010, costs of new solar photovoltaic power have come down by 70% and
wind by 25%. A report from IRENA in 2019 has found that onshore wind and solar PV
are now frequently less expensive than any fossil fuel option without financial assistance.
The International Renewable Energy Agency (2019) has provided the latest estimates
of global renewable electricity costs as of 2018 (Table 12.2), and Table 12.3 presents US
Energy Information Administration (US EIA 2019) estimates of levelized costs for new
renewable and conventional generation entering service in 2023 and 2040. The emerging cost competitiveness of low-carbon-generation technologies has been reaffirmed by

Table 12.2 Renewable electricity costs in 2018

	Global weighted-average cost of electricity	Cost of electricity: 5th and 95th percentiles	Change in the cost of electricity 2017–2018
Bioenergy	0.062	0.048–0.243	−14%
Geothermal	0.072	0.060–0.143	−1%
Hydro	0.047	0.030–0.136	−11%
Solar PV	0.085	0.058-.0.291	−13%
Concentrating solar power	0.185	0.109–0.272	−26%
Offshore wind	0.127	0.102–0.198	−1%
Onshore wind	0.056	0.044–0.100	−13%

Table 12.3 US EIA cost projections by energy source (2018$/kWh)

	2023	2040	% change
Dispatchable technologies			
Coal with 30% CCS	0.104	0.107	2.1
Coal with 90% CCS	0.099	0.097	−1.8
Conventional CC	0.046	0.055	18.8
Advanced CC	0.041	0.049	19.4
Advanced CC with CCS	0.068	0.074	9.3
Conventional CT	0.089	0.101	12.5
Advanced CT	0.078	0.086	10.0
Advanced nuclear	0.078	0.074	−5.2
Geothermal	0.041	0.041	−1.2
Biomass	0.092	0.085	−7.7
Non-dispatchable technologies			
Wind, onshore	0.056	0.051	−8.2
Wind, offshore	0.130	0.110	−15.3
Solar PV	0.060	0.053	−12.2
Solar thermal	0.157	0.138	−12.5
Hydroelectric	0.039	0.050	26.9

Key:

LCOE = levelized cost of electricity: the average revenue per unit of electricity generated that would be required to recover the costs of building and operating a generating plant during an assumed financial life and duty cycle

Duty cycle = the typical utilization or dispatch of a plant to serve base, intermediate or peak load; wind, solar or other intermittently available resources are not dispatched and do not necessarily follow a duty cycle based on load conditions

O&M = operations and maintenance

CCS = carbon capture and sequestration

CC = combined cycle (natural gas)

CT = combustion turbine

PV = photovoltaic

Dispatchable technologies = those able to vary output to follow demand

Non-dispatchable technologies = less flexible sources using intermittent resources to operate

Note: Total system LCOE including capital, fixed and variable O&M and transmission costs

a joint report of the International Energy Agency and the Nuclear Energy Agency in 2020. Research has also demonstrated the job-producing potential of a renewable energy economy (EcoWatch 2014; Georgeson and Maslin 2019).

Uninternalized externalities of conventional power sources

Systems theory informs us that renewable and conventional power sources are not competing on the same playing field. The critical issue is one of comparable total cost, and this implies a formal accounting of externalities as well as present and past

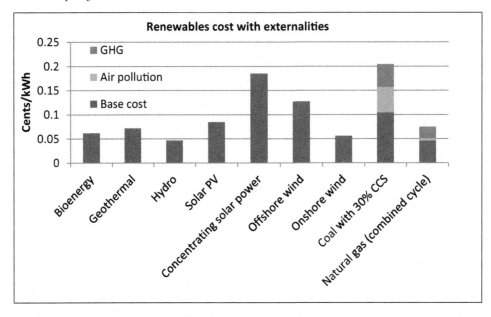

Figure 12.3 Cost of electricity generation with costed externalities

subsidies for each type of energy (Koplow and Dernbach 2001). Table 12.4 presents estimates of the cost of externalities for air pollution and climate change for 2005 and 2030 (NAS 2009; Delucchi and Jacobson 2011; see also Alberici et al. 2014). Figure 12.3 combines the data from Tables 12.3 and 12.4, after adjustment for inflation, to produce an estimate of costs of major electricity-producing systems with estimated externalities included.

In fact, Figure 12.3 is somewhat incomplete, as it suggests that GHG are only associated with fossil fuel–based energy systems. While renewable sources operate without producing carbon dioxide, the inputs into these systems are not GHG free. Systems analysis, which looks at the entire system from cradle to grave, is required to identify the total GHG emissions of any one system of producing energy. Life-cycle analysis is the foremost method of so doing (Nugent and Sovacool 2014). In 2004, the World Energy Council commissioned a LCA report to compare major energy systems. They concluded: "The objective of LCA is to describe and evaluate the overall environmental impacts of a certain action by analysing all stages of the entire process from raw materials supply, production, transport and energy generation to recycling and disposal stages" (WEC 2004, p. 3). This type of analysis can be conducted for a variety of pollutants, including SO_2, NOx, VOCs and particulates. Here we focus on their system-wide production of carbon dioxide. Figure 12.4 is derived from their analysis. It should be noted that the bulk of GHG emissions from fossil fuel plants is produced during their operation; in contrast, GHG emissions from renewables, including nuclear, originate in the pre-operation stages.

Table 12.4 Cost of externalities (cents/kWh in 2007)

Cents/kWh 2007	Air pollution 2005			Air pollution 2030	Climate change (2005/2030)		
	5th%	Mean	95th%	Mean	Low	Mid	High
Weighted by net generation							
Coal	0.19	3.2	12.0	1.7	1.0/1.6	3.0/4.8	10.0/16.0
Natural gas	0.001	0.16	0.55	0.13	0.5/0.8	1.5/2.4	5.0/8.0
Equally weighted							
Coal	0.53	4.4	13.2				
Natural gas	0.004	0.43	1.7				

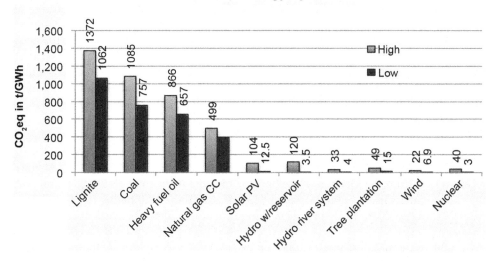

Figure 12.4 LCA of energy systems (CO_2 only)

In 2013, the International Monetary Fund published a report which estimated the implicit subsidies of the economic damage caused by fossil fuels, which totaled $800 billion in 2011. Another study from the University of Cambridge (Hope et al. 2015, p. 1) estimated the implicit climate subsidies and found they totaled $883 billion in 2012. They observed that "for all companies the implicit subsidy exceeds their post-tax profit (averaged over five years). For all pure coal companies, the implicit subsidy exceeds their total revenue." A more recent report by IRENA (2020b) suggests that as of 2017, the costs of unpriced externalities and the direct subsidies for fossil fuels equaled $3.1 trillion, although the IMF (2019) estimated a value as high as $5.2 trillion.

While there can be a significant margin of uncertainty concerning estimates of externalities, it should be apparent that market-based comparisons of per kWh cost can seriously misrepresent the relative costs of alternative electricity-generating sources. By way of example, a comprehensive full-cost accounting study of coal used for electricity production estimated the cost of externalities to be double or even triple the price of coal-fired power, with a range of 9.36 to 26.89 cents per kWh in 2008US$ (Epstein et al. 2011).

What market-based cost studies also omit is the distorting effect of historical and current subsidies for fossil fuels and nuclear power (Alberici et al. 2014). While many renewables currently receive government subsidies, they are not of the same order of magnitude as the direct and indirect grants, tax concessions, depletion allowances and other forms of de facto subsidies received by fossil fuels over the past decades. The case of nuclear power is another case in point, as this industry has profited from extensive historical co-research and development with military programs and the extraordinary limited liability provided by the US Price-Anderson Act of 1957. In addition to the aforementioned limit on total industry liability, the maximum liability limits for individual operators are between $400 and $500 million (US EIA 2007).

The fact that the nuclear industry has lobbied hard for this legislation and the insurance industry is unwilling to assume unlimited exposure suggests they take seriously the risk of a major catastrophe even if the probability is considered very low. An early report by the US Nuclear Regulatory Commission (1982), which estimated potential financial costs of a nuclear disaster by individual plants in the US, posited a worst-case scenario of $314 billion damages at the Indian Point 3 reactor in New York State. A subsequent study by NRDC (2011) estimated that the costs could range from $600 billion to $6 trillion.

It is not an easy task to measure the historical magnitude of such subsidies to fossil fuels and nuclear power, but several studies have tried to do so. (See Table 12.5.) The remarkable range of these estimates is the consequence of cost categories included or excluded from the calculations (Koplow and Dernbach 2001). One estimate of global subsidies for oil and gas production placed the value in excess of $650 billion (ODI 2013). A more recent report from the Overseas Development Institute (Gencsu et al. 2019) found that the G20 countries had increased their subsidies to coal from $17.2 billion to $47.3 billion from 2013/14 to 2016/17 despite their commitment to address the challenge of climate change.

In light of the uninternalized economic externalities associated with the nuclear fuel cycle and fossil fuel production, the superficial comparison of costs per kW or kWh becomes meaningless. Some forms of renewable energy are not only competitive at current market prices but have an even greater cost advantage when the comparison is cast – as it should be – in terms of total social cost.

Table 12.5 Estimates of subsidies

Commodity	Average estimated subsidy range
Oil (annual 1999$)	$562 million–$367 billion–$1.7 trillion
Coal (annual 1999$)	$438 million–$10.5 billion
Natural gas (annual 1999$)	$1.35 billion–$6.60 billion
Nuclear (cents/kWh)	0.74 (ongoing)–11.42 (new)

Source: Koplow and Dernbach (2001) and Koplow (2011)

A brief note on adaptation and global food supplies

With numerous efforts being undertaken by business and various levels of government to mitigate the causes and effects of climate change, increasing attention is being paid to adaptation. The latter focus is borne of the realization that even if all GHG emissions were to somehow cease tomorrow, the effects of climate change would continue to increase because of the residence time in the atmosphere of greenhouse gases already emitted. Two major reports from the United Nations Environment Programme have reported both an emission gap and an adaptation gap. The emission gap is defined as the difference between "where we are likely to be and where we need to be" (UNEP 2020a). The conclusion of the report is that we are not on track to bridge the gap and meet the maximum target of 1.5–2.0 degrees Celsius set by the IPCC but that the post-COVID-19 era may offer a one-time opportunity to address this problem. According to the report (p. xiv):

> Although 2020 emissions will be lower than in 2019 due to the COVID-19 crisis and associated responses, GHG concentrations in the atmosphere continue to rise, with the immediate reduction in emissions expected to have a negligible long-term impact on climate change. However, the unprecedented scale of COVID-19 economic recovery measures presents the opening for a low-carbon transition that creates the structural changes required for sustained emissions reductions. Seizing this opening will be critical to bridging the emissions gap.

The companion UN report devoted to the adaptation gap (UNEP 2020b) paints a somewhat more somber picture, concluding that while adaptation actions in the form of nature-based initiatives have been growing worldwide to address coastal hazards, intense precipitation, drought and rising temperature, there is very limited evidence of climate risk reduction. The report calls for the adoption of increased use of various financial instruments to enhance adaptation planning and implementation and limit climate damages, particularly in developing countries. They conclude that "despite an increase in finance available for adaptation, the adaptation finance gap is not closing." Inger Anderson, the executive director of UNEP, has been quoted as stating:

> We are not saying we can adapt our way out of climate change, but the impacts of failing to invest in adaption to climate change will be very severe, and it is the poorest in wealthy countries and the poorest in the world who will pay the highest price, and who are most exposed to these impacts.
>
> (*Guardian* January 14, 2021)

Up until fairly recently, little serious attention has been given to the vulnerability of our food supplies to climate change. Even if such vulnerability was acknowledged, a common refrain was that the sector could adapt to global warming. It is hypothesized here that such a faith is misplaced and that food supply is the Achilles' heel of adaptation. (See also Nemetz 2022b.) Despite emerging research on developing heat- and drought-resistant plants, there is little evidence to suggest that these efforts can blunt the projected increase in global temperatures in the next few decades. The threats are multifaceted and include: drought, heat, the direct effect of GHGs on plant nutritional content, flooding and storms.

For example, one recent scientific study (Pal and Eltahir 2016) has forecasted that given the current trajectory of global warming, the Persian Gulf region will be unable to support human habitation within this century due to predicted *wet-bulb* temperatures (i.e. combining *dry-bulb* readings temperatures, or conventional thermometer readings, and humidity) in excess of 35 degrees Celsius. At this temperature, the human body is incapable of maintaining a homeostatic temperature balance and faces death in a short period of time (Sherwood and Huber 2010). Recent dry-bulb temperatures in the Gulf region have already surpassed historical records with readings of 54 degrees Celsius – or 129.2 degrees Fahrenheit – during the summer of 2017 in the Iranian city of Ahvaz (*Independent* June 30, 2017).

A similar dire situation faces major agricultural and densely populated regions of South Asia and China, specifically around the Ganges and Indus River basins (Im et al. 2017) and the North China Plain (Kang and Eltahir 2018; see also Chen et al. 2018; Zhou et al. 2018; McKinsey Global Institute 2020a, 2020b).

The issue is not only high average temperatures; it is the occurrence of heat waves of short duration or sustained periods which can have devastating impacts on crops and human health. In statistical terms, this is the distinction between mean and variance, but, in this case, the increased variance of temperature under global warming is asymmetrical, with a much greater probability of extreme heat rather than cold (Bathiany et al. 2018, *New York Times* July 28, 2017; Coumou and Robinson 2013; Fisher and Knutti 2015).

Such events are not restricted to the developing world, however. Within the past few years, and particularly during the summer of 2017, southern Europe sustained an elevated rate of mortality due to excessive heat (Kew et al. 2018). A recent in-depth study has attempted to quantify the number of excess deaths in twenty developed and developing countries due to heat waves under various climate change scenarios (Guo et al. 2018). Their findings tend to support other recent observations that global warming has a disproportionality higher effect on the poorer regions of the world (*New York Times* March 12, 2018).

Some historical data have already provided evidence of the negative effect of extreme heat on crop yields. Lesk et al. (2016) examined data on weather and crop yields over the period 1964–2007 and found that droughts and extreme heat significantly reduced national cereal production by 9%–10%. Another study covering the period 1980 to 2008 (Lobell et al. 2011a) concluded that weather events contributed to a global maize and wheat production decline by 3.8% and 5.5% respectively. Battisti and Naylor (2009) reviewed the effects of severe heat in Europe during the summer of 2003 and reported that Italian maize yields dropped 36%. In addition, France experienced significant decreases in several commodities: maize and fodder (–30%), fruit (–25%) and wheat (–21%). These observations of past events have been complemented by the development of several models which attempt to predict future declines in the face of rising global temperatures. Liu et al. (2016) predict that an increase of 1 degree Celsius in global temperature will lead to declines in wheat yields of between 4.1% and 6.4%. Zhao et al. (2017) broaden their focus to include the four major crops which provide two-thirds of human caloric intake. Their results predict reductions in yields for each degree Celsius increase in *global mean temperatures* as follows: wheat 6.0%, rice 3.2%, maize 7.4% and soybeans 3.1%. Additional evidence on the negative effect of heat on crop yields has been provided by Schauberger et al. (2017) and Tack et al. (2017).

More detailed research has examined (1) crop yields on the basis of time of day and (2) assumptions of linearity in temperature-yield functions. Mohammed and Tarpley (2009, p. 999) observe:

Although the global increase in nighttime temperature is at a faster rate than daytime temperature and it is well-known that high temperatures are a major constraint to crop productivity especially when temperature extremes coincide with critical stages of plant development, most of the studies on crop growth and grain yield are based on daily mean air temperature, which assumes no difference in the influence of day versus night temperatures.

They cite the work of Peng et al. (2004), who found that a decline in rice yields could be attributed to increased nighttime temperature associated with global warming.

Of particular note is evidence to support the theory that ecological processes are frequently not linear. Lobell et al. (2011b) used historical data on African maize yields to demonstrate that the effect of heat on these yields was non-linear. These results are even more pronounced under drought conditions than under optimal rain-fed management. Schlenker and Roberts (2009) conducted a similar analysis of US corn, soybean and cotton yields and found that the resulting curvilinear function is concave to the x-axis whereby yields increase up to 29–32 degrees Celsius and then decline steeply above these levels. Their conclusions, based on scenario-based modeling results, are not encouraging as they conclude that "area-weighted average yields are predicted to decrease by 30–46% before the end of the century under the slowest warming scenario and decrease by 63–82% under the most rapid warming scenario."

Unfortunately, the significant negative direct effects of rising temperatures on crop yields are accompanied by at least one major indirect effect: insect predation. Deutsch et al. (2018) use a spatially explicit insect population metabolism model to estimate losses to rice, maize and wheat. Insect consumption of crops is driven by metabolic rates and population size, both functions of temperature. Projected global yield losses are estimated to increase by 10% to 25% per degree of global mean surface warming, with the highest losses expected in the grain-producing regions of the Northern Hemisphere. Riegler (2018) concludes that this pessimistic assessment may be an underestimate as many insect pests are vectors of plant pathogens, which could further increase crop losses due to global warming.

None of these findings are particularly encouraging in light of expected global population growth and increased incomes with their concomitant changes in taste toward more ecologically damaging foods. Principal among these is meat consumption, whose production relies heavily on grain as an input. Optimistic assessments that increasingly heat-stressed grain production could simple move further north toward a more benign environment are problematic for several reasons: first, the regions no longer hospitable for crop production will face increased economic hardships; second, as global temperatures continue to rise, geographic limits to further northern progression will be reached; and finally, not all soils at more northerly latitudes may be capable of supporting large-scale, intensive crop production. As Overpeck and Conde (2019, p. 807) observe, "absent climate change mitigation, adaptation strategies will in many cases become overwhelmed, leading to unacceptable costs to both human and natural systems."

The principal conclusion about the future of agriculture in the face of climate change is somber. There is mounting evidence, as detailed prior, to suggest that even if major changes in food production systems were undertaken to reduce the array of negative externalities and make these systems more sustainable, continuing releases of greenhouse gases and resulting global warming, if left unabated, would inevitably create a crisis which would seriously, if not irreparably, threaten global food supplies and the continued viability of modern civilization as we know it. These pessimistic conclusions have been reaffirmed by the recent report of the IPCC (2019), titled *Climate Change and Land*, that our current system of industrial agriculture is unsustainable. We have pursued a narrow vision of efficiency at the expense of resilience. But the challenge facing our agricultural system transcends the multitude of problems associated with the myriad of negative externalities. Intensified efforts to develop new hybrid strains of crops that are resistant to flood, drought, salinity and pest infestation will not alleviate the profound risk from increasing global temperatures. In fact, if the NASA projections of future temperatures prove to be correct, much of current agricultural production may not be possible. In extremis, our modern societies may regress to a social structure typical of the early post–agricultural revolution period. In these circumstances, we could return to a dystopian world where the majority of the population, possibly much fewer in number, devotes most of its time to eking out a bare subsistence from the land.

Conclusion

The earth appears headed toward significantly higher temperatures with all their potentially devastating consequences. No single technological solution has yet been demonstrated that can reverse or significantly slow this progression in the immediate future. Nothing less than an extraordinary coordinated effort by civil society, business and government can stem this tide. This will require overcoming the economic, political and social inertia that characterizes our modern society and achieving a profound change in patterns of both production and consumption at the global level using an integrated array of creative economic instruments, regulations, off-the-shelf technologies and the pursuit of new technologies contingent upon the application of the precautionary principle with the ultimate aim of decarbonization of our economic systems (McDonough and Braungart 1998, 2002; Pacala and Socolow 2004; Socolow 2011; Griscom et al. 2017; LSE 2018; Davis et al. 2018; Falk et al. 2019; International Monetary Fund 2019; World Bank 2019; Gaffney et al. 2019; Paul et al. 2019; Lempert et al. 2019; Quantis 2019). As the most recent IPCC report (2018, p. 17) concludes:

> Pathways limiting global warming to 1.5 °C with no or limited overshoot would require rapid and far-reaching transitions in energy, land, urban and infrastructure (including transport and buildings), and industrial systems (high confidence). These systems transitions are unprecedented in terms of scale, but not necessarily in terms of speed, and imply deep emissions reductions in all sectors, a wide portfolio of mitigation options and a significant upscaling of investments in those options.

Failing this unprecedented and ambitious undertaking, we are all in for an extremely rocky ride.

References

Agora Energiewende and Ember (2020) *The European Power Sector in 2020.*
Alberici, Sacha et al. (2014) *Subsides and Costs of EU Energy*. An interim report, European Commission.
Anderson, Kevin and Glen Peters (2016) "The trouble with negative emissions," *Science*, October 14.

Anderson, Ray (2007) "Mid-course correction: Toward a sustainable enterprise," in Peter N. Nemetz (ed.) *Sustainable Resource Management: Reality or Illusion?*, Chetenham: Edward Elgar, pp. 88–114.

Austria et al. (2011) Joint declaration issued in Vienna, May 25.

Bathiany, S. et al. (2018) "Abrupt climate in an oscillating world," *Scientific Reports*, March 22.

Battisti, David S. and Rosamond L. Naylor (2009) "Historical warnings of future food insecurity with unprecedented seasonal heat," *Science*, January 9.

BBC (2019) "Fukushima: Radioactive water may be dumped in Pacific," September 10.

BBC News (2018) "Key 'step forward' in cutting cost of removing CO2 from air," June 7.

BBC News (2019) "Climate change: 'Magic bullet' carbon solution takes big step," April 3.

Blackstock, J.J. et al. (2009) "Climate engineering responses to climate emergencies," *Novim*, July 29, Santa Barbara, CA. http://arxiv.org/pdf/0907.5140

Broecker, Wallace S. and Robert Kunzig (2008) *Fixing Climate,* New York: Hill and Wang.

Carbonbrief (2014) "Around the world in 22 carbon capture projects," October 7.

Carbon Capture & Storage Association (CCSA), "International CCS Projects" (n.d.) (accessed October 16, 2019).

Chen et al. (2018) "Anthropogenic warming has substantially increased the likelihood of July 2017-like heat waves over central Eastern China," *AMS*, December.

China Statistical Yearbook 2020.

Circle Economy (2018) *The Circularity Gap Report.*

Coady, David et al. (2019) "Global Fossil fuel subsidies remain large: an update based on country-level estimates," IMF Working Paper WP/19/89.

Coumou, Dim and Alexander Robinson (2013) "Historic and future increase in the global land area affected bimonthly heat extremes," *Environmental Research Letters*, 8(034018).

Crutzen, Paul (2006) "Albedo enhancement by stratospheric sulfur injections: A contribution to resolve a policy dilemma?," *Climate Change*, 77, pp. 211–219.

Cusack, Daniela F. (2014) "An interdisciplinary assessment of climate engineering strategies," *Frontiers in Ecology*, 12(5), pp. 280–287.

Davis, Steven J. et al. (2018) "Net-zero emissions energy systems," *Science*, June 29.

Dean, Cornelia (2008) "Handle with care," *New York Times*, August 11.

Delucchi, Mark A. and Mark Z. Jacobson (2011) "Providing all global energy with wind, water, and solar power, Part II: Reliability, system and transmission costs, and policies," *Energy Policy*, #39, pp. 1170–1190.

Deutsch, Curtis A. et al. (2018) "Increase in crop losses to insect pests in a warming climate," *Science*, August 31.

Dowell, Niall Mac et al. (2017) "The role of CO2 capture and utilization in mitigating climate change," *Nature Climate Change*, April.

Earth's Future (2016) "Crutzen +10: Reflecting upon 10 years of geoengineering research," Special Issue, May 16, updated February 2, 2018.

Ecowatch (2014) "Renewable energy 'creates more jobs than fossil fuels'," November 11.

Ellen MacArthur Foundation (n.d.) *Towards a Circular Economy: Business Rationale for an Accelerated Transition.*

Epstein, Paul R. et al. (2011) "Full cost accounting for the life cycle of coal," *Annals of the New York Academy of Sciences*, #1219, pp. 73–98.

Falk, Johan et al. (2019) Exponential Roadmap 1.5 Future Earth. Scaling 36 solutions to halve emissions by 2030.

Fisher, E.M. and R. Knutti (2015) "Anthropogenic contribution to global occurrence of heavy-precipitation and high-temperature extremes," *Nature Climate Change*, April 27.

Fleming, James Rodger (2010) *Fixing the Sky*, New York: Columbia University Press.

Gaffney, Owen et al. (2019) "Meeting the 1.5 C climate ambition: Moving from increment to exponential action," *UN Climate Action Summit*, New York.

Gencsu, Ipek et al. (2019) *G20 Coal Subsidies. Tracking Government Subsidies to a Fading Industry*, Washington DC: Overseas Development Institute (ODI), NRDC, IISD, Oil Change International.

Georgeson, Lucien and Mark Maslin (2019) "Estimating the scale of the US green economy within the global context," *Palgrave Communications*, 5, p. 121.

Globe and Mail (2012) "Alberta's carbon capture efforts set back," April 26.

Griscom, Bronson W. et al. (2017) "Natural climate solutions," *PNAS*, October 31.

Guardian (2011) "Longannet carbon capture project cancelled," October 19.

Guardian (2021) "Countries adapting too slowly to climate breakdown, UN warns," January 14.

Guo, Yuming et al. (2018) "Quantifying excess deaths related to heatwaves under climate change scenarios: A multicountry time series modelling study," *PLOS Medicine*, July 31.

Hamilton, Cline (2013) *Earthmasters: The Dawn of the Age of Climate Engineering*, New Haven, CT: Yale University Press.

Hansen, James et al. (2017) "Young people's burden: Requirement of negative CO2 emissions," *Earth System Dynamics*, 8, pp. 577–616.

Hegerl, Gabriele C. and Susan Soloman (2009) "Risks of climate engineering," *Science*, 325, August 21, pp. 955–956.

Hope, Chris et al. (2015) "Quantifying the implicit climate subsidy received by leading fossil fuel companies," University of Cambridge, Judge Business School, Working paper No. 02/2015.

Im, Eun-Soon et al. (2017) "Deadly heat waves projected in the densely populated agricultural regions of South Asia," *Science Advances*, August 2.

Independent (2017) "Temperatures in Iranian city of Ahvaz hit 129.2F (54C), near hottest on Earth in modern measurements," June 30.

Intergovernmental Panel on Climate Change (IPCC) (1996) "Technologies, policies and measures for mitigating climate change," IPCC Technical Paper I, November.

Intergovernmental Panel on Climate Change (IPCC) (2005) *Carbon Dioxide Capture and Storage*, Geneva: IPCC.

Intergovernmental Panel on Climate Change (IPCC) (2018) *Special Report: Global Warming at 1.5C*, October 21.

Intergovernmental Panel on Climate Change (IPCC) (2019) *Climate Change and Land*.

International Atomic Energy Agency (IAEA) (2020) *Nuclear Power Reactors in the World*, Vienna: IAEA.

International Energy Agency (IEA) (2018) *World Energy Outlook 2018*.

International Energy Agency (IEA) (2019a) *The Energy Mix: Renewables 2019*, Paris: IEA (accessed October 21, 2019).

International Energy Agency (IEA) (2019b) *Renewables 2019, Analysis and Forecast to 2024*, Paris: IEA (accessed October 21, 2019).

International Energy Agency (IEA) (2019c) *Renewables Information Statistics*, Paris: IEA.

International Energy Agency (IEA) (2020) *Global Energy Review 2020*, Paris: IEA.

International Energy Agency (IEA) and Nuclear Energy Agency (NEA) (2020) *Projected Costs of Generating Electricity*, Paris: IEA.

International Monetary Fund (IMF) (2019) "Global fossil fuel subsidies remain large: An update based on country-level estimates," Working paper 19/89.

International Renewable Energy Agency (IRENA) (2019) *Renewable Power Generation Costs in 2018*, New York.

International Renewable Energy Agency (IRENA) (2020a) *Renewable Power Generation Costs in 2019*, New York.

International Renewable Energy Agency (IRENA) (2020b) *Energy Subsidies: Evolution in the Global Energy Transformation to 2050*, New York.

Irvine, Peter et al. (2019) "Halving warming with idealized solar geoengineering moderates key climate hazards," *Nature Climate Change*, March 11.

Kang, Suchul and Elfatih A.B. Eltahir (2018) "North China plain threatened by heat waves due to climate change and irrigation," *Nature Communications*, July 31.

Keith, David W. (2010) "Photophoretic levitation of engineered aerosols for geoengineering," *PNAS*, September 21.

Keith, David W. et al. (2018) "A process for capturing CO2 from the atmosphere," *Joule*, 2, pp. 1573–1594.

Keller, David P. et al. (2014) "Potential climate engineering effectiveness and side effects during a high carbon dioxide-emission scenario," *Nature Communications*, 5, February 25, p. 3304.

Kew Sarah F. et al. (2018) "The exceptional summer heat wave in Southern Europe 2017," *AMS*, December.

Kintisch, Eli (2010) *Hack the Planet*, Hoboken, NJ: John Wiley & Sons.

Kirchsteiger, C. (2008) "Carbon capture and storage-desirability from a risk management point of view," *Safety Science*, 46, pp. 1149–1154.

Koplow, Doug and John Dernbach (2001) "Fossil fuel subsidies and greenhouse gas emissions: A case study of increasing transparency for fiscal policy," *Annual Review of Energy and the Environment*, #26, pp. 361–389.

Koplow, Douglas (2011) "Nuclear power: Still not viable without subsidies," Union of Concerned Scientists, February, Cambridge, MA.

Kunzig, Robert (2008) "A sunshade for planet earth," *Scientific American*, November.

Lempert, Robert et al. (2019) *Pathways to 2050: Alternative Scenarios for Decarbonizing the U.S. Economy*, May.

Lesk, Corey et al. (2016) "Influence of extreme weather disasters on global crop production," *Nature*, January 7.

Liu, Bing et al. (2016) "Similar estimates of temperature impacts on global wheat yield by three independent methods," *Nature Climate Change*, September 12.

Lobell, David B. et al. (2011a) "Climate trends and global crop production since 1980," *Science Express*, May 5.

Lobell, David B. et al. (2011b) "Nonlinear heat effects on African maize as evidenced by historical yield trials," *Nature Climate Change*, April.

London School of Economics (LSE) (2018) "What is a carbon price and why do we need one?," My 17.

McDonough, William and Michael Braungart (1998) "The next industrial revolution," *Atlantic Monthly*, October, pp. 82–92.

McDonough, William and Michael Braungart (2002) *Cradle to Cradle: Remaking the Way We Make Things*, New York: North Point Press.

McKinsey Global Institute (2020a) "Will India get too hot to work?"

McKinsey Global Institute (2020b) "Will the world's breadbaskets become less reliable?"

Mohammed, A.R. and L. Tarpley (2009) "High nighttime temperatures affect rice productivity through altered pollen germination and spikelet fertility," *Agricultural and Forest Meteorology*, 149, pp. 999–1008.

Mulligan, James et al. (2018) "Technological carbon removal in the United States," World Resources Institute, working paper, September.

National Academy of Sciences (NAS) (2009) *Hidden Costs of Energy: Unpriced Consequences of Energy Production and Use*, Washington, DC: NAS.

National Academy of Sciences (2019) *Negative Emissions Technologies and Reliable Sequestration: A Research Agenda*, Washington, DC: NAS.

Natural Resources Defense Council (NRDC) (2011) "Nuclear accident at Indian point: Consequences and costs," October, New York.

Nemetz, Peter N. (2022a) *Corporate Strategy and Sustainability*, London: Routledge.

Nemetz, Peter N. (2022b) *Unsustainable World: Are We Losing the Battle to Save Our Planet?*, London: Routledge.

New Scientist (2011) "UK's carbon-capture failure is part of a global trend," October 24.

New York Times (2011) "Japan says decommissioning damaged reactors could take 40 years," December 21.

New York Times (2011a) "Utility shelves ambitious plan to limit carbon," July 13.

New York Times (2011b) "AEP move to stop carbon capture and sequestration project shocks utilities, miners," July 15.

New York Times (2011c) "Obstacles to capturing carbon gas," July 31.

New York Times (2012a) "Growing doubts in Europe on future of carbon storage," January 16.

New York Times (2012b) "With natural gas plentiful and cheap, carbon capture projects stumble," May 19.

New York Times (2017) "It's not your imagination: Summers are getting hotter," July 28.

New York Times (2018) "Hotter, drier, hungrier-how global warming punishes the world's poorest," March 12.

Nugent, Daniel and Benjamin K. Sovacool (2014) "Assessing the lifecycle greenhouse gas emissions from solar PV and wind energy: A critical meta-survey," *Energy Policy*, 65, pp. 229–244.

Overpeck, Jonathan T. and Cecilia Conde (2019) "A call to climate action," *Science*, May 31.

Overseas Development Institute (ODI) (2013) *Time to change the game. Fossil fuel subsidies and climate*, November, London.

Oxford University (2020) *Our World in Data* (OWID) "Renewables as % of energy production," downloaded off website, ourworldindata.org, Oxford University.

Pacala, S. and R. Socolow (2004) "Stabilization wedges: Solving the climate problem for the next 50 years with current technologies," *Science*, August 13.

Pacala, S. and R. Socolow (2006) "U.S stabilization wedges," *Scientific American*, July 27.

Pal, Jeremey S. and Elfatah A.B. Eltahir (2016) "Future temperatures in Southwest Asia projected to exceed threshold for human adaptability," *Nature Climate Change*, October 26.

Parkinson, Claire L. (2010) *Coming Climate Crisis? Consider the Past, Beware the Big Fix*, Blue Ridge Summit, PA: Rowman & Littlefield.

Paul, Mar et al. (2019) *Decarbonizing the US Economy: Pathways toward a Green New Deal*, June.

Peng, Shaobing et al. (2004) "Rice yields decline with higher night temperature from global warming," *PNAS*, July 6.

Pielke, Roger, Jr. (2010) *The Climate Fix*, New York: Basic Books.

Proctor, Jonathan et al. (2018) "Estimating global agricultural effects of geoengineering using volcanic eruptions," *Nature*, August 23.

Quantis (2019) *The Quantis Food Report 2020*.

Riegler, Markus (2018) "Insect threats to food security," *Science*, August 31.

Robock, Alan (2008) "20 reasons why geoengineering may be a bad idea," *Bulletin of the Atomic Scientists*, 64(2), May/June, pp. 14–18, 59.

Rochon, Emily (2008) *False Hope: Why Carbon Capture and Storage Won't Save the Climate*, , Amsterdam: Greenpeace.

Royal Society of the United Kingdom (2009) *Geoengineering the Climate. Science, Governance and Uncertainly*, September, London.

Schauberger, Bernhard et al. (2017) "Consistent negative response of US crops to high temperatures in observations and crop models," *Nature Communications*, January 19.

Schlenker, Wolfram and Michael J. Roberts (2009) "Nonlinear temperature effects indicate severe damages to U.S. crop yields under climate change," *PNAS*, September 15.

Scientific American (2008) "The hidden dangers of geoengineering," October 3. Editorial.

Sekera, June and Andreas Lichtenberger (2020) "Assessing carbon capture: Public policy, science, and societal need," *Biophysical Economics and Sustainability*, October 6.

Sherwood, Steven C. and Matthew Huber (2010) "An adaptability limit to climate change due to heat stress," *PNAS*, May 25.

Smil, Vaclav (2010) *Energy Myths and Reality: Bringing Science to the Energy Policy Debate*, Washington, DC: AEI Press.

Socolow, Robert (2011) "Wedges reaffirmed: A short essay and ten solicited comments on the essay," *Bulletin of the Atomic Scientists*, September 27.

Sovacool, Benjamin K. (2011) "Questioning the safety and reliability of nuclear power," *GAIA*, 20(2), pp. 95–103.

Stahel, Walter R. (2016) "Circular economy," *Nature*, March 24.

Strauss, Lewis L. (1954) "US AEC, remarks prepared for delivery at the founders' day dinner," *National Association of Science Writers*, September 16.

Tack, Jesse et al. (2017) "Disaggregating sorghum yield reductions under warming scenarios exposes narrow genetic diversity in US breeding programs," *PNAS*, August 29.

The Earth Institute, Columbia University (n.d.) *Klaus S. Lackner, Director of the Lenfest Center for Sustainable Energy*.

Thomson, Graham (2009) "Burying carbon dioxide in underground saline aquifers: Political folly or climate change fix?," Munk Centre for International Studies, University of Toronto.

Trisos, Christopher H. et al. (2018) "Potentially dangerous consequences for biodiversity of solar engineering implementation and termination," *Nature Ecology & Evolution*, January.

United Nations Environment Programme (UNEP) (2010) *Emerging Issues: Environmental Consequences of Ocean Acidification: A Threat to Food Security*, Nairobi: UNEP.

United Nations Environment Programme (UNEP) (2020a) *Emissions Gap Report*.

United Nations Environment Programme (UNEP) (2020b) *Adaptation Gap Report*.

US Energy Information Administration (EIA) (2019) *Levelized Cost and Levelized Avoided Cost of New Generation Resources*, February.

US Energy Information Administration (EIA) (2007) *Federal Financial Interventions and Subsidies in Energy Markets*, April, Washington, DC.

US Environmental Protection Agency (EPA) (2008) *Vulnerability Evaluation Framework for Geologic Sequestration of Carbon Dioxide*, July 10, Washington, DC.

US General Accounting Office (GAO) (2011) *Climate Engineering: Technical Status, Future Directions and Potential Response*, July.

US Nuclear Regulatory Commission (NRC) (1982) *Calculation of Reactor Accident Consequences for US Nuclear Power Plants, CRAC-2 Report*, Sandia Labs, New Mexico.

US Nuclear Regulatory Commission (NRC) (n.d.) *Backgrounder: Nuclear Insurance: Price-Anderson Act*.

Weitzman, Martin L. (2009) "On modeling and interpreting the economics of catastrophic climate change," *The Review of Economics and Statistics*, February.

Wilday, Jill et al. (2011) "Hazards from carbon dioxide capture, transport and storage," *Process Safety and Environmental Protection*, 89, pp. 482–491.

World Bank. *World Development Indicators* (WDI) (accessed October 2019).

World Bank (2019) *State and Trends of Carbon Pricing*, Washington, DC: World Bank.

World Energy Council (WEC) (2004) *Comparison of Energy Systems Using Life Cycle Assessment: A Special Report of the World Energy Council*, July.

World Nuclear Association (WNA) (2020) *Nuclear Power in the World Today*, February.

World Resources Institute (WRI) (2020) "5 Strategies That Achieve Climate Mitigation and Adaptation Simultaneously," February 10.

Zhao, Chuang et al. (2017) "Temperature increase reduces global yields of major crops in four independent estimates," *PNAS*, August 29.

Zhou, Chunwu et al. (2018) "Carbon dioxide (CO2) levels this century will alter the protein, micronutrients, and vitamin content of rice grains with potential health consequences for the poorest rice-dependent countries," *Science Advances*, May 23.

Index

Page numbers in *italic* indicate a figure and page numbers in **bold** indicate a table on the corresponding page. Page numbers followed by 'n' indicate notes.

economics *see* ecological economics; environmental economics; macroeconomics; microeconomics; neoclassical economics

The Economics of Ecosystems and Biodiversity (TEEB) 173

The Economics of Happiness (Anielski) 75

economic valuation methodologies: alternative evaluation paradigms *174*; ARIES project and 173; assumptions of 168–170; biophysical evaluation 175; cumulative effects 169; European Commission and 173; incomplete scientific knowledge and 169; InVEST model and 173; MIMES and 173; monetary models for ecosystem services and 173; non-linearities 169–170; TEEB and 173; time horizon in 169

ecosphere 17, *18*

ecosystems 17; characteristics 215–218; as complex adaptive systems 11–12, **12**; of Earth 17–19; Third World living standards and 43, 57

Ecosystems and Human Well-Being: Wetlands and Water 157

ecosystem services 241, *247*; analytical methodologies for estimating values of 243, **245**; biomes and 243, **245**; boreal forest and 259–261; monetizing 251–255; Nature's bill for *245*; New York City's water supply and 181–182; of North America's boreal forest 259, *260*, **261**; payment for (*see* payment for ecosystem services (PES)); revised estimates of value of 243, **246**; shrimp and 262–263, *263*; thresholds and 199; wetlands and 157, **158**

ecotourism 202, 206

EDF *see* Environmental Defense Fund

EDs *see* endocrine disruptors (EDs)

Edwards, Steven F. 11

EEA *see* European Environment Agency

EF *see* ecological footprint (EF)

efficiency: and resilience 321; resilience and 247, *248*

effluent charges 120

Ehrenreich, Barbara 100

elasticity of demand 149n1

Elhacham, Emily 39

Elkington, John 199

emergent behavior 11

emission fees 120, 123–124

emission gap 331

emissions: fees and 120–124; libertarian paternalism and 141; Sheldahl's TRI data for 142–143

Emission Trading System (ETS) 137–138

endocrine diseases 43

endocrine disruptors (EDs) 42, 290–291

energy consumption 37; UK *38*; US *38*, 39

environment: business impact on 11; of Easter Island 16–17; ecological footprint and 218;

fundamental forces in 25; human historical impact on 29–33; human historical impact phases on 29; mangroves and 262; *Silent Spring* and 113; *Techno-Fix: Why Technology Won't Save Us or the Environment* and 215; UN and 119–120; UNEP and 4, 119, 331; WTP *versus* WTA valuations and 165; *see also* Environmental Protection Agency, US; European Environment Agency

environmental benefit estimation 152–153

Environmental Defense Fund (EDF) 144

environmental despoliation: China's cost of 301; conventional economic thinking and 113; Third World's rising standard of living and 39

environmental disasters, Union Carbide and 142; *see also* nuclear reactor accidents

environmental economics 129; command and control 115–116; common property resources 114, 115; ecological economics and 153, 246–248, **247**; emission fees 120, 123–124; externalities and 113; marketable permits 120, 124–127; model of 239, *240*, *241*; open access resources and 115; pollutants and 239, **240**; polluter pays principle and 116–117; public goods and 114

environmental Kuznets curve *40*, 40–41, *41*, 44

environmental neuroscience 289

environmental non-governmental organizations (ENGOs) 320

environmental policy instruments 119–120, **120**, 123

Environmental Protection Agency, US (EPA) 116; Acid Rain Program 130; air pollution inventory of 65; CAA and 177–179; CCS and 324; chemical regulation and 288–289; fish-eating guidelines 217; Greenhouse Gas inventory database of 65; health effects, types of 128; lead exposure and 217–218; mortality risk reduction report of 193; public water system requirements of 181; regulatory tiering, SO_2 127; relative toxicity and 147; requirements for public water systems 181; RSEI of 142–143, **147**; toxicity weighting metric of 147; TRI data reported to 147; WTP and WTA 165

environmental regulation: CAC and 116; chemicals and 288–289; marketable permits and 125; moral suasion and 141; SO_2 and 127; stock values and 148; TRI and 141

environmental risk transition 43–44, *43*, *44*

EPA *see* Environmental Protection Agency, US

EPA Waste Minimization Prioritization Tool (WMPT) 144

epidemics 296, 309

equivalent social cost 275

Erickson, Jon D. 85

An Essay on the Principle of Population (Malthus) 21

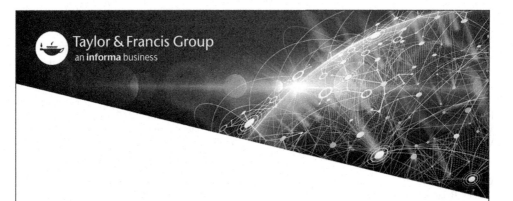

Printed in the United States
by Baker & Taylor Publisher Services